HOW CAPITALISM WILL SAVE US

HOW CAPITALISM WILL SAVE US

Why Free People and Free Markets Are the Best Answer in Today's Economy

Steve Forbes

AND ELIZABETH AMES

► UPDATED AND REVISED EDITION

CROWN
BUSINESS
NEW YORK

Crown Business books are available at special discounts for bulk purchases for sales
promotions or corporate use. Special editions, including personalized covers, excerpts of
existing books, or books with corporate logos, can be created in large quantities for
special needs. For more information, contact Premium Sales at (212) 572-2232 or e-mail
specialmarkets@randomhouse.com.

Library of Congress Cataloging-in-Publication Data
Forbes, Steve, 1947–
    How capitalism will save us / Steve Forbes and Elizabeth Ames.
       p. cm.
    Includes index.
    1. Capitalism—United States. 2. United States—Economic policy.
    3. United States—Economic conditions. I. Ames, Elizabeth. II. Title.
    HB501.F646   2009
    330.12'20973—dc22   2009032751

ISBN 978-0-307-46310-4
eISBN 978-0-307-46311-1

Printed in the United States of America

BOOK DESIGN BY BARBARA STURMAN

10 9 8 7 6 5 4 3 2 1

First Paperback Edition

To the millions of individuals whose energy, innovation, and resilience built the Real World economy. Their enterprise, when unleashed, is always the answer.

CONTENTS

PREFACE TO THE UPDATED
AND REVISED EDITION

This book is a conversation about why free people and free markets are the foundation of a vibrant economy. That statement is as true today as ever. However, when we began this project, in the fall of 2008, it looked as though the idea was on the verge of being discredited. The nation was in the throes of the first major financial panic most of us had experienced in our lifetime. It led to a profound loss of faith in our system of open markets and democratic capitalism.

The introduction that follows describes that period, when, in the view of many, the economy and very possibly the social fabric seemed ready to unravel. Even those who had supported open markets had serious doubts about free enterprise. A new administration came to power that advocated "change you can believe in." To a very great degree, "change" meant a repudiation of the belief in economic freedom that built America's prosperity over four hundred years.

Flushed with the success of the 2008 election, an idealistic president began an expansion of government said to be as profound and sweeping in its way as the tax- and regulation-cutting "Reagan Revolution" of the 1980s. A new administration set about engineering what it considered to be bold solutions. They included a virtually government-run health insurance system, breathtaking new regulations and bureaucracies for the financial sector, a government takeover of two of the nation's Big Three automakers (Washington's power over these companies will last long after these shares are divested), unprecedented government control of the Internet, and federal spending at a level never before experienced in peacetime. The newcomers were lauded by many in the media for their audacious vision. Out with the old and in with the new. Capitalism, after all, had "failed." Too much free enterprise, some people insisted, had been the cause of our problems. A European-style social welfare state was, supposedly, the only answer.

That was then.

As of early 2011, the nation continues to suffer abnormally high unemployment—almost twice the rate immediately before the recession, and the highest rate for a longer duration than at any time since the 1930s. Despite two years of jaw-dropping Washington spending, business leaders remain reluctant to hire. Federal Reserve Chairman Ben Bernanke admits it may be years before we ever see pre-recession 5 and 6 percent jobless rates.[1] Banks have yet to resume lending at healthy levels. The administration's much-heralded "fix" of the health-care system has already led to still higher health-care premiums, while adding immeasurably to the nation's debt burden.

In addition, the stock market has not returned to where it was before the crisis began in 2007. Most people agree that, while things may get a little better, there's not likely to be a return to the roaring prosperity of the past three decades.

Some pundits have openly admitted to being perplexed over the anemic recovery. But those who read this book when it first appeared, or who have a genuine understanding of markets, would not have been at all astonished by how events have unfolded.

You could say that the past two years have been a succession of so-called "teachable moments" illuminating the inconvenient truth about government intervention in an economy. Very simply: it doesn't make things better. And most of the time it makes things worse. Every major systemic crisis, from the Great Depression to the current slowdown, has resulted from government mismanagement.

This book explains that government intervention does not generate jobs. It does not—and cannot—fix problems in health care or the financial sector or any other part of the economy through massive new rules or de facto takeovers. Nor has it ever, throughout history, created greater prosperity or abundance.

Government is good at maintaining order. But it lacks the imagination and creativity to produce the kind of innovations that have always created jobs and driven genuine growth.

Policy makers may be intelligent. They may have gone to the best schools. Their prognostications may sound lofty and compelling. But ultimately, they are outgunned by the ingenuity and problem-solving ability of millions of individuals in an open market. The latitude of a free market is essential for this collective creativity to flourish.

Only a free market, with its millions of inventive and determined entrepreneurs, is capable of generating and successfully allocating the capital that ends up funding entrepreneurial, job-creating innovations that enhance our standard of living.

Our purpose is to dispel the myths and misconceptions that are part of the "Rap" on free enterprise. This book takes the form of an informal conversation addressing the classic concerns and questions about open markets that people have had for generations.

Many of the points made in our discussions have turned out to be prescient, such as the failure of the administration's multi-trillion-dollar spending to "stimulate" a paralyzed economy. In several chapters, we recall the classic explanation—the "broken window fallacy" described by nineteenth-century French economist Frédéric Bastiat, one of the many free-market voices, past and present, heard in this book. He colorfully makes the point that repairing a baker's hypothetical broken window may *appear* to create jobs for neighborhood tradesmen, merchants, and others in the community. But in the end there is a net loss because the baker is out the money he spent on a new window, and even lost some business while the window was being repaired.

Like the spending for the baker's broken window, Keynesian spending never creates new value. That's because it's rarely if ever invested in efficiency-improving technologies that produce genuine gains in employment. Instead it is taken from individuals and business to fund ongoing activities—in President Obama's words, those "saved jobs." Like the baker's money, it ends up producing a net loss, the same kind of loss to the economy as repairing the broken window of every American.

The book's original chapter on health care anticipated the damaging effects of Congress's 2010 legislation, which abruptly increased insurance premiums by adding new layers of distortion to what was previously a market made dysfunctional by tax laws and overregulation. That chapter has been updated.

Health care unfortunately is an all-too-powerful example of what happens when government ends up directly or indirectly dominating a market. You get less competition and innovation—which translates into higher prices, declining quality, and shortages.

The book has also been changed to reflect other developments that have occurred since the publication of the hardcover in 2009, including the takeover of the auto industry. We originally said that the bailout of GM and Chrysler could be seen as emergency relief for a disaster largely created by bad government policy. It could be justified as long as the administration didn't go too far and attempt to run the auto companies. Unfortunately, that is precisely what has happened. In chapter 2 we note that, contrary to spin put out by the administration, the effort can hardly be called a success. The government ended up selling the "new" GM back to the public for less money than taxpayers had paid to bail it out.

The auto bailout and subsequent temporary takeover illustrate another key theme that runs through our book's conversation: Government solutions to economic problems often don't work because they're shaped by political agendas. Businesses in a free market attempt to meet the needs of the greatest number of customers and shareholders. In contrast, government takes action based on the needs of the politically powerful. In the case of GM and Chrysler, both were restructured to benefit favored unions and other favored parties at the expense of private-sector creditors and shareholders. Those interests will drive decisions at the automakers, not the needs of the market.

Our discussion anticipated another topic that has attracted growing attention over the past year—the effects of government-created uncertainty on an economy. Charles Gasparino wrote in the *New York Post* in late 2010: "The massive retrenchment in hiring over the past two years . . . is the direct result of business worries about the future costs of the president's social agenda, which only *begins* with universal health care."[2]

Chapter 8 explains how such fears end up paralyzing an economy. Among those highlighted in the chapter is Amity Shlaes, who has written persuasively about the role of uncertainty in prolonging the Great Depression. Similar paralysis is also produced by a fluctuating "fiat" currency—a reason why a stable dollar pegged to gold is fundamental to a healthy economy.

The good news is that Big Government failures of the past two years are causing a new appreciation of free-market principles. More people are beginning to see through the Rap on capitalism. Not only the Tea Party movement, but millions of independents are attempting to halt the slide into a European-style government-dominated economy. They're speaking out in support of lower taxes, limited government, and more economic freedom.

They're coming to realize that government, when it intervenes in a market, kills innovation and imposes rigidity—delivering services that are behind the curve and not ahead of it. Think FedEx compared with the post office, not to mention how government has mismanaged the public schools, problem-plagued Amtrak, and even, if you live in New York, Off-Track Betting.

Where government dominates a market, such as health care, it produces the kind of supply and price distortions that occur with a monopoly. Where it regulates with a heavy hand, you get less diversity and choice. We explain in several places that regulations intended to promote "fairness" instead encourage "crony capitalism": they end up favoring powerful incumbents—that is, those best able to afford complying with costly rules and deploying high-powered lobbyists. And they crush newcomers or prevent them from starting up in the first place.

Contrary to those who buy into the negative Rap on capitalism, supporting open markets and economic freedom does not mean promoting the interests of "Big Business" or "The Rich." As management expert Court Huber wisely put it, "I'm not pro-business, I'm pro-competition."[3]

The opposition tsunami of the 2010 midterm elections was widely interpreted as a repudiation of the Keynesian expansion of government that began in the middle of the past decade. A president who had openly disdained the private sector was pressured into acknowledging the connection between reasonable tax rates and economic growth, extending what he had once characterized as "tax cuts for the rich."

Some observers see the start of a new era. We hope so. But several political victories are only a beginning. While more skeptical of Big Government, people are still a long way from trusting markets. We hope this book helps restore faith in the free-enterprise system that has enabled the United States to generate a level of opportunity and prosperity unparalleled in history.

STEVE FORBES
ELIZABETH AMES
March 2011

HOW CAPITALISM WILL SAVE US

INTRODUCTION

Why Capitalism Is the Answer: The iPod Economy

"Laissez-faire capitalism should be as dead as Soviet communism."
—Arianna Huffington, *Huffington Post* in December 2008

"Laissez-faire is finished. The all-powerful market that always knows best is finished."
—French president Nicolas Sarkozy

"The worst financial crisis since the Great Depression is claiming another casualty: American-style capitalism."
—*Washington Post*

Has capitalism failed? The events of the last few years have left Nicholas Sarkozy, Arianna Huffington, the *Washington Post*, and countless others ready—some might say eager—to write the obituary of our free-enterprise system. Even to those who aren't declaring its demise, capitalism has seemed on the verge of cardiac arrest. The economy has been roiled by one catastrophe after the next: the failure of financial institutions, the housing-market meltdown, a roller-coaster stock market, decimated 401(k)s, high unemployment, obscene CEO pay, and massive corruption.

As the crisis deepened in late 2008 and early 2009, Wall Street "greed" was blamed daily for the near implosion of the world financial system. Business executives were interrogated like criminals at congressional hearings. For a time, grim economic forecasts and job losses seemed endless. To many people, such events provided proof that "unfettered" markets produce just instability and devastation.

The economic crisis that began in the summer of 2007 produced a momentous crisis of confidence in our free-enterprise system. *Capitalism* and *free markets* suddenly became dirty words. Paul Krugman, the Nobel Prize–winning economist and *New York Times* columnist, ever critical of free markets, seemed to reach an entirely new level of indignation when he excoriated Wall Street for being a "Madoff economy" whose executives are little better than monster Ponzi schemer Bernard Madoff.

Even the faith of some of capitalism's best-known adherents, including former Federal Reserve chairman Alan Greenspan, had been shaken. A well-known supporter of markets whose friend and early mentor was the late libertarian thinker Ayn Rand, Greenspan testified before Congress in 2008 that he should have done more to regulate the financial system, whose breakdown was bigger than anything he could have foreseen: "Those of us who have looked to the self-interest of lending institutions to protect shareholders' equity (myself especially) are in a state of shocked disbelief."[1]

Indeed, the gloom seemed readily justified. In the fourth quarter of 2008 and again in the first quarter of 2009, the U.S. gross domestic product (GDP) declined around 6 percent—back-to-back declines not seen since the late 1930s. The contraction was worldwide. In the first quarter of 2009, Japan's GDP plunged an astonishing 9 percent. Germany's crashed 7 percent. Emerging economies were also hard-hit.

It was easy to see how all of this could rattle Greenspan and others. For many, massive spending by both the Bush and Obama administrations on a succession of corporate bailouts underscored the growing perception that the private sector had collapsed. Billions of dollars from the Troubled Asset Relief Program (TARP) and other sources were pumped into banks and insurance companies like AIG, once deemed "too big to fail." Several of the nation's leading financial institutions were nationalized in all but name. Then came the auto bailout and the government-forced bankruptcies of General Motors and Chrysler. The *Wall Street Journal*'s banner headline "GM Collapses into Government's Arms" did not merely convey the humiliating fall of a once-great company. It seemed to suggest, beyond all doubt, that the private sector needed to be "rescued."

By early 2009, the boundless "irrational exuberance" of recent decades had been replaced by despair that seemed as bottomless as the ever-sinking Dow Jones Industrial Average. People wondered: What was going on? Could the free-enterprise system have been truly responsible for the near collapse of the American economy?

Noted legal scholar, author, and federal judge Richard Posner wrote that the crisis and the economy's subsequent "descent into depression" was "a failure of capitalism"—the title of his book. He predicted that the meltdown would result in a modified, more heavily regulated version of our current system—free enterprise, only less free.

Time magazine columnist Justin Fox, author of *The Myth of the Rational Market*, resolutely insisted that a sea change was taking place: the idea that "financial markets can be relied upon to get things right," he claimed, had been discredited even among its one-time adherents. The long-standing view of markets as "rational" was not only wrong but "dangerous."

Are they right?

We originally decided to write this book before the financial crisis, in the summer of 2007, to address the misunderstanding—and frequent hostility—to our system of democratic capitalism expressed by so many affluent, educated people. As we will discuss later, the economist Joseph Schumpeter observed this irony: that the "capitalist class," which benefits most from free enterprise, has a tendency to "turn against its own."[2]

The financial crisis reached gale force in the fall of 2008. Not only did it amplify classic doubts about our system, but the disaster had been caused to a very great degree by those very misunderstandings which had shaped many bad government policies.

In her classic novel *Atlas Shrugged*, Ayn Rand famously depicted how this takes place. The public and policy makers blame government-created economic devastation on "free markets" and then pile on still more regulations that only worsen the damage and further increase the blame and recriminations.

This book will illuminate the underlying principles of democratic capitalism that even people sympathetic to free markets can be at a loss to explain, in addition to addressing concerns raised by the worst economic crisis of the past seventy years.

Today's rage is anything but a new phenomenon. Capitalism has received a bad rap since before the days of Karl Marx. During troubled economic times, the natural impulse is to hold someone responsible.

Throughout history, private-sector "villains" have been pilloried during periods of economic turmoil—from the "evil bankers" who supposedly caused the real-estate bust of the 1830s, to the "speculators" blamed for the 1929 crash and the Great Depression, to the "predatory lenders" and "hedge-fund billionaires" accused of causing the financial crisis and "Great Recession." This book will show that such perceptions, though understandable, are almost always misguided.

We all know the Rap on capitalism: That it is fundamentally greedy and immoral. That it enables the rich to get richer at the expense of the poor. That open markets are Darwinian places where the most ruthless unfairly crush smaller competitors and where the cost of vital products and services like health care and energy are almost beyond the reach of those who need them. Capitalism has also been blamed for a range of social ills—from air pollution to obesity.

Not only have educated, successful people bought into capitalism's bad Rap, but the Rap is taught in our schools. It has molded the thinking and analyses of our most influential opinion leaders, writers, thinkers, and policy makers of both political parties. Long before the stock market meltdown, before AIG executives and automotive CEOs were being tarred and feathered by Congress, Democrats and Republicans alike regularly blamed "overpaid" executives and "Wall Street greed" for the problems ailing America's economy.

Antibusiness bias has long been rampant at our top universities, where Marx occupies iconic stature, where free-market thinkers are seldom taught—and where careers in nonprofit sectors like academia or the arts are widely regarded as morally superior to those in "money-grubbing" private industry. The Rap is pervasive in the entertainment industry. Scheming business executives are a favorite villain in the story lines of television and motion pictures—ranging from films like *Erin Brockovich* to TV programs like *Dirty Sexy Money*.[3]

Even some of capitalism's leading beneficiaries have bought into the Rap. Warren Buffett, number two on the 2010 annual *Forbes* list of world billionaires, has asserted that his wealth as the world's most successful investor is "disproportionate." At the World Economic Forum in 2008, Bill Gates called for, in the words of the *Wall Street Journal*, a "revision of capitalism." Gates told reporter Robert Guth that he believed that the fruits of capitalism—i.e., advances in areas such as health care, technology, and education—were not reaching the world's poor and primarily helped the rich.

Capitalism's bad Rap has helped to shape a lot of bad economic policy. People who believe it look to government to "create jobs," whereas the most powerful job-creating machine has always been the private sector. They believe that the best way to generate more revenues for government is through raising taxes on the so-called rich and on "profit-hungry" corporations. Yet history shows, time and again, that punishing the entrepreneurs and businesses that create jobs and capital is a sure route to economic devastation, while lowering taxes—not with one-shot reductions that politicians like, but by substantially cutting rates—is always the best economic stimulus.

Thanks to capitalism's bad rap, people bash big private-sector companies like Wal-Mart for supposedly excessive "market power," while they are blind to the massive market power of government and its role in today's economic disasters.

The two biggest examples: the central role of government-created mortgage behemoths Fannie Mae and Freddie Mac in the subprime-mortgage meltdown and financial crisis and the mammoth impact of giant government insurers Medicare and Medicaid in shaping today's dysfunctional health-care market.

Partly because of the Rap on capitalism, many people today are convinced that the way to economic health is protectionist policies that supposedly preserve jobs—when such policies have been shown, not only in the United States, but in nations around the globe, to be job killers.

The emotionally charged rhetoric of the Rap has precluded a clear-eyed understanding of the fundamental principles of economic behavior. People don't understand, for example, how markets work in the Real World or, for that matter, how wealth is created. They believe "wealth" is solely something "greedy" rich people make for themselves—when it is also the source of the capital that is invested in new businesses that create jobs.

The drumbeat against "greed" and "free markets" on the part of the media and politicians has also served to prevent a clear understanding of just what really constitutes a "free" market. Thus, people blame capitalism for economic disasters such as the mortgage meltdown and the astronomical cost of health insurance—when they have in fact been caused by government not allowing markets to function.

Because of the Rap, people are blind to the Reality—that far from having failed, democratic capitalism is the world's greatest economic success story. No other system has improved the lives of so many people.

The turmoil of the past few years by no means mitigates the explosion of prosperity that has taken place since the early 1980s, when President Ronald Reagan enacted promarket reforms to free the economy from the Carter-Nixon stagnation of the 1970s. Those reforms—lowering tax rates and loosening regulations—unleashed job-creating capital. The result: a roaring economy that produced a flood of innovations—from personal computers and cellular phones to the Internet.

Indeed, we may one day look back on the period of 1982 to 2007 as an economic golden age. Many conveniences we take for granted today—from automatic teller machines and DVD players to home computers and CAT scans—did not exist or were not widely used as recently as the 1970s and early '80s. It's not just that we have more and better gizmos. All you have to do is watch an old movie from the 1970s. Even when the past is glamorized by Hollywood, it's obvious—looking at everything from appliances to cars to homes—that living standards back then were lower. We've come a long way. Not only "the rich" but people of all incomes today are doing better.

No system has been as effective as capitalism in turning scarcity into abundance. Think of computers. Forty years ago, only business and government could afford the old massive mainframes. A single machine filled an entire room. Today the BlackBerry device in the palm of your hand has even more computing power than those old machines.

Thanks to capitalism, Americans as a nation are living dramatically better and longer than they did at the beginning of the twentieth century. In *The Greatest Century That Ever Was: 25 Miraculous Trends of the Past 100 Years*, noted economist Stephen Moore and the late business professor Julian Simon make the powerful observation that since the early twentieth century, life expectancy has increased; infant mortality rates have fallen tenfold. Major killer diseases—from tuberculosis to polio, typhoid, and pneumonia—have in most parts of the world been, if not eradicated, drastically reduced; agricultural productivity has soared. The en-

vironment is also cleaner in many parts of the world. Air quality has improved about 30 percent in American cities since 1977.

Not only that, Moore and Simon write, "the affordability and availability of consumer goods have greatly increased. Even most poor Americans have a cornucopia of choices that a century ago the Rockefellers and
the Vanderbilts could not have purchased."[4]

Until the credit crisis, tens of millions of people a year worldwide
were joining the middle class. Between 2003 and 2007, the growth of the
American economy alone *exceeded the size of the entire Chinese economy.*
We grew the equivalent of China in four and a half years. China's growth
rates are higher—but they're coming from a much smaller base.

Free-market economic reforms—especially since the fall of the Berlin wall—have brought an unprecedented explosion of wealth to India,
China, Brazil, and nations in central and eastern Europe as well as in
Latin America and Africa. Capitalism has helped to usher in an era of
wealth and economic growth that failed foreign-aid programs since
World War II were never able to accomplish. In China, for example, over
two hundred million people now have discretionary income. The country
has a burgeoning middle class. The current recession should be seen historically as an interruption, not an end, of this extraordinary economic
expansion.

Along with bringing prosperity to millions, democratic capitalism
has undermined political tyranny and promoted democracy and peace
between nations of the world. It is, without doubt, the world's most
moral system.

This last statement may raise eyebrows in an era that has seen scandals from the collapse of Enron to the devastation of personal and charitable wealth caused by Bernard Madoff. That is not to minimize the
crimes of individuals like Madoff and others or the damage they cause. As
we explain, the off-the-charts criminality of individuals like Madoff
no more reflects the immorality of free enterprise than the murderous
crimes of a Ted Bundy or a Jeffrey Dahmer reflect a fundamental breakdown of democratic society. Democratic capitalism, *as a system*, is more
humane than government-dominated economies, including those in
countries that are otherwise democracies.

Nations that liberalize their economies, that allow people greater
economic self-determination, end up moving, sooner or later, toward

democracy. Since the nations of the world began to liberalize their economies in the mid-1980s, the percentage of democratically elected governments has surged from 40 percent to more than 60 percent today. China, for example, is not yet a Western-style democracy. But the nation is freer today than it was during the era of Mao Tse Tung and the repressive Cultural Revolution.

Despite all the gloom and doom voiced by its critics, the free-enterprise system is—and has always been—the best way to unleash the creativity, inventiveness, and energy of people and mobilize them to meet the wants and needs of others. That's because free-market transactions, far from being driven by greed, are about achieving the greatest possible mutual benefit, not only for the parties directly involved but eventually for the rest of society.

The question remains: Why does capitalism's bad Rap exert such a powerful hold on the American psyche—not only in bad times but in good? Indeed, it's a spectacular irony that so many of the people who have benefited most from our market economy, who have been smartest about using it to their advantage, disdain the very system that produced their success. In his seminal book *Capitalism, Socialism and Democracy*, economist Joseph Schumpeter explained that capitalism's prosperity and democratic values sooner or later cause the "capitalist class" to question the system.[5]

> The capitalist process, so we have seen, eventually decreases the importance of the function by which the capitalist class lives. . . . Capitalism creates a critical frame of mind which, after having destroyed the moral authority of so many other institutions, in the end turns against its own; the bourgeois finds to his amazement that the rationalist attitude does not stop at the credentials of kings and popes but goes on to attack private property and the whole scheme of bourgeois values.[6]

People also question capitalism because free markets are messy and unpredictable. Jobs are lost (and also created) in ways people don't expect. Companies like Google and Wal-Mart become large and successful without the permission or anticipation of bureaucrats and experts. People become wealthy who offend the sensibilities of the more cultivated establishment.

The cultural roots of today's anger go back thousands of years. In ancient times, people struggling to survive amid disease, famine, and other harsh conditions resented the relative wealth of "money changers." Christ believed rich people had less chance of going to heaven. These beliefs were not limited to Westerners. In feudal Japan, merchants were regarded as parasites because they dared to make a profit by charging more for the goods they sold than what they had paid for them.

Economist and scholar Thomas Sowell has written extensively about the universal mistrust of people he calls "middleman minorities" in retail trade or in money lending whose work "takes place somewhere between producers and consumers."

> Retailing and money-lending have long been regarded by the economically unsophisticated as not "really" adding anything to the economic well-being of a community. . . . Both medieval Europe and the Islamic countries regarded the charging of interest as a sin and, in other societies in Asia and Africa, it was considered morally suspect, even without a religious prohibition against it.[7]

Ostracized middleman minorities have included the Jews, Asian immigrants in the United States, the Ibo in Nigeria, and the Parsis in India, among many others. But Sowell says that the prejudices against them were not really based in ethnic hatred.

> An often-cited article by a British economist who was a prisoner of war in Germany during World War II pointed out how middleman economic activities arose spontaneously among the POWs—and how the individuals who engaged in those activities were resented by the other POWs, even though these individuals were not from some middleman minority, but ranged from a Catholic priest to a Sikh.[8]

While less hostile, America's attitude toward its merchant class has long been ambivalent, dating back to the political rivalry of Founding Fathers Alexander Hamilton and Thomas Jefferson. A plantation owner and believer in the agrarian model, Jefferson distrusted cities and commerce. He envisioned a more socially stratified, agrarian society. Hamilton, by contrast, believed in an America based on vibrant commerce, where people, regardless of their birth, would have a chance to move ahead economically.

Their opposing visions partitioned the nation's soul: America became a country based on capitalist principles and free markets, where some of its most successful entrepreneurs are nonetheless considered "robber barons." And corporations are seen as mechanistic oppressors of the human spirit.

But there's more to today's rage than cultural ambivalence. The truth is that a surprising number of people simply don't understand how our economy works. Despite America's preeminence as the world's foremost innovator and wealth creator—whose economy is the envy of other nations—many of us are remarkably uninformed about the system that produced our prosperity.

Little wonder economics is referred to as the "dismal science." "Dismal" describes how it is taught in most classrooms—a jumble of bloodless equations and technical terms like *frictional unemployment, GDP,* and *income elasticity of demand.* It's difficult to imagine that these subjects have any relation to the lives of real people.

According to a 2007 study by the National Council on Economic Education, just seventeen states require students to take an economics course.

Many Americans have had no formal instruction in the economic principles that govern everything from the price of milk to the interest rate on your home mortgage to where you are most likely to find employment. Research has shown that in "test after test," more than 60 percent of the nation's high school seniors were unable to define the word *profit.* Only half of all college seniors could define *inflation, productivity,* and *fiscal policy.*[9]

Several years ago the *Washington Post,* the Henry J. Kaiser Foundation, and the Harvard University Survey Project compared the views of more than 1,500 average Americans with those of 250 economists on various economic matters. George Mason economics professor Bryan Caplan reported that average citizens surveyed were far more prone than economists to emotional, negative perceptions and "anti-market bias."[10]

In other words, the less people know about how the economy works, the more likely they are to take the darkest possible view of free markets.

This book will answer classic questions about democratic capitalism, addressing the central contentions that are a part of capitalism's bad Rap—that cause people to distrust or dislike free markets. Using examples from recent events, we illuminate what we call Real World Economics, the principles of how markets work, highlighting Real World Lessons that people all too often miss about democratic capitalism—that help explain where we are today.

We've written this book as an informal conversation, the kind of discussion of hot-button topics that you might have at the dinner table or in the classroom. The first chapter asks the question, is capitalism moral?

Fundamental to the Rap on capitalism is the insidious notion that free-market transactions are based on "greed," where one party "exploits" the other. The reality is quite the opposite: capitalism is based on trust.

Transactions in free markets are about achieving the greatest possible advantage—but that advantage must be mutual. To cite the classic example from eighteenth-century economist and philosopher Adam Smith, the baker or the butcher sells you food in exchange for your money. True, as Smith points out, this relationship is based on self-interest. They provide your dinner because they seek your money. However, for a transaction to occur, each side must benefit. The deal they strike may not necessarily be the one originally envisioned by both parties—but it is nonetheless the one of greatest mutual benefit based on the realities of supply and demand. As the late free-market economist Murray N. Rothbard once wrote,

> Both parties undertake the exchange because each expects to gain from it. Also, each will repeat the exchange next time (or refuse to) because his expectation has proved correct (or incorrect) in the recent past. Trade, or exchange, is engaged in precisely because both parties benefit; if they did not expect to gain, they would not agree to the exchange.[11]

Smith's description of what takes place in a market, Rothbard wrote, supplanted antiquated notions held by mercantilists of sixteenth- to eighteenth-century Europe, who argued that "in any trade, one party can benefit only at the expense of the other, that in every transaction there is a winner and a loser, an 'exploiter' and an 'exploited.' " After all, a trade does not take place if it is a zero-sum game where only one person gains.

A free-market economy is a latticework of these mutually beneficial exchanges. Together they form what Adam Smith referred to as "the invisible hand," directing resources to where they are most needed.

How does this take place? That's the miracle of the free market—it just does. Free markets are spontaneous. No central planner or bureaucrat is needed to determine the needs of others—or how they must be met.

The classic illustration of how the invisible hand mobilizes people and resources is found in the children's story *I, Pencil*, written in the 1950s by Leonard Read of the Foundation for Economic Education, and cited by Milton Friedman and other free-market economists. The pencil narrates the story of how it came to be. It started out as a tree—"a cedar of straight grain that grows in Northern California and Oregon." The pencil goes on to describe the countless people and processes involved in its production—from cutting and transporting logs to supplying electrical power to mining graphite and extracting the rapeseed oil from the Dutch East Indies that goes into making erasers.

> Actually, millions of human beings have had a hand in my creation, no one of whom even knows more than a very few of the others. . . . Each one wants me less, perhaps, than does a child in the first grade. Indeed, there are some among this vast multitude who never saw a pencil nor would they know how to use one. Their motivation is other than me. Perhaps it is something like this: Each of these millions sees that he can thus exchange his tiny know-how for the goods and services he needs or wants. I may or may not be among these items.
>
> There is a fact still more astounding: the absence of a master mind, of anyone dictating or forcibly directing these countless actions which bring me into being. No trace of such a person can be found. Instead, we find the Invisible Hand at work.[12]

This is how wealth is produced in society: countless individuals seek to meet their own needs by meeting the needs of others. Forming networks of cooperation, they create businesses that produce innovations—not only the pencil, but inventions from laptops to washing machines. In the process of providing for themselves, people generate the capital and innovations that yield economic growth, improving living standards and enabling society to advance.

Those who buy into capitalism's bad Rap, who believe free markets are based on "exploitation" and "greed," fail to appreciate how the invisible hand works. People in a free market are mobilized not by greed but by self-interest. As we will discuss in chapter 1, there's a big difference between the two.

Greed means taking what does not belong to you or simply taking too much of something. Texas mom Catherine "KK" Patton was motivated by anything but greed when she set out to find a way to minimize the unpleasantness of daily insulin injections for diabetes patients. She perceived a need and a potential market. Patton was mobilized by more than the prospect of financial gain: she herself was a diabetes patient who hated the sticks and bruising of daily needles. Her "self-interest"— both financial and personal—propelled her to invent the i-port injection port, a device worn by patients that reduces the pain of injections. Users inject insulin into a little disk implanted in their skin that delivers medication into their bodies. Recently approved by the FDA, the invention is beginning to catch on with a growing number of diabetes patients.

Steve Chen, Chad Hurley, and Jawed Karim, three young employees of PayPal, were also motivated to fill a need based on self-interest. They wanted to share their home videos over the Internet. In 2005 the three founded YouTube, which virtually overnight became one of the Internet's biggest success stories, sold to Google after only one year for $1.65 billion. YouTube, of course, has gone far beyond meeting the simple need for which it was invented. It took the Internet revolution one step further, bringing the Web closer to television in its ability to deliver video content. Countless Web sites, including those of major news organizations, now use YouTube to deliver not only taped but live webcasts.

That's how growth occurs in a free-market economy. No one "orders" it to take place. It happens spontaneously, almost by accident. But it always happens. That's what people who buy into capitalism's bad rap don't get. When there is a need, entrepreneurs will step in to fill it, appearing seemingly out of nowhere.

Take, for example, what happened in the mid-1980s, after budget cuts forced the U.S. Coast Guard to scale back some services. The guard could no longer provide nonemergency marine assistance to recreational boaters.

Almost immediately, small entrepreneurs took up the slack. In Southold, New York, Joseph J. Frohnhoefer founded Sea Tow, an AAA for boats. His small business grew from a single vessel into a thriving franchise network with 121 locations in the United States, Asia, Europe, the Bahamas, and Puerto Rico.

Before Frohnhoefer and other entrepreneurs appeared, government was thought to be "needed" to assure nonemergency boater safety. But Frohnhoefer's private-sector business filled the need for this service as well as, if not better than, government. Frohnhoefer is called on by the Coast Guard to assist in finding lost boaters and major emergencies; his operation aided in the recovery of victims of the crash of TWA Flight 800. But his business is more than a private version of the Coast Guard. It offers a variety of other services such as boat financing and insurance.

Of course, there will be criminals and greedy individuals in a free-market economy. That is where government is critical to a free market—to enforce contracts, protect property rights, and maintain order, as it does in the rest of society.

However, most of the time, democratic capitalism's self-interest compels people to act responsibly and predictably, to work together in networks of cooperation based on trust. After all, it is in people's self-interest to act reliably if they want to succeed in the marketplace.

These roots in a voluntary, open market are what make democratic capitalism more moral than a state-dominated economy—even if the state-run economy is a democracy. Why? Because state-imposed economic solutions reflect the interests of a group of bureaucrats or politicians who are currently in power.

You may happen to agree with those government solutions. And the designers of those solutions may have good intentions. But when you get down to it, their ideas reflect the wishes and interests of a relative few more than they reflect the broad-based needs of people.

▲   REAL WORLD LESSON   ▲
Markets are people voting with their money.

In many ways, a market is an ecosystem. There is no way to know all the forces and factors that propel it forward. Just as no one person can fully fathom all the people and processes that go into making a pencil, no one individual—including the smartest policy wonks and bureaucrats—can have complete knowledge of why a market for any product works as it does.

We are not the first to point out that if government were charged with creating a pencil, bureaucrats at the Department of Pencils would probably order up too many logs in order to please their lumber-industry constituents. (Or they might order too few because of demands from environmentalists.) The graphite miners would be overpaid as a result of political pressures. People involved in the manufacture of pencils would have to comply with an assortment of government rules and regulations, some sensible but many arbitrary. They'd have to spend hours filling out forms to show compliance. Costs would spiral out of control, as they do on so many government projects. Pencils would be priced to reflect those spiraling costs. No one would be able to afford them. You'd have a surplus. Or maybe pencils would be priced too low by the Department of Pencils. Demand would be excessive and there'd be a shortage.[13]

As this book will show, efforts by politicians to manage markets have consistently produced similar consequences. You see this in the government-dominated economies of nations such as Venezuela, North Korea, Cuba, and, years ago, the Soviet Union—as well as in heavily regulated sectors of our own economy, such as health care. Bureaucrats and politicians don't realize that the market has already allocated resources in the most broadly beneficial way possible, based on existing conditions of supply and demand. Thus, their attempts to make markets work according to how people think they should work generally never succeed.

Hugo Chávez, the increasingly dictatorial president of Venezuela, a socialist and ardent believer in the Rap, imposed price controls on hundreds of goods to make food and other essentials more affordable for low-income people—an admirable goal and one that has endeared him to some critics of capitalism in the United States. But what he didn't understand is that the price of a product reflects the costs of the countless transactions and processes required to make it. The prices that he imposed may have pleased his political constituencies and won him votes, but they did not reflect the Real World costs of making those products. As a result, they threw the markets for these products, and his nation's economy, out of whack.

The only place where many food staples can be obtained in Venezuela today is on the black market—where they are now many times more expensive than before price controls. That's typical of the economic solutions devised by people who dislike free markets. They almost never remedy perceived problems or, to use the economists' lingo, the "market failure" they were supposed to correct. Instead they create even worse market failure.

A friend who emigrated from Bulgaria to the United States recently described government-controlled health care in his former country: "Health care is free," he said. "But you can't get it."

As we will see throughout this book, government intervention rarely solves economic problems, because it *politicizes* them. The solutions it imposes to promote fairness are designed primarily to satisfy the desires of those in power, not the Real World needs of people in a market.

What could be a better illustration of this than the Detroit bailout and government's takeover of GM? We discuss in chapter 2 that GM would probably have been able to cut its staggering labor costs and plot out a recovery strategy had the Obama administration allowed the market to work; GM would have taken the usual route and restructured in bankruptcy court. But with the government taking control, GM has been prevented from making the kind of tough Real World decisions needed to bring about a true turnaround.

Wall Street Journal columnist Holman W. Jenkins Jr. wrote in the spring of 2009 that the true priority of GM's new government-appointed management was not the needs of the marketplace but "first and foremost, making sense of GM's relationship with Washington." GM's decisions were likely to be driven not by what will succeed with customers but by what will please its political bosses, as well as the people who *they* need to please, the labor unions.

We explore the unintended consequences of government micromanagement in our chapters on government policy: "Don't Regulations Safeguard the Public Good?" and "Isn't Government Needed to Direct the Economy?"

Overbearing regulations by bureaucrats—from price controls to draconian accounting rules—produce damaging economic distortions that hurt people. The foremost example, which we explore in detail, is health care. In our chapter "Is Affordable Health Care Possible in a Free Market?" we show how government participation in the health-insurance market and layers of regulation have produced a tangled market with runaway costs that benefits fewer and fewer participants.

▲   REAL WORLD LESSON   ▲

Efforts to impose political constraints on market forces end up producing unintended consequences that hurt those they were supposed to help.

Efforts in the United States and other nations to make health care more available and affordable have helped only to drive up prices and lead to rationing. Sadly, the economics of health care remain the least understood of any market.

Almost as poorly understood is the process of wealth creation in democratic capitalism. That is the focus of our chapter "Isn't Capitalism Brutal?" which explores the disruptive and often painful dynamic change that is part of economic growth. Economist Joseph Schumpeter, as we have mentioned, called this process "creative destruction." The very technologies and businesses that produce new industries and jobs can also devastate old industries they render obsolete.

Think about personal computers. They wiped out demand for typewriters, and no doubt thousands of jobs. This is why, even in good times, there will be disturbing stories of corporate layoffs. Businesses and jobs created in a capitalist economy don't always spring up in the sectors where you expect them.

Take a more recent product spawned by the growth of personal computers: the iPod. Apple's revolutionary innovation (which includes not only the iPod but the iTunes software that works along with it) has become a cultural icon. It has created, by one count, more than 40,000 jobs; and that number does not include those related to selling its countless accessories. The technology has brought numerous benefits: It enables consumers to buy single songs instead of pricier CD compilations, making their music dollars go further. It allows smaller artists access to the market without having a record label. And it has generated opportunities beyond the music industry, providing a new way to sell or distribute video content—such as movies and informational "podcasts."

Yet there's no question the iPod has been destructive. It helped accelerate the boom in music downloading that devastated music retailers, forcing many to close down or dramatically alter their businesses. Record labels and recording artists are increasingly having to make their money from the sales of singles rather than more profitable CD compilations. The iPod has also presented challenges for makers of traditional stereo equipment that had to tailor their offerings to the new technology.

For those negatively affected, these changes are unquestionably painful. But does that mean we would have been better off had Apple's innovation never been developed? When all of the benefits are taken into account, most people would probably agree that the iPod has been a plus, not only for the economy but for the broader society. Even well-known recording artists admit that the changes, though disruptive, also offer opportunities, like the ability to be financially and artistically independent.

Contrary to what is commonly perceived, the iPod did not magically spring from the mind of Steve Jobs. Like YouTube, KK Patton's iport, the pencil, and countless other innovations, it emerged from people looking to fill a perceived need. In 2003, journalist Rob Walker noted in the *New York Times Magazine* that the iPod came not from "a specific technological breakthrough" but from the innovations of other companies. Jobs himself acknowledges in the article that he basically brought the pieces together.[14] That's typical of the process of creation that takes place in a free market—it's spontaneous and unpredictable. You'll never know where it will take place.

The widespread inability to perceive the full picture of free-market wealth and creation has encouraged many of the beliefs that are part of capitalism's bad rap. For example, it drives opposition to free trade. As we discuss in our chapter on globalization, commentators who bemoan "outsourcing" and "trade deficits" fail to see that trade with other nations also results in billions of dollars coming back to the United States in the form of foreign investment—producing jobs in other sectors of the economy. Our trade with China, for example, is what generates all those dollars that the Chinese plow back into U.S. Treasury bonds—the investment that the Obama administration now seeks to help underwrite its massive spending and keep our government financially afloat.

What capitalism's critics ignore is the fact that until the current recession, U.S. unemployment in the last three decades had gone down, not up. America's unemployment rate through most of this decade has been substantially lower than during the years of the 1950s and early

'60s—hovering between 4 and 5 percent. And this is true even though "labor force participation"—the proportion of adults in the workforce—is higher than it was forty years ago.

That's right, over the past thirty years, despite all the millions of jobs destroyed by the rise and fall of companies and industries in our democratic capitalist economy, over forty million net new jobs have been created. Overall personal incomes have increased from $2 trillion to $12 trillion. The net worth of American households (that is, assets minus liabilities such as home mortgage debt) has increased dramatically, from $7.1 trillion to $51.5 trillion. The economy as a whole has expanded mightily. Our standard of living has soared.

Yet unlike government programs that are launched with press releases and media fanfare, there is usually no "official" announcement of the jobs and standard-of-living improvements produced by capitalism's invisible hand. No speeches or bill signings in the Oval Office. Most of the time, things simply just happen.

▲   REAL WORLD LESSON   ▲

It is easier to see the "destruction" that takes place in democratic capitalism than it is to recognize the creation and growth that also occurs.

Still, there's no getting around the fact that business failure, the downside of risk-taking and innovation, is part of the process of wealth creation in dynamic capitalism. No one denies it can be painful. Yet, as we discuss in this book, the consequences of not allowing it—a lower standard of living and even greater joblessness—are far worse.

Some people who have lost jobs in the recession may be feeling hot under the collar about now. However, as we will show repeatedly, the financial crisis and recession was anything but a case of normal free-market creative destruction. It was exactly the opposite. History's most devastating economic upheavals have never been caused by the normal cycles of free market; they have been caused by catastrophic distortions that occur when government doesn't allow markets to work.

In a healthy, open economy, when there is an imbalance—too much or too little of something—the market eventually corrects it. Take cell phones. They were once rare and exceedingly expensive. Now everyone has them. Consumers no longer faint at the sight of their cell-phone bills. Prices have come way down, and many companies are struggling to make a profit.

Because a market is about serving the needs and wants of others, it will eventually do so—if people are given sufficient economic freedom. However, when government imposes artificial constraints, through regulation or through its own direct participation, it creates an imbalance—a distortion—that market forces aren't permitted to correct.

The result can be severe dysfunction, as we have with today's government-dominated health care. Or in the case of the larger economy, it can produce the meltdown we experienced in the past two years.

Distortionary federal policies have played a role in every historic economic disaster. This was the case with the Great Depression, the disastrous consequence of the Smoot-Hawley Tariff. That levy, intended to save American jobs, ignited a trade war between the United States and other nations, killing global employment. And it is the case today, with the subprime-mortgage mess and subsequent financial-sector meltdown. Both began with the massive distortion of the mortgage market engineered by misguided federal policies and the giant government-created mortgage corporations Fannie Mae and Freddie Mac.

These two behemoths were created with the worthy goal of boosting home ownership. Their immense size—larger by far than all private-sector competitors—and their ties to the federal government enabled them to create massive distortions in the mortgage, housing, and financial markets that brought the nation's financial system to near collapse.

A still bigger role was played by the Federal Reserve System, which lowered interest rates to boost the economy after the dot-com bust of the early 2000s—but ended up keeping them too low for too long. Without this error in monetary policy, the housing bubble never would have reached the catastrophic size that it did.

Rather than free markets betraying Alan Greenspan's faith, it was the other way around. Greenspan's low-interest, weak-dollar policies as head of the Federal Reserve Bank undermined free markets. Ayn Rand would not have succumbed to the temptation to believe that a government agency like the Fed could fine-tune the American and global economies. Nor would she have forgotten that a key component of a free market is a strong, stable, and reliable currency.

Bad economic policy can cause economic upheaval far more brutal than any disruption caused by the normal operation of markets.

There's another misunderstanding that's common to believers in the Rap. Just as they tend to see free-market destruction and ignore the bigger creation that's simultaneously taking place, they also tend to see certain government activities as fostering "creation" and prosperity—when in fact they're doing exactly the opposite by *destroying* wealth and jobs.

Job programs and other government spending may create some employment. But they do so by siphoning off tax dollars from countless individuals and corporations—resources that would have otherwise provided the capital for new job-creating ventures. What happens when there isn't enough capital? Companies can't expand—and often can't stay in business. New ventures remain on the drawing boards. Jobs that would have grown the economy can't be created—and in many cases are destroyed.

Thus, the massive public-works programs of the 1930s created some temporary employment, but not enough to end the Great Depression, which eventually faded with World War II. Nor did some ten economic stimulus programs, which created infrastructure-building jobs in Japan throughout the 1990s, succeed in pulling the nation out of its decade-long economic slump, despite almost quadrupling the national debt.

In 2009, people of all political stripes decried the massive government spending of the Obama administration on the grounds that it would create an enormous debt to be paid for "by the next generations."

Actually, they're wrong. Government spending is not some green-eyeshade accounting matter to worry about in the future. It has *immediate* impact in the here and now—by producing increased taxes and borrowings that drain the economy of private-sector capital.

Chapter 3, "Aren't the Rich Getting Richer at Other People's Expense?" explores common misconceptions surrounding "the rich" and the role they play in driving a democratic capitalist economy, creating wealth not only for themselves but for everyone else.

What if people like Steve Jobs and Bill Gates—or for that matter, Henry Ford and Thomas Edison—had been prevented from amassing

the capital they needed to expand their businesses or bring their innovations to the world? Millions of jobs and livelihoods never would have come
into existence. Throughout history, countries that have punished or banished their commercial class have discovered what happens—the economy
stagnates or actually collapses.

Our chapter on taxation, meanwhile, asks the question, aren't higher
taxes the price we pay for a humane society? Of course we need to pay
taxes. But contrary to the claims of politicians, they're not an "investment."
Government initiatives rarely deliver a return like a private-sector investment. Even government bonds that repay investors divert capital that
likely would have been better invested in growth-creating businesses.

Taxes make work and other transactions more expensive. Thus, fewer
of them take place. As we discuss, the best way to generate tax revenues is
through policies that encourage a growing tax base by allowing entrepreneurs and businesses to generate the capital to expand. And the best way to
do this is to keep tax rates reasonable—or through a low flat tax.

Some may recognize the ideas in this book as free-market economics.
We call them Real World Economics because we believe that is a
more accurate term. The U.S. economy, after all, is not a totally free
market. It is made up of many markets. Some are freer than others. The
markets that are freer, that give the greatest latitude to entrepreneurs
and innovators, that let buyers and sellers work out price and supply solutions, create more wealth for more individuals than any controlled by
government.

Real World economics is beyond partisan politics. Presidents and
politicians on both sides of the political spectrum have shown both
understanding and ignorance of Real World economic principles. John F.
Kennedy's tax cuts ignited the booming economy of the 1960s. Kennedy
also understood the need for a strong dollar, declaring, "The dollar should
be as good as gold."

Unfortunately, Richard Nixon didn't feel the same way. Nixon's
abandonment of the gold standard, combined with his wage and price
controls, ushered in the stagflation of the 1970s. He failed to heed the
market-based policies that have been associated with his party. Bill Clinton also defied political stereotypes—with better results. Unlike his
party, he believed in reducing international trade barriers. He success-

fully enacted the North American Free Trade Agreement. And he understood the dangers inherent in a weak dollar.

On the negative side, like Jimmy Carter and George W. Bush, Clinton pushed banks to make uneconomical mortgages. When he first took office, he raised income taxes, nearly aborting the recovery that was under way. He made amends for that error early in his second term, supporting a big capital gains tax cut that helped produce a vibrant economy and stock market.

Clinton's successor, George W. Bush, got it right on taxes with his 2003 rate cuts, which convincingly pulled the United States out of the 2000–2001 recession. But his weak-dollar policy and other mistakes made in 2008 produced the worst economic disaster since the 1930s.

Ronald Reagan slashed income-tax rates and, working in tandem with Paul Volcker at the Federal Reserve, killed the devastating inflation that had pockmarked the 1970s. Together these achievements—not to mention winning the cold war—set off a great, long boom in America and the world that didn't end until the crash of 2007.

Real World economics isn't about "left" or "right." It's based on tried-and-true principles that offer the best explanations of how the economy—and daily life—really works.

Ironically, as many in the U.S. question capitalism, nations that have been held up as models of "Third Way" democratic socialism are increasingly embracing Real World free market principles. Prime Minister Fredrik Reinfeldt of Sweden openly blames high taxes and welfare state policies for the problems of his nation's economy. As he noted in a speech in 2008, his country's much-vaunted affluence was built before the nation turned to socialism.

> At the beginning of the 1970s Sweden also had the fourth highest GDP per capita measured in purchasing power parity. Sweden was blooming.[15]

Thanks to Swedish socialism, Reinfeldt said, the wealth that "took a hundred years to build was almost dismantled in twenty-five years." As he recounts, "Growth fell off. Unemployment rose. The quality of welfare declined."

Between the 1970s and the 1990s, Sweden fell from fourth to eighteenth place among nations belonging to the Organisation for Economic Co-operation and Development (OECD). As we discuss in chapter 2, not only Sweden but other Nordic nations have a lower material standard of living than many people think, with dramatically less disposable income and fewer basic necessities. Reinfeldt's government, elected in 2006, is working to turn things around with initiatives like tax cuts, smaller government, and privatization—Real World pro-market policies.

➤Whole Foods founder John Mackey confesses he once thought that "business and capitalism were based on exploitation: exploitation of consumers, society and the environment." At one time an ardent believer in capitalism's bad rap, Mackey admits, "I believed that 'profit' was a necessary evil at best, and certainly not a desirable goal for society as a whole." However, when he founded Whole Foods, his view of the world began to evolve.

> Becoming an entrepreneur completely changed my life. Everything I believed about business was proven to be wrong. The most important thing I learned about business in my first year is that business wasn't based on exploitation or coercion at all. Instead I realized that business is based on voluntary cooperation. No one is forced to trade with a business; customers have competitive alternatives for their labor; investors have different alternatives and places to invest their capital. Investors, labor, management, suppliers—they all need to cooperate to create value for their customers. If they do, then any realized profit can be divided amongst the creators of the value through competitive market dynamics. In other words, business is not a zero sum game with a winner or loser. It is a win, win, win game—and I really like that.

Mackey's transformation was helped along by exposure to free-market thinkers: "I stumbled into reading Milton Friedman, Friedrich Hayek, Ludwig von Mises, Ayn Rand—I read all of them. I said to myself, 'Wow, this all makes sense. This is how the world really works. This is incredible.' "[16]

All of this caused him to conclude: "Business, working through free markets, is possibly the greatest force for good on the planet today. When executed well, business increases prosperity, ends poverty, improves the quality of life, and promotes the health and longevity of the world population at an unprecedented rate. . . . How many people in our greater society comprehend [this]?"

The noted playwright David Mamet attracted media attention when he wrote about a similar awakening:

> I began reading not only the economics of Thomas Sowell (our greatest contemporary philosopher) but Milton Friedman, Paul Johnson and Shelby Steele, and a host of conservative writers, and found that I agreed with them: a free-market understanding of the world meshes more perfectly with my experience than that idealistic vision I called liberalism.[17]

Both Mackey and Mamet realized that, as we'll show in this book, free-market principles are, for better or worse, the best description of how people go about their business each day and how markets actually function in the Real World.

Today, Americans are contemplating entering a new age of unprecedented government control of the economy—and their lives. Politicians have sold it as the answer to today's searing recession. But government micromanagement of an economy has seldom if ever succeeded in the Real World. As we show in this book, government solutions may benefit certain narrow sectors and interests. But they end up short-changing the larger society—reducing prosperity and living standards and creating different inequities and "unfairness."

In every single case, democratic capitalism is still the answer: it provides economic and social solutions that, while not always perfect, are ultimately better for society than the command-and-control economies advocated by proponents of "big government."

Traditional economists will tell you that economics is fundamentally about scarcity—how people go about allocating scarce resources. This idea does not describe what takes place in the Real World economy, which routinely turns scarcity into abundance.

Consider Henry Ford. He took the car, then a scarce commodity and exotic toy for the rich, and through his innovation, the assembly line, transformed it into something that could be mass-produced and affordable for working people. In other words, he turned scarcity into abundance.

Not only did Ford and his company prosper, but so did the millions of automobile buyers who benefited from using the car in their personal and professional lives.

People who don't like capitalism and, surprisingly, many economists, fail to fully appreciate the power of innovation, an intangible, to drive—indeed to transform—the economy.

No one, for example, anticipated that automobiles and trucks would largely supplant railroads. Or that the Internet would transform the news business. Conventional economic wisdom, the prognostications and solutions of "experts," too often assume fixed conditions—which is why they are so often wrong.

Giving people the maximum latitude to meet their own desires and the desires of others through innovation is a more potent wealth creator than a cornucopia of natural resources. This freedom is the reason that Hong Kong—a small territory with few national resources—became an economic powerhouse. The late economist and Nobel Prize winner Milton Friedman once observed:

> Compare Britain—the birthplace of the Industrial Revolution, the nineteenth-century economic superpower on whose empire the sun never set—with Hong Kong, a spit of land, overcrowded, with no resources except for a great harbor.[18]

University of Illinois business professor Andrew Morriss recounts in an excellent article in the magazine *The Freeman* that no one thought much of Hong Kong's prospects when the British acquired it as part of a settlement of a minor war in 1842. Shanghai, on the mainland, was a better natural port. Hong Kong seemed of little consequence, and so "Britain did relatively little with its new colony, beyond establishing public order and extending the rule of law." Hong Kong's economic freedom, however, made it a magnet for entrepreneurs from the repressive mainland. In the twentieth century, the tiny colony ended up outstripping its onetime "mother country"—per capita income went from 28 percent of Britain's in 1960 to 137 percent of Britain's in the late 1990s, when the colony was formally turned over to China.[19]

Neighboring mainland China was far larger and more resource rich. But its centrally controlled economy lagged for decades under communist rule until it finally began to liberalize.

This book will illuminate a fundamental Real World Lesson: *the needs and wants of society are most effectively met when individuals are free to harness their powers of creativity to provide the goods and services most desired by others.*

Some may say that this sounds like Adam Smith's classic notion of the power of self-interest to drive people and markets. But saying that the free market is solely about self-interest is a woefully blinkered perception. Self-interest alone did not invent the automobile, the Internet, the personal computer, the cell phone, or countless other wealth-creating inventions. These and other innovations are the product of the brilliance and creativity of individuals—and an economic environment that gives these people sufficient freedom to take risks and pursue their visions.

Far from being a Madoff economy, democratic capitalism is an iPod economy, a dynamic marketplace where people seek to get ahead by finding new ways to meet the wants of society through the constant process of trial and error. Yes there are greedy individuals, and there is destruction that takes place as well as creation. But through this process of innovation and growth, the standard of living is raised and wealth is created. More people live better. Society advances. Indeed, it is no accident that few revolutionary inventions have originated in authoritarian nations. As we note in chapter 1, when new technologies do emerge, such as in China centuries ago, the stranglehold of government bureaucracy prevents would-be entrepreneurs from bringing them to society and maximizing their potential.

This book will explore and explain these and other facts of economic life in the Real World. Many of the ideas we discuss are illustrated with examples drawn from the financial crisis and other recent events. These stories will continue to develop. But the principles do not change. We will show that, throughout history, capitalism has consistently disproved the doubters—and is the most radically constructive force in American life.

Forbes magazine founder B. C. Forbes, a near-penniless Scottish immigrant, came to this country in the early part of the last century. He began every set of editorials in *Forbes* with a phrase from Proverbs—"With all thy getting, get understanding." We hope this book promotes a true understanding of our economic system—with answers that will motivate you to move ahead and fulfill your dreams and aspirations.

CHAPTER ONE

"Is Capitalism Moral?"

THE RAP ► Capitalism is an amoral, dog-eat-dog system founded on greed and the survival of the fittest.

THE REALITY ► Capitalism is the world's most humane economic system, promoting the democratic values of a free and open society: hard work, cooperation, generosity, charity, and devotion to the rule of law.

Is capitalism moral? The question has been debated for generations. But it has more relevance today than ever in the wake of the recent financial crisis and recession.

Capitalism's critics insist that evidence of its "immorality" is everywhere—from the collapse of Enron in the early 2000s to the "predatory lending" that helped bring on the subprime-mortgage meltdown and ꞈꞈꞈꞈꞈꞈ ꞈꞈꞈꞈꞈꞈ ꞈꞈ ꞈꞈꞈꞈꞈꞈꞈꞈ ꞈꞈꞈꞈꞈ Bꞈꞈꞈꞈ Mꞈꞈꞈꞈ'ꞈ ꞈꞈꞈꞈꞈꞈꞈꞈ $50 billion Ponzi scheme that wiped out personal and institutional fortunes around the globe. These and other events, they say, demonstrate that the free market is a winner-take-all jungle, a place where the most ferocious and dishonest triumph, where nice guys finish last, where greed rules and people get ahead by exploiting others.

No doubt there can be bad behavior in a capitalist system. There is bad behavior in any society. However, when viewed as a *system*, capitalism is more moral than any and all alternatives.

Capitalism has produced the world's highest standard of living by promoting the moral values of cooperation, democracy, and free choice. Nobel Prize–winning economist and noted free-market advocate Milton Friedman frequently made the point that capitalism's foremost historic contribution has been its moral influence.

As we started to discuss in the introduction to this book, capitalism is not about selfishness, but about the needs and wants of others. Former U.S. ambassador, noted theologian, and author Michael Novak makes this point:

> The capitalist economy is *not* characterized, as Marx thought, by private ownership of the means of production, market exchange, and profit. All these were present in the precapitalist aristocratic age. Rather, the distinctive, defining difference of the capitalist economy is enterprise: the habit of employing human wit to invent new goods and services, and to discover new and better ways to bring them to the broadest possible public.[1]

Adam Smith explained in his classic work *The Wealth of Nations* that the exchange of goods and services in a market takes place only if both sides benefit. Such mutually beneficial exchanges, multiplied by the hundreds of millions, form what Smith referred to as "the invisible hand." The classic example of the pencil illustrates how these exchanges spontaneously allocate resources in a way that benefits more and more people.

To see the benefits of the Invisible Hand, one need only look around at the profusion of entrepreneurial businesses in most American communities. The vast array of goods and services generated by our vibrant democratic capitalist economy is unequaled: from 24-hour gyms and copy centers to supermarkets with countless varieties of food to even day spas in airports. The open markets of democratic capitalism meet needs that people don't even realize they had. Who ever would have imagined, for example, that we would need social networking sites such as Facebook? Or that you'd want to get a massage at an airport? Millions of Americans—and people around the world—now use Facebook and other similar sites every day, and they benefit from an Internet industry that began in the United States.

Free markets don't just meet the needs of the majority. If there's something people want or need, entrepreneurs in an open market will figure out a way to provide it—from size 22 shoes to hard-to-find spare parts for home appliances.

Since the emergence of democratic capitalism in the last three hundred years, humankind has made more advances—in incomes, standard of living, social mobility, and longevity—than in all the previous centuries put together.

Those who buy into capitalism's bad rap fail to see the moral significance of democratic capitalism's ability to provide for people's material well-being. And yet, would anyone question the *immorality* of regimes such as Venezuela, North Korea, and the former Soviet Union, where restrictions on personal and economic freedom have caused citizens to suffer extreme deprivation, food shortages, and even famine?

Democratic capitalism is moral precisely because it gives people the greatest latitude to meet their needs and desires by serving those of their fellow citizens. Through doing so, it generates broad-based prosperity.

Many people today have forgotten that, for centuries, China was technologically ahead of Europe in metallurgy and shipbuilding. Both Europe and China, for example, developed the compass. But Europeans were the first to use it in navigating and exploring the earth. Why? Because Europe had a religious belief in the necessity of progress that eventually became a key underpinning of capitalism.

Milton Friedman wrote that capitalism is about being "free to choose."[2] That's why free markets have caused people around the world to move in the direction of democracy. Michael Novak has observed: "Every democracy on earth that really does protect the human rights of its individual citizens is based, in fact, upon a free capitalist economy. Empirically speaking, there is not a single contrary case."[3]

Free markets are about people expressing their desires, saying yes or no to a product or service by essentially voting with their money. Economist Walter Williams has written that, in contrast to state-dominated societies, capitalism respects "the sanctity of the individual" and is "rooted in voluntary relationships rather than force and coercion."[4]

In a democratic capitalist economy, people interact in networks of cooperation that teach discipline and moral lessons—from the importance of showing up for work and handling money responsibly to the value of teamwork. Americans take capitalism's moral ethos for granted. Cynics may ridicule chirpy fast-food servers who greet them with "Have a nice day." But this etiquette reflects an emphasis on meeting the needs of others that is not present in other societies.

For example, twenty years after the fall of the Soviet Union, visitors to Russia still complain about the sullen customer service. That's because

Russia's formerly communist society was run by a repressive govern-ment that controlled all resources and imposed its agenda on citizens. People had to accept what they got, take it or leave it. The idea of freely meeting people's needs—and being polite to them—in an open market was largely alien to this culture.

Russians are only now learning customer-service values from Western businesses like McDonald's that have managed to gain a foothold in the country's difficult business environment. The story is often told that when McDonald's started in Russia twenty years ago, company trainers had to overcome the famously dour attitude of service personnel whose at-titude was "We've got the hamburgers. The customers don't."⁵

The value capitalism places on meeting the needs of others doesn't stop with the marketplace. It has made America a more charitable na-tion. No citizens give more of their income and time than the American people. According to New York University professor Claire Gaudiani, the U.S. gives twice as much as the next most charitable country—about $300 billion each year. This generosity extends throughout all income levels and is not limited to domestic charities. Americans have sent hun-dreds of millions of dollars overseas to help those in need after natural disasters ranging from the Burmese cyclone to the Asian Tsunami.

To fully appreciate the morality of democratic capitalism, it helps to have lived in other societies. Author and human rights activist Ayaan Hirsi Ali was born in Somalia, spent time in Saudi Arabia, and later lived in the Netherlands, where she served as a member of parliament. She now lives in the United States. Having experienced a repressive terror state, a Middle Eastern feudal society, and a European social welfare sys-tem, she believes that the moral standards of American free enterprise "are far higher than those of history's other great powers."

Why? Because, she says, democratic capitalism is a "meritocracy" that offers people the greatest opportunity to pursue their own goals, to in-novate and excel, both in their business lives and at home in their com-munities. Not only does Ali believe democratic capitalism to be more moral than the oppressive systems of the former Soviet Union, prereform China, and Saudi Arabia. She writes that it is also superior to the welfare states of Western Europe, whose statist economies "corrode" individual re-sponsibility by encouraging dependency.

In a free-market society, where liberty comes first, individuals tend to be more creative and to innovate; in welfare states that assign priority to equality, the natural resourcefulness of human beings is perverted. To become successful, you must learn how to "work the system" rather than how to develop a better product. Risk is avoided, and individual responsibility is thwarted. Although superficially the system may appear fair, it promotes mediocrity and a sense of victimhood, and it discourages those who want to excel.[6]

Ali believes that the innovation and open exchange of ideas that take place in democratic capitalism make people more likely to seek remedies to social problems. For example, she says, moral debates about issues such as pollution are conducted mainly in free-market societies. And in her experience capitalism's entrepreneurs solve problems more efficiently than the bureaucrats of any government.

Ali readily acknowledges that our system of democratic capitalism is far from perfect—"There are many wealthy, decadent, and vapid people in America." However, she warns that the quest for moral perfection in a society can itself have immoral consequences:

In the course of history, the search for perfect societies—that is, the failure to acknowledge human imperfection—almost always ended in one or another form of theocracy, authoritarianism, or violent anarchy. But for those who seek to work with human flaws of every stripe, and to increase the sum total of individual happiness, the free market, combined with political freedom, is the best way.[7]

We wholeheartedly agree.

Q ► BUT DON'T FREE MARKETS RELY ON GREED?

A ► FREE MARKETS RELY ON TRUST.

Greed, for lack of a better word, is good. Greed is right. Greed works. Greed clarifies, cuts through and captures the essence of the evolutionary spirit. Greed, in all of its forms—greed for life, for money, knowledge—has marked the upward surge of mankind."

That's how Gordon Gekko, the iconic Wall Street financier in the 1980s film *Wall Street*, famously—and cynically—summed up a widespread view of the free market economy—a place where all economic transactions, for good and ill, occur because of greed, the darker side of human nature.

Modeled on the notorious corporate raiders of the 1980s, Gekko was a fictional character. But his belief is shared by numerous individuals who see capitalism as immoral and based on greed.

Those who equate capitalism with greed will sometimes quote from the eighteenth-century Adam Smith classic *The Wealth of Nations*: "Nobody but a beggar chooses to depend chiefly upon the benevolence of his fellow citizens."

True, Adam Smith's brewer and baker give you dinner for a self-interested reason: they want your money. But self-interest isn't greed.

One of the seven deadly sins, greed means taking too much of something that you may not rightfully deserve. That is what Bernard Madoff was accused of doing, and that is why he went to jail. But his behavior, like that of any criminal, is an exception. People don't get ahead in a democratic capitalist economy by taking what they don't deserve. They may for a while, but, as the story of Bernard Madoff shows, sooner or later they pay the price.

Most of the transactions that take place every day in free markets are actually based on the opposite of greed: millions of people exchange goods and services in mutually beneficial transactions based on verbal promises or written agreements, cooperating with one another in "webs of trust."

We rely on this trust each day: The knowledge that the overwhelming majority of customers will pay. Or that we will get a paycheck from our employer every two weeks. Or that the dry cleaners will return our clothing cleaner than it was before. Without this kind of reliability and predictability, our economy couldn't function.

A prime example of capitalism's "web of trust": the auction site eBay, where customers buy and sell to one another anonymously, based on little more than a thumbnail product profile, a seller rating, and a credit card number.

EBay's sellers and buyers are not always honest. But most often they are. Without this expectation of reliability there could be no commerce. People would not be able to buy, sell, and create wealth—not only on eBay, but in any market.[8]

Trust, not greed, was the reason that so many people were duped by Bernard Madoff. Few could anticipate his over-the-top villainy because such a willful violation of the rules is relatively rare. Madoff's annual returns to clients also appeared reasonable.

The idea that capitalism is based on greed is belied when taking a closer look at the great fortunes of the people on the Forbes 400 list of wealthiest Americans. Number 18 on the 2010 list, Jeff Bezos, founded the hugely successful Internet bookstore Amazon.com, which has since become an online megastore selling virtually anything. He built his $12.6 billion fortune not because of greed, but because he correctly saw the potential of emerging Internet technology to do a better job selling books than bricks-and-mortar retailers.

And what about Oprah Winfrey (number 130 in 2010, with a net worth of $2.7 billion)? Her story is well-known: born in Mississippi, she rose to become a TV talk show host, actress, producer, publisher, and owner of a media empire. Her productions and publications promote positive values of self-improvement. She has also built her fortune by bringing wealth to others, launching the media careers of personalities like Dr. Phil and Rachael Ray. As if all of this were not enough, she has donated millions to charity, including starting a school for girls in South Africa.

Henry Hillman (number 170 in 2010, with a net worth of $2.1 billion) was not self-made. He inherited his family's steel fortune. But he, too, has been anything but greedy. He has invested in real estate, medical technology, and other high-tech companies. Hillman has been one of Pittsburgh's most active philanthropists—a heavy supporter of medical and computer research. He has given some $20 million to cancer research and recently gave $10 million for a new computer science research building at Carnegie Mellon University.

Number 68 on Forbes' 2007 list was James Sorenson. The inventor, who passed away a year later at age 86, made a $4.5 billion fortune from medical devices, including a patented plastic catheter and a disposable surgical mask. Sorenson had more money than he could ever spend and nothing to prove. Yet he started another new venture, Sorenson Forensics, in 2006, shortly before his death. The company's genome-based technologies have helped solve cold-case murder mysteries. Asked why he risked his capital so late in life to start yet another new business, the habitual entrepreneur replied, "It soothes the soul to help people."

John Drummond isn't on the *Forbes* 400 list. His business, Unicycle.com, started out as a hobby. Drummond discovered that the unicycling he'd loved as a child could help him take off weight.

Yes, Drummond had a self-interested reason for building his business—he had been laid off by IBM and needed a job. But he also wanted the sense of personal fulfillment that comes from bringing something good to others. Drummond felt that people would enjoy unicycling and appreciate its unique, if quirky, value as a fitness workout. He succeeded because he was an innovator: he made a hard-to-find product more easily available over the Internet.

Today Drummond's business has franchises in eight countries, and he recently started another business, Banjo.com.

The claim that capitalism is based on greed is often used by politicians to sell solutions to economic problems that are supposed to be more moral—from taxes on windfall profits to government health insurance. These government-imposed remedies are supposed to deliver greater morality and fairness. But as we will show repeatedly in this book, they generally do neither. That's because political solutions are not developed to serve the Real World needs of people who make up a market but the narrower concerns of those who happen to be in power. They're frequently less fair, and less moral, than grassroots market solutions.

If greed is the one-sided taking of what does not belong to you, then what does one call pork-laden stimulus packages and other legislation that channel taxpayer money into things like "low bush blueberry research" and a water taxi service in, yes, Pleasure Beach, Connecticut—politicians' personal projects that produce few if any economic benefits. Whatever you may call them, such "solutions" divert capital that could have been put into productive innovations that would have created more wealth for more people. Is that moral?

▲   REAL WORLD LESSON   ▲

The self-interest driving democratic capitalism is profoundly different from greed, which ignores the needs of others and is the opposite of what succeeds in a free market.

Q ► IF CAPITALISM ISN'T GREEDY, THEN WHY DO SOME COMPANIES CHARGE
EXORBITANT PRICES FOR CRITICAL PRODUCTS LIKE GASOLINE AND
LIFESAVING DRUGS? AREN'T THEY GOUGING TO REAP EXCESSIVE PROFITS?

A ► PROFIT IS A CRITICAL INDICATOR OF CONSUMER DEMAND AND THE
ONLY WAY TO ENSURE THAT THERE WILL BE A SUFFICIENT SUPPLY OF
ANYTHING. BY THE WAY, PROFIT IS AMONG THE SMALLEST
COMPONENTS OF DRUG AND OIL PRICES.

When gasoline prices soared between 2004 and 2008, people were enraged by the profits being made by oil companies. A Gallup poll found that more Americans believed the high price of gasoline was due to oil company greed rather than to other factors, including the Middle East conflict. Politicians from California senator Barbara Boxer to then New York senator Hillary Clinton called for measures to "get tough" on "Big Oil." Vermont senator Bernie Sanders sputtered in an editorial: "Exxon-Mobil has made more profits in the last two years than any company in the history of the world."[9]

Similar indignation has been directed at the pharmaceutical industry. Critics accuse drug companies of "gouging," among other transgressions, calling for various government regulations to rein in "Big Pharma." "Other countries don't allow prescription drug companies to gouge their customers," complained former Congressman Tom Allen (D-Maine).[10]

The critics aren't entirely wrong. Bernie Sanders is correct when he says that oil company profits were the highest in history. And it's true, as Tom Allen suggests, that newly developed brand-name drugs can cost more in America than in other countries. The cholesterol-lowering medicine Lipitor, for instance, costs about sixty cents a pill in Paris and around four dollars in Philadelphia.[11]

Yet these emotional accusations reflect a misunderstanding of the myriad and complex factors affecting pricing and profit. People who decry oil company profits, for example, don't understand that a major factor driving up oil prices was the weak value of the dollar on currency markets, a result of the Federal Reserve Bank printing too many greenbacks. Also driving up prices was the high demand for oil, driven by rapid growth in India, China, and eastern and central Europe.

Both factors, of course, have little to do with profit. In nonrecessionary times, the typical net profit margin of oil companies—what they make off each dollar of revenue—is only around 8 percent. That's far less than the profit margins of banks (over 19 percent), software companies (17 percent), and even food producers (more than 9 percent). And it's just a little higher than the profit margin of Starbucks, which is around 7 percent.

Pharmaceutical profit margins are ordinarily around 18 percent or 19 percent, only nominally higher than those in the software industry. Yet they're especially reasonable considering that only about one in a hundred drugs ends up on the market. Each drug that makes it must generate enough revenue to cover the development costs of the ninety-nine drugs that didn't—as well as the cost of future drugs. And bringing a single drug to market costs a major pharmaceutical company anywhere from $800 million to $1.5 billion.

If a drug company does not come up with new, successful drugs, profits stagnate—and stock plummets. Pfizer, for example, has had a dearth of blockbuster drugs in recent years. The result: the stock had plunged over 70 percent in value between 1999 and 2008.

Yet some people believe that pharmaceutical makers and oil companies shouldn't be allowed to make a profit—or that their profits should be limited through taxation or price controls. They don't understand how profit functions and the role it plays in a Real World economy.

Profit does more than make some people rich by generating dividends and capital gains. It is also the way our economic system mobilizes people to provide for others. This goes beyond merely serving as an incentive: profit is a critical barometer of demand, telling producers where they should invest—or where they should cut back. It keeps supply flowing smoothly.

For example, if demand soars for, say, coffee, producers will raise their prices. And why not? Java is in greater demand and thus more valuable. So what happens? The lure of higher profits encourages producers to grow and process more. New coffee suppliers may also be enticed to enter the market. The result: supply increases.

Then something else happens: profits create competition. Higher profits bring more players into the market. To compete, producers have to slash prices. The result: profits eventually fall.

An example: Xerox, inventor of the modern photocopying machine. The enormous profits the company made with its first copiers soon attracted countless competitors, including Canon, Ricoh, and Mita (now Kyocera), to name a few. At one time only large offices could afford these machines. Today they're so cheap that even students can afford desktop models. And not only do they copy, they scan and print, too.

Scores of other examples are provided by the electronics industry. A few years ago flat-screen TVs cost ten thousand dollars or more. Now you can get many for under five thousand dollars.

What happens when companies aren't allowed to generate profits? No barometer exists to adjust supply to meet demand. Politicians like to think that punishing profits serves the public interest. But the Real World economic truth is that it does the opposite. You end up with shortages of essential products—and sometimes surpluses of things no one wants.

Many people today are too young to remember what happened after President Richard Nixon imposed controls on the price of oil in the 1970s. Immediate shortages of gasoline resulted, which led to gas lines. People had to fill up on given days, depending on whether they had odd- or even-numbered license plates.

Taxing profits to punish "greedy" companies doesn't work, either. That's because profit is a key source of the investment capital companies use to expand operations, innovate, and create jobs.

In the case of oil companies, taxes on profits destroy capital that would otherwise go toward exploration and new oil production. In 1980 President Jimmy Carter enacted the Windfall Profit Tax to punish supposedly avaricious oil companies. What happened? Domestic production plunged. With oil companies producing less, the levy generated far less for Uncle Sam than proponents had predicted. The Windfall Profit Tax was widely considered a disappointment and was eventually repealed.

Decades later, when gasoline prices skyrocketed from 2004 to mid-2008, there were no gas lines. Why? Because there were none of the kind of profit-punishing price controls imposed by President Nixon in the 1970s—something antiprofit protesters have failed to notice.

As for drugs, a major reason newly developed medications are more expensive in the United States is not because of "gouging." It's because drug makers charge more in this country to recover the costs of selling to Canada and European nations whose state-run heath-care systems keep drug prices artificially low.

So what do Canadians and Europeans get for their "fairer" drug prices? As we will explore in chapter 7, they get fewer new medicines and treatment with older, frequently less effective drugs.

Critics say profit is merely a bribe to get businesspeople to provide products and services. Actually, profit is essential to achieving innovation and a higher standard of living.

The late renowned management guru Peter Drucker repeatedly emphasized this key, oft-ignored point: without profits, there is no capital to build the advances of the future. If you don't have profit, you don't get change.

Profit is not only moral. It's essential to a healthy economy. What's immoral is not allowing people to make it.

▲   REAL WORLD LESSON   ▲

Profit isn't a greedy surcharge but a vital barometer of demand and supply, and a source of capital critical to a smoothly functioning economy.

Q ► HOW CAN CAPITALISM BE HUMANE WHEN LOW-INCOME PEOPLE
SUFFER THE MOST FROM MARKET FLUCTUATIONS LIKE THE
SUBPRIME-MORTGAGE CRISIS?

A ► THE SUBPRIME-MORTGAGE CRISIS IS A CLASSIC CASE OF THE "MORAL
HAZARD" THAT RESULTS WHEN GOVERNMENT INSULATES PEOPLE
FROM THE CONSEQUENCES OF RISKY BEHAVIOR.

It's a question often raised by free-market critics: how can capitalism be a moral system when low-income people are so often harmed by the fluctuations of "unfettered" markets?

For many, the subprime-mortgage debacle provided the most painful example in years of this moral pitfall of capitalism. According to the popular narrative, "predatory" lenders trapped low-income borrowers with lenient subprime loans. Ridiculous introductory terms seduced thousands of unsuspecting homeowners into signing on the dotted line—only to be slammed later with higher interest rates.

The result: hundreds of thousands of subprime borrowers went into default. Bad subprime loans were blamed for a 53 percent rise in delinquencies and foreclosure proceedings on 1.5 million homes in 2007, a situation that only got worse in 2008.

Media reports about the crisis highlighted heartbreaking personal stories of poor people facing the loss of their homes. During her presidential primary campaign, Hillary Clinton called for curbs on "abuses" by "unscrupulous brokers." Her Democratic rival John Edwards compared the mortgage market to "the wild, wild West."

Of course, poor people were hardly the only ones hurt. The crisis ripped through the economy. Several major lenders, such as New Century Financial and American Home Mortgage, were forced into bankruptcy. Even the largest mortgage company, Countrywide Financial Corporation, was laid low. It was ultimately sold to Bank of America at the fire-sale price of about five dollars per share—a stark contrast to its forty-three-dollar-a-share price in 2006, before the bubble burst.

The financial crisis has been a global disaster, but the collapse and economic devastation were not the fault of "unfettered markets." It was a classic case of what economists refer to as "moral hazard," the damage that occurs when government artificially protects people from the consequences of their high-risk behavior.

Cato Institute senior fellow Gerald P. O'Driscoll explains:

> Government programs and policies often serve to insulate individuals from the full consequences of their actions. For instance, subsidized federal flood insurance leads individuals to build more homes in flood plains than would otherwise be the case. The public naturally feels sympathy for homeowners who are the victims of flooding, and supports more assistance for those caught up in these dreadful situations. The "help" often exacerbates the problem, however, by removing incentives for homeowners to build on higher and drier land.[12]

In the case of the subprime crisis, overly low interest rates and an overabundant money supply, combined with well-intentioned though misguided policy, encouraged lenders to engage in risky behavior. They made ill-advised loans that they wouldn't have made under normal circumstances to too many unqualified borrowers, ultimately causing a collapse.

It all began several years back after the dot-com bust of 2000 and 2001. Seeking to boost the economy, the Federal Reserve Bank made two critical mistakes. First, it kept interest rates too low for too long. Second, it started printing more money, triggering an inflation in home values.

Suddenly the market was on steroids. Prices kept rising with no end in sight. These upwardly spiraling prices—rather than "greed"—were one reason that lenders lowered their standards. People figured, *So what if you weren't really qualified to receive a loan?* There was a way out: you could sell your house for more money or refinance later.

Inflating the bubble still further were the government-created mortgage giants, Fannie Mae and its cousin, Freddie Mac. We go into additional detail about these two giants in later chapters. President Franklin Roosevelt set up Fannie Mae during the Great Depression to indirectly boost a flagging housing market. Freddie Mac, a Fannie Mae clone, was launched in 1970. Fannie and Freddie were eventually spun off by the government, selling shares and becoming enormous publicly held corporations. Their mission is to indirectly help the housing market by buying mortgages from banks, bundling them into packages to be sold to investors. The idea was to generate money for banks that would increase mortgage lending and help more Americans achieve the dream of owning their homes.

Fannie's and Freddie's money comes from selling their own bonds, as well as stock, to investors. However, the two companies owe their enormous size—as well as their immense political and market power—to their ties to government. They had emergency lines of credit with the U.S. Treasury Department. Investors thereby believed that the companies were implicitly backed by the government. As we mentioned in the introduction to this book, they are larger than any private-sector competitors.

The impact of these enormous corporations on the housing market cannot be overstated. Fannie and Freddie were responsible for some $1.6 *trillion* worth of less-than-prime mortgages by 2008 from banks and mortgage brokers, packaging them as securities and selling them to investors.

With money flooding the market, some lenders didn't bother documenting whether borrowers had any real income. These were dubbed "no doc" loans. Anyone breathing seemed to be able to obtain a mortgage. Sometimes no down payment was required.

Contrary to the impression conveyed by politicians like Congressman Barney Frank and now-retired senator Christopher Dodd, most lenders were more careless than predatory, making loans with free-flowing capital in a market that seemed certain to keep going up.

The end result was a classic bubble of gargantuan dimensions. Then the Fed started to raise interest rates between 2005 and 2006. Everyone had previously assumed that subprime home buyers could always get a new mortgage with a new teaser rate when the teaser of an existing mortgage expired. But now those ultralow teaser rates would have to go up. Even if a home buyer got a new teaser rate, it was going to be higher than the old one. The market for home mortgages began to cool.

The whole thing crashed in the summer of 2007. Subprime borrowers—particularly speculators or "flippers"—faced increased monthly payments and could not refinance or sell. They were stuck.

Ironically, some of the same people who today criticize subprime lenders condemned banks in the 1970s for not lending to low-income communities. Back then, the practice was demonized as "redlining." The outcry resulted in the 1977 Community Reinvestment Act, which required banks to offer credit to their entire market area and not just wealthier neighborhoods. Until recently, anti-redlining sentiment persisted. It has been credited by many with helping to create an atmosphere that only further encouraged subprime lenders. Moreover, the Department of Housing and Urban Development urged lenders to provide loans requiring no down payment for low-income people right up to the bust.

Had the government not artificially lowered interest rates and done so much to encourage subprime lending, we would not have seen the recklessness that so distorted markets and led to the subprime meltdown. In a truly "free" market, fewer people might have gotten mortgages. But also fewer would have defaulted.

People in the subprime crisis suffered not because of the immorality of free markets, but because of markets that weren't free enough.

▲   REAL WORLD LESSON   ▲

Government actions intended to help people often set the stage for even greater hardship down the road.

Q ► IF CAPITALISM'S FOREMOST HISTORIC CONTRIBUTION HAS BEEN ITS MORAL INFLUENCE, THEN WHY DOES CAPITALISM APPEAR TO ENCOURAGE WHITE-COLLAR CRIME?

A ► IN FACT STATE-RUN ECONOMIES ENCOURAGE MORE CORRUPTION THAN DOES CAPITALISM.

At the height of the corporate-governance scandals several years ago involving Enron, WorldCom, and other companies, *Time* magazine asked: "Why a sleaze wave now? To some extent, it represents the dark side of President Reagan's emphasis on the free market and individual enterprise."[13] William Greider, a writer for *The Nation* and a harsh critic of free markets, called the scandals "a teaching opportunity" reflecting the essentially corrupt and narrow "soul of capitalism."

Such views were not just voiced by the left. Then Federal Reserve chairman Alan Greenspan attributed the scandals to "infectious greed." *Time* also quoted James Gattuso, policy analyst for the conservative Heritage Foundation, who observed, "We have more capitalism now, and it isn't always pretty."[14]

These statements suggest that there would be fewer instances of white-collar crime and corruption if only we had more state control and less open markets. According to this line of thinking, without the temptation provided by the riches of capitalism, there would be less corruption and wrongdoing.

Really? Real World experience suggests the opposite: free markets encourage less corruption. Government control—instead of reducing wrongdoing—produces more.

There are relatively few measurements of white-collar crime. However, one international study by Transparency International, a nonprofit organization dedicated to fighting corruption, found that the United States is one of the *least* corrupt countries in the world when it comes to the crime of bribery. According to the report, about 10 percent of U.S. respondents reported paying bribes—unlike countries like Indonesia, Russia, Venezuela, Greece, and other nations, where as many as 50 percent of respondents reported doing so.

Bribery is a daily fact of life in many of these nations. Annelise Anderson, a former government economist now at Stanford University's Hoover Institution, says a key reason for this is overbearing state bureaucracies. In order to get anything done, people have to pay officials or find other ways to subvert an unreasonable system. Anderson writes:

In general, excessive bureaucratic power and discretion provide the basis for corruption—for bribery, shakedowns, and extortion—especially when the criteria for bureaucratic decisions are unclear and difficult to monitor and evaluate. The corruption of a bureaucratic agency may begin with the clients of the agency, such as the members of a regulated industry. Thus building contractors may seek to speed up the work of the agencies that give building permits. More often, however, the bureaucrats originate the corruption by demanding payment. Getting a government contract may require a kickback; tips or bribes may be necessary to secure a wide variety of government services. In the Soviet Union bribes were necessary to secure everything from drivers' licenses to medical care and even higher education, as well as goods.

Cuba, with its controlled prices and black markets, illustrates just what Anderson is talking about. The *St. Petersburg Times* reported that

> the difficulty of making ends meet has turned ordinary Cubans into petty criminals. . . . Stealing from state workplaces or operating small, illegal businesses is so common that Cubans dismiss it as an almost acceptable part of daily life.[15]

Ironically, one measure being considered in Cuba to remedy the situation is an *expansion* of private enterprise. Philip Peters of the Lexington Institute observed, "These are bitter facts to air in a place where socialist state enterprises are said to represent the revolution's values, delivering services at fair, controlled prices without the exploitation or inefficiency of capitalist systems."[16]

One reason many people think prosperity brings more white-collar crime is that the definition of what constitutes white-collar crime changes with the political climate. In fact, some believe the government has gone too far in criminalizing economic behavior—making what are really regulatory violations into criminal offenses. Writes Paul Rosenzweig of the Heritage Foundation,

> Where once, to be a criminal, an individual had to do an act (or attempt to do an act) with willful intent to violate the law or with knowledge of the wrongful nature of his conduct, today it is possible to be found criminally liable and imprisoned for a substantial term of years for the failure to do an act required by law, without any actual knowledge of the law's obligations and with no wrongful intent whatsoever.[17]

Prosecutors are increasingly launching criminal prosecutions of individuals who do not meet the traditional test of "mens rea," or criminal intent. For example, in the middle of this decade nineteen employees of the accounting firm KPMG were accused of issuing "abusive" tax shelters. In the past, this would have been pursued as a regulatory matter. Instead it wound up in criminal court. But prosecutors couldn't prove their case, and a federal judge threw it out.

Still, wouldn't there be fewer corporate scandals, fewer Enrons and WorldComs, with less capitalism and more state control over markets? More control, of course, means bigger government. And government is even less transparent than the private sector—and has a more dismal record of safeguarding people's money.

According to the World Bank, some $1 trillion worldwide is paid each year in bribes to government officials. In Africa alone, more than $400 billion has been looted by government officials and stashed in foreign countries.

In the United States, taxpayer money is regularly pilfered for questionable and often self-serving purposes through the practice of congressional "earmarks," allocations for frivolous spending that are slipped into appropriations bills with no hearings, examination, or oversight. We don't usually think of earmarks as white-collar crime—indeed, many people would take exception to the idea. Yet some of the worst earmarks are indeed criminal, a result of bribes paid to legislators.

FOX News reported on Pennsylvania congressman Paul Kanjorski, who earmarked $10 million in taxpayer dollars that ended up in a family-run company, Cornerstone Technologies, that eventually went bankrupt. Kanjorski's story shows the double standard that can exist when determining what constitutes white-collar crime. Had the congressman's misdeeds taken place in a public company, they would have been labeled theft.

Yet few news organizations covered Kanjorski the way they did corporate crooks like Enron's Andrew Fastow and Jeffrey Skilling. Fastow and Skilling went to jail. Kanjorski remained in office until he was finally defeated in the 2010 midterm elections.

▲   REAL WORLD LESSON   ▲

There will be dishonesty under any system. However, capitalism's dependence on winning the trust of consumers, as well as the rule of law, discourages corruption and encourages the most transparency.

Q ▸ IF CAPITALISM IS MORAL, THEN WHY DID FREE-MARKET REFORMS APPEAR TO INCREASE CRIME AND CORRUPTION IN POST-COMMUNIST RUSSIA?

A ▸ BECAUSE RUSSIA IS NOT YET A DEMOCRATIC FREE-MARKET ECONOMY.

Free-market critics love to hold up the crime and corruption of post-communist Russia as emblematic of the fundamental immorality of unbridled capitalism. Yet Russia's economy is hardly a democratic free market.

In 2009 the Heritage Foundation, the noted free-market think tank, gave Russia's economy a 50.8 percent rating, calling it "mostly unfree."[18]

Putin's authoritarian "managed democracy" is more intrusive in the economic lives of its citizens than that of his predecessor, Boris Yeltsin. True, things have improved since the lawless 1990s. The Russian economy is growing. There are privately owned businesses and an increasingly affluent middle class. The tax code has been drastically simplified. Steps have been made toward the creation of Western-style property rights. But there is still not the kind of rule of law and property-rights protections that we take for granted in the United States. Nor does Russia's court system effectively mediate disputes.

Russian economist and political leader Grigory Yavlinsky has noted: "We do not have independent courts in Russia. . . . The law enforcement system is corrupt and has been transformed into an instrument of revenge and the grabbing of property."[19]

It is still not easy to launch a new business in that country. According to the Heritage Foundation, getting a new business license still involves plenty of red tape, taking "much more than the world average of 18 procedures and 225 days."[20]

Small wonder that Yavlinsky, while acknowledging reforms, has derided his nation's system as "phony capitalism": success or failure in the Russian marketplace depends on political favors, i.e., paying bribes and protection to officials or their cronies. The contrast with Western-style democratic capitalism, he says, is "stark."

We discuss later in this chapter that Russia's oil wealth has helped to create this appearance of affluence—the "phony capitalism" described by Yavlinsky. Russia's corruption is the product not of free markets, but of an authoritarian government that hasn't permitted them to flourish.

Government-dominated "phony capitalism" suffers from the same corruption as other state-controlled societies.

Q ► Why have Russia, China, and other nations failed to democratize following recent free-market reforms if capitalism promotes more open societies?

A ► Democratization occurs faster in some countries than others.

Freedom House, the nonpartisan organization that monitors political rights around the world, in 2008 announced a disturbing finding: for the first time in years, there had been a "setback in global freedom" in one-fifth of the world's countries. Yet many of the backsliding nations, such as the former Soviet Union, had instituted free-market reforms. Other countries, like China, continue to have "closed" political systems despite economic liberalization. According to the organization, this decline continued as of 2009.[21]

These and other developments have been held up as evidence that free markets don't bring free societies after all. The *New York Times* declared that "both liberal and conservative intellectuals, even once ardent supporters, have backed away" from a belief in capitalism as a democratizer.

Then there are those like Yale law professor Amy Chua who maintain capitalism actually hurts poor nations. She wrote a book with the incendiary title *World on Fire: How Exporting Free Market Democracy Breeds Ethnic Hatred and Global Instability.*

Chua claims that instead of planting the seeds of democracy in struggling countries, capitalism in fact makes things worse, exacerbating ethnic conflicts and widening the gap between rich and poor. She points to nations like Nigeria, that, despite having open markets, continue to experience bloody tribal conflicts and have failed to establish democracy.

Chua's perspective is no doubt partly shaped by personal tragedy: her well-to-do aunt, a Chinese businesswoman living in the Philippines, was stabbed to death by her chauffeur. For some people, her arguments may appear compelling. Yet they reflect a poor understanding of the history of democracy and an ignorance of Real World economics.

No, capitalism does not magically turn nations into American-style republics overnight. But political scientists have documented the relationship between free markets and free societies.

Cato Institute analyst Daniel Griswold has found that "the most economically open countries are three times more likely to enjoy full political and civil freedoms as those that are economically closed. Those that are closed are nine times more likely to completely suppress civil and political freedoms as those that are open."[22]

Griswold cites research showing that since the nations of the world began to liberalize their economies in the mid-1980s, the percentage of democratically elected governments surged from 40 percent to over 60 percent today.[23]

When you think about it, the link between economic and political liberty makes sense. Free markets not only demand, but teach, the skills needed for political self-governance. Griswold explains, "Economic freedom and trade provide a counterweight to governmental power."[24] That is because under capitalism you, and not government, are responsible for most day-to-day economic decisions, from how to raise money to start a business to how to take care of the maintenance of your home.

Sooner or later, people realize that if they can vote with their money and choose their refrigerator or automobile, why shouldn't they have the similar ability to vote at the ballot box and elect their officials?

Truly free markets also require an open flow of information. A Silicon Valley can emerge only when people have the freedom to develop and exchange ideas. Capitalism also fosters democracy by encouraging the growth of a better-educated middle class—people who are more likely to make demands of public officials.

As for Russia and China, it's true that they remain politically repressive. But both nations allow more personal freedoms than they did under communism. In China, the days of murderous Maoist campaigns like the Cultural Revolution and the Great Leap Forward, which took the lives of tens of millions, are over. People now have property rights to their apartments and the ability to travel. Tens of thousands of entrepreneurs have created new businesses.

The *New York Times* reported that China's growing middle class is increasingly pushing back against authoritarian rule: "The new property owners have poured their energy into everything from establishing co-op boards to spar with landlords, to organizing real estate market boycotts to force down prices. Others, meanwhile, have begun running for office in district-level elections, where they hope to make the city government more responsive to their needs."[25]

The *Times* quoted a scholar at the China Development Institute who observed "an awakening of awareness on public issues" and civic leaders who see "a steady growth in citizen involvement." This was clearly the case after the 2008 earthquake disaster in Sichuan Province, which led to an outcry against corruption, which was blamed for the shoddy "tofu construction"[26] that helped cause some seventy thousand deaths and countless other casualties.

In Russia, observers are justifiably alarmed by the crackdowns that have rolled back the democratic reforms that followed the collapse of Soviet communism in the 1990s. Even so, most Russians today have more personal liberties than they ever had in their blood-soaked history. A political demonstration will get you arrested and your head cracked. But you don't have countless thousands of people being arbitrarily rounded up and sent to the Gulag, as they were under the old Soviet authoritarianism.

The reason Russia hasn't democratized is because it is still a state-dominated economy. Most of the country's vast wealth comes not from free markets but from revenue produced by its oil and other natural resources. Experts have called this "the Oil Curse." This resource-driven prosperity creates the illusion of capitalism while preserving the power of oligarchs and an authoritarian government. Like welfare or big inheritances for adolescents, the oil curse removes the incentive for governments to encourage a diversified, entrepreneurial economy.

Russia isn't the only authoritarian society propped up by its natural resources. Since the new oil boom that started in 2004, huge windfalls have bolstered the economies of not only Russia, but also countries like Iran and Venezuela. These are the countries that are the backsliders—or outright failures—on the freedom index. Their resource-rich "phony capitalism" provides a smoke screen for anti-capitalist, big-government policies.

Take a country cited by Amy Chua—Nigeria. Sure enough, it, too, is beset by the oil curse: it produces 10 percent of the oil consumed by the United States. That's lots of petrodollars flooding its coffers. Not surprisingly, the Heritage Foundation/*Wall Street Journal* Index of Economic Freedom rates the country as "mostly unfree." It lags behind in free-market essentials, such as property rights, contract enforcement, ease of setting up legal businesses, and sensible taxation. Therefore, Nigeria can hardly be called a free market, and thus it is no surprise the country continues to experience political turmoil.

The Freedom House report on declining global freedom is really no surprise. The plunge in oil prices between the summer of 2008 and the spring of 2009, halting the oil boom in these nations, is a likely reason that political repression increased in these countries.

What free-market doubters fail to recognize is that the road from economic reform to political liberty can be long and not always smooth. Chile is a prime example. In 1973, the radical Socialist government of Salvador Allende sought to turn Chile into a Cuba-style dictatorship. By the time the Allende government was overthrown in a coup d'état by strongman General Augusto Pinochet, the annual inflation rate was 286 percent.

Pinochet established an authoritarian government that violently suppressed the Far Left. However, at the same time, he instituted free-market reforms such as removing price controls, opening trade, and privatizing some state enterprises. They unleashed a wave of prosperity. The Chilean economy began to diversify, reducing its onetime dependence on copper.

What the strongman didn't grasp was that he was creating conditions for his own political demise. The prosperity created an ever-larger middle class that grew increasingly dissatisfied. By the late 1980s, it was no longer possible to resist demands for more political freedom. General Pinochet agreed to hold a plebiscite on his future. To his own astonishment, he lost the vote. The emergence of a free Chilean economy has been largely credited with helping the nation return to democracy. The moral of the story: prosperity brings democracy and not gratitude to dictators.

▲   REAL WORLD LESSON   ▲

Democratization of authoritarian nations can be achieved only by genuinely free markets and not by the bloated, phony capitalism of resource-rich countries.

Q ► How can our system be moral when a baseball player like
Derek Jeter can make more than 350 times the pay of the
average nurse?

A ► Derek Jeter has a skill that makes him uniquely valuable
in the job market.

Nurses save lives. Yet the median income for a nurse is only around
$65,000.[27] New York Yankees shortstop and team captain Derek
Jeter plays baseball. In 2010 he earned around $23 million—more than 350
times a nurse's pay.

Jeter's immense earning power may have dropped some with his latest
contract, signed in late 2010. Nonetheless, he still stands to earn an astounding $51 million over three years.

Is the free market immoral because it rewards an athlete more highly
than someone who saves lives, especially when there are not enough
nurses to fill jobs in the U.S. health-care system?

The value that the market places on someone like Derek Jeter is astonishing. We may not personally agree with it. But it is fair.

How did Jeter get to be paid $23 million a year? Only about 1,000
people in the world are qualified to play major league baseball. Jeter,
captain of the Yankees and an eleven-time All-Star, is widely acknowledged to be among the best shortstops in baseball's history. He holds
five Gold Glove awards, including his most recent award in 2010 at age
thirty-six—the oldest for an American League shortstop since 1970. He
has been among baseball's elite since 1996, when he was the league's
Rookie of the Year.

One of the most talented players in baseball, Jeter is a top attraction in
a sport that is not only America's national pastime but a multibillion-
dollar industry, generating revenue from everything from ticket and
hotdog sales to promotional deals and broadcast rights.

To win in this high-stakes business, baseball teams need the best
players and will pay mightily to get them. With so much money flooding
into the sport, they can afford to pay a lot. The Yankees are more than the
richest club in baseball. They were fourth on the Forbes 2010 list of the ten
most valuable teams in all of professional sports worldwide. The result:
Jeter's eight-figure salary.

Comparing Derek Jeter's out-of-the-ballpark compensation with a nurse's pay calls to mind a question once posed by the great economist Adam Smith: Why do diamonds, which have very little practical use, command a higher price than water, which is essential to life? This disparity is known as the paradox of value, or the "diamond-water paradox."

Some economists explain this apparent contradiction with what they call the theory of marginal utility. What matters is not the value of water or diamonds to society, but their worth *to the individual consumer.* Yes, H_2O is essential to life. But as individuals we find it to be nonetheless abundant. Therefore a glass of water is less valuable than a single diamond, which is extremely scarce and provides enormous satisfaction to its owner.

Few baseball players have the skills of Derek Jeter, whose performance has made baseball history. Fortunately for society, there are many more nurses with life-saving skills than there are baseball players with his level of skill. So, in terms of the labor market, Jeter was more valuable than a nurse and plenty of others as well, including many highly paid executives.

A market is a public forum where people vote, but instead of casting ballots, they vote with their money.

And this market is efficient. Jeter may have been disappointed in his latest contract. But it was no accident: In the final stage of his athletic career, he's not likely to repeat the kind of performance that earned him the title of Most Valuable Player in 2009.

That said, he remains a stellar player and major attraction. His still-stratospheric compensation reflects the value placed on him by the millions of people whose dollars flood into major league baseball. The alternative would be to have some centralized government entity decide Derek Jeter's salary. That would be less democratic and less fair.

▲   REAL WORLD LESSON   ▲

Dramatic pay disparities, even when they appear unfair, are a reflection of very real market conditions and the value-setting "votes" of participants.

Q ► ISN'T ADVERTISING IMMORAL BECAUSE IT MANIPULATES PEOPLE INTO BUYING THINGS THEY REALLY DON'T NEED?

A ► NO. BY CONVEYING INFORMATION AND HELPING COMPANIES SELL PRODUCTS, ADVERTISING PLAYS AN IMPORTANT ROLE IN A FREE-

MARKET ECONOMY. AND IT IS OFTEN LESS PERSUASIVE THAN
PEOPLE THINK.

People who buy into capitalism's bad rap often hold up advertising as yet
another example of the immorality of free markets. Ads, they claim,
seduce and mislead people. They're an annoying, unwanted intrusion
on TV, in cyberspace, newspapers, magazines—and every corner of our
lives. Americans are defenseless against such pervasive "propaganda."

The late historian Arnold Toynbee has been quoted as saying, "[I]
cannot think of any circumstances in which advertising would not be an
evil."[28] Advertising has a long list of critics. Among the most influential
was the late economist John Kenneth Galbraith. In The Affluent Society,[29] he
asserted that advertisers applied "ruthless psychological pressures" to
artificially create demand for products. Galbraith's contemporary, social
critic Vance Packard, wrote about how advertisers used psychological research and techniques to manipulate consumers. In the 1970s, Wilson
Bryan Key, in a book titled Subliminal Seduction, advanced the notion that
advertising contained hidden, seductive images. He famously claimed
that a liquor ad's alluring photo of a vodka on the rocks contained subliminal images of a woman's breasts hidden in the ice cubes.

This thinking has led to bans on TV commercials for products like
cigarettes and hard liquor. A few years ago, Senator Tom Harkin tried
through his Healthy Lifestyles and Prevention America Act to get the
Federal Trade Commission to restrict junk-food advertising to children.
Americans haven't heard the last of efforts like this. Bans against advertising certain toys and foods to children are already in effect in Europe.
Sweden has outlawed all TV advertising to children under twelve.

Actually, evidence suggests that advertising is often far less persuasive than people think. For a large segment of the population, ads are
more annoying than convincing. A study by Yankelovic Partners found
that a substantial majority, 69 percent, claimed that they "are interested in
products and services that would help them skip or block marketing"—
hence the rise of devices like TiVo that let TV viewers skip the commercials.

Ask people in the industry, and they'll tell you that the real problem
is that, in fact, many ads fail. Today more ads than ever compete
for viewer attention, a condition known as "clutter." According to Rex
Briggs, CEO of Marketing Evolution, a marketing research and consult-

ing firm, and Greg Stuart, former CEO and president of the Interactive Advertising Bureau (IAB), so many ads flop that the pair decided to write a book called *What Sticks: Why Most Advertising Fails and How to Guarantee Yours Succeeds.*

One rule of thumb is that you need to run at least three ads before people can even remember your brand. You need to run seven before consumers consider making a purchase. That's when people understand what your ads are about. And believe it or not, studies show they often don't.

The problem of creating awareness has become so great that advertisers have been resorting to so-called guerrilla advertising—placing ads in unusual locations, such as on train station stairsteps, people's cars, or building scaffolding. But even these guerrilla approaches have become so common that they are losing their impact.

But what about those ads that you do remember—the ones that generate buzz and that, for all appearances, seem seductive? They often don't work, either. Who can forget the Pets.com sock-puppet dog—star of one of the most memorable ad campaigns in the last decade? Most people remember those commercials. They told you why you should shop online for pet food at Pets.com: "because pets can't drive."

The sock-puppet character was such a hit that it ended up doing interviews and talk show appearances on its own outside the commercials. The problem was that while pets couldn't drive, people could. The ads were good, but they were based on a faulty business premise. People preferred to pick up pet food as they shopped for groceries. Despite a brilliant multimillion-dollar ad campaign, Pets.com was one of the great failures of the dot-com era. The company was bought out by Petsmart.com, which was more successful because it had something people wanted—stores.

Other much-advertised but failed product launches have included New Coke, the Ford Edsel, Levi's Type1 jeans, and McDonald's Deluxe sandwich line. All had brand-name backers and big bucks behind them. But they failed. Why? Because despite their expensive, alluring ads, they could not create desires that consumers simply did not have.

Advertisers clearly cannot create demand for things people don't want. What Professor Galbraith and others failed to understand back then—and what many don't realize today—is that entrepreneurs in a free market often rush to meet the needs and wants of people before those needs are conscious. Fifteen years ago, for instance, did you ever think you needed e-mail? Yet today most people would insist that they can't live without it. In other words, the visionaries who invented e-mail perceived your needs before you did. The same goes for countless other products.

But what about the claims that advertising manipulates children? Aren't they more impressionable? That's not borne out by the Real World experience in places like Sweden, Norway, and Quebec, where bans on advertising have failed to reduce childhood obesity. In Sweden, where such a prohibition has been in effect for more than ten years, obesity rates are comparable to those in the rest of the European Union.[30]

For all the criticisms of advertising, people who buy into capitalism's bad rap overlook its critical role in the economy. Jerry Kirkpatrick, marketing professor at California Polytechnic State University and author of *In Defense of Advertising*, writes, "Advertising is, at once, a rational, moral, productive, and above all, *benevolent* institution."[31] In fact, he says, ads enabled America's early entrepreneurs to build the nation's young economy, and provide more of what people needed:

> Throughout the nineteenth century, as production expanded and transportation improved, manufacturers started distributing their goods hundreds and thousands of miles away from their factories. To assist their commercial travelers and Yankee peddlers, "announcements" (as early advertisements were called) were placed in newspapers to reach many more people at one time. The result was a reduction in the cost of communication over what it had been using travelers and peddlers exclusively. Thus, mass communication through advertising made it possible for manufacturers to sell their goods at a faster rate, enabling them to recover their investments more quickly. The faster recovery of investments, in turn, provided a strong incentive for the manufacturers either to reach out to still more distant markets or to develop new products.
>
> Thus, advertising came into existence as a form of specialization in the division of labor. . . . Advertising is an accelerator—it speeds up the acceptance of new products, thus encouraging the development of still more new products.[32]

Ads continue to be a critical driver of our economy, building the brands of America's companies and spurring the buying and selling that creates wealth for millions. According to a recent study by the economic consulting firm Global Insight, advertising helps generate more than $5.2 trillion in sales and economic activity throughout the United States, supporting more than twenty-one million jobs, or 15.2 percent of our U.S. workforce.

But there is another benefit that people seldom mention: advertising is the reason that the U.S. media is larger, more vigorous, and more outspoken than the media in most other nations. Ads underwrite the vital institutions that provide outlets for free speech. Take the travails of newspapers. Their revenue base—classified ads—has been eviscerated by the Internet, particularly craigslist. With such a sharp loss in advertising dollars, most daily newspapers are in a precarious financial position, with their very survival in question.

Think about it: where did you hear those experts talking about the evils of advertising? Most likely on advertiser-supported television, radio, newspapers, magazines, and Web sites. Without advertising, media would be more expensive or government supported. Either way, free speech would be less free. Is that really the more moral alternative?

▲   REAL WORLD LESSON   ▲

Advertising fills a very real need for information in a democratic, free-market society. But it can't create desires people don't already have.

Q ► AREN'T McMANSIONS SYMBOLIC OF THE GREED AND SELFISHNESS OF CAPITALISM?

A ► No. LIKE THEM OR NOT, McMANSIONS REFLECT THE INCREASING DEMOCRATIZATION OF WEALTH.

About ten years ago, a little-known industrialist named Ira Rennert caused an uproar when he started building the ultimate McMansion, a mammoth residence in Sagaponack, a hamlet within Long Island's affluent Hamptons resort area.

The *New York Times* reported: "Ira Rennert's dream house in the Hamptons will have 29 bedrooms, 39 bathrooms, a 164-seat theater and a restaurant-size kitchen with 5 refrigerators, 6 sinks and a 1,500-gallon grease trap."[33]

The sixty-three-acre seaside compound was also to include two tennis courts, two bowling alleys, and a basketball court; a garage sufficient for two hundred cars; and a power plant with four huge water tanks, a 2.5 million–BTU furnace, and a maze of underground tunnels, among other amenities.

Asked the *Times*: "Can a complex of such staggering dimensions be considered a single-family home?"[34]

National publications like the *Times* and *Vanity Fair* predicted that the house would destroy property values and ruin the neighborhood. They quoted people who feared the home was secretly being built as a hotel or a religious retreat. Rennert's McMansion, and others like it, have come to signify over-the-top ostentation, greed, and selfishness. A reporter from the *Austin Chronicle* dubbed them "Chateau du Screw You."[35] For many people, they are symbols of what's wrong with capitalism.

Indeed, McMansions are almost universally reviled—except, of course, by those who live in them.

McMansions may not be architectural masterpieces. We may not like them or like the idea of one springing up next door. But they are anything but indicators of capitalism's moral malaise. They are the result of the democratization of wealth over the last three decades, enabling more people to enjoy luxuries once reserved only for the very rich. Noted author and commentator Dinesh D'Souza wrote about this trend in his book *The Virtue of Prosperity*:

> The real story in real estate isn't the McMansions and "starter castles" of the nouveau riche; it is the fact that the average house built in the United States today is nearly double the size of its counterpart of the 1950s. In Levittown, New York, the archetypal 1950s suburban development, the average home was 1,100 square feet; today's homes average 2,150 square feet. And most of our homes are fully loaded; they have dishwashers, two-car garages, multiple color TV sets, full indoor plumbing, and central heating and air-conditioning, which relatively few homes in the 1950s had, as well as microwave ovens, personal computers, videocassette recorders, CD players, cell phones, and answering machines that nobody in earlier generations had because they didn't exist.[36]

D'Souza emphasizes that these luxuries have proliferated not because there are more rich people, but because middle-income people have more buying power:

> I once asked the novelist Tom Wolfe if he was awed at the levels of opulence that he observed in New York society. "What I find even more remarkable," Wolfe said, "is that at this very moment, your plumber or my electrician is vacationing with his third wife in St. Kitts. . . . Soon they will take a walk along the shore, sipping glasses of designer water and getting ready to sample the local cuisine."[37]

Look what's happened to luxuries: they're cheaper. *Wired* magazine found that the real, inflation-adjusted prices of a number of luxury goods and services have declined dramatically over the last twenty-five years. The inflation-adjusted cost of chartering a plane, for example, has declined nearly 40 percent between 1980 and 2004. An around-the-world cruise on the QE2 declined 45 percent. A BMW 3 series that cost $40,945 in 1995 was 25 percent less expensive in 2004. Even dinner at New York's tony 21 Club, which cost an average of $114.66 in 1987, costs 23 percent less today in inflation-adjusted dollars.[38]

McMansions are a reflection of the fact that capitalism allows more people to enjoy luxuries once reserved for the rich. Isn't that good— indeed moral? Over the last thirty years, free markets have made life better for people on all rungs of the social ladder. That doesn't mean everyone will have the best of taste. The controversy over McMansions is emblematic of the social tensions that typically occur when large numbers of people move up the income ladder, causing discomfort to those both above and below.

Should there be laws against McMansion building in a free market? We will see in chapter 5 that regulation of the free market often ends up producing unintended consequences. By restricting property sales and development, anti-McMansion laws can discourage prospective home buyers, bringing down property values in an entire neighborhood. Efforts to outlaw such homes have also been criticized for being arbitrary. Exactly how does one define a McMansion, anyway?

The story of Ira Rennert suggests that not only can McMansions be excessive, but the passions against them can be, too. Since building his monster house, Rennert has faced a bruising bankruptcy of a subsidiary and the loss of millions to Bernard Madoff. Meanwhile people are less angry about his home. A decade later, some of those who once opposed it admit they got carried away. A local newspaper editor, Dan Rattiner, so regretted the brouhaha that he actually published a letter of apology. It turned out that the house was a family residence and not a religious retreat, as Rennert had contended. Rattiner acknowledged that, thanks to a "forest" later planted on Rennert's property, even the most diligent curiosity seekers today can hardly see the place.

Love 'em or hate 'em, McMansion building began to slow even before the housing bust. People are increasingly opting for quality amenities instead of sheer space. In other words, the very free market that critics blame for McMansions has begun to encourage higher standards and a cooling of the trend toward monster homes.

▲   REAL WORLD LESSON   ▲

Prosperity can be socially disruptive as new groups arrive in communities and professions once reserved for established elites.

Q ► CAN CAPITALISM BE MORAL WHEN CORPORATIONS RUN BY HIGHLY
PAID CEOs LAY OFF THOUSANDS OF PEOPLE, DISRUPTING LIVES
AND COMMUNITIES?

A ► YES. PAINFUL THOUGH THEY ARE, EMPLOYEE LAYOFFS CAN BE
CRITICAL TO A TROUBLED COMPANY'S SURVIVAL, AS WELL AS
FUTURE ECONOMIC GROWTH AND JOB CREATION.

Capitalism could not have seemed more brutal during the 2009 recession, with companies like Caterpillar laying off tens of thousands. "These days mass layoffs are sadly unsurprising,"[39] Randy Cohen, ethics columnist of *The New York Times Magazine*, grimly acknowledged. But are they ethical?

His view: "They are not, at least until more benign tactics have been exhausted. Caterpillar may not simply pile a bunch of unwanted workers into a van, drive across town, drop them on the doorstep of a flourishing company, ring the doorbell and run away."[40]

Cohen's belief is shared by many—and it is especially understandable at a time of increased mass layoffs and high unemployment. Layoffs carried out by highly paid executives can be especially difficult for some to accept. University of Arkansas finance professor Craig Rennie found that CEOs who laid off employees between 1993 and 1999 got 13 percent more in total pay than the CEOs of firms that did not have layoffs.[41]

Layoffs are immensely disruptive to lives, families, and communities. They seem cruel and unfair. And they are all of these things. However, not to lay off people means a company or industry may not survive—in either the near or the long term. And, sooner or later, there will be fewer jobs.

We see this playing out today in the collapse and downsizing of the Detroit automakers. Their inability to lay off people is one of the reasons why GM and Chrysler ended up in bankruptcy in 2009—and why a government bailout was necessary to keep them alive.

One widely acknowledged reason that the U.S. auto industry lost its competitive edge was the burden of billions of dollars of "legacy costs"—including union-pleasing programs that force companies to hang on to unneeded employees. The *Wall Street Journal* told of the Jobs Bank, a windowless room where employees who otherwise would have been laid off are paid six-figure salaries to sit idle. The program cost the auto industry as much as $2 billion annually.

Traumatic though they may be, layoffs can often be the only way a company can survive in a competitive market. A corporation may have to cut its workforce after revenues decline in bad times. Or else it may need to reallocate resources—shut down one division so it can start a new one that requires a new workforce with different skills. Either way, the auto protect the vast majority of jobs.

Of course, not all layoffs succeed in saving companies. Even when they do, that may be cold comfort if you're unemployed. So what if a layoff helps the guy sitting next to you keep his job? But if CEOs could not respond to economic conditions, you would be less likely to get another job because fewer new ones would be created elsewhere.

The ability of U.S. companies to respond to a changing market and lay off people is one reason our economy is more flexible, better able to respond to change—and, as a result, a far more robust job creator than the sluggish nations of Western Europe. A study by the International Monetary Fund in 2000 found that "strong systems of job protection," which make it more difficult to lay off people, tend to decrease a nation's ability to create new jobs. The United States, with its flexible workforce, was far and away the biggest job creator. Nations with worker-protection laws, such as Germany and France, ranked on the bottom half of the list. Sweden was dead last. IMF researchers observed that America's level of job creation was especially remarkable, considering the high level of low-skilled immigration to this country.

> [The] United States has truly experienced an employment miracle, creating many more jobs than needed to keep pace with population growth and bringing a dramatic decline in unemployment. Over the last 20 years the country's ratio of employment to working-age population rose by more than 7 percentage points, despite sizable immigration.[42]

Until the 2007–2009 economic slowdown, U.S. unemployment had been lower than in most developed countries.

Allowing companies to lay off people during a recession can help a company bounce back and enable a downturn to end sooner. History provides numerous examples of corporations that have made major comebacks and hired new people after laying off thousands. One recent example: Boeing, which closed plants and laid off thousands in order to divert resources into the design and production of its 787 Dreamliner. Despite production delays, the plane has been a major financial success, possibly the biggest-selling plane ever, outselling competitor Airbus.

An even more compelling example is IBM. For decades, Big Blue dominated the mainframe computer market and was enormously profitable. It was immensely powerful—the Microsoft or Google of its day. But in the 1980s the company faltered because of the rise of mini computers and PCs. By 1993, IBM had one foot in the corporate graveyard, having lost $16 billion in three years. A desperate board of directors brought in an outsider, Lou Gerstner, who had formerly turned around American Express credit card operations and RJR Nabisco. Among his moves, Gerstner laid off sixty thousand workers. He fundamentally changed the company. IBM became profitable and innovative. As the company's fortunes improved, Gerstner was able to add new jobs. By the time he retired in 2002 he had hired sixty-five thousand people. Not only did Lou Gerstner save IBM, but the company had more employees at the end of his tenure than it had at the beginning.

Ethics columnist Randy Cohen acknowledges the necessity of layoffs in hard times. But he asserts that they shouldn't be "a panicky response to an economic downturn."[43] A company should try everything else first—cutting stockholder dividends and executive pay, for example.

Cohen admits that Caterpillar took some of these steps before its own layoffs. Robert Sutton, author and management professor at Stanford School of Engineering, believes Cohen's criticisms are unrealistic.

> Simply calling layoffs at Caterpillar a "panicky response" is sort of like criticizing people for a "panicky response" to [a] Tsunami. I am sure, in hindsight, that executives might have been better prepared, but I think Mr. Cohen does not show quite enough understanding of how hard it is to manage during times of harsh uncertainty.[44]

Sutton admits that he once shared Cohen's view—until he studied the Real World challenges faced by corporate management. He recalls:

> When I first studied declining and dying organizations in Michigan in the early 1980s, I thought that layoffs were misanthropic and any company that did not spread the pain equally was immoral. But as I have seen the difficult and complex set of constraints that executives face in organizations of all kinds and sizes, I have learned to avoid pointing the morality finger at those leaders who do layoffs—there are too many times when it puts the remaining business at risk or when because of immovable constraints (such as union contracts, work rules, or the nature of the work) cost-cutting short of layoffs is not feasible. . . . Layoffs do massive damage to people, I am not defending them as humane acts, but there are too many times when they are the lesser evil.[45]

▲   REAL WORLD LESSON   ▲

Layoffs are moral. The alternative, not laying off people, would mean more companies going under. The result would be fewer jobs, longer downturns, and less prosperity—with longer-lasting pain and suffering.

Q ► CAN FREE MARKETS BE MORAL WHEN PEOPLE ARE ALLOWED TO GET RICH BY SELLING PRODUCTS THAT ARE NOT GOOD FOR YOU—SUCH AS TOBACCO?

A ► Free markets are moral because they are democratic, reflecting the wishes of people in society. That does not mean that everything that people want is good for them.

It is a familiar conundrum: Cigarettes are known to increase the risk of cancer. Cigarette packets scream health warnings. Yet people persist in smoking. Cigarette makers generate billions of dollars in profits. Until the 2008 crash, their stocks continuously increased in value. And they performed better than the general market in the downturn. It is the free market at work. But is it right?

Free-market critics say no. And yet what would happen if smoking were banned completely? Most likely people would simply continue to smoke, as they have smoked for hundreds of years. And people would most likely still get rich from illegal cigarettes—by selling them on a black market. That's already happening today in states like New York and Michigan, where high cigarette taxes have created a black market for cheaper tobacco. Smugglers are bringing in cigarettes from lower-tax states, such as North Carolina, or from Indian reservations. Law enforcement officials worry that many Middle Eastern smugglers are channeling ill-gotten gains to fund terrorist activities in other countries.

Criminals also profited in the 1920s when the United States banned the sale and distribution of alcohol, another addictive and "immoral" substance. People turned to homemade "moonshine" made by bootleggers. It was not only more potent and dangerous, but more expensive. Hard-core drinkers turned to even more destructive substances like opium.

As Mark Thornton of the Ludwig von Mises Institute has pointed out, banning booze had no effect on the widespread employee absenteeism of the time or on abuse of alcohol. Consumption dropped at first but then rose steadily. Violent crimes such as murder actually increased.[46] The expanded black market for booze also helped to bolster organized crime. Prohibition was widely considered to be a failure. Alcohol was legalized again in 1933.

When it comes to cigarettes, the real moral question is: which is preferable, allowing people to voluntarily buy a product with negative health effects—or imposing a ban that is not likely to work? Instead it would criminalize millions of otherwise honest people, in addition to helping real criminals get richer.

But what about drugs? Some libertarians say we shouldn't ban marijuana and other addictive drugs for the same reasons we don't ban alcohol and cigarettes. Yet society has opted for criminalization because it has judged drugs to be, on the whole, a greater threat to public health and safety. Experiments with looser drug laws have not exactly been successful. Even Holland, which legalized marijuana to great fanfare, is now rethinking its liberal drug laws, shutting down some of its marijuana-selling "coffee shops."

▲   REAL WORLD LESSON   ▲

Free markets can sometimes mean making moral trade-offs.

CHAPTER TWO

"Isn't Capitalism Brutal?"

THE RAP ► The free market is brutal: Big players with too much power crush smaller competitors. People are laid off without warning or protection. Individuals are vulnerable to ups and downs in remote sectors of the economy that have little apparent connection to their daily existence, suffering untold disruption to their lives and businesses.

THE REALITY ► Democratic capitalism can be disruptive and unpredictable. But the process of "creative destruction" is critical to a healthy economy and society. New products and industries render old ones obsolete. Some jobs may be destroyed. But other jobs—more of them—are created. In this way, individuals and resources go where they are most needed by people and businesses, and wealth-producing innovations are developed. Without creative destruction, the economy would stagnate. Living standards would be lower and unemployment would be far higher.

Wealth is produced not by continuing the old ways of doing things but from change, developing products and services that are cheaper, faster, and better—or that do new things altogether. These innovations offer benefits so powerful that they compel people to abandon the "old"— products, services, business practices, and, sometimes, social customs.

A thousand years ago in medieval Europe, advances in agriculture, such as the collar harness, the wheelbarrow, and the axle-based horse-drawn wagon, increased farm productivity. Farmers were able to grow more food than they needed and sell their products to others. They moved beyond subsistence to a surplus economy. Medieval monasteries also traded with one another, specializing in certain crops and relying on bookkeeping techniques, becoming prototypes of modern corporations. The wealth they generated helped bring about the rise of city-states, undermining the power of the ruling feudal lords.

Advances that are today considered progress were seen as destructive by the nobles and aristocrats of that era. We see creation. They saw destruction.

Industrialization brought similarly disruptive changes in the nineteenth century: the rise of mechanical looms boosted textile production, but they rendered traditional hand weavers obsolete. The result: riots in England. Craftsmen smashed the machines they saw as job killers. One riot was led by Ned Ludd. His opposition was so virulent that his name became synonymous with resistance to all technology. Hence the term *Luddite*.

The spread of railroads throughout America and Europe enabled people to travel and transport freight faster. Yet railways also replaced the canals that had been used for commercial transport. Many canal operators went broke, stiffing bondholders. People who made their living from canals had to find new lines of work. Contractors had to switch from digging canal trenches to laying rails and building railroad cars.

Joseph Schumpeter, the great twentieth-century Austrian economist, recognized the disruptive power of innovation. He understood that advances wrought by entrepreneurs and others are not only beneficial. They also shatter the old order. Schumpeter called this process "creative destruction" and explained that it is essential to a healthy economy.

Creative destruction can provoke a yearning for a simpler way of life. Industrialization in the nineteenth century raised living standards and made life easier. But it also disrupted the agrarian rhythms of the countryside with smoke-belching factories. People like the writer William Blake called the large textile plants "satanic mills."

Like Blake, many people today are upset by the process of change—especially politicians. Ohio congressman Dennis Kucinich calls for protections against foreign competition. New York senator Charles Schumer wants China to revalue its currency to slow exports to the United States. Unfortunately, the instinct of such free-market opponents is to condemn what is changing and attempt to preserve the old order. They don't see the process of creation simultaneously taking place in the economy.

Think of where we'd be today if, to preserve jobs, we had to continue using old-fashioned typewriters instead of word processors. Or if we had to use human operators instead of electronic routers to direct our telephone and cell-phone calls. Or if we still had to ship goods via canals— instead of by trucks, rails, and air. Or if we continued using those mammoth old mainframe computers instead of today's PCs and handhelds. Or, finally, if we still used the telegraph instead of communicating by fax, phone, or e-mail. Some jobs would have been saved. But many more never would have been created. And our general standard of living would have been far lower.

People who complain about the "brutality" of free markets fail to appreciate that over time, democratic capitalism has resulted in more job creation than destruction. The U.S. economy is constantly creating and destroying jobs. Each week in normal times 540,000 jobs are lost while some 580,000 new ones are created.

Between 1980 and 2007, despite fluctuations, the United States overall gained jobs. Employment rose to 130 million from 91 million, a net gain of nearly 40 million jobs, far more than the rest of the developed world put together. Productivity, measured by output per worker, increased more than 56 percent, despite three recessions during this period.[1] Thus, even though there are serious job losses as of this writing in 2009, history shows that the United States will remain a vigorous job-creating machine because we don't have the job-killing regulations and taxes of Western Europe—at least not yet.

Many of these new jobs barely existed just a short time ago. For example, no one had ever heard of a "webmaster" in 1990. But in 2002 there were 280,000 of them, in addition to programmers, network operators, and the millions of other jobs created by the Internet in the last two decades.

Sometimes labor-saving devices end up creating more jobs than they destroy. Take ATMs, which were meant to replace most bank tellers. There are now more bank tellers than there were when ATMs were introduced thirty years ago. Why? The machines handle routine banking transactions, allowing branch personnel to focus on providing customers with specialized services.

For decades, until the current recession, U.S. unemployment has been significantly lower than in most nations of Europe, where hiring and firing and new business formation and closings are heavily regulated by government in the name of creating a kinder, gentler capitalism.

Competition can be rough in a free market. But it also compels people to do things better. Individuals hone their skills; companies improve quality and cut costs. The result tends to be better, cheaper products. Society as a whole benefits. A study by the McKinsey Global Institute, for example, suggested that competition was at least as important as technology in improving a business's productivity and innovation—its effectiveness in serving its customers.[2]

Thanks to growth created in part by the "brutality" of democratic capitalism, a middle-class American commands a greater variety of goods and services and better health care than any monarch in the nineteenth and early twentieth centuries. No doubt individuals as well as organizations can experience failure in a free market. And for some, those failures are acutely painful. Yet because of our economy's flexibility, those who suffer setbacks have a greater chance of recovering and eventually succeeding.

Q ► BUT DOESN'T CAPITALISM PRODUCE DEVASTATING ECONOMIC TRAUMAS SUCH AS THE FINANCIAL CRISIS OF 2008, WHICH DESTROYED TRILLIONS OF DOLLARS OF WEALTH AND MILLIONS OF JOBS?

A ► NO. THE WORST HISTORIC DOWNTURNS ARE TYPICALLY CAUSED BY MASSIVE GOVERNMENT INTERVENTION IN THE ECONOMY. UNCLE SAM'S LOOSE MONEY POLICIES AND ITS DOMINATION OF THE MORTGAGE MARKET SET THE STAGE FOR THE CRISIS— ENCOURAGING RECKLESS LENDING AND OVERHEATED FINANCIAL MARKETS.

When the economy goes through a major downturn, politicos and pundits inevitably blame capitalism. The last few years have been no exception. The collapse of the subprime-mortgage market and the credit crisis that followed have been widely blamed on "unfettered markets." Congressman Barney Frank, chairman of the House Financial Services Committee, declared the crisis the fault of "the private sector"[3] and "predatory lenders."[4] "Wall Street greed" was blamed not only by Democrats but Republican candidates in the 2008 presidential campaign.

John McCain attributed the crisis in part to "a casino on Wall Street of greedy, corrupt excess—corruption and excess that has damaged them and their futures."[5]

Finger-pointing like this, however, obscures a Real World economic truth: what is often blamed on free enterprise is in fact the result of price or supply distortions created by government.

We're not saying that all downturns are government created. There's a distinction to be made between catastrophes like the 2008 credit crisis and ordinary business cycles produced by the forces of marketplace creative destruction. Normal downturns can be caused by—to give an example—too many companies entering a market. In the early 1980s numerous players jumped into the personal-computer business. Most failed. This kind of turbulence, while painful, is part of the economy's process of change, whereby new technologies and ways of doing things supplant the old, creating more jobs and higher levels of prosperity.

Recessions produced by such normal cycles, though, are usually not long lasting. But the very biggest traumas, such as the meltdown of the credit and housing markets, are not made by free markets. They result from government intervention that didn't allow markets to work.

Few people fully appreciate the extent to which the behavior of markets is influenced by government, with its mammoth powers of regulation and taxation and ability to direct, indeed to print, trillions of dollars. This immense power was a key determinant in both the subprime collapse and the credit crisis.

We began to outline government's role in the crisis in chapter 1. The financial crisis in fact was the by-product of not one but three government-created disasters. The first was in monetary policy. The housing bubble would not have reached its immense size without the Federal Reserve's low-interest-rate, "easy money" policy of the early 2000s. In 2003–2004, the Federal Reserve made a fateful miscalculation, believing that the U.S. economy was much weaker than it was. The Fed therefore pumped out excessive liquidity, printing dollars and keeping interest rates artificially low. That affected not only housing, but also the entire economy.

When too much money is printed, the first area to feel it is commodities. (They're traded globally on a daily basis in dollars and are therefore more sensitive to changes in the money supply than, say, a fixed asset like a home that is sold every few years or months.) Thus the Fed begat a global commodities boom as the price of oil, copper, steel—even mud—shot up. The price of gold roared above its average of the previous twelve years. For nearly four years the dollar sank like a rock in water against the euro, yen, and pound.

The already booming housing market exploded. Housing was experiencing above-average price rises because of a favorable change in the tax law in 1998 that virtually eliminated capital-gains taxes on the sale of most primary residences. Now with money easy, a bubble mentality took hold. The reasoning was that housing prices always go up; therefore, lending standards could be safely lowered.

We described in chapter 1 how people were swept up in this manic optimism: so what if a dodgy borrower defaulted? It didn't matter—the value of the house would always be higher.

No doubt some lenders became aggressively reckless. One homeless man reportedly got to buy a $700,000 house. Mortgage underwriters in institutions like Washington Mutual were under severe pressure to process mortgages, quality be damned. So-called teaser rates proliferated. A borrower would be given a very low rate at the beginning of the mortgage, which would be jacked up after a given period. Such a higher rate might be beyond the borrower's ability to pay. But not to worry. Many of these borrowers were assured that they could refinance with a new teaser rate.

The housing debacle could never have happened on such a catastrophic scale without the government's easy money policy. Yet the Fed's error was studiously ignored by most policy makers as well as the mainstream media.

Disaster number two: government-created mortgage giants Freddie and Fannie helped inflate the balloon still further. As we mentioned in chapter 1, Fannie and Freddie dominated the subprime market. With $1 trillion in assets and more than $53 billion in revenues, Fannie Mae was in 2004 the nation's twentieth-largest corporation and the second-largest financial institution in the country, right behind Citigroup. Freddie Mac, meanwhile, held some $800 billion in assets in 2007.

By 2008, Freddie and Fannie bought, packaged, and guaranteed more than $1 trillion worth of less-than-prime mortgages, selling them as securities to investors. These securities—remarkably—were rated "triple A" by rating agencies, in an extraordinary bout of hallucination.

The third government disaster bringing on the financial meltdown was a succession of regulatory failures. The worst by far was the refusal by regulators to back off "mark-to-market" or "fair value" accounting rules, which gratuitously destroyed banks and insurance companies. A concept floating around since the 1990s, mark-to-market accounting got a push from the corporate scandals that engulfed Enron and others. The intent was to compel public corporations to increase accounting transparency.

Mark-to-market required financial companies to adjust the value of their regulatory capital—to mark it down or up—to what they would command on the open market. These changes would "have to flow through" the companies' profit-and-loss statements. In other words, if the value of a bank's securities went down, it would have to show a charge. The rule meant that the bank had to raise capital in order to restore its balance sheet.

One fundamental problem was that not all assets on a balance sheet are necessarily saleable at a given moment. For example, what if you had to state the value of your home based on what you would get if you had to sell it today? That number might be zero. But if you sold it under normal conditions, the house's ordinary value might be $400,000.

In much the same way, mark-to-market accounting forced banks and insurers to adjust their capital accounts to reflect what their financial assets were worth, as though they suddenly had to be sold on the open market. During the financial crisis, it encouraged undervaluation of assets—including perfectly good loans.

Yet regulators and lawsuit-fearing auditors insisted that solvent financial institutions drastically write down the value of their entire mortgage portfolios, the good loans as well as the bad. This meant banks had to raise more capital, sending distress signals to the market that forced down their stock prices. Result: hedge funds smelling blood started shorting financial stocks.

The frenzy of short selling sent financial stocks into a death spiral. Companies saw their credit ratings downgraded by agencies that had lurched from easy indulgence to mindless overreaction.

Of the $600 billion financial institutions wrote off between the summer of 2007 and the fall of 2008, almost all were book—or artificial—losses and not actual cash losses. If the mark-to-market rule had been in effect during the banking crisis of the early 1990s, almost every major commercial bank in the country would have gone under. There would have been a second Great Depression.

Tragically, the Bush administration did not comprehend the damage caused by mark-to-market. Not only banks but also life insurers had to raise capital to cover the supposed decline in the value of their financial reserves, even though those assets had little or no relation to their day-to-day operations or viability. They were intended to cover liabilities arising from future claims. No matter. Otherwise healthy companies such as Hartford Financial found themselves in a near death spiral. Hartford saw its stock plunge from $72 a share in 2008 to a low of $3 before state insurance regulators stepped in with their own accounting relief that reduced pressure on life insurers.

The maniacal short selling that helped drive down both insurance and banking stocks was made possible by still another governmental misstep—removal of the uptick rule that had provided a critical speed bump to slow short selling.

The uptick rule was enacted back in 1938 to stop the bear raids that devastated companies in the 1920s and '30s. Raiders would pick a stock, spread rumors that it was in trouble, and sell it short relentlessly, hoping to create panic. In this way they would force the price into a downward "death spiral," then they would buy the stock back at a considerably lower price and make a profit. Allowing a short sale only after a stock went up from its previous price, the uptick rule had served as a critical speed bump, preventing or slowing bear raids. Suspending it heated up volatility, deepening the atmosphere of anxiety and uncertainty.

The 2008 economic meltdown precipitated by these mistakes is just the latest economic catastrophe caused by the less-than-invisible hand of government.

Missteps of a different kind helped produce the Great Inflation of the 1970s. Contrary to what many believe, neither oil speculators nor OPEC caused the soaring fuel prices of that era. The true culprits were the Federal Reserve and Washington politicians like President Richard Nixon, who weakened the dollar by severing its anchor to gold. That set off massive printing of money not only in this country but around the world, causing three ever-more-debilitating bouts of inflation and stagnation.

The most powerful example by far is the Great Depression. More and more people are becoming aware of the government's role in that disaster, brought on in the fall of 1929 by the introduction in Congress of the Smoot-Hawley Tariff. That protectionist bill was designed to shield American farmers from foreign competition, keeping out or restricting agricultural goods from Canada and elsewhere. It was later expanded to protect a vast array of industrial products. Even imported olive oil was hit with huge taxes, although the U.S. was not a producer. Markets try to anticipate the future, and with this disaster looming, the stock market crashed. When Smoot-Hawley looked as though it would be sidetracked, the stock market rallied and ended the year almost where it had begun.

The bill reemerged in 1930 and stocks plunged again. When President Hoover finally signed it that June, decline turned to disaster. Countries retaliated and trade shriveled. International flows of money dried up, severely damaging countries' financial systems.

Then, President Herbert Hoover proposed and Congress passed a gargantuan tax increase in 1932. The top income-tax rate was boosted from 25 percent to 63 percent. There was even an excise tax on checks. You had to pay a tax each time you wrote a check! The intention was to "restore confidence" by balancing the budget. Not surprisingly, confidence was anything but restored. Strapped consumers responded by using more cash. These withdrawals from banks nearly broke the financial system, forcing the new president, Franklin Roosevelt, in 1933 to close every bank in America for several days.

Roosevelt then made numerous mistakes of his own—such as instituting industrial codes that tried to micromanage prices, wages, and even selling practices throughout virtually every sector of the economy—that further retarded economic recovery. Yet it was the "economic royalists" and "plutocrats"—the selfish rich people—who were blamed for the miseries of the 1930s.

True, there had been excesses in the private sector in the heady precrash days of the 1920s. But these alone could never have caused a decade-long catastrophe that encompassed the entire economy.

Stock market breaks in and of themselves do not bring economic downturns. In spring of 1962, Wall Street had the biggest stock market bust since 1929. But no depression followed. Unlike Roosevelt, President John F. Kennedy backed off some of his earlier antibusiness actions, such as the raids by his attorney-general brother on steel company executives. JFK actually introduced major tax cuts, which helped make the 1960s the most prosperous decade up until that time in American history.

And why was there no depression or even recession in 1987 after stocks had their worst one-day crash in history—down 23 percent? That's because President Ronald Reagan did not respond to that crash with tariffs or taxes. Nor did he enact obese stimulus packages. Instead he allowed his scheduled tax cuts to take effect. Stocks recovered. And the economy continued to grow.

People blame the private sector during economic disasters. Yet government policy causes the worst instances of economic brutality.

One final example: the momentous government blunders—again in monetary policy—that were made in Germany during and after World War I. Instead of paying for the war through a judicious mix of taxes and borrowing, Berlin simply turned on the printing press. The resulting flood of money into the economy created raging inflation that was blamed initially on the need to pay for the war—and later on the need to raise money to pay reparations to the Allies. Instead of fully comprehending the cause, the public as always sought scapegoats. Blame shifted to Jewish financiers, "speculators" who "stabbed" Germany in the back. After catastrophic inflation wiped out the foundations of the middle class, Germany became ripe for both Nazism and communism when the Great Depression hit in 1929.

▲   REAL WORLD LESSON   ▲

The biggest economic catastrophes result not from unfettered capitalism but from interventions by government.

Q ► CREATIVE DESTRUCTION MAY HELP THE LARGER ECONOMY, BUT WHAT ABOUT THE PEOPLE WHO LOSE THEIR JOBS?

A ► MOST PEOPLE REBOUND RELATIVELY QUICKLY. EVEN IN A RECESSION, JOBS ARE NOT ONLY DESTROYED, BUT ALSO CREATED.

Losing a job is painful. But it is particularly scary in a down economy. Media headlines such as "Job Losses Worst Since 1974" and "Worst Financial Crisis Since the Great Depression" convey the impression that things are only going to go downhill. That you'll never get another job.

Even during the period of growth that preceded the 2008 crisis, when unemployment was barely 5 percent, gloom sayers complained about a "jobless recovery"; others complained that the jobs being destroyed were being replaced by low-wage, menial jobs like chain-store cashiers and burger flippers.

Media stories characteristically focus on mass layoffs and jobless statistics. This is not only an immense disservice, but also a distortion of what is taking place in the Real World economy.

The Real World truth is that even in the worst recessions, jobs are being created as well as lost. And most people find new employment, sooner rather than later.

At the end of 2008 the median amount of time a person was unemployed was ten weeks, or two and a half months, according to the Bureau of Labor Statistics. That means half the people were jobless for less than that amount of time.[6] In 2009 the length of joblessness increased because government blunders—like the Federal Reserve's failure to revive credit markets—seriously hobbled the normal forces of recovery. Even so, only a little more than a fifth of those jobless were classified as long-term unemployed, that is, out of a job for twenty-seven weeks or more.

During the severe 1980–82 recession, when unemployment reached nearly 11 percent, most people found new jobs in a relatively short period of time. Most, in fact, found jobs as good as or better than the ones they had lost. Unlike the administration today, Ronald Reagan enacted pro-growth tax cuts.

In addition to jobless statistics, the Bureau of Labor Statistics recently has started measuring what it calls Business Employment Dynamics—the number of jobs both created and lost in the economy. During the second quarter of 2008, when the country had slid into what was believed to be the worst downturn since the Great Depression, 7.8 million jobs were lost. But at the same time some 7.3 million were created.[7]

This is what economists refer to as "churn," which is always taking place. Economists Clair Brown, John Haltiwanger, and Julia Lane report that from the mid-1990s to the mid-2000s—a period encompassing the 2000–2001 recession—private-sector job creation and job destruction rates each have averaged almost 8 percent of employment per quarter.[8] About one in thirteen jobs is destroyed every quarter. But a slightly higher number of jobs are created on average, resulting in relatively moderate increases in the overall number of jobs.

The economists believe that the media's tendency to emphasize the negative—even in good times—may result from the fact that more than two-thirds of job destruction occurs in blocks, i.e., mass layoffs at companies that downsize by more than 10 percent in a quarter. Job creation occurs in blocks, too. But the media are predisposed to write about conflict. And in those terms, job loss makes for the better story.

This churn is part of the economy's process of reallocating people and capital. As economists W. Michael Cox and Richard Alm put it, the job loss that results is "the way the macro economy transfers resources to where they belong."[9]

What happens then? People take new jobs in high-demand sectors. Entrepreneurs emerge to meet the needs in underserved markets. Innovations are developed. More jobs are generated. The economy recovers.

What does that mean for us today? As we've noted, the 2008–2009 recession was the result not of the economy's normal creative destruction brought about by new technologies, but destructive government decisions. Nonetheless, spontaneous reallocation of resources still takes place. Two areas of the economy where, according to the Bureau of Labor Statistics, jobs continued to be created in 2008: education and health services.

Whether or not maximum growth occurs in the future will depend in large part on what the government does, such as creating a strong and stable dollar, lowering taxes, enacting sensible regulation (no more mark-to-market distortions, for example), and instituting positive systemic reforms of health care and Social Security.

As Alm and Cox explained in a 2003 op-ed in the *New York Times*, "It is the paradox of progress: a society can't reap the rewards of economic progress without accepting the constant change in work that comes with it. Efforts to soften the blows, by devising policies or laws to preserve jobs or protect industries, will lead to stagnation and decline, the biggest threat to American workers."[10]

Alm and Cox's intent was to reassure people that job growth would resume after the 2001 recession. It did. And what they said back then is just as true of the current downturn: "Facing unemployment and rebuilding a life can be hard on families, but the United States today is better off for allowing it to happen. . . . Job growth will come, as it always has in the past. The economy, meanwhile, is as busy as ever in shifting labor from one use to another to make the country richer and more productive."

▲   REAL WORLD LESSON   ▲

Job destruction, as well as job creation, is critical to economic growth in democratic capitalism.

Q ► Doesn't Google's growth and power on the Internet
   demonstrate how big companies can gain an unfair
   advantage?

A ► No. Sooner or later in the Real World, smaller, innovative
   competitors eventually outstrip big players.

What doesn't Google dominate? In just ten years, the company, which grossed almost $17 billion in 2007, has become a power in Internet search, online advertising, and media. It has helped to remake the news business through virtually inventing the concept of content aggregation, providing readers with the best offerings of a wide range of new media on a single page. Along with selling its own ads, the company in 2008 expanded its reach with its $3.1 billion acquisition of DoubleClick, the largest online ad agency that brokers advertising across the Internet. Google has entered the hardware business with a touch-screen handheld to compete with the iPhone. It is also making deals with computer makers such as Toshiba to provide its desktop search software.

Little wonder that software makers, telecommunications firms, advertisers, book publishers, and others have expressed fears of this growing power. Indeed, Google seems to swallow everything in its path. Doesn't its domination of the Internet attest to the brutality of free markets, where big companies crush their competitors and keep getting bigger?

This thinking lay at the heart of antitrust legal actions that are the price of success for many of the nation's biggest companies, which each year spend millions of dollars diverting—indeed, wasting—valuable intellectual resources on defending themselves and sometimes paying penalties, in federal, state, and private antitrust cases.

We discuss in our chapter on regulation that antitrust actions usually have less to do with issues of corporate power and more to do with retaliation by other competitors. As for the notion that big companies like Google and others can gain "too much market power," it may be true that some companies can for a time dominate their markets. But in the competitive Real World economy this dominance never lasts.

Free-market opponents and antitrust supporters fail to appreciate an essential principle of Real World economics: *so-called monopolies are almost always temporary.* Sooner or later, smaller, more nimble competitors enter the market and supplant established players. This competition can come not just from within an industry, but *from competitors with previously unforeseen new technologies.*

The *Forbes* 500 list of best big companies is a powerful illustration of the vulnerability of big players to market forces: of the top 500 companies in 1983, only 202 were on the list twenty years later. The rest were outgrown or, in some cases, put out of business by competitors.

In the early 1960s, General Motors was so powerful that it decided to scale back production of its cars and trucks to avoid a federal antitrust suit. Once the world's most powerful company, the automaker by 2008 was a hobbled giant that had to plead for a bailout from a hostile Congress, only to later be forced into government-orchestrated bankruptcy. At one time, no one could have possibly imagined that the initials of the great GM would years later stand for "Got Money?"

In his classic analysis *The Innovator's Dilemma*, Harvard professor Clayton Christensen explains that in the Real World economy, "seemingly unaccountable failures," like those of GM and others, take place all the time. In fact, they're inevitable.[11] Why? Christensen makes the seemingly counterintuitive point that great companies almost always fail not because they did something wrong but because they do everything right. They focus so heavily on serving their customers that they become myopic, failing to perceive competitive threats.

Christensen cites the classic case of Sears. The retail chain at one time accounted for 2 percent of all retail sales in the United States. The chain was a vibrant innovator, in many respects the Wal-Mart of its day: "It pioneered several innovations critical to the success of today's more admired retailers: . . . supply chain management, store brands, catalogue retailing, and credit card sales."[12]

Sears was doing a great job serving its market. The problem was that it did not see a new threat emerging from a new type of retailer—discounters. "Sears received its accolades at exactly the time—in the mid-1960s—when it was ignoring the rise of discount retailing and home centers, the lower-cost formats for marketing name-brand hard goods that ultimately stripped Sears of its core franchise." The company was also losing its lead in the use of credit cards in retailing to two emerging players—Visa and MasterCard.

The computer industry is rife with similar cases of huge players being usurped by smaller newcomers. Few people today have heard of Digital Equipment, Commodore, Tandy, and other big names that were prominent in the 1970s and '80s but have since lost out to subsequent waves of innovation.

IBM, "Big Blue," was at one time the world's leading computer innovator. The company dominated the market for big mainframes. But Christensen says that it "missed by years the emergence of minicomputers, which were technologically much simpler than mainframes."[13] IBM became a leader in the market for personal computers. But it was slow to market laptops, fell behind competitors, and eventually sold its PC business to a Chinese company. It was overshadowed by innovations from companies like Apple and Microsoft. Big Blue managed to survive after a brush with insolvency in the early 1990s and today is a large, profitable company. But it is proportionately far less powerful than it was in its heyday.

The problem with industry leaders like IBM, Christensen says, is that *they tend to work on improving their existing products and services, rather than trying to anticipate the next big thing.* This emphasis is not due to a lack of foresight. To a big industry leader, cutting-edge products can appear less attractive, at least at first: "disruptive products are simpler and cheaper; they generally promise lower margins, not greater profits." That's because

> disruptive technologies typically are first commercialized in emerging or insignificant markets. . . . leading firms' most profitable customers generally don't want products based on disruptive technologies. By and large, a disruptive technology is initially embraced by the least profitable customers in a market.

Hence most companies with a practiced discipline of listening to their best customers and identifying new products that promise greater profitability and growth are rarely able to build a case for investing in disruptive technologies until it is too late.[14]

A prime example: the failure of Xerox to anticipate the rise of desktop copiers.

Xerox once dominated the market with its complex, expensive machines. Employees needing photocopies had to wait at the corporate copy center until the operator could get around to the job. But then Ricoh and Canon brought their slow but inexpensive tabletop photocopiers to the market in the early 1980s. Xerox at first ignored these poorly performing machines; they were not good enough to address the needs of the customers who wanted better, faster machines for their high-volume, centralized copy centers. Yet as with minicomputers, the tabletop copiers allowed a larger population of unskilled people to make copies in closets and nearby supply rooms. From those disruptive beginnings, photocopying has become so convenient that easy access to high-quality, feature-rich, and low-cost copying is now viewed as a constitutional right. High-speed photocopying facilities still exist, but they thrive by disrupting conventional printing businesses—enabling low-skilled operators to copy and bind printed matter on demand, which once required the time-consuming skill of professionals.[15]

What free-market opponents fail to grasp is how bigness most often becomes a disadvantage in a marketplace that demands agility to compete. The investment research firm CommScan looked at stocks of the thirty biggest corporate mergers over five years during the late 1990s. On average, they underperformed the Standard & Poor's 500 index.

Remember when Internet powerhouse AOL merged with Time Warner in 2000? People feared that the new company would dominate media markets. Instead, AOL–Time Warner is now considered one of the biggest failed mergers in history, a corporate behemoth burdened with debt. The synergies expected between the company's old and new media divisions failed to materialize and produce any new value for shareholders. The final blow: in spring 2009 Time Warner announced that it was getting rid of AOL.

Antitrust advocates fail to appreciate how rapidly a market can change. This is especially true in technology. Since supplanting Yahoo!, Google has been the acknowledged "master of the online universe." Today it faces growing competition from Facebook for eyeballs and ad dollars.

All of this is not to imply that small companies are always capable of outstripping bigger ones. Smallness is a disadvantage when a start-up tries to do things pretty much the same way big companies do. After World War II, construction magnate Henry Kaiser invested considerable resources into developing a new auto company. But his foray into autos flopped because he offered no real technological breakthroughs. Nor were his models seen as any better than what was already in the market-place. "Me too"–ism won't work.

By contrast, a big company can give another big company a renewed run for its money. Microsoft, having badly trailed in the search-engine business, is making a rejuvenated and innovative run at Google with its new search engine, Bing.com.

Ironically, companies with the greatest control over their markets are those whose power is enforced by government fiat. Few question the "market power" of their local utility. When government creates a monopoly, no one complains.

▲   REAL WORLD LESSON   ▲

"Market power" is temporary because of the natural creative destruction of free markets.

Q ► IF CREATIVE DESTRUCTION IS ESSENTIAL TO A HEALTHY ECONOMY, WASN'T IT A BAD IDEA FOR THE GOVERNMENT TO BAIL OUT THE FINANCIAL SECTOR IN 2008 AFTER THE SUBPRIME-MORTGAGE COLLAPSE?

A ► THE BAILOUT WAS A NECESSARY EVIL TO AVOID THE COLLAPSE OF THE GLOBAL ECONOMY.

In 2008, many people were incensed when the federal government passed a $700 billion bailout of financial companies on the verge of imploding from the subprime-mortgage collapse. Opposition was voiced not only by those ordinarily hostile to business, but also by many who saw the bailout as a betrayal of Schumpeter's principles. After all, they insisted, isn't this supposed to be a free-market economy? Aren't companies that make bad decisions—in this case, investing in high-risk mortgage-backed securities and derivatives—supposed to suffer the consequences? Shouldn't they be allowed to fail?

Most of the time we'd say yes. But, as we've noted, by fall 2008, a series of government errors had put the whole financial system on the verge of collapse. That's why, in the Real World, the bailout was critical. Very simply: had the government not stepped in, the impact on the worldwide economy, on billions of people, would have been cataclysmic.

The financial sector is not just another industry. It is the lifeblood of our system. Without banks and other credit providers you don't have an economy. By September 2008 the U.S.—and global—financial system was on the verge of cardiac arrest. Allowing the financial sector to implode would have unleashed a cascade of calamity: People fearful of losing the money in their checking or money-market account would have withdrawn their cash. Banks would have stopped lending to one another and to solvent borrowers. Merchants wouldn't have been able to get financing for inventories. Buyers wouldn't have been able to get credit for their purchases. Entrepreneurs would have been denied capital for start-ups. There would have been no money available for business expansion. Capital and credit flows would have dried up. Companies everywhere would have been forced to liquidate their debts, and many would have gone under. Unemployment would have soared. Economic activity would have imploded.

Some of these events were beginning to unfold after the crash of 2008. Worried clients of money-market funds were already withdrawing massive amounts of money in the panic that began in mid-September. Banks were ceasing to lend to other institutions for fear that they could end up losing their money in another Lehman-style collapse. Many financial institutions regularly borrow short-term—including just overnight—in the course of their normal operations. Suddenly these transactions began to seize up. Otherwise solvent entities suddenly found themselves on the brink of ruin. The big example was General Electric, whose extensive financial businesses had short-term debts of tens of billions of dollars.

Had Congress allowed the panic to continue and major financial institutions like AIG and others to go under, we would have suffered not just a serious recession but a worldwide depression of untold magnitude. Tens of millions would have seen their jobs destroyed. Countless solvent companies would have gone under. Beyond the devastation of the worldwide economy, the political repercussions would have been uglier than they were in 2009. The resulting government intrusion into the U.S. economy would have vastly exceeded anything the Obama administration will be able to do.

The repercussions would have been felt outside the United States. In some less stable countries, free markets and democracy itself would have been discredited. Tyrants would have had new opportunities to rise up. Let us not forget that Hitler would never have come to power had it not been for the Great Depression of the 1930s. Before that crisis, the Nazis had carried only 2 percent of the vote in 1928.

Another reason government had to intervene was that, as we explained in the first question in this chapter, this was not a disaster created by free markets. Companies did not melt down because of "natural causes"—i.e., losing out in the rough-and-tumble competition of the marketplace. This was government-made destruction. There was nothing "creative" about it.

Low interest rates and a too-abundant money supply, courtesy of the Federal Reserve Bank, stoked an overheated housing market. Government-created Fannie and Freddie helped promote low-interest lending to unqualified borrowers. Federally mandated mark-to-market accounting rules added fuel to the fire, making basically healthy banks and insurers appear in worse shape than they were, encouraging write-downs that set off maniacal short selling of financial stocks.

The bottom line is that bad government policies distorted the decision making and market behavior of these financial institutions. Thus, government intervention should be seen as *an effort to reestablish the normal functioning of the market.*

Unfortunately, both the Obama and the Bush administrations badly bungled this emergency response.

Bush Treasury Secretary Hank Paulson responded by instituting the Troubled Asset Relief Program (TARP). It was originally designed to buy toxic assets from banks—those so-called bad subprime loans. However, it can be argued that the panic could have been halted simply by suspending the destructive mark-to-market rules that had destroyed bank balance sheets. When Congress finally forced regulators to do that six months later, in March and April of 2009, the markets roared back.

Things got worse under the Obama administration. As then–chief of staff Rahm Emanuel famously observed, "You never want a serious crisis to go to waste." TARP money was used as a tool to micromanage institutions. For a while, banks were—astonishingly—not allowed to repay the TARP loans that Treasury Secretary Paulson had forced them to take. They had to get government permission. Had there not been the pressure of public opinion, the administration would probably not have taken the repayments. They would have continued to control these financial institutions.

Thanks to TARP, the administration was able to force banks to accept the subsequent reorganizations of Chrysler and GM that heavily favored the UAW. It caused them to take actions based on politics and not their true interests.

TARP and Detroit were just a warm-up. What started as a temporary emergency bailout turned into the first step in an unprecedented expansion of government control over the economy. It was followed in 2010 by Congress's huge power grab over health care (detailed in chapter 7) and financial "reform" legislation that gave government enormous discretionary power over not only banks, but any corporation judged to be a "threat" to the financial system.

All of this did not have to happen. Democrat as well as Republican administrations have reduced government power after other interventions into the economy. Not only Ronald Reagan, but Jimmy Carter and Bill Clinton also scaled back some of the rigid regulations and programs that had been a response to the Great Depression. Under Jimmy Carter there was airline and railroad deregulation. In 1999 the administration of Democrat Bill Clinton repealed the Glass-Steagall Act, which had been instituted during the Great Depression to separate commercial and investment banking. Clinton also signed welfare reform, another Depression-era program, in 1996, proclaiming "the end of big government as we know it." If only that were true.

▲   REAL WORLD LESSON   ▲

The 2008 bailout of the financial sector was not corporate welfare but critical disaster relief for a a financial "Katrina" that was largely the government's making. It should never have led to the massive expansion of government power that took place under the Obama administration.

Q ► SHOULD GOVERNMENT HAVE STEPPED IN TO SAVE THE DETROIT
     AUTOMAKERS?

A ► A SHORT-TERM BAILOUT COULD HAVE BEEN JUSTIFIED TO CUSHION
     THE RAPIDLY DECLINING ECONOMY. BUT THEN WASHINGTON SHOULD
     HAVE LET GM AND CHRYSLER REORGANIZE UNDER EXISTING
     BANKRUPTCY LAWS.

The government bailout and the subsequent takeover of GM and Chrysler in 2009 angered not only staunch free-market supporters. Plenty of other Americans wondered whether it was truly necessary to rescue Detroit automakers on the taxpayers' dime.

Seizing on widespread public anxiety stoked by the economic crisis, the administration helped foster the perception that the only option for struggling Detroit automakers was decisive action from the federal government. This could not be further from the truth.

There's a whole body of law and procedures to deal with troubled companies. When a large company goes bankrupt, it does not cease to exist. Courts often make provisions for short-term payments to suppliers to minimize disruptions.

Every major air carrier except one—American Airlines—has survived one or more bankruptcies. You'd think if an airline went broke, passengers would stay away. Yet each of these carriers emerged from bankruptcy to compete again.

Most likely, GM and Chrysler would also have recovered in a similar restructuring. But they never had the chance. Government took control of both companies in a historic power grab that trampled the rule of law and mainly served the interests of the administration's political supporters.

This is not to say that we opposed all aid to Detroit. Let's back up a bit. In 2008, a free-market argument could be made for the temporary assistance the automakers initially received. This was justified for two reasons: the number of jobs at stake and the fact that Detroit's decline is not entirely a case of marketplace creative destruction. Government policies were partly to blame for Detroit's problems.

Federal Reserve monetary policies that weakened the dollar were extremely damaging. They sent commodity prices soaring and substantially increased the price of gas. High gasoline prices killed the market for Detroit's most profitable product, sport utility vehicles (SUVs).

There's no question that Detroit is responsible for numerous mistakes. Many American auto offerings in recent decades have failed to excite consumers. Auto companies also acceded to crushingly expensive labor agreements that dampened productivity. But that is not the only reason these companies are in the trouble they are today. A relatively little-known irony is that GM and Ford do well selling small, fuel-efficient cars in foreign markets. They are unable to include those cheaper, foreign-made cars in their fuel-efficiency averages because the U.S. government, responding to pressure from politically powerful labor unions, requires that 75 percent of their models be made with at least 75 percent domestic parts to count in their Government Corporate Average Fuel Economy, or CAFE, averages. Thus, to meet government standards, automakers are forced to manufacture more vehicles here, forgoing needed profits.[16]

CAFE standards currently require fleet fuel efficiencies averaging twenty-seven miles per gallon for cars and twenty-two miles per gallon for light trucks. Originally enacted in 1978 in response to the Arab oil embargo of the 1970s, CAFE standards are set to increase to thirty-five miles per gallon as a result of the Energy Independence and Security Act signed into law by George W. Bush in 2007. President Obama proposes to increase the cost burden of these regulations still further by raising CAFE standards to thirty-nine miles per gallon by 2016.

Of course, European governments get people to buy small, energy-efficient vehicles in a more direct way—they tax the heck out of gasoline. But American politicians know they can't do that. So they try to achieve the same result via fuel-efficiency regulations.

The other problem, of course, has been excessive labor costs. Detroit exemplifies what happens when companies are kept from responding to Real World market pressures, when they're forced by unions to pay for labor they don't need and "legacy"—i.e., health-care and pension—costs they can't afford. The late *Forbes* automotive editor Jerry Flint observed in 2009 that while billions of taxpayer dollars were poured into unionized Detroit manufacturers, nonunion automakers in other parts of the country—subsidiaries of overseas automakers like Toyota and others—did fine without bailouts. It took a while, Flint wrote, for American "trans-plants" to learn how to manufacture here. But eventually they did.

Toyota solved its problems, while the Detroit automakers col-lapsed. One reason: the unions.

The Detroit auto plants are all unionized (United Auto Work-ers), and union stewards are on the company payroll at every car plant, at a cost of millions of dollars. The UAW works to keep the production pace down. One transplant plant manager who used to work for Detroit figures his people were working 10% faster than at a Detroit plant. If Detroit workers did 50 jobs an hour, his people did 55.

Detroit pay and benefits ran about $55 an hour, vs. an aver-age of $45 for the transplants, with Korean automakers paying less. Those "legacy" costs—health care and pension payments to retirees—add another $16 an hour to the domestics' costs. So Detroit's total labor runs about $70 to $75 an hour, vs. $49 for Japanese transplants.[17]

Flint said it's not only about money. Japanese and German compa-nies that manufacture here also "put particular emphasis on teamwork and quality."[18] And the products show it.

Because government helped create the mess, a limited bailout to keep Chrysler and GM from collapsing could be justified. Unfortunately the Obama administration went way beyond that, engineering what one observer called "one of the most radical moves in the history of American industry."

The government ended up investing some $50 billion in taxpayers' money and owning more than 60 percent of GM. And the United Auto Workers Union got some 17.5 percent of GM stock, in addition to $2.5 bil-lion in cash *plus* $6.5 billion in preferred stock carrying a dividend of about 9 percent. Mark Modica and Hal John recount in the *New York Post*:

The UAW got three to four times as much as the bondholders for a smaller claim on GM's assets. The union even boasted to its mem-bers in May 2009 that it had made no concessions on pay, health care or pensions in the restructuring. In effect, the government divided up GM's creditors into favored and unfavored groups, then gave a fat stake in the reorganized business to the favored (aka longtime Democratic Party donors). On top of that, Washington also ordered the shutdown of 1,650 GM dealers and another 1,000 Chrysler dealers as part of its takeover.[19]

Chrysler, meanwhile, was forced into a government-designed solution in which the UAW took 55 percent of the company. Italian automaker Fiat took 35 percent. The U.S. government got 8 percent and the Canadian government 2 percent. Private-sector investors saw their holdings wiped out. Modica and John write ruefully:

Small bondholders are essential to funding US industry. How eager will they be to invest their savings after seeing how the administration misappropriated the federal government's vast power and ignored long-standing bankruptcy law to reward its supporters at the expense of the less powerful?

And then there's the Real World question of how well the two companies will do when management is forced to place demands of politicians and unions before their customers. What do politicians, many of whom have never worked in the private sector, know about successfully selling cars? In the spring of 2009, administration officials temporarily barred Chrysler from spending money on marketing. How does anyone sell anything successfully if they can t market it?

One of the "accomplishments" of the so-called "new GM" has been the Chevy Volt, an electric car that you can drive off the lot for $33,000. The problem is, as *Forbes*'s Rich Karlgaard has noted, the car actually costs $41,000 to produce—in other words, taxpayers are subsidizing every car to the tune of $8,000. Meanwhile, there are plenty of great cars you can buy "honestly" for less, without costing taxpayers a dime—including such esteemed brands as Cadillac, Audi, and BMW.

The debacle of Detroit offers a painful Real World lesson about what happens when politicians and others attempt to micromanage a market and reduce the "brutality" of capitalism. They inevitably fail—and produce even more brutal consequences. In the case of the automakers, the effort to save Detroit from itself resulted in the needless spending of billions of the hard-earned dollars of countless taxpayers, and it wiped out holdings of creditors and shareholders—not just equity funds but individuals who had invested in GM stock. It forced dealers to close and lay off employees. And it will still result in the loss of worker jobs. The new GM will be smaller, with at least 20,000 fewer workers. In 1970, at the peak of its power, GM employed 395,000 blue-collar workers. That number is slated to go to 38,000 after the reorganization.

Not only will Detroit jobs be lost. Many more in the larger economy will never come into being, because of the higher taxes or borrowings necessary to pay for this "rescue."

Forbes's Detroit Bureau Chief Joann Muller summed up what taxpayers laid out for all of this as of September 2010:

- ► $19.4 billion in emergency bridge loans for GM under President Bush
- ► $4.0 billion in emergency funding for Chrysler under Bush
- ► $5.9 billion in emergency funding for GMAC under Bush
- ► $1.5 billion in emergency funding for Chrysler Financial under Bush
- ► $30.1 billion to finance GM's bankruptcy under Obama
- ► $8.1 billion to finance Chrysler's bankruptcy under Obama
- ► $11.8 billion to recapitalize GMAC under Obama
- ► $0.6 billion for GM and Chrysler vehicle warranties under Obama
- ► $0.4 billion to prop up auto suppliers under Obama

Total for the above: $81.8 billion.[20]

How wisely were these dollars spent? When the Obama administration sold "new GM" back to the public in 2010, the total amount of money Washington had lent or given to the GM bailout was estimated at the equivalent of $43 a share. However, the administration was able to sell its government-restructured automaker for only $33 a share. What does that tell you?

Meanwhile, Ford Motor Company, the one automaker that did not take a bailout and avoided a government takeover, weathered the "brutality" of the market. As of late 2010, sales were up more than 20 percent and the company was on track to gain market share for the first time in almost twenty years.

▲   REAL WORLD LESSON   ▲

Detroit's collapse under the burden of government regulations and excessive labor costs illustrates how efforts to soften the "brutality" of markets can end up producing far more destructive consequences, destroying companies and jobs.

Q ► WHY SHOULDN'T THE GOVERNMENT STEP IN AND CREATE JOBS
    DURING AN ECONOMIC CRISIS?

A ► BECAUSE GOVERNMENT-CREATED JOBS DIVERT RESOURCES AWAY
    FROM ENTREPRENEURS AND BUSINESSPEOPLE WHO CREATE
    REAL JOBS PRODUCING GOODS AND SERVICES THAT CUSTOMERS
    ACTUALLY WANT.

Barack Obama promised during his presidential campaign to create "five million new jobs that pay well and can't ever be outsourced."[21] Shortly before taking office, he announced his solution to the mounting unemployment resulting from the economic crisis. His administration would generate or preserve 2.5 million jobs over two years by spending billions of dollars to rebuild roads and bridges, modernize public schools, and construct wind farms and other alternative sources of energy.

The first attempt to make good on this promise was the 2009 American Recovery and Reinvestment Act, $862 billion in government spending that was supposed to create jobs and bring down soaring unemployment. The move boosted federal spending to its highest peacetime level ever.

But by late 2010, the nation's unemployment rate, instead of trending downward, had only increased—to nearly 10 percent. Some Keynesian economists said that the problem was that the stimulus wasn't big enough. But the failure of the stimulus as a job creator came as no surprise to anyone with an understanding of Real World markets.

It's easy to see why so many people believe that government-created jobs are a solution to a down economy. Job programs sound like a swift and decisive response to high unemployment. Why not put people to work expanding and repairing the nation's infrastructure or working on "green" projects? Aren't these worthy undertakings that would have to be done at some point anyway?

The only problem is that in the Real World, public-works programs—contrary to what many believe—have rarely, if ever, been shown to be an effective solution to economic recession or even depression.

French economist Frédéric Bastiat explained why back in 1850. He wrote about what he called the "broken window fallacy." This story is famously retold by economist Henry Hazlitt in *Economics in One Lesson*.[22] A boy throws a brick through the window of a local bakery, shattering the window and raining glass over cakes and pies. The bakery owner is enraged by this vandalism. Bystanders tell him to look on the bright side. What looks like an act of destruction will end up creating work for people.

> It will make business for some glazier. As they begin to think of this they elaborate upon it. How much does a new plate glass window cost? Two hundred and fifty dollars? That will be quite a sum. After all, if windows were never broken, what would happen to the glass business? Then, of course, the thing is endless. The glazier will have $250 more to spend with other merchants, and these in turn will have $250 more to spend with still other merchants, and so on ad infinitum. The smashed window will go on providing money and employment in ever-widening circles. The logical conclusion from all this would be, if the crowd drew it, that the little hoodlum who threw the brick, far from being a public menace, was a public benefactor.[23]

Wait a minute. It may look like work and wealth are being created by the broken window. In fact they're not. As Hazlitt retells Bastiat's tale:

> The shopkeeper will be out $250 that he was planning to spend for a new suit. Because he has had to replace the window, he will have to go without the suit (or some equivalent need or luxury). *Instead of having a window and $250 he now has merely a window* [our italics]. Or, as he was planning to buy the suit that very afternoon, instead of having both a window and a suit he must be content with the window and no suit. If we think of him as part of the community, the community has lost a new suit that might otherwise have come into being, and is just that much poorer. *The glazier's gain of business, in short, is merely the tailor's loss of business.* No new "employment" has been added.[24]

The broken-window fallacy is the idea that destroying wealth—the baker's window—can produce new wealth for those who rally to replace it. What really happens is that wealth is transferred from one group of individuals (the baker and the tailor) to another (the glass maker and his suppliers). And the baker ends up with a loss—the $250 he would have spent on a new suit.

The same can be said of government job programs: People see the work and jobs that are being created. What they don't see is the wealth that is destroyed so that this activity can take place.

Government finances its job programs through heavier taxation of people and businesses. Or, as Obama initially plans to do, through borrowing. Either way, the government takes funds that otherwise would have been used for new business investment and consumer spending. People being recruited to work in government-sector jobs would otherwise have been available to work in growth-producing private-sector businesses. In other words, money and jobs are simply transferred from one sector to another to fix the "broken window" of the economy.

Fox Business News host and commentator John Stossel has a good explanation of why government job programs are ultimately useless.

> Creating jobs is not difficult for government. What is difficult for government is creating jobs that produce wealth. Pyramids, holes in the ground, and war do not produce wealth. They destroy wealth. They take valuable resources and convert them into something less valuable.[25]

Stossel points out that President Obama's plan to put people to work in so called green jobs, weatherizing buildings, and other public works projects, doesn't create growth or produce innovations that raise living standards and help society advance.

> Instead of iPods, great art, cures for diseases, and machines that replace back-breaking work, we get the equivalent of digging holes and filling them up.[26]

Economist Thomas Woods Jr. compares the process to using a bucket to move water in a pool from the deep end to the shallow end. Government is generally not in the business of creating innovative goods and new technologies that make the economy expand.

In those rare instances when it does, usually in the military, the application remains narrow. Job and wealth creation are limited or virtually nonexistent.

Case in point: the Defense Advanced Research Projects Agency (DARPA) invented the Internet in the late 1960s to facilitate communication among universities doing defense-related research. But the network encompassed only a handful of academic computers until the late 1980s, when it was opened to commercial Internet service providers like CompuServe and others. Only when the private sector gained access did the Web truly take off and become the revolutionary force and job creator that we know today.

Government originated the computer during World War II to help calculate the trajectory of artillery shells. Obviously, computers have wider applications than aiding artillery officers. It was the private sector that ultimately made computers into necessities we cannot live without.

In contrast, it did not take twenty years for Apple to create thousands of jobs after inventing the iPod. Researchers at UC Irvine estimate that the revolutionary device has created more than 41,000 jobs—from engineers to retailers. That's probably a conservative estimate, as their study leaves out thousands of people who make and sell iPod accessories, as well as those who are in the business of creating and marketing podcasts and other content.

Proponents of government job creation point to FDR's famed public-works programs of the New Deal, which, they say, helped pull America out of the Great Depression. This is a myth. Economist Amity Shlaes is one of an increasing number of historians who make a powerful argument that the public-works programs of that era actually kept the economy from recovering.

Shlaes acknowledges that those projects "created enduring edifices," such as New York's Triborough Bridge, the Mountain Theater of Mount Tamalpais State Park near San Francisco, and the Texas post office murals. But they ultimately failed to fix the economy. The reason: "Public jobs did their work inefficiently. That was because the jobs were scripted to serve political ends, not economic ones."[27]

In the Real World, the economy grows and creates wealth by innovating and improving efficiency. Increased efficiency results in profits that can then be invested in growth and expansion, replacing capital destroyed elsewhere. But the government during the Depression was doing exactly the opposite: creating wasteful, make-work jobs that produced little economic benefit for anyone other than the people being paid to create them.

While researching her widely read book *The Forgotten Man: A New History of the Great Depression*, Shlaes came across the example of a government farm in Casa Grande, Arizona, that employed workers who were "poor— close to 'Grapes of Wrath' poor—but sophisticated." She recounts,

> They knew that the government wanted them to share jobs. But they saw that the only way for the farm to get profits was to increase output and to stop milking by hand. Five dairy crewmen approached the manager to propose purchasing milking machines to increase output. They even documented their plea with a shorthand memo: "Milking machine would save two men's labor at five dollars per day. . . . Beginning in September would save three men's wages or $7.50 on account of new heifers coming in."[28]

What was their manager's response to their efforts to save labor and boost the farm's profit? He fired them. "The government man was horrified at the idea of killing the jobs he was supposed to create."

Making matters worse, these public-works jobs were being created with capital that could have generated real jobs. Government taxation and the sale of bonds, Shlaes says, effectively sucked all the air out of the economy, appropriating capital that would have been available for growth-producing private-sector investment:

> Utilities are a prime example. In the 1920s electricity was a miracle industry. There was every expectation that growth in utilities might pull the country through hard times in the future.
>
> And the industry might have indeed done that, if the government had not supplanted it. Roosevelt believed in public utilities, not private companies. He created his own highly ambitious infrastructure project—the Tennessee Valley Authority (TVA). The TVA commandeered the utility business in the South, notwithstanding the vehement protests of the private utilities that served that area.[29]

Ultimately, Shlaes writes, public jobs were a Band-Aid solution: "The New Deal's emergency jobs were short term, lasting months, not years, so people could not settle into them. This led to further disruption." Shlaes notes that in the best years of Roosevelt's first two terms, unemployment remained at severe recession levels. In fact, unemployment averaged almost 15 percent before the United States entered World War II. Roosevelt's treasury secretary, Henry Morgenthau, admitted, "[A]fter eight years of this Administration we have just as much unemployment as when we started."

Depression-era programs are far from the only examples of government failure to stimulate a flagging economy by spreading the work around. Over a more than decade-long recession, Japan launched at least ten stimulus programs—including public-works projects. But none delivered any lasting boost.

Forbes.com columnists and economists Brian Wesbury and Robert Stein observe that, if history tells us anything, it's that government spending produces *unemployment*:

> Contrary to popular belief, government spending is not stimulus— it's anti-stimulus. Look back at the US in the 1970s, or Europe (and Canada) over the past 30 years. Whenever government spending rises as a share of GDP, unemployment rises too. Government must tax and borrow from the private sector to fund itself. The larger the government, the smaller the private sector, and the fewer jobs there are.[30]

And then there is the question: do people *really* want all those products and services—green or otherwise—being created? John Stossel points out:

> Since government services are paid for through the compulsion of taxes, they have no market price. But without market prices, we have no way of knowing the importance that free people would place on those services versus other things they want.[31]

Government "stimulus" programs are supposed to deliver a quicker, more immediate boost to the economy than simply allowing the economy's "invisible hand" to create jobs spontaneously. In fact, it can take years for government programs to work. Many policy makers in 2009 were stunned when a report from the nonpartisan Congressional Budget Office predicted that the $358 billion in proposed infrastructure projects could take as long as ten years to work its way into the economy.[32] The report predicted that only about a third of the infrastructure money would be spent by the end of 2010. Most of the government's rescue package, and jobs, would most likely be delivered after the economy recovered.

So just what jobs were created by the 2009 "stimulus"? Senators Tom Coburn and John McCain attempted to answer this question in 2010 with their report "Summertime Blues." It singled out one hundred "job-creating projects" funded by the 2009 stimulus billions. The jobs created included repairing an 1846 brick fort marooned on Dry Tortuga, a remote national park in the Florida Keys; creating a museum in an abandoned train station in Glassboro, New Jersey; and installing new windows in the Mount St. Helens visitors center in Amboy, Washington. Unfortunately, the report pointed out that, since 2007, the building has been closed and has no plans to reopen. Bastiat would have been amused.

Keynesians, however, maintain that a job is a job. Stalwarts, including President Obama, insist that without the government's spending, unemployment would be far worse. In July of 2010 the White House insisted that some three million jobs were "created or saved."

This claim, however, was dismissed by many experts, including Harvard economist Greg Mankiw: "There is no way to measure how many jobs are saved. Even if things get much, much worse, the President can say that there would have been 4 million fewer jobs without the stimulus."[33] He called the notion of "saved jobs" "an act of political genius" but ultimately a "non-measurable metric" that is essentially meaningless.

▲   REAL WORLD LESSON   ▲

Government job programs don't create sustainable economic growth.

Q ► Doesn't Wal-Mart's impact on mom-and-pop businesses show that sometimes the "destruction" of capitalism exceeds "creation"?

A ► No. Wal-Mart may have hurt some businesses, but it has created opportunities for other entrepreneurs, in addition to lowering costs for consumers.

To many, Wal-Mart is not only America's leading discount chain. It's a retailing juggernaut that crushes competitors and symbolizes the brutality of the free market. In a *New York Times* op-ed piece, former Clinton labor secretary Robert Reich, expressing this view, complained that the retailing giant has turned "main streets into ghost towns by sucking business away from small retailers."[34]

A *Wall Street Journal* online poll found that an astonishing number of Americans, more than 47 percent, believed that the mammoth retailer was "bad for the American economy."[35] Al Norman, one of the chain's most vocal opponents, crowed in the *Huffington Post* that between 2007 and 2008, local citizens' groups were directly responsible for killing some nineteen of sixty-four new locations that had been on the drawing board.[36]

Norman and others may be patting themselves on the back for helping to protect America's mom-and-pop businesses from the giant retailer. The problem is that America's small businesses did not need their "help."

Andrea M. Dean and Russell S. Sobel of West Virginia University say studies that show Wal-Mart to be a destroyer of small business are "misleading" on many fronts.[37] The researchers acknowledge that Wal-Mart has hurt certain small neighboring competitors that compete with the store directly. However, they found that something else is also happening: "the emergence of other small businesses—both in other sectors and in other counties." For example, a Wal-Mart store might cause a nearby small competitor to close. But another small business, like an antique store or a restaurant, would open in its place.

Dean and Sobel observed this taking place around the country, including in their own hometown:

Morgantown, W.Va., is just one of many cities that have witnessed, first-hand, the process of creative destruction unleashed by Wal-Mart. Shortly after a new Wal-Mart store opened, Morgantown's popular downtown area was wrought with empty storefronts. However, after only a brief period of time, the once-empty storefronts filled with new small businesses. A former women's clothing shop transformed into a high-end restaurant. A former electronics store converted into an ice cream parlor. One by one, each of the vacant stores filled with new businesses, such as coffee shops, art galleries, and law firms. This process of creative destruction is able to increase economic efficiency by the reallocation of resources. Downtown retail space, which prior to a Wal-Mart store opening would be extremely competitive and

allocated mainly to general merchandise stores, becomes an economically viable location for more elaborate types of small businesses once a Wal-Mart enters the area.[10]

If anything, Dean and Sobel say, Wal-Mart indirectly has created opportunities for some smaller entrepreneurs "who once could not afford the
high rents of the limited downtown retail space" but "are now granted an
affordable opportunity to open their own businesses."

The researchers take issue with a study by Wal-Mart Watch, one of the
chain's most dogged opponents, that claims that the expansion of a single
Iowa store in 2005 was responsible the closing of no less than 1,581 small
firms, "including 555 grocery stores, 298 hardware stores, 293 building
suppliers, 161 variety shops, 158 women's stores, and 116 pharmacies."
Sounds bleak, right? But the numbers don't add up.

The data would imply a failure of 11.3 percent of all businesses
in the state of Iowa. If computed as a percentage of only small
businesses, Wal-Mart would be responsible for the failure of almost 30 percent of all Iowa small businesses.

If this kind of devastation had occurred, you'd think it would be reflected in national statistics measuring small-business formation. That's
anything but what happened. Dean and Sobel found that during the years
of Wal-Mart's growth the number of self-employed entrepreneurs—
mom-and-pop business owners—actually soared!

Over the time period in which the number of Wal-Mart stores
dramatically increased from just a few to over 2,500, there was
also a continual increase in the rate of self-employment. This
overall upward trend in self-employment is just as strong in the
1980s when Wal-Mart was rapidly expanding as it was in the
1970s. . . . Rather than a dramatic drop, the raw data suggest a
nearly 50 percent increase in self-employment during the time
frame.

But what about self-employment in areas where there are more Wal-
Mart stores? "The lack of statistical significance indicates that the number
of Wal-Mart stores has no significant effect on small business activity in a

state, measured by either self-employment or small establishments." In fact, "*bankruptcy rates are actually lower in states with more Wal-Marts.*"

Nor are the stores replacing failed Wal-Mart competitors lower-quality businesses. Dean and Sobel found that they "have higher revenue, and are more profitable, than in the past (in real terms)."

The two conclude: "The previous research on Wal-Mart's effects did not correctly model the welfare-enhancing process of 'creative destruction.'" The chain hurt some small businesses. But it created opportunities for others.

Dean and Sobel conclude that in terms of the overall economy, Wal-Mart is a net gain. The low prices and available goods, not only from Wal-Mart but from other stores like it, "benefits consumers and . . . frees money and resources that can then give rise to new businesses and further advancements."

Dean and Sobel are not the only ones to find small-business growth in the shadow of Wal-Mart. A 2004 *BusinessWeek* story about Wal-Mart's opening amid the struggling mom-and-pop stores in South Central Los Angeles found that the retailer's presence turned out to be *good* for its smaller neighbors:

> Now that people can stay in the neighborhood for bargains, something else interesting is happening: They're stopping at other local stores, too.
>
> "The traffic is definitely there. We're seeing more folks," says Harold Llecha, a cashier at Hot Looks, a nearby clothier. The same is happening at other nearby shops, say retailers. They acknowledge that these shoppers don't always buy from them. On some items, Wal-Mart prices can't be beat. And a handful of local shops have closed. But the larger picture is that many that were there before the big discounter arrived are still there. There are new jobs now where there were none. And a moribund mall is regaining vitality. In short, Wal-Mart came in—and nothing bad happened.[39]

The magazine cites 2003 research that confirms Dean and Sobel's findings: "Emek Basker at the University of Missouri found that five years after the opening of Wal-Marts in most markets, there is a small net gain in retail employment in counties where they're located, with a drop of only about 1% in the number of small local businesses." Not only did the chain bring more jobs, but it helped to lower prices some "5% to 10%" in the neighborhood.

Another anti–Wal-Mart argument advanced by opponents is that the retailer strong-arms suppliers to produce its products at such low margins that it practically forces them out of business. It's true that the chain is a tough negotiator. But if doing business with Wal-Mart was so bad for vendors, it's doubtful that so many tens of thousands would be lining up for the privilege. According to the *Wall Street Journal*, ten thousand companies each year compete to become Wal-Mart suppliers and only about two hundred, or 2 percent, get accepted. Those who do can see their business skyrocket overnight.[40]

The idea that a retailer that employs 1.4 million people in the United States and helps consumers stretch their earnings could be bad for the economy is an upside-down notion with no grounding in any Real World facts or economic argument. Several years ago, documentary filmmaker Robert Greenwald made a documentary, *Wal-Mart: The High Cost of Low Price*. One of the people he profiled was Don Hunter, owner of H&H Hardware, a Middlefield, Ohio, business supposedly forced out of business by Wal-Mart. The only problem was that, as journalist Byron York reported later, H&H closed before Wal-Mart ever opened. And there's a surprising ending to the story: "The H&H property has been sold to new owners, who have opened it as . . . a hardware store."[41]

▲   REAL WORLD LESSON   ▲

Because markets are spontaneous ecosystems, creation and destruction can occur in ways—and in sectors—that people can't anticipate.

Q ► Isn't the free market too brutal to trust with people's retirement funds?

A ► Since they were introduced, 401(k)s have created wealth for millions of Americans. Private-sector investment of retirement funds delivers far better returns than Social Security, where financial mismanagement has resulted in a near-bankrupt system.

The bear market of recent years hasn't been a good place for anyone's money. But the financial meltdown has been especially painful for retirees living off equity investments. Between October 2007 and early 2009, the Dow Jones Industrial Average declined by some 50 percent, shrinking the 401(k) retirement accounts of millions of Americans.

This isn't the only time that 401(k)s have taken a beating. A few years ago, in the early 2000s, Enron's scandal and subsequent implosion wiped out the 401(k)s of thousands of the company's employees, who'd invested their savings primarily in company stock.

Thus, politicians and others have expressed misgivings about 401(k) retirement plans, which let people invest their own savings in stocks where they can grow tax deferred. U.S. Representative George Miller, a California Democrat, called them "little more than a high-stakes crap-shoot." John Bogle, the highly respected founder of the Vanguard group of mutual funds, testified before Congress in 2009 that the nation's system of retirement security is headed "for a serious train wreck."[42]

Some critics believe that we're better off with lower-risk programs, such as government-run retirement accounts composed only of government bonds. One alternative to 401(k)s that received considerable attention was proposed by Teresa Ghilarducci, professor of economic policy analysis at the New School for Social Research. Ghilarducci has proposed replacing 401(k)s with a guaranteed retirement account administered by the Social Security Administration. Workers would get a six-hundred-dollar annual inflation-adjusted subsidy from the U.S. government and would have to invest 5 percent of their pay into the account. That money in turn would be invested in special government bonds that would pay about 3 percent a year.

Such a plan may sound appealing in today's environment. But in the Real World it's a bad idea for a variety of reasons. Foremost among them: do we really want to entrust our retirement savings to government policy makers or, for that matter, to the Social Security program—which does not exactly have the best track record for sound financial management?

The Social Security Trust Fund was founded to provide a safety net to workers in retirement. You would put money in during your working life and draw on it when you retired, much like an annuity. It was supposed to be an insurance system—hence the term *trust fund*. But if a private-sector company were run like Social Security, its executives would probably get jail time.

You've paid countless thousands of dollars into Social Security over your lifetime. But unlike the funds in your 401(k), the money isn't being held in a dedicated account that's yours and guaranteed to be there at your retirement. Unlike a traditional annuity, no reserves are set aside to meet future obligations. Thus, as baby boomers draw on their benefits, the system faces insolvency.

In 2008, a Heritage Foundation report stated that "in net present value terms, Social Security owes $6.5 trillion more in benefits than it will receive in taxes." Many doubt the government will have the funds to make good on those IOUs when baby boomers start retiring in greater numbers.[43]

Since government is not a business, it has little if any understanding of how to preserve, much less to grow, capital. Its domestic core competency is what it does most often—spend taxpayer money. That's the reason Social Security dollars aren't there. As the Cato Institute's Michael Tanner has explained:

> Congress treats that money like its own: free to spend on whatever the members choose. And spend it they do, on everything from the war in Iraq to the International Fertilizer Development Center. In return, the Social Security Trust Fund is given a bond, essentially an IOU, which will eventually have to be repaid out of future taxes. . . . This has been going on for more than 20 years, under both Democratic and Republican administrations.[44]

Not only that, Social Security's rate of return has, in the words of the Heritage Foundation, "decreased steadily and dramatically." According to its report, "a worker born around 1920 could expect a rate of return from Social Security taxes of about 7 percent after inflation. A worker born in the mid-1980s, however, could expect a return of less than 2 percent."[45]

Even when retirement funds are managed for the government by an independent system, investment decisions are not always about what's good for investors, but are about the priorities of politicians. Around the country, state-run pension systems have been criticized for politically motivated investments—for example, deciding to invest in struggling companies to save union jobs or, alternatively, declining to invest in companies that have done business in politically sensitive countries.

Since they were introduced in 1978, 401(k)s have helped to create the most affluent generation of retirees in U.S. history. According to the Federal Reserve's Survey of Consumer Finances, in 1983, the average retiree (aged sixty-five to seventy-four) had a median income of $16,100 and median assets of $76,300. Stocks made up 26 percent of these financial assets. Over twenty years later, in 2004, the average sixty-five- to seventy-four-year-old had a median income of $33,300 and median assets of $190,100. Stocks made up 51.5 percent of these financial assets.

Investing always involves risks. As individuals, and as a society, we're better off learning to manage those risks ourselves rather than letting the government take over our savings and getting a miserable return on our money.

The fact that equity markets can go up and down does not mean people would be better off handing their retirement savings over to government bureaucrats. It means that people need to learn the basic principles of prudent investing. The first thing you're taught in any finance course is diversification—that it's essential to spread your investments among different companies and sectors—as well as the importance of making age-appropriate investments.

Young people can invest their 401(k)s entirely in equities because they have time after a down market to wait for their portfolios to recover. As you get older, more of your money should be invested in less volatile, short-term instruments like bonds and certificates of deposit. Retired mutual fund visionary John Bogle of Vanguard says that the portion of your 401(k) invested in such fixed-income securities should match your age. For example, if you're sixty years of age, 60 percent of your nest egg should be in short-term bonds. Thus, if the market crashes, your losses are minimized. If you decide to retire, you can draw down on your fixed-income side while letting time heal your equity side.

Critics of 401(k)s don't realize that some of the current pain has been created not by the market slide but by government rules forcing 401(k) owners and IRA owners to make withdrawals every year after the age of seventy and a half. (How Washington came up with seventy and a half is anyone's guess.) When the market crashed in 2008, many beneficiaries wanted to not withdraw from their retirement funds, feeling that they would forego current income to let their capital build up again. But Washington forces them to withdraw assets that have been depressed in value. Why? So the government can tax their money, of course.

Even with market swings like the crash of 2008, studies have shown that stocks are the best long-term investment. Wharton School finance professor Jeremy Siegel has studied the hypothetical performance of stock and bond investments going back to the 1800s: "Over twelve-month periods, stocks outperform bonds only about 60 percent of the time. But as the holding period becomes greater, the frequency of stock outperformance becomes very large. Over twenty-year periods, stocks outperform bonds about 95 percent of the time."[46]

How many Americans, even today, would eagerly embrace the feeble 3 percent returns of a mandatory government program like that outlined by Teresa Ghilarducci? One can understand apprehensions about investing in a sometimes volatile stock market—especially among those nearing retirement. But stocks are not the only private-sector option for retiree investments. In the early 1980s, the county government of Galveston, Texas, and two other Texas counties pulled out of the federal Social Security program. Fearful of stock market fluctuations, the counties invested their employee money in annuities, guaranteed-interest contracts from sound insurance companies.

Former judge Ray Holbrook, who oversaw the creation of the program, wrote that twenty-five years later, "our results have been impressive: We've averaged an annual rate of return of about 6.5% over 24 years. And we've provided substantially better benefits in all three Social Security categories: retirement, survivorship, disability." Depending on their salaries, county workers get returns that are anywhere from 50 percent more than to three times the amount they would have gotten under Social Security. The judge recounts,

> We sought a secure, risk-free alternative to the Social Security system, and it has worked very well for nearly a quarter-century. Our retirees have prospered, and our working people have had the security of generous disability and accidental death benefits. Most important, we didn't force our children and grandchildren to be unduly taxed and burdened for our retirement care while these fine young people are struggling to raise and provide for their own families.[47]

▲   REAL WORLD LESSON   ▲

The federal government, which allocates resources based on political inter-
ests, provides less effective protection for retirement funds than private-
sector solutions dedicated to safeguarding and growing capital.

Q ► Don't Nordic countries demonstrate that free markets can
   coexist with protections against "unfettered capitalism"?

A ► Citizens of Nordic countries, like those in other European
   nations, pay a high price and have a lower standard of
   living than most Americans.

Scandinavian nations—Sweden, Norway, Denmark, and Finland—are
often held up as proof that a social welfare state can be economically
successful. Writing in *Scientific American* magazine, Columbia University
economist Jeffrey Sachs voiced the view, held by many free-market skeptics, that these countries show you can have high taxes and regulation and
still be prosperous.[48]

Sachs writes, "On average, the Nordic countries outperform the Anglo-
Saxon ones on most measures of economic performance."[49] Citizens are
protected by social welfare programs and labor regulations yet enjoy the
benefits of a private sector with competitive, open markets.

Cato Institute senior fellow Dan Mitchell agrees that "there is much to
applaud in Nordic nations. They have open markets, low levels of regulation, strong property rights, stable currencies, and many other policies
associated with growth and prosperity. Indeed, Nordic nations generally
rank among the world's most market-oriented nations."[50]

Denmark, Sweden, and Finland have enjoyed economic growth levels
higher than European nations such as Germany and France. Prior to the
2008 recession, Mitchell wrote,

> Average annual growth rates over the past 10 years range from
> 2.1 percent in Denmark to 4.3 percent in Iceland. Unemployment
> rates are all below 9 percent, with Iceland enjoying a jobless rate
> of just 2.6 percent. [This was before the country's economic col-
> lapse.] Per capita GDP also is reasonably impressive, especially com-
> pared to most parts of the world, ranging from nearly $43,600 in
> oil-rich Norway to slightly more than $34,400 in Sweden.

What the numbers don't show, however, is a Scandinavian standard of living far below that in the United States. The average Nordic citizen has about half the disposable income of the average U.S. resident. Mitchell cites a 2003 study by the Organisation for Economic Co-operation and Development (OECD) showing that

> the average person in the United States had more than $27,000 of disposable income while the average person in Nordic nations (no data available for Iceland) had disposable income of barely $14,300, less than 53 percent of the U.S. level. Even Norwegians, bolstered by oil wealth, had per capita disposable income of less than $16,800, barely 62 percent of the American level. Danes and Finns are at the bottom, with less than 50 percent of the disposable income of the average American.

Mitchell elaborates:

> Americans have twice the household wealth of Swedes, Finns, and Norwegians. . . . Americans also own more consumer products, particularly durable equipment such as automobiles and household appliances. Americans also enjoy more housing. Indeed, poor people in the United States have as much housing space as the average European.

What does this mean in terms of daily life? Writing in the *New York Times*, Bruce Bawer, an American freelance journalist living in Oslo, Norway, reports that evidence of a lower living standard is everywhere:

> Library collections are woefully outdated, and public swimming pools are in desperate need of maintenance. News reports describe serious shortages of police officers and school supplies. When my mother-in-law went to an emergency room recently, the hospital was out of cough medicine. Drug addicts crowd downtown Oslo streets, as the *Los Angeles Times* recently reported, but applicants for methadone programs are put on a months-long waiting list. . . .
>
> After I moved here six years ago, I quickly noticed that Norwegians live more frugally than Americans do. They hang on to old appliances and furniture that we would throw out. And they

drive around in wrecks. In 2003, when my partner and I took his teenage brother to New York—his first trip outside of Europe— he stared boggle-eyed at the cars in the Newark Airport parking lot, as mesmerized as Robin Williams in a New York grocery store in "Moscow on the Hudson."[51]

Writing before the recession, Bawer was amazed at how many Norwegians—"from classroom to boardroom"—brown-bagged their lunches.

It is not simply a matter of tradition, or a preference for a basic, nonmaterialistic life. Dining out is just too pricey in a country where teachers, for example, make about $50,000 a year before taxes. Even the humblest of meals—a large pizza delivered from Oslo's most popular pizza joint—will run from $34 to $48, including a delivery fee and a 25 percent value added tax.

Bawer says his experiences bear out studies reflecting the glacial economic growth of both Scandinavia and the European Union. According to one study, "Economic growth in the last 25 years has been 3 percent per annum in the U.S., compared to 2.2 percent in the E.U. That means that the American economy has almost doubled, whereas the E.U. economy has grown by slightly more than half."

Another study from the international accounting and consulting firm KPMG "indicated that when disposable income was adjusted for cost of living, Scandinavians were the poorest people in Western Europe. Danes had the lowest adjusted income, Norwegians the second lowest, Swedes the third."[52]

Dan Mitchell of Cato writes, "If Sweden were part of America, it would be the sixth poorest state."[53]

The key culprit behind this wealth gap—taxes. Scandinavians have less disposable income because they have to fork over so much to their welfare states. According to the Brussels Journal, "Between 1990 and 2005 the average overall tax burden was 55% in Finland, 58% in Denmark and 61% in Sweden. This is almost one and a half times the OECD average."[54] Dramatically higher personal income taxes are combined with a VAT (value-added tax) on consumer goods of as much as 25 percent, much higher than any U.S. state sales tax. The only bright spot—and one that is helping to sustain economic growth—are corporate tax rates, which are lower than in the United States.

Unemployment has been lower in Scandinavia than in other EU nations such as France and Germany, with their rigid worker-protection laws. But jobless rates have generally been higher than in the United States because of the high cost of hiring workers. And long-term unemployment has been far higher. Even before the recession, Dan Mitchell writes, "more than 18 percent of the unemployed in Nordic nations have been out of work for more than 12 months. In the United States, by contrast, fewer than 12 percent of the unemployed [had] been jobless that long."[55]

Per Bylund, a Swedish libertarian writer, reports that concern over joblessness was so great in the the middle of this decade that

> the national trade workers' union demanded the state "redistribute" jobs through offering people in their 60s state pensions if they step down and their employers employ young, unemployed people in their stead. In the labor union's calculations, such a stunt would "create" 55,000 jobs. What this shows is that the only perceivable way of finding jobs for the young seems to be to "relieve" older people of theirs.[56]

In fact, Scandinavia generated much of its vaunted wealth in the 1960s, before it instituted its high taxes and massive social-welfare bureaucracy. For example, according to Dan Mitchell, unemployment in Sweden averaged 2 percent twenty years ago. It has since more than tripled. He quotes an analyst at a Brussels-based think tank who observed, "Not a single net job has been created in the private sector in Sweden since 1950."[57]

Mitchell and others report that—despite its attractiveness to some Americans—Scandinavia's high-tax welfare is driving away entrepreneurs and businesses. Mitchell writes, "Many productive people have departed for lower-tax jurisdictions. Others remain, but they move their assets so they are hidden from tax authorities."[58]

Sweden has lost much of its pharmaceutical industry, which has moved abroad. Volvo and Saab, its automakers, were taken over by Ford and GM. Even IKEA, the giant furniture retailer that to many is a symbol of Swedish enterprise, relocated to the Netherlands. Company founder

Ingvar Kamprad moved to Switzerland. According to one estimate, emigration since 2000 has grown at five to seven times the growth rate of the population as a whole. At least half—or more—of those leaving are college graduates.[59] No wonder Sweden's per capita income has fallen to about 80 percent of that of the United States. When the Swedish Tax Authority recently produced TV commercials to promote paying taxes online, it outsourced them to low-tax Estonia to save on labor costs.

Scandinavia's own citizens have become increasingly disaffected with the economic stagnation that afflicts their economies. Sweden, as we noted in our introduction, has recently adopted pro-market policies. What about Denmark? Fans say that even though the country has a high income-tax rate of 63 percent the economy still prospers. It is true that the country has lower unemployment because businesses are allowed to shed redundant workers, thus giving its economy greater flexibility. And because of its small economy, government job-retraining programs are more focused and successful than similar programs elsewhere.

What they don't mention is that there is growing dissatisfaction with the tax burden. Many Danes find ways around high tax rates, such as incorporating themselves so that some of their income is taxed at lower rates. They overlook the fact that, like other Scandinavian countries, Denmark has experienced emigration to lower-tax nations.

Even accounting for Scandinavian countries' national health-care programs, their overall economic well-being still isn't a match for those of many other western European countries, or indeed many parts of the United States.

Ironically, free-market bashers in the United States are touting the virtues of the "third way" just as its own practitioners are discovering that, when it comes to producing true prosperity, it's not the best way at all.

▲   REAL WORLD LESSON   ▲

Nordic countries' lower living standard is the little-known price paid for high taxes and social protections.

CHAPTER THREE

"Aren't the Rich Getting Richer at Other People's Expense?"

THE RAP ► The rich are a privileged group that prospers at the expense of everybody else, exploiting employees and customers to stay on top, while getting special treatment and tax breaks. Meanwhile, the poor get poorer and the middle class struggles to keep from falling behind.

THE REALITY ► Rich people make their fortunes by creating opportunity and wealth for others. They do this by launching businesses that generate jobs, by investing in new ventures, or by spending money on other people's products and services. The rich are not a fixed aristocracy. Who is rich and who is poor is always changing. You can't have a prosperous or innovative economy unless people are allowed to become rich.

It's true: the rich have been getting richer. Recent decades have seen an unprecedented expansion of worldwide prosperity. Until the credit crisis, there was an extraordinary explosion in asset values. Between 1982 and 2007, for example, the stock market went up more than fifteen-fold. The typical price of a house went from $69,000 to $247,000. In 1982 it took a mere $125 million to get you on the *Forbes* list of richest Americans. In 2008 it took $1.3 billion. Even in the current recession we see breathtaking displays of personal wealth—from ten-thousand-square-foot "McMansions" to privately owned jets to luxury cars that cost more than many single-family homes. The 2008–2009 downturn was most likely an interruption, not the end, of this long boom.

Free-market opponents—including many who are rich themselves—

say the growing number of rich proves that our economy is divided into "two Americas." One is made up of the wealthy, who keep moving ahead at the expense of everybody else. Barbara Ehrenreich, a vociferous critic of capitalism, summed up this view in the *Nation* magazine. She called the rich "a bloated overclass" who in certain ways "drag down a society as surely as a swelling underclass. . . ."

> Every year, four or five of the people on *Forbes* magazine's list of the ten richest Americans carry the surname Walton, meaning they are the children, nieces, and nephews of Wal-Mart's founder. You think it's a coincidence that this union-busting low-wage retail empire happens to have generated a $200 billion family fortune?[1]

She writes scornfully, "A lot of today's wealth is being made in the financial industry, by means that are occult to the average citizen and do not seem to involve much labor of any kind, we all pay a price, somewhere down the line."

Those who do not share Ehrenreich's anger nonetheless have plenty of complaints. Among them: the rich make life miserable for others by driving up the price of everything. A few years ago, *New York* magazine ran a cover story, "Don't Hate Them Because They're Rich."[2] According to the article, Manhattan was a place where, if you weren't spectacularly wealthy, you were jealous of someone who was: "The more rich people there are, the tougher it is for everyone else to get by, to afford apartments and live the New York life they dreamed of. How wonderful is Central Park if you live an hour away by train?"[3]

The article observed, "It's almost as if the superrich have cordoned off much of Manhattan for their own personal use, distancing themselves from the workaday rich and building a social class all their own."

The financial collapse of 2008 deepened this resentment still further, with many blaming "hedge-fund billionaires" and greedy Wall Street for the nation's economic woes. The downturn seemed to provide the most powerful proof yet that America is a land where the poor and middle class keep falling further and further behind and are victimized by the selfish rich. Barack Obama seemed to suggest this when he insisted that the 2008 financial crisis was the result of "a philosophy we've had for the last eight years—one that says we should give more and more to those with the most and hope that prosperity trickles down to everyone else."

Columnist Daniel Henninger has noted that the president's tax and spending policies have been shaped by this view of the rich and "everyone else" as being two distinct groups on opposite sides of some imaginary divide, with rigidly disparate economic interests. He cites commentary included in the administration's budget document that asserted, "There's nothing wrong with making money, but there is something wrong when we allow the playing field to be tilted so far in the favor of so few. . . . It's a legacy of irresponsibility, and it is our duty to change it." An appalled Henninger writes,

> The rancorous language used to describe these taxpayers makes it clear that as a matter of public policy they will be made to "pay for" the fact of their wealth— no matter how many of them worked honestly and honorably to produce it.[4]

Bashing "rich people" may be good for getting votes during political campaigns. But in the Real World, the rich do not get rich at the expense of the poor. The opposite is true: they make their fortunes by meeting the needs and wants of other people—by building or providing capital for innovative, job-creating businesses whose goods and services make life better.

There's no question that those who contribute innovations in our entrepreneurial economy can reap immense rewards. Bill Gates had virtually no wealth at all when he set up Microsoft in 1976. By the turn of the twenty-first century, he was worth over $60 billion. The boom in high technology, finance, and other sectors over the past thirty years has created numerous newly rich individuals. But this wealth was not made at the expense of the poor. Entrepreneurship and capital investment by rich people are responsible for businesses that created 1.4 million jobs annually over the last decade. Americans couldn't live without cell phones, laptops, BlackBerrys, high-definition TVs, and new medical procedures—innovations produced from the investments of wealthy individuals that have helped people throughout society get richer.

Take the favorite target of Ehrenreich and other capitalism bashers—Wal-Mart. A drag on the economy? The company employs some 1.4 million people, 1 percent of the U.S. workforce, and two million worldwide. It has generated billions for countless vendors and suppliers, not to mention thousands of stockholders, helping to finance the retirement and college savings of countless families through 401(k)s and college funds. By selling its products—including food, and recently, medicines—at 15 percent to 25 percent less than the average prices, Wal-Mart also helps its customers live better by getting more for their money. Even the most fervent adversaries of the retail giant acknowledge these benefits. In the 2008 recession, customers flocked as never before to Wal-Mart precisely because of its low prices. In that sense, Wal-Mart does more for strained household budgets than any government program.

Wal-Mart is just one of the wealth-creating contributions to our economy from members of the *Forbes* 400 in 2010. There's also Facebook, launched by Mark Zuckerberg, the list's youngest member at age twenty-six (net worth $6.9 billion); Home Depot, cofounded by Arthur Blank ($1.2 billion); Kenneth Langone ($1.1 billion); and Bernard Marcus ($1.5 billion). There's also Fidelity Investments (Edward and daughter Abigail Johnson, worth $7.1 billion and $11.3 billion respectively). And that's to name a very few.

History books portray the rich of the nineteenth century as rapacious oligarchs—"robber barons"—who amassed their immense wealth through their ruthless treatment of workers and nearly everyone else. The reality was more complex. Most of the robber barons made their fortunes building railroads or opening mines, oil fields, or retail chains. What is underemphasized, or just plain ignored, is the degree to which these innovations dramatically raised the living standard of what was then a hardscrabble, rural society where backbreaking labor was the rule and the average American faced a level of hardship unknown today. It was this new affluence, some observers believe, that helped to stoke subsequent labor movements by encouraging *rising expectations*, impatience with the pace of change.

Tom Sowell rightly observes that people who start businesses are actually the *last* to benefit from the wealth they create. They reap their profits after paying off their workers, creditors, and investors—and that's when things are going well. If business isn't thriving, they may never see a dime.

You don't get rich off the sweat of others in a free-market economy—

unless you're former college football player Kevin Plank, who founded Under Armour, the perspiration-absorbing athletic-apparel maker that went on to make him a fortune in little more than a decade.

Contrary to the claims of populists, high earners pay the largest share of taxes. According to the Tax Foundation, the top 10 percent of households—with incomes roughly $100,000 or greater—pay roughly 70 percent of all federal income taxes. That share is up from just below 50 percent in 1980.

Critics of capitalism like to give the impression that "rich people" are a fixed aristocracy. Yet only 19 percent of families on today's *Forbes* 400 list have inherited their wealth. When the rich list appeared in 1982, it was populated by Rockefellers and du Ponts. Today there is only one Rockefeller—ninety-four-year-old David. As rich families proliferate, wealth is divided and often depleted. It's hard for families to stay rich for more than a generation or two.

Fail to invest successfully or work productively and your net worth will quickly decline. People hold up free-spending Paris Hilton as an example of the selfishness and self-indulgence of wealth. What they don't understand is that, unless she buckles down and actively builds up what she inherited she will become an example of downward mobility. One especially sad example is the once-mighty Astor fortune. At its height, the family wealth exceeded, relatively, that of Gates and Buffett put together. The Astors owned a big chunk of Manhattan. But as the family multiplied, their business acumen declined. The late Brooke Astor in fact took pride in giving away most of what remained of the fortune to a variety of charities, such as the New York Public Library. Since then, the family's sad, scandalous story has become tabloid fodder: her son, eager for the remnants of this once-colossal fortune, was accused of abusing his aging and ailing mother, providing her with inadequate care, and forging changes to her will.

The moral? Even the most seemingly massive, solidly based pools of wealth eventually evaporate. Entrepreneurial genes are rare indeed, and no family has a heredity claim on them.

Bottom line: people get rich by working hard, innovating, and investing. The only ones who get rich at other people's expense are bank robbers.

Q ► Aren't the abuses of subprime mortgages the perfect
    example of how rich people make fortunes on the backs of
    the poor? In this case, they reaped profits from predatory
    lending and issuing mortgage-based securities while low-
    income people lost their homes.

A ► Subprime-mortgage abuses proliferated as a result of
    market distortions created by government in the name of
    helping poor people.

During the 2008 financial meltdown—the stock market crash and credit crisis brought on by the collapse of the subprime-mortgage market—then House of Representatives speaker Nancy Pelosi made an angry speech placing the blame for the disaster squarely on the shoulders of the rich: "On Wall Street people are flying high, they are making unconscionable amounts of money. They make a lot of money, they privatize the gain, the minute things go tough, they nationalize the risk. They get a golden parachute as they drive their firm into the ground, and the American people have to pick up the tab. Something is very, very wrong with this picture."[5]

Pelosi's outburst on the eve of the first vote on Congress's bank bailout was driven by election-year politics. Nonetheless, it reflected a view of free enterprise shared by critics and cynics on both left and right—that free markets essentially "privatize the profits, nationalize the losses." To them, 2008's financial Katrina was just one more example of the perils of capitalism, where people, propelled by greed, heedlessly and callously enrich themselves at the expense of others.

Such an explanation may resonate with those who have seen too many Hollywood movies about corporate America, with cartoonish portrayals of demonic corporations and greedy Wall Street villains. But it bears no resemblance to what happened in the Real World.

As we have pointed out, the most extreme economic downturns usually take place after government intervention ends up distorting markets. The subprime meltdown was not the result of runaway capitalism and the greedy machinations of "rich people." It was the result of well-intentioned government interventions—including some intended to help poor people—that ended up wreaking havoc in the housing and financial markets.

Most people fail to fully appreciate the roles of the two "government-sponsored enterprises" at the center of the debacle—Fannie Mae and Freddie Mac. We have discussed their activities in preceding chapters, and we will be returning to them again. We explained in chapter 1 that the mission carried out by Fannie and Freddie originated with government during the Depression. Fannie was a government agency created to boost the resources of banks to enable them to lend more and thus increase homeownership. Freddie Mac was a Fannie clone created in 1970. Alan Reynolds of the Cato Institute explains that the two corporations themselves did not provide mortgages:

> They just buy bundles of mortgages from lenders and swap them for mortgage-backed securities. They also invest in private mortgage-backed securities, paying for them by getting deeper in debt.[6]

Fannie and Freddie fueled the trend toward securitization, the bundling of home loans into mortgage-backed securities that were bought and sold on Wall Street. In and of itself, securitization was a very positive financial innovation. The pool of money available for mortgages was now the entire financial system—instead of just local banks. Securitization spread the risk; if a mortgage went bad, one bank wouldn't take the whole hit. The impact would be spread all over the country and throughout the world. Lower risks meant lower, more affordable mortgage rates. But unfortunately, like many essentially positive innovations, securitization could be misused and abused.

We mentioned in chapter 2 that Freddie and Fannie began as federal agencies. They were later spun off by the government so that they could sell shares to the public and generate more mortgage money. But they weren't truly privatized. Noted economist Alan Reynolds explains that Fannie and Freddie were vastly different from other private-sector corporations:

> They're exempt from state and local taxes. And their required "core capital" (mainly stock) is merely 2.5 percent of assets, compared with a 6 to 8 percent norm for banks. As a result, their $5.3 trillion of debt is piled precariously atop a thin cushion of only $81 billion in core capital. It's risky business. But who bears the risk? Fannie and Freddie pay an artificially low interest rate

on their bonds because everyone assumes that, if it came to it, the U.S. Treasury would bail them out. The artificially fat spread between interest rates earned on mortgages and interest rates paid on bonds amounts to a big subsidy. That thwarts competition. It also undermines market discipline, because creditors have little incentive to monitor the firms' borrowing and investments.[7]

Fannie and Freddie had been created to serve as helpful resources in the housing market. Instead, the two giants virtually became the market. They recklessly expanded their indebtedness. Who cared? Uncle Sam stood behind them.

During the administration of Bill Clinton, Fannie and Freddie became true behemoths. As Terry Jones recalled in *Investor's Business Daily* in September 2008,

> [President] Clinton . . . extensively rewrote Fannie's and Freddie's rules. In so doing, he turned the two quasi-private, mortgage-funding firms into a semi-nationalized monopoly that dispensed cash to markets, made loans to large Democratic voting blocs and handed favors, jobs and money to political allies. This potent mix led inevitably to corruption and the Fannie-Freddie collapse.[8]

By the mid-2000s, some people were warning of the enormous risk to the economy Fannie and Freddie had created. A report from the Heritage Foundation warned in 2005: "Fannie Mae and Freddie Mac have abused their generous federal privileges to the point that they now control as much as half of the nation's residential mortgage market. Their commanding presence exposes U.S. financial markets to excessive risk and instability."[9]

Calls to rein in Fannie and Freddie went unheeded. Enriched by their government ties and special privileges, these government-sponsored monsters had enormous lobbying power. Between the late 1990s and 2008, the two spent some $200 million to buy political influence. Fannie and Freddie made themselves the most potent lobby in Washington—more powerful than any corporate interest from the private sector. Political contributions flowed everywhere. "Affordable housing" charities with ties to Fannie and Freddie had a presence in virtually every congressional district. Relatives of influential politicos could often find a cushy perch in these organizations.

Fannie and Freddie were a favorite landing place for ex-officials and staffers from Congress seeking lucrative jobs after government careers. The hours were easy. And the pay was lavish. Fannie and Freddie soon had more million-dollar executives than virtually any company in America. In 2004, Fannie Mae's then CEO Franklin Raines was seventy-seventh on *Forbes* list of most highly paid executives, with an annual compensation of $11.6 million.

Fannie and Freddie didn't even have to make the financial disclosures required of every other publicly held company in America. This gravy train began to slow in 2004, when Raines and his executives were accused of manipulating Fannie's books, overstating earnings and understating risk in an obvious ploy to inflate their bonuses. After an SEC review, Fannie had to cut its dividend to bolster its shaky finances. Raines and others were made to resign. Did they go to jail, as they would have in the private sector? Not a chance.

While Fannie and Freddie were building their government-sponsored mortgage empires, Washington politicians were working to lower lending standards to homeowners. Lenders were pressed to abandon the standard they had developed based on decades of market experience, which had proved effective in filtering out too-risky borrowers—requiring homeowners to put 20 percent down. Why put 20 percent down? Why not 3 percent? That's what Washington started to do in the 1970s. By the 2000s, President George W. Bush's administration was urging lenders to write mortgages requiring no down payment.

People who blame Wall Street for the subprime crisis conveniently forget that in the 1970s, banks were demonized for "redlining"—failing to lend to low-income neighborhoods. Congress, in 1977, during the Carter administration, responded by passing the Community Reinvestment Act, designed to pressure banks to make more loans. Banks could not get government approval to merge unless they had a CRA rating that showed they were in compliance with the law. Critics at the time warned that the act would lead to unsound lending and distort markets.

The Community Reinvestment Act did not create today's crisis, but it established a critical government priority that influenced lending for the ensuing decades, increasing pressure on banks to make loans they would not have made under normal circumstances. Thus, Uncle Sam institutionalized the very practices that are today labeled "predatory."

Government pressure on banks to lower lending standards and the creation of Fannie and Freddie were just two of the unfortunate interventions that helped inflate the subprime bubble. As we explained in chapter 2, misguided Federal Reserve policies of too much money and low interest rates also helped to fuel the lending mania.

Clearly, no one in either government or the private sector could have foreseen that such a perfect storm could occur. There was plenty of blame to go around. But the Real World truth is that the subprime meltdown and its corruption was not caused by a private sector looking to get rich at the expense of the poor, but by government efforts to influence markets in the name of well-meaning social policies.

▲   REAL WORLD LESSON   ▲

Private-sector "greed" is all too often blamed for calamitous market distortions engineered by government in the name of helping the poor.

Q ► DON'T THE NUMBERS SHOW THAT THE POOR ARE SLIPPING WHILE
    THE RICH ARE GETTING RICHER?

A ► NO. THE REAL WORLD TRUTH IS THAT OVER RECENT DECADES,
    ALL GROUPS HAVE GOTTEN RICHER.

The era of 1982–2007 may well go down in history as a golden age of growth produced by a succession of promarket government reforms—most notably, the tax cuts of Ronald Reagan and George W. Bush, as well as the capital gains tax cut of Bill Clinton. A boom in high technology, finance, and other sectors created numerous newly rich individuals. This wealth was not at the expense of the poor. Everyone profited from millions of new jobs, products, and services.

Yet even in good times, despite countless positive economic indicators, critics of capitalism insisted that the longest boom in the nation's history benefited only "the rich," while the poor lost ground.

Exhibit A, some say, is the Gini coefficient, a government ratio measuring income distribution. According to the U.S. Census Bureau, the U.S. Gini index was nearly 0.47 in 2009, reflecting a historic level of "income inequality," an unprecedented gulf between rich and poor. Further proof, they say, is provided by Census Bureau statistics showing that the percentage of Americans living below the poverty line has remained virtually unchanged since the 1960s—around 12.5 percent.

These numbers supposedly provide irrefutable evidence that the free-market policies of the past three decades simply haven't worked. In the words of Hillary Clinton, they've delivered "trickle-down economics without the trickle."

The problem is that many experts—on both ends of the political spectrum—say the government's poverty numbers are frequently misrepresented. Some believe they're just plain wrong.

Let's look at those income inequality numbers. Yes, there is a wider gulf between poor and rich incomes today than in years past. But it's not because the poor are falling behind, but because more low-income people than ever are coming here.

Between 500,000 and more than one million immigrants, many of them poor, are admitted to the United States each year. This does not include the one million to two million illegals who annually enter the United States. (Obviously, in times of recession, particularly a severe one, the number of newcomers temporarily declines.)

According to Brink Lindsey of the Cato Institute, author of *The Age of Abundance: How Prosperity Transformed America's Politics and Culture*, the portion of the total U.S. population born in foreign countries jumped from 5 percent in 1974 to 12 percent in 2004.[10] Today's top points of origin are not the European nations as they were in years past, but the world's poorest countries, such as Mexico, Haiti, Cuba, the Dominican Republic, Nicaragua, and El Salvador, among others.

Even the most mathematically challenged among us would acknowledge that the influx of so many tens of thousands of low-skilled, low-income people is going to widen the extremes of income in this country.

This flood of immigrants raises the question, would so many be breaking their necks to come here—sometimes paying small fortunes to smugglers and risking their lives—if they believed the United States was a place where *the poor got poorer?* Media fantasies of American affluence are not the only thing drawing so many hundreds of thousands, legally and otherwise, to our shores and across our borders. They are motivated by the experiences of relatives, friends, and friends of friends who have conveyed an irresistible message: America is a place *where you have a better chance to get ahead and even get rich.*

That's what the income inequality numbers don't show: *income mobility*, the movement between income levels in our economy. Few of us remain at the same income level throughout our lives. We move up and sometimes down depending on our age, our career advancement, and fluctuations in the economy.

When you look at the statistics for income mobility, the numbers show that the poor are doing anything but standing still. America's democratic capitalist society is more upwardly mobile than at any other time in history.

According to a U.S. Treasury Department study of American taxpayers, about half of those in the lowest income group when filing their tax returns in 1996 moved into a higher income category by 2005. Twenty-five percent moved into a middle- or upper-income group, while more than 5 percent moved into the highest quintile.

Diana Furchtgott-Roth, former chief economist at the U.S. Department of Labor, says that this upward mobility is reflected in a dramatic improvement in living standards among low-income people over the past two decades:

> In 1985, 38% of poor households owned a home—by 2005 it was 43%. And these homes were of better quality than the 1985 homes. In 1985, 17% of these homes had central air conditioning, and in 2005, 50% did. Fifty-six percent of homes owned by poor households had washing machines in 1985, and in 2005, it was 64%.[11]

The *Wall Street Journal* observed that mobility runs in both directions. Among those with the very highest incomes in 1996—the top $^1\!/_{100}$ of 1 percent—only 25 percent remained in the group in 2005.[12]

Michael Barone of the American Enterprise Institute writes in the *Washington Examiner* that those who bemoan supposed "income inequality" are totally missing the point and don't fully comprehend the impact of higher living standards:

> I bought my first electronic calculator in 1970 for $110. Today you can buy the same gadget for $1.99 at your local drug store. The consumer electronics widely available today at declining prices simply didn't exist in the 1980s.

In addition, as George Mason University economist Tyler Cowen writes in the *American Interest*, "The inequality of personal well-being is sharply down over the past hundred years and perhaps over the past twenty years as well." Bill Gates may have a bigger house than you do. But you have about the same access to good food, medical care and even to the Internet as he does.

Or consider something as prosaic as food. The supermarkets of the 1960s and 1970s didn't come close to matching the amazing selection of produce, meats and exotic foods as you find in supermarkets today—and not just in high-income neighborhoods but in modest-income places all over the country.[13]

Nor does greater income equality mean a fairer society. Journalist Hedrick Smith discovered this as a *New York Times* correspondent in the communist Russia of the 1970s. On paper, there may not have been income inequality. But there were still dramatic disparities:

Money is a poor yardstick in Russia. Earnestly, I asked Intourist guides, queried my Russian office interpreters, went to factories or engaged people in conversation in restaurants, inquiring how much they earned, how much they spent on food or rent, how much it cost to buy a car, trying to compare living standards. I busily went on making computations until Russian friends tipped me off that it was not money that really mattered but access or *blat* . . . influence or connections.[14]

"Rich people" in the old Soviet Union may not have had American-style bank accounts. But they enjoyed special privileges off-limits to most Russians—like access to special stores with rare consumer goods, as well as the right to travel. Incomes in Russia may have been more equal. But there was less fairness: power and material wealth were concentrated in the hands of a tiny elite whose position was based on political favors and power.

And what about that other oft-cited statistic—the 12.5 percent of Americans who have supposedly been stuck for decades at an income below the poverty line? In 2007, American Enterprise Institute analyst Douglas J. Besharov testified before the House of Representatives

Ways and Means Committee that "many on the left as well as the right" believe the methodology used to produce that Census Bureau number is highly flawed and is very likely overstating the nation's level of poverty.[15]

The Census Bureau's formula for calculating "income" understates things like self-employment income, which is not always reported. It also does not include numerous "in kind" benefits from government programs, such as food stamps and Medicaid. Nor does it encompass cash payments from government programs such as unemployment insurance and workers' compensation. Besharov says that's only the beginning of a dizzying list of flaws. Not all errors involve underreporting. But when they're all tallied up, Besharov says the net effect is a dramatic understatement of real income.

What would the poverty rate be if the Census Bureau used a Real World methodology? According to Besharov, the percentage of Americans living in poverty is probably a fraction of the government's estimate— around 5.4 percent.

Even Democrats on the congressional Joint Economic Committee agree that there has been "much greater progress in poverty reduction over the last two decades than the official poverty measure would indicate."[16]

Some go beyond Besharov's critique to question the government's fundamental definition of *poverty*. Nicholas Eberstadt of the American Enterprise Institute says the problem with the oft-cited poverty numbers is—as the critics noted above have suggested—they confuse "income" with standard of living.

He explains, "For lower-income people especially, income tends to be an unreliable predictor of true living standards." Many people who are today labeled as "poor" by the U.S. government actually have a higher living standard than those *above* the poverty line in the 1960s and '70s. "In 1999, nearly 36 percent of all 'poverty level' African American households had central air conditioning—well over twice the figure for America's white *nonpoverty* population in 1970."[17]

The government has also branded as "poor" levels of material wealth that would be considered affluent elsewhere in the world. For instance, according to the Census Bureau, over three-quarters of a million "poor" persons own homes worth over $150,000; and nearly 200,000 "poor" persons own homes worth over $300,000.[18] These numbers do not reflect the hundreds of thousands of people who became homeowners during the subprime binge of 2004–2006. Even with substantial defaults of these particular mortgages, the fact remains that hundreds of thousands of supposedly poverty-stricken people owned valuable homes.

A study in the 1990s found that an American considered "poor" in the eyes of the Census Bureau has one-third more living space than the average Japanese citizen and four times as much living space as the average Russian.[19] Eberstadt believes "the poverty rate misleads the public and our representatives, and it thereby degrades the quality of our social policies. It should be discarded for the broken tool that it is—and a poverty rate worthy of the name should be crafted anew in its place."[20]

Another seldom-appreciated fact is that the gap between rich and poor often grows, at least temporarily, when an economy is expanding. Economist Brian Wesbury offers an enlightening explanation of why this happens:

> [I]ncomes at the top (earned by entrepreneurial innovators or early-technology-adopters) rise more rapidly. This divergence happens whenever growth picks up due to technological innovation. And it is even more pronounced in recent decades because of technology.
>
> For example, Michael Jordan and Tiger Woods earn much more than Larry Bird or Jack Nicklaus ever did because of the global reach of television. A rising income gap signals growth and opportunity for investors and the economy, and should not be viewed as a problem in a free economy. Income gaps in third-world countries, ruled by dictators, are a more serious development because they reflect exploitation and an abuse of political advantage.[21]

As we've noted, equal incomes do not necessarily signify a healthy economy—and often they mean just the opposite. There was little inequality in the old Soviet Union, or, for that matter, economically impoverished communist Cuba. There was a lot less income inequality in the United States during the Great Depression—and there's probably less now, during the current recession. There's little income inequality when almost everyone is poor.

▲   REAL WORLD LESSON   ▲

Statistics measuring poverty and "income inequality" are snapshots in time and essentially meaningless as measures of fairness or mobility.

Q ► IF THE RICH ARE NOT GETTING RICHER AT THE EXPENSE OF OTHERS, WHAT ABOUT CEOs WHO GET MASSIVE PAY PACKAGES MANY TIMES THEIR WORKERS' SALARIES—EVEN WHEN THEY'RE NOT DOING A GOOD JOB?

A ► CEO PAY REFLECTS THE SCARCITY OF THE HIGHEST LEVEL OF MANAGEMENT TALENT. CEOs CAN DELIVER ENORMOUS BENEFIT TO THEIR COMPANIES. YET DESPITE THE LARGE NUMBERS, THEY COST WORKERS AND SHAREHOLDERS RELATIVELY LITTLE.

The decades-old controversy over CEO pay reached a new level of intensity during the financial crisis. Jaws dropped in 2008 when then CEO John Thain suggested that he should still get his $10 million bonus from Merrill Lynch, even as the struggling, money-losing company was about to be taken over by Bank of America. Thain was hardly the only executive whose pay incited outrage. Some $18 billion in bonuses was paid by Wall Street firms that had been bailed out with taxpayer money. President Obama called the situation "shameful" and imposed a $500,000 cap on the pay of top executives of banks that received federal TARP funds.

As some later pointed out, not all the executives who received bonuses were highly paid CEOs, and Wall Street firms were contractually obligated to pay them. Nonetheless, the firestorm over bailout bonuses served to focus public attention on the broader issue of executive pay. Congress and the Obama administration have been mulling ways to restrict CEO pay at all public companies, not only those that are recipients of government largesse.

Even in good times, it can be hard for people to comprehend the immense compensation paid to CEOs—including those as successful as Larry Ellison of Oracle. Number one on the *Forbes* 2008 list of top-paid executives, Ellison received a six-year average annual pay of $71 million, and he received a total of $192 million in 2007.

Oracle, the software company that he founded, in addition to creating enormous wealth for stockholders, employs some 86,000 people. Although Oracle's stock price has declined with the market, investors nonetheless have done well in the long term. If you had invested $100 in Oracle in 1990, it would be worth $4,000 today, despite the volatile ups and downs of the market.

Ellison created immense wealth for shareholders before the stock market meltdown. Shareholders considered Ellison a sufficiently good deal in 2008 to vote against a "say on pay" provision that would have enabled them to curtail his compensation. They decided that Ellison's package—high though it may appear—was not an overly steep price for leadership that has produced a financially healthy company generating more dollars for salaries and jobs.

Another way to look at Ellison's pay is to boil it down to the cost of each share of stock. Ellison's $71 million average annual pay amounts to a cost of less than two cents per share.

CEO compensation should be viewed in terms of the billions of dollars top executives help their companies generate. Executive-compensation consulting firm Watson Wyatt calculates that the top-five executives at U.S. companies receive only about 2 percent to 3 percent of the value they create for shareholders.

Of course, not every CEO is a Larry Ellison. Few would dispute that Countrywide Financial CEO Angelo Mozilo was a miserable deal for employees and shareholders. The lender's concentration in risky subprime mortgages was a disastrous strategic decision that led to the ultimate implosion of the company and its distress sale to Bank of America. At the bottom of the *Forbes* list of worst-performing CEOs, Mozilo ran his company into the ground while being paid around $66 million a year.

What about Robert Nardelli? Before becoming head of troubled Chrysler, he received an astounding $210 million golden parachute after being fired from Home Depot, setting off a firestorm of public outcry.

What's going on here? Isn't the stratospheric compensation of some CEOs the perfect example of "the rich getting richer" at other people's expense—in this case, the bosses making a fortune at the expense of the workers and shareholders of their companies?

The real question should be "Why do these pay packages persist in spite of decades of criticism?" The reason is that despite emotional claims to the contrary, they make sense in Real World economic terms. The benefits that good CEOs can deliver are enormous and far exceed the dollar value of their compensation.

Unfortunately, CEO pay packages are negotiated before an executive takes a job and his or her performance is known. High pay can be necessary to get a talented executive to give up an existing position with enormous pay and benefits. To get a top-tier CEO to take on a risky assignment, you have to pay what he or she is commanding on the open market. That was the case with Robert Nardelli. Home Depot had to entice him to come over from GE, where he had been one of three finalists to succeed the legendary Jack Welch. Almost all of his $210 million severance package was what Nardelli would have received had he stayed at GE. Controversial Ford CEO Alan Mulally—who received $28 million in his first four months on the job—had to be persuaded to give up a highly lucrative job and successful career at Boeing.

Actually, most CEOs who get fired don't get massive payouts. Mega-million-dollar golden parachutes are exceptional, which is why they make news. The average CEO makes about $14 million per year in total compensation—i.e., salary and the gains from the sale of stock options.[22] Still, for most people, this is enormous. But so is the CEO's job. A top executive of a public company can preside over a corporation the size of an American city. As we mentioned, Oracle has 86,000 employees. That's nothing compared to Procter & Gamble, which has 138,000. These massive corporate communities—for that's what they are—encompass divisions and thousands of people in countries around the globe. Guiding them requires a singular combination of skills. A good CEO needs to know far more than how to make and sell a company's products. He or she needs to understand finance and where global markets are going. Chief executives must also communicate with countless constituencies—workers, unions, customers, and suppliers, as well as regulators and media that are constantly scrutinizing their activities. It's more than a twenty-four-hour-a-day job.

Just as there are few people who have the skills and talent of a top baseball player like Alex Rodriguez or a singer like Rihanna, there are probably even fewer people who can run companies like IBM or P&G and do so successfully. Ford CEO Mulally, for example, aggressively downsized Ford—selling Jaguar for $2.3 billion while competitor GM was dithering about what to do with Saab and Hummer. Mulally also aggressively raised cash, both to develop new products and to give the company a financial cushion. As a result, Ford did not need a government bailout, while GM and Chrysler were forced into government-orchestrated bankruptcies costing taxpayers billions of dollars. GM defaulted on its debts. Meanwhile Ford in 2010 paid down a third of its debt and announced the most profitable quarter in its history, with new models like the Fiesta subcompact in high demand, without help from government bailouts. It's unclear what the future holds. However, few would question that the millions paid to Mulally were a good investment not only for Ford but for the American taxpayer.

Contrary to what activists allege, CEO pay is usually not the result of executives cutting sweetheart deals with crony boards of directors. Boards today are more independent than they once were. Shareholders can—and sometimes do—hold the line on pay considered excessive.

Proof that market forces are what's driving executive pay is provided by the fact that even higher CEO salaries are paid by private equity funds like TPG, Kohlberg Kravis & Roberts, and the Blackstone Group, firms run by veterans of corporate suites and sharp-eyed MBAs who have to answer to sophisticated clients obsessed with investment returns. American-style CEO salaries and bonuses are increasingly being paid in Europe, including in socialist France, where top executive compensation at the biggest companies increased 58 percent in 2007.

Another reason CEO salaries have gotten bigger is because American corporations have gotten larger. According to a report from the National Bureau of Economic Research, "the sixfold increase of CEO pay between 1980 and 2003 can be fully attributed to the sixfold increase in market capitalization of large U.S. companies during that period." Why this increase? One reason is the boom in stock ownership that has taken place over the past three decades. Sixteen million American households owned stock in 1983; 57 million do so today. Thus, today's CEOs are responsible not only for managing bigger corporate entities, but for creating more value for more investors.

Should there be caps on CEO pay? As we have said, executives command high pay because of their value in the marketplace. Corporations will therefore seek to pay desirable executives what they are worth, regardless of the efforts of bureaucrats. For this reason, past attempts by government to override the market and impose unnatural constraints on executive pay haven't worked and have only made things worse. In 1993, President Clinton signed legislation designed to discourage high CEO pay by allowing deductions of no more than $1 million in CEO salary on corporate tax returns. What happened? Companies started paying executives with bonuses and stock options that can balloon in value. CEO pay packages grew even bigger.

A more fruitful way to exert pressure on executive pay would be to remove certain barriers to shareholder challenges to management. Hundreds of publicly held companies protect themselves against hostile takeovers with "poison pill" measures—such as making it harder to get board control by limiting the number of directors who can come up for election each year. If companies could not resort to such poison-pill measures, managers would be less able to insulate themselves from shareholders seeking to install new management. They might be more sensitive to the appearance of their pay packages.

This approach is distinct from "say on pay" measures, which give shareholders approval rights on individual executive compensation packages. Shareholders can't micromanage companies. Businesses must have flexibility to operate day to day. If they don't perform over time, shareholders should be able to make changes.

There's no question that some CEOs are overpaid. But the bottom line is that CEO compensation, astonishing as it may be to some, reflects market forces—high demand for top-level talent that's in extremely short supply.

▲   REAL WORLD LESSON   ▲

CEO pay reflects the value placed by the market on the handful of individuals equipped to lead global corporations.

Q ► Hedge-fund trader John Paulson stunned even Wall Street by earning $3.7 billion, essentially by betting that the housing market would fail. Does he really deserve that kind of money?

A ► Paulson profited from shrewd analyses that enabled him to foresee the coming crash of the mortgage market.

HIS HUGE PAYDAY REFLECTED THE ENORMITY OF THE DOLLARS
HE WAS INVESTING, THE SINGULAR BRILLIANCE OF HIS TRADING
MOVES, AND THEIR EXTREMELY HIGH RISK.

When stories about Paulson came out in late 2007, even free-market believers wondered: How could anyone legitimately make $3.7 billion *in one year*? Could this be a spectacular case of, to use a favorite term of left-leaning economists, "market failure"—a socially destructive fluke that should not have happened and that really should be prevented?

Our reply: not only does Paulson "deserve" his $3.7 billion; his profit makes sense in Real World economic terms.

Paulson operates in the complex, high-risk world of hedge funds, a far cry from your traditional mutual fund. Hedge-fund managers employ mind-boggling arrays of strategies, using puts, calls, options, and short sales. They deal in everything, including, of course, stocks, bonds, commodities, and currencies. What makes hedge funds high-octane vehicles is their use of borrowing on a scale that can take your breath away— a process that can magnify gains and losses.

Paulson earned his historic reward because his hedge fund invested with exceptional success for the multibillion-dollar pension funds that are his clients. His investments in 2007 yielded an astounding $15 billion gain—a 600 percent return. His subsequent trades generated more than 17 percent gains for his clients despite a down market in 2008.

The news media has characterized his trades as a "bet," as though Paulson was playing the slot machines in Vegas. But his investment decisions were based on anything but luck. Paulson's analysis led him to conclude that the housing market—fueled by so many low-interest, ill-advised subprime loans—was dangerously overheated. As he told journalist Gary Weiss, "We felt that housing was in a bubble; housing prices had appreciated too much and were likely to come down."[23] Mortgage-backed securities created by investment firms from bundles of mortgage loans were, as a consequence, drastically overvalued. His trades were predicated on the belief that the market would eventually tumble, and that banks like Lehman Brothers, Washington Mutual, and Wachovia would find themselves in major trouble.[24]

Paulson's two-year "megatrade"—as it has been described—involved an assortment of tactics and financial instruments. One strategy was to sell short, risky, mortgage-backed securities called collateralized debt obligations, or CDOs, betting their value would soon decline. Another tactic was to buy credit-default swaps, which are a form of insurance against the failure of mortgage-backed securities if their underlying mortgages go bad. Paulson steadily bought credit-default swaps before the housing bubble showed any sign of bursting—when the instruments were cheap.

He took on a staggering amount of risk. According to one account, he invested some $22 million in credit-default swaps alone long before the financial crisis hit.

As all of us know by now, he was right big-time: homeowners began defaulting on their loans, and the value of Paulson's credit-default swaps soared. When the federal government declined to rescue Lehman Brothers[25] his $22 million investment in credit-default swaps paid $1 billion.

Paulson made a fortune for himself and his clients precisely because he went against the then-prevailing wisdom. The very fact that most others lost in the market attests to the fact that he served his clients better than other money managers did.

Paulson was hardly the only trader to see the downside of the subprime market. But unlike others, he surmised correctly that banks were not fully aware of its potential perils. Weiss writes:

> Other traders refused to short the big banks because they couldn't believe that such huge institutions would be so unaware of their own risks. Once that fact dawned on Paulson, he bet, fast and big, that the banks would fail.[26]

While appreciating this foresight, Weiss questions "the moral dimension of Paulson's achievement." He asks, "If he saw all of this coming, was it right for him to keep his own counsel, quietly trading while the financial system melted down? Do traders who figure out a way to profit from our misery deserve our contempt or our admiration, however grudging?" What Weiss and others should remember is that many bright people thought Paulson was wrong. Several economists, including New York University's Nouriel Roubini, warned of the impending housing disaster and were routinely ignored.

Paulson did not really "keep his own counsel." His massive invest-

ment of client money in positions predicated on a market decline constituted a powerful signal to other big investors that trouble was brewing.

Short sellers traditionally play an important role in helping to cool
overheated markets. Without traders like Paulson signaling to more traditional investors that a decline is coming and it's time to slow down,
markets would be prone to even more violent swings. Had he remained
on the sidelines, the overheated trading in mortgage-backed securities
would likely have gone on longer than it did, funding more bad mortgage lending.

If more people had the foresight of John Paulson, some of the excesses that produced the financial crisis might have been avoided.

As we explain elsewhere in this chapter, the wealth created by hedge
funds like Paulson's benefits not only the "fat cats" on Wall Street. It
quickly makes its way to Main Street, boosting the coffers of pension
funds that support millions of retired employees, as well as endowments
that fund university budgets.

Paulson made money for his clients in a dangerous market at a time
when other hedge funds were racking up losses. He may have netted a
multibillion-dollar reward. But he's one in a million in terms of his acumen, the wealth he created, and his critical role in the economy.

Some observers have complained that short sellers like Paulson benefited from the weakness in financial stocks artificially created by the removal of the uptick rule and the advent of mark-to-market accounting. It's
true that these short sellers made immense amounts of money because of
those two factors. But you can't blame the short sellers for successfully responding to distorted market conditions that the government created.

▲   REAL WORLD LESSON   ▲

There's a world of difference between lotteries, slot machines, and other gam-
ing activities and investing. Gambling is a form of entertainment; investing is
how we finance future innovation and growth.

Q ► DOES SOCIETY REALLY NEED RICH PEOPLE?

A ► YES. EXPERIENCES OF NATIONS THAT HAVE DESTROYED THEIR
    MERCHANT CLASS ILLUSTRATE THE IMPORTANCE OF WEALTH
    BUILDERS IN AN ECONOMY.

The title of author Hunter Lewis's recent book posed a question that has been asked by the critics of capitalism: *Are the Rich Necessary?* The book, which looks at both sides of the debate, offers a good explanation of why, in the Real World, "rich people" are not only necessary but essential:

> An economy expands by becoming more productive. We become more productive by learning how to produce more and more, better and better, with the same number of workers. Productivity increases as we give workers better tools. In order to afford these tools, we need . . . to save, so that we can invest the savings in the tools we need.[27]

> The poor cannot be expected to save, because they need every dollar for basic needs such as food and shelter. Middle class people will save something for emergencies, children's education, or old age. The rich, however, are different. They have so much money that, in aggregate, they simply cannot spend it all. They are, in effect, forced to save.[28]

The author is essentially saying that because they are "forced" to save, the rich have the capital to invest in the tools—the businesses and innovations—that increase productivity and economic growth. What happens when there aren't enough rich people? There isn't enough investment capital. The economy suffers.

People who buy into the Rap on capitalism fail to see the role that the rich play in an economy as society's entrepreneurs and investors. All too often, they see "rich" and "poor" as fixed groups with opposing interests. In her 2007 essay in the *Nation* on the "bloated overclass," Barbara Ehrenreich angrily declared that "it no longer takes a Marxist, real or alleged, to see that America is being polarized between the super-rich and the sub-rich everyone else."[29] Ehrenreich, as we saw earlier in this chapter, holds rich people culpable for countless sins, ranging from "exploiting" low-wage labor and displacing people through gentrification to enriching themselves and not others through their fortunes.

Society would be better off, she says, if these selfish rich people weren't around. In her piece, Ehrenreich quotes a fellow writer, Roger Lowenstein, who, while more accepting of inequality, acknowledged that the nation might be a more "egalitarian" place if "the upper crust were banished to a Caribbean island."[30]

Ehrenreich does him one better. The Caribbean, she insists, is not a sufficiently remote location: "why give the upper crust an island in the Caribbean? After all they've done for us recently, I think the Aleutians should be more than adequate."[31]

Well, about thirty-five years ago, Idi Amin, the dictator of Uganda, more or less did what Ehrenreich is proposing. In 1972, the dictator expelled the nation's population of Indians, who made up the merchant class. Amin accused them of being "bloodsuckers" who had undermined the nation's economy, avoiding taxes and not investing their profits back in the economy. He gave them ninety days to leave. Some eighty thousand did.

Amin rid his country of most of the people who were supposedly the cause of its woes. The result? Deprived of the services and capital produced by these entrepreneurs, Uganda's economy collapsed. An account in the British daily *The Independent* describes what happened:

> After the expulsion, Uganda's inflation soared and imported goods became impossible to get hold of. Few Ugandans saw material benefits from the expulsion. Instead of equally distributing the property and land the [Ugandans of Asian descent] left behind, Amin gave the confiscated property to a handful of his favourite soldiers who had no business skills or money for investment. Uncared for, the shop fronts crumbled and farmlands returned to the jungle, and international investors became increasingly reluctant to put their money in the country.[32]

More than a decade later, the bloodthirsty Amin, a man who had butchered tens of thousands of his own people, had gone into exile and a new regime attempted to undo the damage that the Asian exodus had done, returning confiscated property and inviting the exiled Asian Ugandans back. So much for the notion of the rich being a drag on the economy.

Some people might be tempted to believe that expelling the rich was such an economic disaster because Uganda was a small country. But as Thomas Sowell has written, other countries that have scapegoated and destroyed their merchant class—Sowell calls them "middleman minorities"—have suffered much the same effects:

In many times and places, middleman minorities have been forced to flee for their lives from mobs or have been expelled en masse by political authorities. Yet the departure of these supposed "parasites" and "exploiters" has not been followed by a more prosperous life by the rest of the population but usually by economic decline—sometimes catastrophic decline.[33]

The Jews of Spain five centuries ago were similarly resented for their affluence. In 1492, King Ferdinand and Queen Isabella gave them four months to leave Spain or else convert to Christianity. As many as four hundred thousand emigrated. Most went to the Ottoman Empire. Fortunately, Sultan Bayezid II was smarter than the Spanish king and queen and had a better understanding of the role wealth producers play in a Real World economy. According to historians, he knew it. "How can anyone call Ferdinand wise when he impoverishes his own kingdom to enrich mine?" he reportedly declared.[34]

The economic and cultural damage of the Jewish exodus is felt by Spain even today. A *New York Times* story marking the five-hundredth anniversary of the expulsion acknowledged, "Educated Spaniards commonly lament the 1492 expulsion as a horrible mistake that contributed to Spain's later decline."[35] It was one reason that the development of the Spanish economy woefully lagged behind that of the others of Western Europe.

The Real World principle that rich people are critical to everyone's prosperity is borne out by history. We will show in chapter 4 that tax cuts enacted by both Republican and Democrat administrations, which opponents said would mainly benefit "the rich," have consistently produced more tax revenue, along with economic growth—not only for the upper income earners, but for everyone else.

As Lincoln also said: "You cannot help the wage earner by hurting the wage payer."[36] Or as author and economist Ben Stein puts it today, "No society ever got anywhere by using envy of the rich as a tool of social policy. No society has ever helped the poor by crusading against the rich."[37]

▲   REAL WORLD LESSON   ▲

Rich people are essential to economic growth because they can amass and invest the capital needed to create and develop businesses, jobs, and innovations.

Q ► Don't the recent financial crisis and high oil prices show
how hedge funds and private equity investors, with their
concentrated pools of unregulated wealth, end up hurting
the economy?

A ► No. Hedge and equity funds provide a vital source of capital
in the economy. With proper oversight, their trading
activity can in fact help moderate markets.

Hedge funds and their close cousins, private equity funds, have become emblematic of the evils of great wealth and unfettered markets.
These vast, unregulated pools of capital have faceless clients and employ
mysterious-sounding high-risk trading strategies like arbitrage or short selling equities or derivatives. Critics portray them as invisible monsters run
amok, "speculators" and short sellers wreaking untold havoc in markets.

Hedge funds in particular came under withering attack for helping to
cause the financial meltdown of 2008 by trading in credit-default swaps
and other financial instruments, and short selling the stocks of companies like Bear Stearns, Lehman Brothers, Washington Mutual, and AIG.
Hedge-fund trading in oil futures contracts was also blamed for driving
up oil prices when gas prices were at their height. Hedge funds have also
been involved or associated with headline-making financial scandals
and, occasionally, wrongdoing—such as the implosion of the fraudulent
Bayou Group of funds, which defrauded investors of some $450 million.

This dubious image has been exacerbated by media portraits over the
past decade of the out-of-this-world wealth of "hedge-fund billionaires"
who make obscene fortunes even higher than those of overpaid CEOs of
public companies. The top twenty private-equity and hedge-fund managers pocketed an average of $657.5 million in 2007, a sum inconceivable
even to many highly paid executives.

Hedge funds are unregulated because clients are supposed to be financially sophisticated, high-net-worth individuals or pension funds
that can take care of themselves. The minimum investment that most
funds accept is $1 million. For their services, hedge funds will charge
high fees, usually 2 percent of assets under management and 20 percent of
all gains. The idea is that high-risk investments, capably managed, will
produce high returns.

In contrast to hedge funds, the primary focus of private equity funds is longer-term positions in undervalued companies. They will often install a new management team, turn the companies around, and then sell them at a much higher price.

Equity and hedge funds get criticized for "looting" companies, ruthlessly eliminating jobs or moving them out of the country for short-term profit. As UCLA law professor Lynn Stout complained in the *Wall Street Journal*, such funds "use their ownership position to pressure boards into strategies they claim unlock 'shareholder value,' and then dump their stock as soon as the price rises."[38] In this way, investors, such as Carl Icahn and others, launch "activist attacks" against companies "to make money quick." Not only do these funds lower the returns of other investors in a particular stock, she asserted, but they exert downward pressure on the market as a whole.

There have been calls to regulate or to raise taxes on both hedge and equity funds. Equity funds are also criticized because their gains are taxed at capital gains rates instead of regular income-tax rates.

Hedge funds and equity funds play a very useful role in the investment world. By providing clients, particularly investment funds, with exceptionally high returns on their money, they've become a critical source of capital—not only for Wall Street, but, indirectly, for Main Street.

Between 1991 and 2006, private equity firms worldwide created more than $430 billion in net value for investors—which include universities, charitable organizations, and pension plans covering tens of millions of Americans. Thus, the superior investments of private equity firms translate into stronger pension plans, more financial aid, and scholarships at public and private colleges and more funds for research to cure or treat diseases.

The biggest customers of hedge and private equity funds are pension funds, particularly public pension funds like CalPERS. In 2006, the twenty largest pension funds invested in private equity represented some 10.5 million retirees, including plans from California, New York, Texas, Florida, New Jersey, Ohio, Pennsylvania, and Michigan. Their collective private equity investment: $111 billion.

Without these vehicles, there would be less capital available to fund the retirement of these state and union employees. In the case of public employees, that would very likely compel states to resort to higher taxes. It's worth noting that until the crash, states had been able to avoid the budget cuts or tax increases that would have been required to meet their legally mandated pension obligations. There's no protection from tough times and overspending politicians. But without the returns from these funds, many state governments would be in an even deeper financial hole than they are today.

Private equity funds are a critical source of capital for charitable foundations as well as higher education. University endowment funds, most notably those of Harvard and Yale, have received considerable publicity for the rapid growth of their endowment funds thanks to these nontraditional vehicles. In fact, some institutions like Harvard and Yale overdid a good thing in using these funds too extensively. When the downturn came they overcommitted their cash to these funds and thus had to cut back on what they could provide for their operational budgets.

Students at public and private universities get tuition assistance from the return on their universities' private equity fund investments. Schools also use investment income to hire faculty, construct buildings, and fund programs. The University of California, the University of Minnesota, Cornell, Pepperdine, and Emory are just some of the many institutions of higher learning that rely on private equity investment returns to bolster the educational experience they provide their students.

Private equity funds have also been instrumental in the turnarounds of major companies such as Burger King and Continental Airlines, among others.

Another benefit of hedge funds is that their massive pools of capital help reduce the cost of equity trading by increasing market volume and liquidity. For example, if you want to sell a big block of stock, there are more traders capable of handling that volume. Greater trading volume makes it more likely that there will be a buyer when someone wishes to sell, or conversely, that there will be a seller when someone wishes to buy—which is also good for investors.

Under normal conditions, hedge funds can be said to have a moderating effect on markets. The larger trading volume they help produce causes big transactions to have less of an impact. In a market with fewer trades, selling or buying large positions has a bigger impact on price.

Added to all this, as we explained earlier, the activity of hedge-fund short sellers usually provides a vital signal to other investors that a market may be overheating.

Hedge funds did not cause the financial meltdown of 2008. Nor were hedge funds and equity funds the prime movers driving prior commodities bubbles. They did not create subprime mortgages or package them as did Wall Street investment houses. And they did not print the excess money that created the commodities bubble in 2004. After all, there were several commodities bubbles in the 1970s, long before today's hedge funds existed. As previously noted, these events were the consequences of monumental monetary and regulatory mistakes, not to mention the resulting excesses on the part of Wall Street firms and banks.

Hedge funds were also mistakenly blamed for helping to propel the steep rise in the price of oil—another example of shooting the messenger. Hedge funds alone couldn't set the value of a commodity traded worldwide in so many markets. They went along for the ride. Their speculation was prompted by the Federal Reserve Bank's easy-money policy, which sent the prices of all commodities rocketing upward. When the Fed tightened up that policy in the summer of 2008 by not printing excess dollars, commodities, including oil, crashed—and hedge funds were powerless to prevent it.

Given the current economic disaster, there will certainly be new rules and regulations for equity and hedge funds. Whether they will be constructive or destructive remains to be seen. Suffice it to say that big collapses of "underregulated" hedge and equity funds have been far fewer than those of highly regulated banks and insurance companies.

▲   REAL WORLD LESSON   ▲

Hedge funds and equity funds, with proper oversight, are a critical source of investment capital, providing important information about the direction of markets, and increasing the efficiency and precision of commodity and equity pricing.

Q ► Isn't it harder for a two-income family to get by today than it was for a one-income family in the 1970s?

A ► It is harder mainly because of the increased tax burden

ON TWO-INCOME HOUSEHOLDS AND THE RAPID INCREASE IN
HEALTH-CARE COSTS.

Harvard Law School professor and Obama adviser Elizabeth Warren and her daughter Amelia Tyagi did a study comparing an average middle-class family who lived on one income in the 1970s with the two-income family of today. They claimed that even though today's two-income family brings in 75 percent more income than yesterday's one-income wage-earning family, they actually have less disposable income. Why?

According to Warren and Tyagi, five budget items—housing, health insurance, cars, taxes, and child care—now eat up three-quarters of the income of today's two-income families. A generation ago, they assert, these expenses consumed only half the income of a *single*-earner family.

Critics of capitalism also blame tax cuts and free trade for squeezing the middle class. It may be tempting to believe such gloom-saying during the sharp 2008–2009 recession and subsequent sluggish recovery. But it is not borne out by long-term statistics. In the 1980s, the net worth of U.S. households increased 110 percent; in the 1990s, it rose 108 percent. And until the financial crisis of 2007 it increased another 50 percent. In the current downturn, household net worth took a real hit because of the sharp slump in both the housing and equity markets. But this is not a permanent state of affairs. We've had periods in the past of decline followed by rebounds that exceeded the previous highs. The only exception, of course, was the 1930s, when, as we've seen, government policies hurt recovery.

Before the financial crisis and recession the nation was, in the view of some, nearly at full employment, with unemployment rates lower than they had been throughout most of the past thirty years.

Critics of capitalism have long insisted that Census Bureau numbers reflecting a smaller percentage of middle-income earners since 1980 suggest the decline of the middle class. Author Bruce Bartlett, a former Treasury official, dismisses "the clear implication that the percentage of those defined as the 'middle class' has fallen because many of those who used to be considered middle class have become poor." That idea, he claims, is essentially hogwash. "In fact, the ranks of the poor have fallen along with those of the middle class" over the past three decades.[39]

The reason, he says, is that more of them are richer. Multiple studies confirm this trend, including the 2007 U.S. Treasury Department study mentioned earlier in this chapter. It reported that "roughly half of tax-payers who began in the bottom income quintile in 1996 moved up to a higher income group by 2005."[40]

Bartlett asks, "How can it not be a good thing for society that fewer people are now making low incomes and more are making high incomes?"

But what about those people left in the middle? Aren't they being squeezed by higher health-care, education, and insurance costs? Yes, those things are more expensive. But it's taxes that are causing the problem.

Writing in the *Wall Street Journal*, George Mason University professor and bankruptcy expert Todd Zywicki shows how Warren and Tyagi's study downplays the tax issue. "When a spouse enters the workforce, he or she is immediately taxed at a higher marginal rate than one worker would be alone."[41] Not only that, he says, family budgets are stretched still further by rising state and local taxes, especially property taxes.

Mortgage payments, health insurance, and car payments have increased since the seventies. However, "the increase in tax obligations is over three times as large as the increase in the mortgage payments and almost double the increase in the mortgage and automobile payments combined. Even the new expenditure on child care is about a quarter less than the increase in taxes."[42]

Zywicki takes a closer look at the numbers in Warren and Tyagi's comparison. He finds that the tax bill for their present-day middle-class family had increased by $13,086—an incredible 140 percent. Meanwhile, "the percentage of family income dedicated to health insurance, mortgage and automobiles actually declined between the two periods." In other words, he says, today's middle class families are not in a "two-income trap" but in a "two-income-tax trap."[43]

"The typical family in the 2000s," he says, "pays substantially more in taxes than the combined expenses of their mortgage, automobile and health insurance." Some may wonder how this can be the case in light of the tax cuts that have taken place since the 1970s. It's because until the 1970s, most income earners were not in high tax brackets, especially after President Kennedy cut taxes in the 1960s. Then, too, Social Security and Medicare taxes were very low. In 1970 the payroll tax for FICA ate up a maximum of 6.9 percent of your income; by 1980 it was 8.1 percent; in 2009 it was 15.3 percent.

Moreover, the value of standard exemptions (deductions for kids and spouse) was higher in real terms in the 1950s and 1960s than afterward. When you have two income earners, especially among professionals, you fall into a very high tax bracket. People didn't hit those brackets as often in those early days, and exemptions were richer. Add increased payroll taxes, zooming property taxes, and burgeoning state income and sales taxes, and you have yourself a heavy burden indeed. For example, New Jersey had no sales tax until the mid-1960s. Today it is 7 percent. The Garden State had no income tax until the mid-1970s, and then the maximum rate was 2.5 percent. In 2009 the highest rate was almost 11 percent. (Under Governor Christie, the top rate has fallen to just under 9 percent.)

As for rising health and education costs, they are anything but the result of too much capitalism. As we shall see in chapter 7, health-care costs are the result of layers of laws and regulations distorting markets for medical care. And isn't government responsible for those substandard schools that families are economically stretching themselves to escape?

Today's middle-class squeeze is partly the result of another development that the gloom sayers don't necessarily like to acknowledge: today's higher level of material affluence and opportunity that has raised consumer expectations and standards. Yesterday's innovations and luxuries have become today's necessities. As personal-finance writer Laura Rowley puts it, it's harder to live on one income today because there is "so much more stuff to say 'no' to."[44]

Take higher education. Spiraling college costs were not an issue decades ago when the majority of people did not go to college. But now many more do.

Another modern convenience that was not part of life back in the 1950s: credit cards. Few people realize that they became a major factor only in the 1960s. Before, people often used personal-loan companies to borrow money for household purchases. Their rates made credit cards look like bargains. "Plastic" lowered the cost and availability of credit. You didn't have to run to the bank to get cash. It made buying things a whole lot easier. But the downside was that you could misuse these powerful tools and incur too much consumer debt.

The truth is that there *are* middle-income families that are living on one income. How do they do it? Through prudent budgeting and consumption. Living like a one-income family in the 1970s can sometimes mean scaling back consumption to something resembling 1970s standards. This sounds harsh. But those who have managed to do it insist that it isn't. One typical post on Wise Bread, a blog for people "living large on a small budget":

> We have had only one income for 19 years and are raising three kids. Everything we own is paid in full including our house now valued at $450,000. We take vacations every year and every two years we fly to Florida to Disney World. My husband has a blue-collar job. I don't think it's a status symbol to live on one income. I think it's just the best for our family.[45]

Carl, a single-income earner, opines that, in the end, family life on a single income ends up being cheaper because there aren't the costs associated with a second job—like child care and transportation.

> We are a single-income family, saving more money than most dual-income families. I think the time when dual-income families have more money than a single-income family [is] gone. We live in a larger house and are saving more money than my brother while our income is 40% less than his dual-income . . .
>
> The idea that an average family has more money with a dual-income than a single-income is a myth. Of course there are always exceptions, but if you run the numbers with all the expenses— a single-income family actually has the edge.[46]

Writes Paul, a stay-at-home dad, living on his wife's income "allows me to garden, take care of the chickens, take care of the bees, plan and cook good meals, write poetry, walk with the kids, etc."

He concludes, "I have to say that I do feel, often, that the sensual enjoyment of our lives, the fact that we have no consumer debt and an emergency fund, and the time we can spend with our kids, raises our quality of life well above that enjoyed by most people making a little above $40,000 a year. I FEEL rich."[47]

▲   REAL WORLD LESSON   ▲

Progressive tax rates penalizing two-income families are the primary driver of the middle-class squeeze.

CHAPTER FOUR

"Aren't Higher Taxes the Price We Pay for a Humane Society?"

THE RAP ► Taxes are an investment in the common good. They are the price we pay for a humane society. Taxes are essential to funding federal, state, and local governments, which maintain social order. Not only do tax cuts deprive government of needed revenue, they mainly help the rich, who need them the least.

THE REALITY ► Taxes are necessary to pay for critical government services. But excessive taxation undermines the common good. Overly high taxes keep individuals from building personal wealth and advancing in the economy. They deprive society of the capital needed to fund investment in new businesses and jobs. History shows that, time and again, tax cuts, by unleashing economic growth, have generated more—not less—money for government.

No one doubts that we need government for essential services such as ensuring law and order, providing a national defense, providing disaster relief, and building and maintaining roads and highways, among other functions. But to pay for government, you need a healthy, growing economy. Excessive taxes defeat this objective by slapping an enormous financial penalty on work and enterprise. This penalty is even higher than most people realize. On top of what you or your business pays the government, there's the additional cost of compliance—the thousands of dollars spent on accounting and sometimes legal fees, not to mention the hundreds of hours you spend gathering data and filling out your returns and other records—the W-2s, 1099s, and so on. In 2004, the Office of Management and Budget estimated the cost of the nation's total tax compliance to be some $200 billion.[1]

Billions of dollars in money and human resources are wasted on taxes and tax compliance that could have gone into launching or expanding business-creating jobs. Taxes also end up making economic transactions more expensive. So what happens? Fewer of them take place. That's why high taxes sooner or later produce a stagnant economy, with fewer and poorer taxpayers who generate less money for government coffers.

Politicians love to talk about taxes being an "investment" in society. Sometimes taxes are supposed to be a way of "protecting jobs"—as in the case of tariffs on imports. Other times they're proposed as a way of encouraging what certain groups deem to be "desirable" behavior—for example, so-called obesity taxes discouraging consumption of sugary foods and beverages. Proponents of these taxes often don't understand that markets are millions of people expressing their desires. Trying to control their behavior through what is basically a coercive measure usually backfires.

No matter how they're sold to the public, taxes rarely produce the market outcome their advocates want. As Andrew Chamberlain, Gerald Prante, and Patrick Fleenor of the Tax Foundation explain, taxes tend to produce unexpected economic effects:

> Economists teach that, in general, taxes do not stay where lawmakers put them. Instead, some portion of taxes are generally shifted onto others.[2]

For this reason, taxes intended to protect the economy almost always do just the opposite—they kill jobs. The classic example, mentioned in chapter 2: the devastating Great Depression that ensued after the Smoot-Hawley Tariff slapped oppressive taxes on imports.

Smoot-Hawley was supposed to help preserve American jobs by making a vast array of imported products more expensive. What it produced was a trade war that made countless products unaffordable. Consumers simply stopped buying. Manufacturers had to cut back on employment. Millions of jobs were destroyed. Profits shriveled and investment capital dried up, undermining banks and precipitating the economic slump. The massive tax increases enacted in 1932 in the name of balancing the budget crushed an enfeebled economy and made the Great Depression even worse.

Taxes also helped create the infamous economic "malaise" of the 1970s. The Great Inflation of that decade pushed up salaries, forcing people into higher tax brackets. What did Congress do? It squeezed people and businesses further by, among other things, substantially boosting the capital gains tax. Would-be ventures couldn't get financing. Productivity fell. A family making $18,000 a year in 1979 was less well off than a family that had made $7,000 in 1968.

When tax rates are cut, however, the opposite takes place: the economy booms. Tax revenues grow. This has happened after every major tax cut in the last eighty-five years. Economist Arthur Laffer explained this continuum effect in the 1970s using what came to be known as the "Laffer curve." Higher taxes may initially increase government revenues. But they retard economic growth.

A classic case was the Clinton tax increases of 1993. They cut in half the 5 percent growth rate the economy had achieved by the end of 1992. This slowdown—combined with a rejection of Clinton's proposed plan for national health care—helped defeat the Democrats in 1994. With the Republicans in charge of Congress, the capital gains tax was slashed by 29 percent. The capital gains levy on people's primary residences was virtually eliminated; new taxes on the then-emerging Internet were barred. Welfare was also reformed and the growth of government spending was curtailed. The tax reductions, combined with slower spending, set the stage for a boom decade.

Would-be tax hikers forget that high tax rates hinder productive work, risk taking, and capital formation. That means a slower-growing economy generating less government revenue than it otherwise would have. But when tax rates are cut, more economic activity produces more tax revenues.

To observe the beneficial impact of tax cuts on the economy, all you have to do is look at history. In 1921, when President Warren Harding took office, the nation was in a depression, the result of the Federal Reserve raising interest rates to fight the inflation triggered by World War I. Unemployment had reached 13 percent.

Harding's plan for a "return to normalcy" included a major income-tax cut. After his untimely death from food poisoning, his successor,

Calvin Coolidge, pushed through additional tax cuts. The result: the Roaring Twenties. The federal budget surged into surplus. Increased revenues plus spending restraints saw the national debt shrink by one third. Real GDP growth went from 2 percent to 3.4 percent.

John F. Kennedy's proposed income-tax cuts, enacted in 1964, had much the same effect: real income-tax revenue growth surged from 2.6 percent to 9 percent. GDP growth increased to a robust 5.1 percent. Same for the Reagan tax cuts legislated in 1981: income-tax revenue, which had been shrinking by 2.6 percent a year, grew by a robust 3.5 percent. Real GDP growth soared from 0.9 percent to 4.8 percent, ushering in an era of prosperity that lasted almost three decades.

Not all tax cuts, however, are created equal. Some officeholders seeking political credit for cutting taxes will attempt to portray nominal rate cuts or rebates as Kennedy- or Reaganesque tax reduction. But these one-time gimmicks do not have the effects of substantial, across-the-board cuts in rates. The Bush tax cuts of 2001, for example, were largely useless. The tax rebates provided a small, one-shot boost to the economy and then fizzled, as rebates always do. The rate cuts that were enacted were phased in over so many years that their initial impact was virtually nil. The result: the economy treaded water in 2001 and 2002.

However, the Bush administration did get it right with its second round of tax cuts in 2003. Income-tax rates were reduced by an average of 10 percent. The capital gains levy was slashed; the personal income tax on dividends was meat-axed over 60 percent, from almost 40 percent to 15 percent. Small businesses were given incentives for investment by being allowed to write off capital expenditures of up to $100,000 immediately, instead of over several years. The economy bloomed.

The consistently salutary effects of tax cuts on the economy have been documented in a powerful study by Christina Romer, who served a stint as chair of President Obama's Council of Economic Advisers. She and her husband, UC Berkeley economist David Romer, studied all federal tax cuts and tax increases from 1947 to 2005. They found that tax cuts have a direct and pronounced impact on our economic output. A tax cut of 1 percent will increase GDP by about 3 percent.[3]

The real issue is not whether we should have high taxes or have no taxes. It is what level of taxation is necessary to fund essential services while enabling society to grow at its full potential. A 2009 annual poll by the Tax Foundation showed that Americans, on average, believe taxes should be only around 16 percent of their income.[4] Unfortunately, we're a long way from that.

Taxes don't just stifle economic activity. They're used by politicians to influence behavior that might otherwise be considered beyond the reach of government. Political debates over taxes frequently center on whether or not to impose a particular incentive—say, a tax credit for "caregiving" or for hiring American citizens. Libertarians like Yaron Brook, president of the Ayn Rand Institute, question whether the government should really be in the business of using taxes to influence what are essentially personal decisions:

> Tax policy works by attaching financial incentives to a long list of values deemed morally worthy. If you want to maximize your wealth come tax time—and who doesn't?—you must look at the world through tax-colored glasses, "voluntarily" adjusting your behavior to suit social norms and thereby qualify for tax breaks. In this way, the social engineers of tax policy preserve the impression that you're exercising free choice, while they're actually dispensing with your reason and your judgment.
>
> [T]here's nothing wrong with caring for grandparents, hiring local people or spending on R&D—if a rational thought process leads you to conclude that those choices actually serve the self-interest of you or your company.[5]

Taxes also let policy makers dispense political favors. How did the sale of lumber by the timber industry come to be taxed—and stay taxed—at the capital gains rate instead of the normal tax rate? One factor: Weyerhaeuser Company, a leading forest products company, had huge properties in Washington State, represented in the 1950s and '60s by powerful senators Henry "Scoop" Jackson and Warren Magnuson.

Equity funds have benefited from a similar tax break, thanks in part to the efforts of Senator Charles Schumer of New York, who has helped preserve the capital gains rate for the industry—at least until the financial crisis hit. These tax breaks can be defended objectively—as we've done on occasion. But they never would have been enacted without powerful political lobbying.

With government spending soaring as a result of the financial crisis and recession, even some conservatives are saying that taxes must go up. After all, they argue, a top tax rate raised to 40 percent of income would still be far below the 70 percent that Reagan found when he took office. That would give us about the rate we had in the prosperous 1990s. Others advocate a European-style consumption levy called the Value Added Tax (VAT). These individuals have fallen into the trap of concluding that government outlays are inevitable and that therefore, we have no choice but to raise tax levies to "help pay for it all." They have forgotten their basic lesson—that low, reasonable rates generate a wealthier economy.

It is precisely because of coming crises in Social Security and health care that we need more incentive for innovation and growth. A moderate increase in tax rates may produce higher revenues. But it will nonetheless stifle economic expansion, resulting in a smaller economy and lower tax receipts.

No one denies that the services of government are vital and must be paid for. But the only way we will continue to afford them is through reasonable taxation that allows people control of their behavior and leaves them free to generate wealth—for themselves and others.

Q ► Shouldn't the rich pay more taxes? (Or: Why should Warren Buffett pay a lower tax rate on his income than his secretary does?)

A ► The rich already pay more.

In late 2010, a fierce debate was waged over whether to extend the Bush tax rates. Supporters of the administration proposed that the old lower rates should apply only to those with incomes below $250,000. Those with higher incomes should get a tax increase. It was the latest debate over the long-standing question: Do the rich pay their fair share of taxes?

The conventional wisdom of many politicians is that they don't. Investor Warren Buffett made headlines when he complained about this to an audience of wealthy executives at a Democratic fundraiser in 2007: "The 400 of us [here] pay a lower part of our income in taxes than our receptionists do, or our cleaning ladies, for that matter. If you're in the luckiest 1 per cent of humanity, you owe it to the rest of humanity to think about the other 99 per cent."[6]

Buffett explained that he had been taxed on only 17.7 percent of the $46 million he had made the previous year. Meanwhile, his secretary had to fork over 36 percent of her sixty-thousand-dollar salary.

Buffett and others who deride "tax cuts for the rich" ignore a little-known fact: rich people already pay more in taxes. And their share of the nation's total tax bill has *increased* since Ronald Reagan cut taxes in 1981.

Consider this: In 1980, before the Reagan tax cuts, the top 1 percent of American income earners paid 18 percent of federal income taxes. Then rates were reduced from a high of 70 percent to a low of 28 percent. What happened? The share of the national tax burden paid by the wealthy actually *went up*. They produced 23 percent of national income and paid 36 percent of federal income taxes.

They pay even more today. That top income tax rate is now 35 percent. The top 10 percent of income earners pay 71 percent of the federal income taxes. And the top 1 percent of America's income earners paid 38 percent of all federal individual income taxes.[7]

What about those who say that the rich should pay a higher percentage of their incomes? They already do. Some 43 percent of the population, overwhelmingly people with lower incomes, pay no federal income taxes.

Warren Buffett's complaint is disingenuous. If he paid himself a salary, he would, indeed, be paying a higher rate than his secretary. That 17.7 percent, however, is not an income-tax rate. It's the capital gains rate he pays on investment income from Berkshire Hathaway, the company he manages and in which he is a major shareholder. Critics like Buffett ignore the fact that dividend income to shareholder/owners is taxed twice, first on the corporate level and then on the personal level. Not only does a shareholder pay personally; his or her company does, too.

Why are the capital gains tax rates that Buffett pays lower than the income-tax rate paid by his secretary? Because, as we discuss later in this chapter, capital gains income is different from salaried income. Salaried income means you get paid regularly, say, every week or twice a month. As long as you are not laid off and your company doesn't go broke, you get that paycheck. By contrast, capital gains are generated only after you have placed your capital at risk and the venture has succeeded. The gain is far from guaranteed. Most new businesses fail. And as people discovered during the financial crisis, investing in stocks is no sure thing. Stocks can plummet in value and you can end up losing money. A lower capital gains rate constitutes your "reward" for taking that risk on ventures that produce jobs and other benefits for the economy.

Conversely, raising capital gains taxes penalizes this kind of risk-taking. You ultimately get less investment and entrepreneurship, a smaller, less wealthy economy with fewer jobs. How does that help the poor? According to *Wall Street Journal* economics writer and editorial board member Stephen Moore, if the tax cuts of 2003 proved anything, it's that cutting taxes is the best way to "soak the rich":

> Between 2001 and 2004 (the most recent data), the percentage of federal income taxes paid by those with $200,000 incomes and above has risen to 46.6% from 40.5%. In other words, out of every 100 Americans, the wealthiest three are now paying close to the same amount in taxes as the other 97 *combined*. The richest income group pays a larger share of the tax burden than at anytime in the last 30 years with the exception of the late 1990s—right before the artificially inflated high tech bubble burst.
>
> Millionaires paid more, too. The tax share paid by Americans with an income above $1 million a year rose to 17.8% in 2003 from 16.9% in 2002, the year before the capital gains and dividend tax cuts. The most astounding result from the IRS data is the deluge of revenues from the very taxes that were cut in 2003: capital gains and dividends. Capital gains receipts from 2002–04 have climbed by 79% after the reduction in the tax rate from 20% to 15%. Dividend tax receipts are up 35% from 2002 to 2004, even though the taxable rate fell from 39.6% to 15%.[8]

Despite myriad statistics from many sources, there is a refusal by many to accept the importance of capital creators to a healthy economy. They point to economic downturns, such as today's fierce recession, as evidence that "trickle-down" has failed. They ignore the decades of prosperity that preceded the downturn—and the fact that, over the long term, the economic pie has grown steadily. Except for the 1930s, every expansion has exceeded the peak of the previous expansion. Even with fluctuations, the standard of living of the American people has moved steadily upward.

Warren Buffett may feel guilty about paying lower capital gains tax and divided rates. But that doesn't mean government should cripple other critical entrepreneurs and businesses whose health is vital to pulling the nation out of bad times.

One result of the recession has been a heightened reluctance to raise taxes on *anyone*—and a growing awareness of the role of the "rich" as job creators. Increasing political pressure, and the resounding victories of pro-market candidates during 2010 midterm elections, forced even the president to see the light. In a significant reversal, he agreed to extend the Bush tax rates for another two years.

▲   REAL WORLD LESSON   ▲

Contrary to public perception, the rich in fact pay the greatest percentage of taxes. Their share of the nation's tax burden has increased, not decreased, when taxes were cut.

Q ► WHAT'S WRONG WITH TAXING CORPORATIONS TO AVOID A HEAVIER BURDEN ON INDIVIDUALS?

A ► HIGHER CORPORATE TAXES END UP BEING PASSED ON TO INDIVIDUALS AND KILLING ECONOMIC ACTIVITY.

Populist politicians traditionally score points by bashing the idea of tax cuts for corporations. In the 2008 presidential campaign, then-candidate Barack Obama said of himself and John McCain, "We both want to cut taxes, the difference is who we want to cut taxes for." Obama said he wanted to cut taxes for the "middle class," while McCain wanted to reduce rates for "some of the wealthiest corporations in America" including the big oil companies. The implication was that McCain was out of touch and cared little for the needs of the average citizen.[9]

However, had McCain been elected and been able to carry out his promise to lower the corporate tax rate to 25 percent, he would likely have delivered a charge to the economy that might have helped to lift it out of the recession brought on by the 2008 financial crisis.

That's because high corporate taxes, like other levies, destroy economic activity. As Thomas Sowell explains so aptly, taxes make transactions more expensive. Thus, fewer take place. In the case of corporate taxes, they leave businesses with less capital to invest. Taxes also lower the net return on investments. Consequently, companies become reluctant to take risks and less likely to expand. High tax rates also increase the mortality rate of small businesses because they have less access to capital. They're less likely to grow large enough to attract outside investment.

American corporate taxes are the second highest in the developed world. According to the Tax Foundation, the total American corporate tax rate—including state taxes—exceeds 39 percent, second only to that of Japan among developed countries. The top statutory corporate tax rate in the United States reaches as much as 47 percent in some states, such as high-tax Iowa.[10]

That's a stark, ironic contrast to the nations of Europe, which, despite high personal income taxes, have lower corporate rates. Even semi-socialist countries such as Sweden, for example, have more reasonable business taxes. They understand that allowing companies to generate profits helps maintain a healthy economy better able to afford government social schemes. Sweden's corporate tax is a moderate 28 percent. Even France's rate is lower than the U.S. statutory rate. In recent years these nations have actually lowered rates to attract business investment.

The consequence? Businesses that might have located or invested here are going elsewhere. After all, why would any intelligent CEO decide to invest here if his corporation will only end up paying taxes that are 5 percent or 10 percent higher than in other countries?

Little wonder companies are moving to places like Ireland, with its corporate tax rate of 12.5 percent. Once the poorest country in Western Europe, that tiny nation has been able to transform itself in barely two generations into an economic miracle. Though it has been hard hit by the recession, Ireland's per-capita income has surpassed that of Britain, France, and Germany.

High corporate tax rates drain businesses not only of capital but of productivity. They divert resources from business development and expansion into tax-avoidance efforts. These include so-called abusive tax shelters—elaborate, often convoluted strategies and transactions created for the sole purpose of avoiding taxes. The Enron fraud was in large part a huge tax-avoidance scheme. The *New York Times* reported that the energy company created 881 subsidiaries abroad, almost all located in tax havens. The strategy enabled the company to evade some $2 billion in federal income tax—and thus report false profits.[11]

In contrast, when corporate taxes are cut, businesses become more productive. More of them spring up. The result: increased tax collections. Cato Institute fellow Alan Reynolds has noted, "countries with corporate tax rates from 12.5% to 25%, such as Ireland, Switzerland, Austria and Denmark, routinely collect more corporate tax revenue as a share of GDP than the anemic 2.1% figure the Congressional Budget Office projects for the U.S."[12]

Politicians like to imply that taxing corporations is "fairer" and will somehow leave individuals with a lighter burden. The reverse is actually the case: higher corporate taxes end up increasing the financial burden on consumers. After all, where do businesses get money to pay those corporate taxes? Where else? From their customers.

When you buy a tie or a blouse, you're not just paying for the fabric and the labor. You're indirectly paying the manufacturer's—and the retailer's—payroll taxes, Medicare taxes, excise taxes, fuel taxes, and the like that are passed on as part of "the cost of doing business."

What does this mean in Real World economic terms? According to the Tax Foundation, the $370 billion in federal corporate income taxes collected in 2007 by Uncle Sam translated into an annual tax burden of $3,190 per family—more than the average household spends on restaurant food, gasoline, or home electricity in a year.[13]

Furthermore, the Tax Foundation's Scott Hodge and Gerald Prante believe that supposedly "invisible" corporate income taxes impose the greatest burden on lower-income households. These low-wage earners have a lower disposable income. They are most sensitive to these pass-along levies. Hodge and Prante conclude:

> A general cut in corporate income tax rates (or other taxes on capital) would provide a greater benefit to low-income households than would further rate cuts in individual taxes. Indeed, there are 43 million Americans who already have no income tax liability after they take advantage of their credits and deductions. Those households would benefit most from a cut in corporate taxes.[14]

Harvard economist Gregory Mankiw predicts that cutting the rate to 25 percent would unleash enough economic activity to generate revenues through other taxes to cover a major part of the $100 billion cost of the reduction. Other experts believe the cut would be self-financing.[15]

Capitalism bashers like to insist that only faceless corporations pay corporate taxes. But in the end, everybody pays.

▲   REAL WORLD LESSON   ▲

Besides reducing economic activity, corporate taxes are in effect a hidden tax that is passed on to consumers.

Q ► WHY WOULD A FLAT TAX BE BETTER THAN THE CURRENT SYSTEM?

A ► A FLAT TAX WOULD LOWER EVERYONE'S TAX BURDEN. IT WOULD REMOVE THE ONEROUS COMPLIANCE COSTS PAID ON TOP OF TAXES, GENERATING MORE REVENUES AND ECONOMIC GROWTH.

Steve Forbes's book, *The Flat Tax Revolution*, outlines the plan for the Forbes Flat Tax: a single-rate federal income tax and corporate tax of 17 percent. Income is taxed once and only once. The flat tax eliminates all double taxation of dividends, as well as taxes on personal savings and capital gains. The tax for individuals and families would apply only after generous exemptions for adults and children. A family of four, for example, would pay no federal income tax on their first $46,165 of income.

Adults would be able to take a $13,200 standard exemption. Single people who make less than that would not be on the tax rolls. Married couples would receive a $26,400 deduction. Heads of single-parent households would have a 30 percent higher exemption of $17,160 to compensate for the additional burden of raising a child alone. Families would receive a $4,000 exemption for each dependent and a refundable tax credit of $1,000 per child age sixteen or younger, as under the current system.

In contrast, the current system is based on a tangle of tax rates: personal rates range from 10 percent for lower-income earners to 35 percent for top earners. There's a 15 percent tax on capital gains and a 35 percent federal corporate income tax. On top of this are piled city, state, and local taxes.

People get concerned that the flat tax would eliminate favorite deductions, such as those for mortgages and charitable contributions. That's why individuals should have a choice between going to the new system or staying with the old. Most people would quickly realize that a simple, low flat tax would give them more resources for housing and charitable contributions.

Why is the flat tax better than the current system? Simplicity, for starters. Lincoln's Gettysburg Address, which defined the character of the American nation, is 272 words in length; the Declaration of Independence, 1,300 words; the Constitution, nearly 5,000 words. The Holy Bible, which took centuries to produce, 773,000 words. The federal income tax code and all of its attendant rules and regulations come to more than *nine million words.* And nobody truly knows what's in the code and what it means. That's why the IRS gives taxpayers on its hotline wrong information at least 25 percent of the time.

The complexity of the code was illustrated several years ago by a *Money* magazine survey. It took a hypothetical family's finances and gave the numbers to forty-six expert tax preparers, the best in the field. What the magazine got back was a shocker: no two preparers could agree on what the family owed. Each had a different estimate, and the differences came to thousands of dollars.[16]

Just about everyone would pay less under the flat tax than they do now. This is true regardless of the deductions they have taken under the old system. This substantial tax cut would unleash economic growth and boost tax collections. Fiscal Associates, a consulting firm specializing in quantitative analysis, estimates that a flat tax imposed in 2005 would have generated some $56 billion more in net government tax revenue by 2015 than the existing progressive code.[17]

The flat tax also eliminates a hidden tax we all currently pay—the enormous cost of compliance, the immense amount of money and manhours that we spend filling out returns and working to reduce our taxes. As we mentioned, the nation's total compliance cost has been estimated by the Office of Management and Budget to be around $200 billion.

With a flat tax, you'd file your return by filling out a single card. No more filling out page after page of tax returns. No more anguished hours spent with your accountant worrying whether you took the right deductions. The flat tax would reduce the need for the armies of accountants and bureaucrats who are part of the public- and private-sector effort of producing and processing tax returns.

Even if the flat tax only reduced compliance costs by half, that would mean, in national terms, a total reduction of $100 billion. This immense cost saving would free up human and financial resources that could then be invested in new jobs and businesses. The billions of dollars businesses spend on tax compliance or avoidance could be reallocated into new business activity and jobs. Think of what this would mean multiplied millions of times throughout the economy. The flat tax would unleash an economic boom that would produce more wealth—not only for individuals but also for government coffers.

The flat tax would also be a great time saver. The IRS reported that in 2008 Americans spent some seven and a half billion hours filling out tax forms, the equivalent of more than three million full-time jobs.

A flat tax would sharply reduce Washington's waste of resources on tax-related activity—the 115,000 agents (and climbing) of the IRS, as well as the lobbying that is the source of so much corrosive corruption. With its endless and ever-changing latticework of loopholes, the current system has spawned an industry devoted to influencing tax policy. One in six private-sector employees in Washington is employed by the lobbying industry. Half of their efforts are directed at wrangling changes in the tax code.

Members of Congress fight like cats and dogs to gain a place on the House Ways and Means Committee, which originates our tax legislation. Those who do are set for their political lives. Courted by lobbyists, trade groups, and individuals seeking to influence the writing of new tax legislation, lucky members rake in more contributions each election cycle than do most of their peers.

The flat tax would do away with the loopholes and tax shelters that produce useless economic activity and often rip people off. According to the Government Accounting Office, some 6,400 individuals and corporations have "bought abusive tax shelters and other abusive tax planning products" in recent years.

The flat tax would also kill off the death tax. It would end the draconian unfairness of the alternative minimum tax. It would lower the tax rate on business profits, while abolishing corporate loopholes and encouraging greater transparency. The personal tax on dividends would be eliminated. Companies would thus be able to increase the dividends they pay to shareholders.

The tax would allow the United States to once again become a business-friendly environment. Nations around the world that have instituted a flat tax—from Lithuania and Romania to Mongolia and Russia—have seen their economies roar almost immediately. Russia's depressed economy boomed after enactment of its flat tax, even before the commodities boom of 2004–2008. All flat-tax countries experienced impressive growth right up until the credit crisis. There's no reason why the United States can't have the same experience.

The flat tax would also return free choice to individuals who are now forced to make financial and personal decisions they wouldn't have made in order to lower their taxes. Yaron Brook of the Ayn Rand Institute writes,

> Government's job is not to dictate your values but to protect them. In a free country, you choose values and then use your own money as a tool to achieve them. But a value-rigged tax policy reverses this cause and effect—it uses your money against you, bribing you with tax breaks that let you keep some of your earnings in exchange for abandoning your preferred values.[18]

The flat tax would end this moral distortion, enabling you to live life in a freer society.

▲   REAL WORLD LESSON   ▲

The flat tax would boost the economy not only by lowering the cost of economic activity but also by freeing up more intellectual energy and manpower for entrepreneurship and innovation.

Q ► WHY NOT A CONSUMPTION TAX LIKE A NATIONAL SALES TAX OR A VALUE-ADDED TAX (VAT)?

A ► BOTH WOULD PRODUCE IMMENSE HIKES IN THE PRICE OF GOODS, PRESENTING SIGNIFICANT ENFORCEMENT ISSUES AND INCREASING YOUR OVERALL TAX BURDEN.

Another plan proposed to address the economic distortions created by today's monstrous federal income tax code is the National Retail Sales Tax—or what proponents call the "Fair Tax." This sales tax is intended to replace the federal income tax and payroll taxes. It would be collected on the sale of new goods and services. But used goods and business purchases would be exempt. Business purchases would also be exempt. The Fair Tax, which has some support among conservative politicians and pundits, calls for a 30 percent tax on virtually all consumption, including new houses, as well as on services from haircuts to legal advice to open-heart surgery.

Supporters of the idea have their hearts in the right place. They understand the economic damage caused by excessive taxes on income. On its face, a sales tax can look appealing. It does not create the social and marketplace distortions created by income taxes. But instituting the Fair Tax would bring numerous, Real World complications.

The enforcement issues are endless. For instance, what is the precise definition of the goods and services that are "new" and therefore should be taxed? What about people selling items on eBay that they claim aren't really new and should be tax exempt? There's also the problem of having to answer the question, *What constitutes a business?* What about individuals who incorporate simply to avoid paying the tax? The plan also assumes that government entities, such as the Pentagon for example, will pay a 30 percent sales tax when they buy an aircraft carrier or purchase supplies for our troops overseas. That's a totally unrealistic assumption.

Exactly how would a national sales tax be collected? Will states really devote resources to collecting a 30 percent tax that goes to the federal government? What federal agency will ensure that the hundreds of thousands of retailers in America are complying? Or that a business is indeed a business?

The greatest argument against the Fair Tax is that it will drastically raise prices. The price of nonexempt goods and services purchased at retail would instantly increase 30 percent. Partisans reply that such price hikes will be offset by the fact that people would have more take-home pay because the income tax and other taxes would be abolished. And companies freed from the burden of corporate income and payroll taxes could charge less. Really? We have to admit we're skeptical. Have you ever heard of a tax—one that's essentially a surcharge—making a product less expensive?

Key sectors of the economy, such as housing, would be devastated.

Who would want to buy a new home, for example, when it would cost 30 percent more than a preowned one?

Critics say that a sales tax, especially one this size, would be highly regressive, hitting hardest those with the least. Designers of the Fair Tax acknowledge this drawback, which is why their plan includes a scheme of monthly rebates to one and all. They call them "prebates," which would give to everyone money equal to poverty-level income to cover necessities such as food and clothing. This "prebate" would require an entirely new bureaucracy, even if we somehow got around the problem of enforcement. Rebates are also likely to further politicize the tax system, with interest groups of all kinds pressing for more favorable rebates based on "need," either real or perceived.

In a recession a national sales tax is especially unfair. Income taxes decrease in hard times if your salary declines. But with a sales tax, you still have to pay a 30 percent tax on your basic living expenses—such as mortgage, food, clothing—even if you're less able to afford it.

Finally, the fair tax requires repealing the Sixteenth Amendment to the Constitution. Otherwise, Washington continues to have the right to impose an income tax in addition to a national sales tax. Without repealing the Sixteenth Amendment, we will end up with the situation that exists in most states and in most other countries—that is, having both an income tax and a consumption tax.

Our Founding Fathers deliberately made amending the U.S. Constitution a time-consuming, cumbersome process. Getting people to accept the idea that a substantial sales tax—either the Fair Tax or a VAT— won't raise their cost of living will require considerable time and powers of persuasion.

Another alternative to income taxes—in use in Europe—is the VAT, or value-added tax. A value-added tax is imposed not only on the retail sale of items to consumers but also on the purchase of materials by businesses to manufacture their products. It is insidious because it imposes an invisible layer of taxation that inflates the cost of living. The French were the first to enact the VAT because it's hard to avoid: it is applied to every transaction, including services. A sales tax applies only on a final purchase, whereas a VAT is incorporated into every step of the manufacturing process—no exemptions anywhere.

A VAT increases the cost of doing business and hits all consumers. Another downside is that a VAT always ends up being an additional tax instead of a replacement tax. France, for example, imposes the VAT in addition to ferocious income taxes. As they say over there, *quel horreur!*

▲   REAL-WORLD LESSON   ▲

A 30 percent national sales tax or a European-style value-added tax would likely end up being an addition to our income taxes—just as such taxes are in most states and virtually every country around the world.

Q ► Aren't "death taxes"—aka, inheritance taxes—necessary to prevent aristocracies?

A ► No. Death taxes have actually helped preserve the fortunes of the wealthiest people, while preventing those on the way up from building wealth and protecting their families.

Originally, the Bush administration wanted to abolish the death tax. But Congress insisted—erroneously—that it would cost too much. To get his tax cuts passed, the president struck what was supposed to be a compromise: the inheritance tax would disappear for one year in 2010. Then it would return at the higher—and onerous—rate of 55 percent. The Bush administration went along with this in the hope that the single year of tax relief would fuel public demand for the permanent abolition of the death tax. They were wrong.

Instead, the need to pay for today's soaring spending has created pressure to keep the tax. President Obama has proposed keeping the top rate at 45 percent in 2010 and thereafter. If nothing is done, then in 2011 the top rate would increase to 55 percent. The levy would also kick in sooner: today's $3 million exemption will decline to $1 million.

Actually, death taxes—or inheritance taxes—raise a minuscule amount of money for government coffers—about 1 to 2 percent of tax receipts for the federal government, if that, according to the Tax Foundation. Then why bother with them? The argument is supposed to be "fairness." The first death taxes were devised in 1916 to raise money to beef up the military as World War I loomed. The tax was supposed to prevent the kind of entrenched aristocracies that dominated Europe by preventing estates from being passed to "unworthy" heirs.

In fact, the death tax has helped to *perpetuate* such fortunes by forcing the wealthy to hire high-powered lawyers and accountants to preserve their money via tax-avoiding trusts. If they were not compelled to resort to such protective devices, large estates would be subject to the normal forces of creative destruction and dissipate more rapidly. Those unworthy heirs would have a far easier time frittering away their inheritances.

Many of the people affected by the tax are far from wealthy. Studies show heirs to be often less affluent than the relatives who leave them their property. Thus, the tax is "much less progressive than its supporters believe it to be."[19]

The Tax Foundation has found that, in many ways, a high death tax functions much like excessive income taxation. It discourages entrepreneurship and wealth creation:

> The estate tax's 55 percent rate . . . had roughly the same disincentive effect as doubling an entrepreneur's top effective marginal income tax rate. . . . At some point the threat of estate taxation causes entrepreneurs to become more likely to retire early rather than continue to work. If the estate tax encourages entrepreneurs to stop working and saving, not only does this reduce federal income and payroll tax revenue, but also results in less overall wealth creation in the U.S. economy.[20]

Fewer jobs and opportunities end up being created for the broader economy by entrepreneurs who end up selling their businesses and retiring sooner than they otherwise would have.

A typical example: fear of the death tax forced the Mavar family of Biloxi, Mississippi, to sell its sixty-two-year-old Mavar Shrimp & Oyster Co., Inc. to H. J. Heinz in the late 1980s. Selling the business at that time allowed the family to pay a lower capital gains levy—avoiding a 55 percent death tax that would have required selling assets and breaking up the company.

The Mavar family had hoped their buyer would have continued to operate the business in Biloxi. But Heinz soon moved the company's operations—and its jobs—out of the state. Family member and former company vice president Victor Mavar recalled in written congressional testimony:

Obviously, most of our employees, who had lived in Biloxi for all of their lives, were not able to simply relocate with the new owners. While a handful did move, the majority simply lost their jobs and had to start new careers. Today, I regularly meet folks on the streets of Biloxi, who tell me that they used to work in our business, and state that they wished it had never been sold. . . .

I've avoided making any investments in other new businesses, which may not turn a profit for several years. I have chosen to do this despite my interest in supporting the rebuilding of Biloxi, which was ravaged by Hurricane Katrina in 2005.

In fact, I have received requests for investments in several local businesses, including a housing development that would help lower and middle income families who lost their housing due to the hurricane. However, I have been forced to turn them all down, lest I burden my children with the same death tax that we sold the business to avoid. As I see it, the death tax has encouraged a "wealth-redistribution," not from the rich to the poor, but from the local community to the national corporations.[21]

Mavar also complained about the overwhelming costs of death-tax compliance:

Even with the sale of our business, I am still concerned about being able to pay for the death tax. I've spent a fortune on attorneys, accountants, life-insurance and tax avoidance measures, such as early gifting to my children and charitable endeavors.

One 1992 study by economists Henry J. Aaron and Alicia H. Munnell estimated the cost of complying with estate taxes to be one dollar for every dollar of revenue raised—nearly five times more costly per dollar of revenue than the notoriously complex federal income tax. According to the authors of the study, "the ratio of excess burden to revenue of wealth transfer taxes is among the highest of all taxes."[22]

In the end, the death tax costs society far more than the trivial revenues it raises. It undermines the very "fairness" its designers were trying to achieve, as entrepreneur and radio commentator Herman Cain can attest to. His late father, Luther Cain, was a grandson of slaves, had no college education, and worked jobs as a barber, janitor, and chauffeur. In the beginning, Luther Cain was the kind of low-income person advocates of tax "fairness" profess to care about—except that he did too well, building a nest egg of slightly under $1 million by the end of his life in 1982. Hermain Cain wrote to Congress,

> By the time of my mother's death in 2005, my father's assets had grown modestly leaving his family with a death tax liability of $1.3 million. My father would have been proud to have known that his hard earnings had been well-managed and used to propel his family to ever greater heights. Somehow, I do not think he would be nearly as pleased to learn that nearly half of it never made it into the hands of his grandchildren.

As his son acknowledges, Luther Cain is a powerful example of how excessive taxes destroy economic growth and hurt the very people they're supposed to help.

> My father is only one example of thousands. Most Americans who have earned over a million dollars in their lifetime have done it through hard work and rigorous discipline. It is easy for members of Congress to talk about wealth disparity and to gloat about their grand schemes to ensure "fairness." It is another matter when they confront the individuals whose "wealth disparity" they are actually seizing.[23]

▲   REAL WORLD LESSON   ▲

Death taxes have the unintended consequence of forcing the very wealthy to protect their fortunes, while keeping individuals of moderate means from building wealth.

Q ► WHY NOT JUST COLLECT MORE MONEY FROM "SIN" TAXES ON
   CIGARETTES AND ALCOHOL?

A ► SIN TAXES AND OTHER ATTEMPTS AT "SOCIAL ENGINEERING"
   THROUGH TAXATION USUALLY FAIL.

If taxes on income are bad for the economy because they discourage constructive, wealth-creating transactions, what's wrong with financing government by taxing behavior most people agree is destructive—like smoking, for example? After all, supporters argue, so-called sin taxes deliver a two-for-one benefit: they generate needed revenue for government while discouraging undesirable activity.

That rationale accounts for the trend over the last twenty-five years toward targeted excise tax increases—sin taxes on tobacco and alcohol—in place of raising income and sales taxes. According to the *New York Times*, "across the country, politicians, eager to avoid anything that looks like a tax increase, are turning to levies on . . . 'unhealthy behaviors' to finance education. Kentucky, Maryland, Missouri, Tennessee, Utah and West Virginia are among the states that have shifted part of the cost of schooling from income, sales and property taxes to levies on gambling and nude or topless dances in the last few years."[24]

Not only are states turning to sin taxes to fund programs and services. They've also begun developing a whole spate of new "sins" to be taxed—from polluting to eating junk food, playing video games, or even drinking bottled water.

As Daniel Clifton and Elizabeth Karasmeighan explain in a recent report on this trend for Americans for Tax Reform, sin taxes are palatable to people who would like to see less of the behaviors the states are taxing. After all, you don't have to pay if you don't indulge in the "sinful" activity being taxed. As the authors point out, "By targeting their tax increases to narrower segments of the population, legislators divide taxpayers into smaller groups and minimize voter backlash."[25]

Sin taxes are what economists refer to as a "Pigovian tax" intended to correct a market's "negative externalities." That's economist speak for undesirable behavior. Sin taxes are supposed to be justified because, the thinking goes, they "adjust" a product's price to reflect its "actual cost" to society.

Pigovian taxes are named not for the swinish behavior they're supposed to control but to honor economist Arthur Pigou, who developed the thinking behind such taxes. Because sin taxes provide a disincentive to negative behavior, many people see them as a more palatable alternative to regulation. Creating a tax disincentive does not require the costly bureaucratic manpower that would be needed to enforce a new law.

The problem is that sin taxes don't really work as advertised. They present a host of unintended economic and social consequences—in addition to raising moral questions.

That cigarette smoking has declined is a consequence less of taxes on smoking than of greater public awareness of its health effects. New York State has the highest cigarette taxes in the nation. And New York City prohibits smoking in public places. But this has not stamped out smoking. What it has done is increase smoker determination to buy cigarettes from cheaper states and Indian reservations and on the black market, increasing opportunities for cigarette smugglers and criminals.

That's why Father Robert Sirico, a Catholic priest and head of the Acton Institute, which studies moral and economic issues, is an outspoken critic of these levies:

> One of the unintended consequences of sin taxes is the increased motivation for people to violate the law. Sin taxes exist as a half-way house to prohibition, and in the same way bootleggers used to smuggle liquor into the United States from Canada from 1919 to 1933, smokers will face greater temptation to engage in black market activities.[26]

He concludes, "The temptation to impose sin taxes is one that should be resisted for economic and moral reasons."[27] Indeed, some sin tax proposals are more than a little morally ambiguous—like when Texas governor Rick Perry advocated funding education by imposing taxes on exotic dancing. Not surprisingly, the plan, ridiculed in the media as "tassels for tots," went nowhere.

Sin taxes often don't work because states end up dependent on the very activities they're supposed to be taxing out of existence. When the activities decline, so do tax revenues. In 2008 the city of Chicago enacted a levy on bottled water. Five months later, experts predicted that it would bring in less than half the revenue estimated in its first year.

The state of Maryland doubled the cigarette tax to two dollars a pack to pay for expanded health-care coverage. But as the *Wall Street Journal* reported in 2008:

> Eight months later, cigarette sales have plunged 25% and the state is in fiscal distress again. A few pols are pretending to be

happy that 30 million fewer cigarette packs have been bought in the state so far this year. As House Majority Leader Kumar Barve put it, fewer people smoking is "a good thing." Yes, except that Maryland may be losing retail sales more than smokers. Residents of Maryland's Washington suburbs can shop in nearby Virginia, where the tax is only 30 cents a pack, and save at least $15 per carton. The Maryland pols are so afraid this is true that they've made it a crime for residents to carry two packs of cigarettes that weren't purchased in the state. In other words, the state says it's legal to smoke, so long as you use cigarettes that the government can tax and thus become a financial partner in your bad habit. But if you dare to buy smokes across state lines, you can be fined.[28]

There's also the issue of "fairness." Like other excise taxes, sin taxes are regressive, which means they take a greater percentage of the income of low earners. A National Center for Policy Analysis Report, "Taxing the Poor," explains why:

> Consider two families, one earning $10,000 a year and the other earning $100,000. If both spend $100 a year on cigarette taxes, the amount constitutes 1 percent of the lower earner's salary, but only 0.1 percent for the higher earner.[29]

Also, lower-income people often spend more on the activities commonly taxed. About one-third of lower-income adults smoke versus one-fifth of middle- and high-income earners, according to the Centers for Disease Control and Prevention. The NCPA points out, "The portion of income spent on alcoholic beverages by the lowest fifth of earners is double that of middle earners and more than three times that of the highest earners, on the average."

Father Sirico asks whether we truly want a tax system that is financially dependent on people's bad habits, while the addiction to wasteful government spending is totally ignored. He concludes,

> We must ask ourselves whether we want to charge politicians and bureaucrats with sanctioning sins in areas that are morally am-

biguous. Or should this task be left to community, family, church, and tradition—social institutions that are often more trustworthy in determining the limits of non-violent behavior?[30]

▲   REAL WORLD LESSON   ▲

So-called sin taxes, like other sales taxes, penalize lower-income people. They rarely produce the revenue expected and undermine freedom and individual choice.

Q ► WHY SHOULD CAPITAL GAINS BE TAXED DIFFERENTLY FROM INCOME?

A ► CAPITAL GAINS ARE TAXED DIFFERENTLY FROM INCOME BECAUSE THEY COME FROM RISK TAKING AND INVESTMENT—ACTIVITIES THAT PRODUCE GROWTH AND BENEFIT SOCIETY.

In 2003, the Bush administration cut capital gains taxes from 20 percent to 15 percent. The cuts are supposed to expire in 2010. Tax hikers—who included Barack Obama when he ran for president—have proposed letting the cuts expire or even raising the tax as high as 28 percent. While a hike would score political points in some quarters, it would be disastrous for an economy struggling to emerge from the worst recession in nearly three decades.

Cutting taxes on capital gains is frequently derided as a giveaway to the rich. In fact it's anything but. Millions of Americans depend on stock market gains for wealth building, savings, and retirement. Thirty years ago, only about 13 percent of Americans owned stock. At least 50 percent of American households do today.

Capital gains taxes, of course, are not paid only on stock sales. They apply to income from the sale of other investments, such as a business or work of art. Some capital gains are exempt from the tax. For example, a couple doesn't have to pay the tax on the first $500,000 of gains from the sale of their primary residence if they buy another home within two years.

The tax is paid on the "gain"—the difference between proceeds from the sale and the asset's original price. One problem with the capital gains tax is that the "gain" is not necessarily real profit. The tax has what policy analyst Stephen Moore and others refer to as an "inflation penalty." Moore explains, "The seller pays tax not only on the real gain in purchasing power" realized by an asset sale, "but also on [an] illusory gain attributable to inflation."[31]

In the 1970s, the cruel reality was that people paid punitively high rates of almost 50 percent on inflated gains that were essentially illusory. In effect, the tax was confiscating principal, wealth that had already been taxed. No wonder the seventies were a decade of stagnation and paltry investment.[32]

Capital gains have traditionally been taxed at lower rates than income. That's partly because, unlike salaried income, the gains are achieved after an individual or corporation has placed capital at risk. Experts like Stephen Moore believe that the reward for risking capital isn't big enough and that the capital gains tax in fact contains a "bias" against risk taking. Why? Because if your risk taking doesn't work out, you get to deduct only part of a loss—up to three thousand dollars a year.

Experts agree that capital gains tax cuts produce an especially large bang for the buck. They're a great way to boost the economy. That's because high capital gains rates cause what is called a "locked-in" effect. Investors hold off on selling assets to avoid the tax. But if capital gains taxes are cut, those same people sell—and invest. "Locked-in" wealth is released. Growth soars, along with a surge in tax receipts.

The Bush administration's 2003 capital gains tax cut was a key reason that the economy finally recovered from the 2000–2001 recession. Donald Luskin, chief investment officer of Trend Macrolytics, LLC, analyzed the Congressional Budget Office's annual "Budget and Economic Outlook" report in 2006. He concluded that the cuts actually ended up generating more money for government, not less, as had been feared. "Instead of costing the government $27 billion in revenues, the tax cuts actually earned the government $26 billion extra."[33]

Nor did the rich get a free ride from those cuts. According to Stephen Moore's study for the National Center for Policy Analysis,

[T]he rich did not get a huge tax cut from the capital gains cut; in fact, the percentage of income taxes paid by the rich increased from 34 percent to 39 percent from 2002 to 2005 (the most recent year for which data are available). The capital gains tax cut did not only benefit wealthy Americans; more than half of all tax filers with capital gains had incomes of less than \$50,000 in 2005 and more than two-thirds had incomes of less than \$100,000.[34]

Many have wondered why capital gains are taxed at all. Capital and income are two very different things. Income is the fruit that comes from ongoing enterprises. Capital fuels the enterprises and investments that drive growth and generate income for many. Reducing the amount of capital through taxation reduces this societal benefit. Free-market skeptics fail to understand this Real World economic truth—the "gain" produced for government by taxing capital is far outweighed by the cost to the economy and to people.

▲   REAL WORLD LESSON   ▲

Capital gains taxes penalize the critical risk taking essential to business investment and growth. Cutting or eliminating capital gains taxes would benefit not only the rich, but people of all incomes.

Q ► WHY NOT JUST GIVE MONEY DIRECTLY TO THE POOR INSTEAD OF GIVING TAX CUTS TO THE RICH?

A ► BECAUSE ACROSS-THE-BOARD CUTS HELP MORE PEOPLE AND ARE THE BEST REDUCERS OF POVERTY.

A question that has been raised by tax-cut opponents is "How are the poor going to be helped by tax cuts when many of them pay little or no taxes?" Barack Obama's campaign tax proposal favoring tax credits to lower-income people—instead of an across-the-board cut in tax rates—was based on this thinking. People who already paid no taxes would receive their tax "credit" in the form of a check from the government.

Giving money to people sounds generous. For politicians it can get votes. But in the Real World it is at best a one-shot solution that doesn't go very far. In fact, Real World experience shows that meaningful cuts in tax rates are the best way to generate more money for the poor.

We've explained in detail why this is so earlier in this chapter: cuts in tax rates boost the economy. Not only do such reductions let entrepreneurs and individuals keep more of what they earn, but even more important, lower tax rates increase incentives to take risks, to work more productively, to succeed. More people are hired. More wealth is produced. The result is a bigger, stronger tax base that produces more tax revenues that can be used to help those in need.

Analyst Brian Riedl of the Heritage Foundation points out that tax cuts between 1979 and 2003 resulted in not less but dramatically more government spending on the poor:

> Anti-poverty spending has leaped from 9.1 percent of all federal spending in 1990 to a record 16.3 percent in 2004. The data clearly show that . . . the people with the highest incomes are paying more of the tax burden while the poor are receiving more [government social] spending. Yet the misperception that the federal government is doing the opposite persists.[35]

John Tamny, editor of *Forbes*'s RealClearMarkets.com and forbes.com Opinions Channel, reminds us that expanding the tax base is the best way to increase funding for the poor because of a Real World principle few people know: no matter how much you raise taxes, they tend to remain at a fixed percentage of the tax base—around 18 percent of GDP.

That's the lesson of the Laffer curve—raise taxes and all that happens is the tax base shrinks. You get 18 percent of a smaller base—in other words, lower collections.

Tamny writes, "What this means is that if we grow the overall economic pie, we expand the taxable base. Sure enough, the reductions in top marginal rates that began in 1981 helped U.S. GDP to grow sixfold over the last twenty-five years and as a result, federal revenues have hit record levels nearly every year since."[36]

▲   REAL WORLD LESSON   ▲

Tax cuts are the best antipoverty measure because they create the economic growth that lifts people out of poverty through employment while generating tax dollars for government.

Q ▸ But don't tax cuts deprive Uncle Sam of the money needed to run the country?

A ▸ Tax cuts or tax increases, there are never enough revenues, because government just keeps growing.

We've all heard the "logic": tax increases are the only way to reduce the deficit and balance the budget of a government strapped for funds and groaning under the weight of debt made worse by "tax cuts for the rich."

The populist narrative has long been that the "massive deficits" of the Reagan years and the second Bush administration were the result of tax cuts. Supporters hearken back nostalgically to the income-tax increases of Bill Clinton, which they insist produced "the Clinton surplus" and an era of prosperity.

This view has persisted even in the wake of the Obama spending binge. In late 2010, Democrats pushed for the expiration of the Bush tax rates. They insisted that the tax increase was the only way to reduce the administration's historic budget deficit, regardless of the condition of the economy. The Real World truth is that deficits are not created by tax cuts. And they can't be fixed by either tax cuts or tax increases—if the size of government keeps growing.

Federal, state, and local government spending grow year in and year out, no matter which party is in power. At the start of the twentieth century, total government spending on all levels was not even 7 percent of the nation's economic output. By 2010 it was nearly 40 percent.

Tax cuts may expand the size of the economy. But a larger economy will never generate sufficient revenues if the growth of our sprawling bureaucracy continues uncontrolled and unabated. The big villains, of course, are entitlements, especially Social Security, Medicare, and Medicaid. All three need systemic reforms or they will end up impoverishing everyone, because they will require horrific increases in taxes to meet their growing liabilities. There are positive, exciting ways to change these programs so that, amazingly, they can provide increased benefits without undermining our future. We discuss these in chapters 7 and 8.

Opposition politicians seek to score points by blaming tax cuts during the Reagan and Bush presidencies for increasing federal budget deficits. But tax cuts—as we have shown above—increased the size of the economy and federal tax revenues. The problem was that Washington spent the extra money and then much, much more.

Despite Ronald Reagan's best intentions to limit the size of government, he was ultimately unable to rein in Congress on domestic spending. Reagan did sharply boost defense outlays—and that investment paid off.

We won the Cold War. Reagan's effort to maintain fiscal discipline was stellar when compared to that of his successors, especially George W. Bush, under whose administration domestic spending growth exceeded that of Democrat Bill Clinton.

According to the Heritage Foundation, "from 2001 through 2008, federal spending surged 60 percent—6.9 percent per year, on average." In 2008 alone, it increased by some $249 billion or more than 9 percent.[37]

Heritage analyst Brian Riedl says Bush would have been able to balance the 2008 budget "had [total] spending increases been limited to 35 percent—4.4 percent annually."[38]

And what about the legendary "Clinton surplus" and prosperity that Paul Krugman—not to mention former Clintonites such as Robert Rubin, Robert Reich, and Larry Summers—tout as being the result of Clinton-era tax increases? People forget that while he raised income taxes (which slowed economic growth for two years), Bill Clinton subsequently cut the capital gains tax from 28 percent to 20 percent. And as we've discussed, he ended up cutting other taxes as well, and kept the Internet a virtually tax-free zone.

If Bill Clinton had not cut capital gains taxes, his economic record would have been far different. In a report prepared for the Heritage Foundation, Dan Mitchell wrote that Clinton administration documents showed that

> in early 1995, nearly 18 months after enactment of the 1993 tax increase, the Clinton Administration's Office of Management and Budget projected budget deficits of more than $200 billion for the next 10 years. Clearly, events after that date—including the 1997 capital gains tax cut and a temporary reduction in the growth of federal spending—caused the economy to expand and the budget deficit to vanish.[39]

Mitchell concluded, "The Clinton tax increase delayed the economy's resurgence and had nothing to do with the budget surplus."

Tax hikers at this point invariably insist that the size of government is a given, that its services are needed, and that there's nothing that can be cut. That's simply not true. Because government lacks the discipline of having to compete in the marketplace, there is no incentive for cost-effective management, as there is in the private sector. Politicians simply keep tapping the public for money. Bureaucratic fiefdoms keep getting bigger. Costs keep going up.

Can the size of government be cut while still preserving essential services for people who need them? You bet they can. Writes Heritage's Brian Riedl: "A real war on government waste could easily save over $100 billion annually without harming the legitimate operations and benefits of government programs."

Riedl offers ten examples of egregious government spending that, if corrected, could slow today's hemorrhage of red ink. We won't list all of them here. But they include:

▶ **"Medicare Overspending."** As Riedl reminds us, "Medicare wastes more money than any other federal program, yet its strong public support leaves lawmakers hesitant to address program efficiencies, which cost taxpayers and Medicare recipients billions of dollars annually." The program pays as much as eight times what other federal agencies pay for the same supplies. Payment errors, frequently the results of fraud as well as plain mistakes, cost more than $12 billion annually. "Putting it all together, Medicare reform could save taxpayers and program beneficiaries $20 billion to $30 billion annually without reducing benefits."

▶ **"State Abuse of Medicaid Funding Formulas."** Says Riedl, "Significant waste, fraud, and abuse pervade Medicaid, which provides health services to 44 million low-income Americans. While states run their own Medicaid programs, the federal government reimburses an average of 57 percent of each state's costs." States overreport their Medicaid expenditures to receive larger reimbursements. Riedl says the problems have begun to be addressed, but more could be done that could produce billions in savings.

▶ **"Redundancy Piled on Redundancy."** Decades of regulation by Washington have produced a jungle of overlapping fiefdoms. As of 2005, Riedl says there were "342 economic development programs; 130 pro-

grams serving the disabled; 130 programs servicing at-risk youth; 90
early childhood development programs; 75 programs funding international education, cultural and training exchange activities; 72 federal programs dedicated to assuring safe water." And that's not even
the whole list. While he acknowledges that some duplication may be
inevitable, consolidating those programs would save money and improve government service.[40]

Those are just three key areas where cuts could produce billion-
dollar cost savings. Additional savings would come from better oversight
in routine administrative matters such as, yes, making sure government
employees turn in their unused airline tickets. An audit in the mid-
2000s found that the Defense Department had purchased approximately
270,000 fully refundable commercial tickets that were never used. No
refunds were issued. Total cost: $100 million. Also wasting your tax dol-
lars: employee abuse of government-issued credit cards. In one case,
employees at the Department of Agriculture were discovered to be using
government cards meant for office purchases to pay for personal items—
like Ozzy Osbourne tickets, tattoos, bartender school tuition, car payments, and cash advances.

Then, of course, there's the looming crisis of underfunded public-
sector pensions. Estimates of unfunded liabilities run into the trillions of
dollars. Already, numerous municipalities and counties are raising property taxes to meet the crisis. Fortunately the public is waking up to the
rampant abuses. In 2008, the New York Times revealed that virtually all
retiring employees of the Long Island Rail Road, healthy people not
much older than fifty, received disability payments on top of their pensions amounting to hundreds of millions of dollars. Dozens of so-called
disabled retirees were found to be enjoying free memberships at a local
golf course.

With government not accountable to taxpayers like a publicly held
company is to shareholders, it's unlikely we'll soon see an end to these
abuses. And no tax increase—or reduction—will be able to prevent the
mother of all deficits expected as a result of Obama administration
stimulus measures combined with already rocketing Social Security,
Medicare, and Medicaid costs. According to a projection by the Heritage

Foundation using data from the Congressional Budget Office, unless spending is slowed, this "coming tsunami" will push debt to inconceivable levels—300 percent of GDP by 2050 and 850 percent by 2082.[41]

▲   REAL WORLD LESSON   ▲

No amount of revenue can cover the debts incurred by spendthrift government.

CHAPTER FIVE

"Don't Regulations Safeguard the Public Good?"

THE RAP ► Without regulations and statutes imposed by government as the referee of capitalism, greed and selfishness would run rampant in unfettered markets. Regulations safeguard the public good. They promote public safety and ethical business practices, preventing businesses from cheating and ensuring that citizens abide by the rules of the road.

THE REALITY ► The rule of law is essential to the successful functioning of democratic capitalism. Certain regulations are necessary in an open economy. Yet others are a response to political pressure from self-interested constituencies. Politically motivated, overly meddlesome regulations and rules produce unintended consequences, hurting the very people they're supposed to protect. They micromanage the economy and stifle innovation, favoring incumbents at the expense of innovative outsiders.

In his book *The Road to Serfdom*, Nobel Prize–winning economist Friedrich Hayek said that the purpose of law in a democratic capitalist economy should be to codify the rules of the road. It should make certain that people travel in an orderly fashion. Rules and regulations should let people set their own path. They should not tell people precisely where and when they should travel—they should not micromanage markets. Hayek believed democratic capitalism was best facilitated by common law that applied to everyone, not by arbitrary laws designed to favor or penalize particular groups, enacted to carry out political agendas.[1]

Milton Friedman thought that the role of government should be to protect people from abuse and coercion by others. "Unless there is such protection we are not really free to choose," he wrote. "The armed robber's 'Your money or your life' offers me a choice, but no one would describe it as a free choice or the subsequent exchange as voluntary."[2]

The problem these days is that too many regulations reach beyond the basic functions of guidance and protection advocated by Hayek and Friedman. They often impose artificial constraints on behavior that distort the normal operation of markets. They end up hurting the people they're supposed to help, at great cost to the economy and society.

Many fear that the free market would degenerate into anarchy without regulation. The truth, though, is that free markets are to a great degree self-regulating.

This may be hard for some to believe, given the financial meltdown of 2008, with its nonstop headlines of wrongdoers and wrongdoings. But overall, in the Real World economy of democratic capitalism, the Bernard Madoffs of the world are the exception. Free-market economist and blogger William Anderson provides a good explanation of why this is so. The free market regulates itself precisely because it is voluntary and, as Adam Smith wrote, governed by self-interest. You can't force someone to do business with you. Thus, it's in your self-interest to act in a responsible way that will help attract and keep customers. After all, what individual or business will thrive by offering shoddy products and poor service?

Anderson reminds us that for about a century after the founding of the republic, businesses in the United States functioned largely without regulation. Settlers established the colonies in part to escape the suffocating rules of the Old World, where the minute workings of the economy could be dictated by government. Anderson gives the example of Louis XIV's finance minister, Jean-Baptiste Colbert, who "regulated the French economy down to the required thickness of threads for textiles."[3]

However, by the late 1800s, old-world regulatory habits began to reassert themselves in this country. Why? People feared that corporations had grown too powerful to be controlled by the usual marketplace checks and balances. In addition, a growing number of people believed that the certainties of science could be brought to bear on politics and economics. Free markets seemed so messy and chaotic. Why couldn't they be efficiently, scientifically managed?

The Progressive Era, which began in the late nineteenth century and ended with World War I, ushered in a new era of regulation. Politicians like Republican Theodore Roosevelt and Democrat Woodrow Wilson believed that Washington should be involved in managing a modern society.

The first major federal agency, the Interstate Commerce Commission, was established in 1887 to regulate the railroads. The market, driven by customer demand and competition, had formerly set rates and rail routes. Now government bureaucrats took over those functions in the name of safeguarding the public good. Routes and rates were now determined by a handful of regulators responding to political forces.

The ostensible purpose of the commission was to protect railroad customers, mainly farmers, from monopolistic practices and unfairly high rates. However, the commission ended up reinforcing the interests of the biggest industry powers—effectively creating a cartel—and destroying what had been an open, competitive market. As Milton Friedman recounts in *Free to Choose*, "Farsighted railroad men recognized that . . . they could use the federal government to enforce their price-fixing and market-sharing agreements and to protect themselves from state and local governments."[4]

Unfortunately, this is all too often a Real World consequence of well-intentioned regulations. They're sold by politicians as solutions to help the consumer or "the little guy." But they end up protecting the biggest industry players and special interests.

What free-market critics fail to appreciate is that markets are merely people expressing—or responding to—one another's needs and desires, based on the current realities of either supply or demand. Free-market transactions seek to achieve the greatest mutual benefit possible under the circumstances. In this way, as Adam Smith observed, the "invisible hand" of the free market ultimately acts in the best interest of the greatest number of people.

This behavior is not always what "the experts" think it should be. That's often because the people who make up a market are responding to imbalances in price and supply created by existing regulations. The most recent example, of course, is the 2008 collapse of the housing and financial markets. As we explained earlier, contrary to the heated claims of House Speaker Nancy Pelosi, Congressman Barney Frank, and others, these events were anything but the results of "unfettered" markets.

They were the result of markets thrown out of whack by layers of government mismanagement.

Overly stringent rules and regulations don't just distort market behavior, they can strangle an economy. Every year, the Heritage Foundation and the *Wall Street Journal* release their Index of Economic Freedom. Nations that rank lowest on the list, with the least economic freedom, are usually the poorest.

For example, number 131 out of 179 on the 2009 list is Indonesia, with a per-capita income of just $3,454 and 9.6 percent unemployment. The report explains that despite recent reforms that have helped boost growth, many obstacles to economic activity persist in that country.

> The overall freedom to conduct a business is significantly restricted by Indonesia's regulatory environment. Starting a business takes more than twice as long as the world average, and regulations are onerous.[5]

The report also noted: "Despite some progress, foreign investment remains restricted, and judicial enforcement is both erratic and nontransparent. Because of pervasive corruption, impartial adjudication of cases is not guaranteed."

Indonesia's corruption is typical of government-dominated nations. That is the irony of an overregulated economy: it ultimately undermines a lawful society. People strive to circumvent rules they perceive as unfair. We observed in chapter 1 that this is the case in Russia, where private businesses skirt an overly meddlesome bureaucratic system by paying bribes in order to operate.

A democratic capitalist economy shouldn't be entirely unregulated. But in today's heated debates, too little attention is focused on the potential impact of a proposed regulation in the Real World. Any well-intentioned rule has benefits, at least for some. The question is whether those benefits are worth their cost. We discuss later in this chapter the largely ignored unintended consequences of the initial CAFE standards enacted in the mid-1970s. These regulations did produce more fuel-efficient cars, but with a major cost—higher accident fatalities.

Another example: the ban on the pesticide DDT. Environmental and health concerns led to prohibition of the insect killer in the 1960s and '70s. Alternative methods for fighting malaria, such as netting, were

supposed to serve as replacements, but they have been comparatively in-
effective. Malaria epidemics have since killed over a million people a
year, with fifty million deaths over twenty-five years. Were the benefits of
banning DDT really worth so many lost lives?

Several years ago, South Africa started allowing judicious use of DDT.
The spraying of small amounts was permitted inside people's residences.
There were no negative health effects. Quite the contrary: the incidence of
malaria declined by 90 percent.

According to the Competitive Enterprise Institute, the cost to the
U.S. economy of complying with the nation's countless regulations came
to almost $1.2 trillion—almost equal to the amount that the federal gov-
ernment collects in personal income taxes.

In 2008, Congress passed and the president signed into law 285 bills.
Federal agencies finalized over 3,800 new rules and regulations. *That's
just in a single year.* Everyone wants rules to protect their welfare, health,
and safety. The question is—how many?

**Q ► Isn't the financial crisis of 2008 a historic example of
the need for far more extensive, rigorous regulation
of free markets?**

**A ► What the crisis demonstrates is the need for sound
monetary policy, better enforcement, and sensible
adjustments to existing regulations.**

The meltdown was anything but the result of too little regulation. It was
the outcome of a "perfect storm" of regulatory mismanagement—
that is, existing rules poorly designed or applied.

A key regulatory failure was the Federal Reserve's low-interest-rate,
"easy money" policy that fed Wall Street's appetite for selling—and
buying—fee-generating packages of subprime mortgages.

We noted in our introduction that government economic and regulatory decisions are ultimately driven by the agendas of politicians and not
the needs of people in a market. Why didn't the Treasury Department—
behind the scenes—tell the Fed to strengthen the enfeebled greenback?
Because the Bush administration liked a weak dollar, believing that it
would improve our trade balance by artificially making our exports
cheaper. Not since Jimmy Carter had the United States had such a weak-

dollar administration. Without the Fed flooding the banking system with too much money, the housing bubble could never have reached the size it did.

There's another part of this story: the failure of bond-rating agencies such as Moody's, Standard & Poor's, and Fitch. They, too, were caught up in the irrational exuberance of the housing boom and gave mortgage-backed securities triple-A ratings. This was hardly surprising. Though private entities, rating agencies are essentially a government-sanctioned cartel. The SEC still must approve which firms will be "nationally recognized." Even today, rating agencies' powers are protected by federal and state law. Pension funds, banks, and insurers, in many cases, must still have certain amounts of securities that are rated investment-grade by these government-sanctioned agencies. Another peculiarity of rating agencies is that the issuers of securities that are being rated—not the buyers—pay for the ratings. This presents a strong potential conflict of interest. Many observers strongly believe that to get business, rating agencies have been tempted to soften criticisms of securities since the issuer is their client. This is the opposite of how stock analysts are compensated—no one would take seriously an analyst's stock recommendation that was paid for by the company being analyzed.

Thus the ultimate alchemy: junk mortgages, bundled together, became prime-grade, triple-A-rated mortgage-backed securities. They were bought up by financial institutions, spreading the risk everywhere. The Fed and other bank regulators stood by as the bubble ballooned.

Another culprit: the Securities and Exchange Commission. If the SEC had not repealed the uptick rule in July of 2007, much of the unprecedented volatility would have been avoided. As we've explained, the rule created a critical road bump by requiring that an investor could short a stock only after it had gone up in price.

Hedge funds, however, wanted the rule repealed. In response, the SEC conducted a study of market activity in recent years to determine if the rule was needed. Unfortunately, that period happened to be one of the calmest ever for stocks. So in 2007 the SEC repealed the seven-decade-old rule. Market volatility soared. A key measure of volatility, the VIX index, quadrupled.

The SEC, meanwhile, compounded this error by inexplicably failing to fully enforce another rule—the ban on so-called naked short selling.

Short sellers are supposed to possess shares by borrowing them for a fee before selling them. Naked short sellers, in contrast, sell the stock without possessing the shares. This makes it far easier for the shorts to hammer a stock into the ground. As of this writing, the uptick rule still hasn't been restored and naked short selling still exists. Why? In no small part because the SEC has an institutional bias in favor of short sellers.

Another regulatory villain was the U.S. Congress, which blocked reforms of Fannie Mae and Freddie Mac, the two government-created mortgage giants that helped fuel the market for subprime mortgages. Washington cronyism allowed these companies to become monsters—and it was also responsible for the regulators' appallingly lax oversight.

Fannie and Freddie were not held to the same SEC standards as other publicly held companies. Moreover, Congress made sure that they didn't have as strict capital guidelines as banks did. For example, banks are supposed to have one dollar of capital for every ten dollars of liability. Fannie and Freddie were allowed to carry a far greater debt burden—forty dollars or more of debt for each dollar of capital. Thus, they were able to buy insane numbers of mortgage loans. No one cared. Everyone assumed that if Fannie and Freddie faltered, Uncle Sam would come to the rescue.

Finally, we've mentioned the role of another regulatory bad guy, "fair-value" or mark-to-market accounting. Mark-to-market required companies to mark down the value of assets to what they would immediately fetch in an open market. These rules were established by the Financial Accounting Standards Board (FASB). They were a result of the politically charged aftermath of the Enron scandal.

Thanks to mark-to-market and the suspension of the uptick rule, short sellers proceeded to shatter financial stocks. The stage was set for the cataclysmic market meltdown and the events that followed.

Regulatory failure also played a key role in the rise of Bernie Madoff. He got away with his momentous fraud for decades not because of "too little regulation" but because of the astonishing failure of the Securities and Exchange Commission's giant regulatory bureaucracy.

Madoff's firm was an investment adviser and broker-dealer registered with the SEC. He employed three hundred people in a sleek New York City office tower. Madoff clients were some of the leading financial institutions around the world, such as HSBC, as well as some of the world's wealthiest individuals. Celebrities like Kevin Bacon were also clients. A former chairman of the NASDAQ stock exchange, Madoff was a social figure who sat on charitable boards. In other words, he could not have been more visible. Despite thousands of regulations and an expanding bureaucracy, the SEC could not detect his wrongdoing—even after multiple investigations and warnings from tipsters. Shortly after Madoff's crime came to light, a *Wall Street Journal* article disclosed that a competitor had actually written to the agency that "Madoff Securities is the world's largest Ponzi scheme" a full ten years earlier.

The SEC had plenty of rules and overseers to prevent a fraud like that of Bernie Madoff. Those who think that new layers of regulation will protect people from economic disasters like those of 2008 should think again. The real question is why so many regulations already in force so frequently fail.

▲   REAL WORLD LESSON   ▲

Regulations do not mitigate risk in markets. Layers of regulation offer no perfect guarantee of protection against marketplace disasters and may create new distortions that result in future problems down the road.

Q ► WASN'T FINANCIAL REFORM NEEDED TO ADDRESS THE CAUSES OF THE FINANCIAL CRISIS?

A ► SOME REFORM WAS NEEDED, GIVEN THE PROLIFERATION OF MANY NEW AND HIGHLY COMPLICATED FINANCIAL INSTRUMENTS OVER THE PAST TWO DECADES. BUT CONGRESS'S SLOPPILY DRAFTED 2,300-PAGE LEGISLATION HAS ONLY ADDED COMPLEXITY AND AMBIGUITY TO ONE OF THE NATION'S MOST HIGHLY REGULATED INDUSTRIES. THIS WILL NEITHER PREVENT MORE MARKET BUBBLES NOR HELP THE CONSUMER.

At the beginning of this chapter, and elsewhere in this book, we describe the toxic cocktail of bad government policies that led to the financial crisis of 2008: excessive money creation that ignited a real-estate boom, fueled still further by government-created mortgage giants Fannie and Freddie pumping hundreds of billions of dollars into the junk-mortgage market; and the insanity of government-mandated mark-to-market accounting that forced banks to excessively write-down the value of their loans, thereby shrinking their capital.

Congress's answer was the Dodd–Frank Wall Street Reform and Consumer Protection Act, signed into law in July 2010. The problem is—it doesn't fix what caused the disaster.

The bill is a typical government overreaction based on the fevered need for politicians to "do something" in response to a crisis. The financial sector is already very heavily regulated. The bill creates a new multiheaded hydra of bureaucracy and restrictions. It sets the stage for more future market dysfunction. That's bad news not only for financial institutions—but for the overall economy that depends on this critical sector.

The new regulations are complicated, vague, and ultimately arbitrary. That's no accident. Congress meant to give regulators enormous discretionary latitude—basically, to give them mandates to do whatever they want. This gives them more power.

Former McKinsey & Company chief economist James S. Henry and Boston University economics professor Laurence J. Kotlikoff put it bluntly on Forbes.com:

> Dodd-Frank is a full-employment act for regulators that addresses everything but the root causes of the financial collapse. It serves up a dog's breakfast covering proprietary trading, consumer financial protection, derivatives trading, executive pay, credit card fees, whistle-blowers, minority inclusion and Congolese minerals. Dodd-Frank also mandates 68 new studies of carbon markets, Chinese drywalls, and person-to-person lending, and many other irrelevancies.[6]

All of this is no surprise. The authors of the Dodd-Frank Act were then-senator Chris Dodd and Congressman Barney Frank, whose ardent support of Fannie and Freddie helped to make them the behemoths that they ultimately became. Both Frank and Dodd resisted calls to restructure the two giants, insisting they were solvent as late as 2008.

Dodd-Frank completely ignores the problem of Fannie Mae and Freddie Mac and their impact on the mortgage market, even though the two giants were two of the largest recipients of federal bailout money, receiving some $150 billion, and are now in federal receivership.

So just how much of a mess does this 2,300-page monster create? Henry and Kotlikoff write:

Dodd-Frank provides government bureaucrats with unrestricted hunting licenses. Only one of the roughly 115 federal and state agencies currently involved in financial regulation has been consolidated. At the same time, the new law creates 12 new regulatory bodies and gives them vast amounts of rule-making discretion. In the next two years these and other financial regulators will hold an estimated 243 new rule-making procedures . . .[7]

Instead of increasing transparency and promoting accountability, Henry and Kotlikoff say, the effect will be the opposite—"regulatory sclerosis," with more opportunities for corruption and crony capitalism. The bill, they say, "is a bonanza for Wall Street lobbyists and lawyers, who will help determine what this law's 283,985 words actually mean."[8]

It's impossible, of course, to go through everything in the bill. Highlights, if you can call them that, include:

▶ **The Financial Stability Oversight Council.** In the words of the bill's authors, this new bureacracy "will be charged with identifying and responding to emerging risks throughout the financial system."[9] *The problem:* The council has been granted power to seize private property. If it arbitrarily decides that a firm is a so-called systemic risk, it can basically take over the company and force it to downsize or liquidate. This enormous and truly frightening power also applies to "non-bank financial companies"—however the council decides to define them—if they are judged to "pose a risk to the financial security of the U.S."

▶ **Bureau of Consumer Financial Protection.** In the words of the bill's authors, this new body is "to autonomously write rules for consumer protections governing all financial institutions—banks and non-banks—offering consumer financial services or products." The ostensible purpose is to shield consumers from everything from unfair late payment charges to overly high interest rates. *The problem:* It's redundant. Congress has already enacted credit card reform. And here, too, there's vagueness. In the words of Brookings Institute analyst Douglas Elliott, "Regulators will decide almost everything about how this works. Congress laid out a broad mandate, a set of criteria to be considered when balancing decisions, and a few limitations."[10] Even though the bureau is under the umbrella of the Federal Reserve, the central bank has no jurisdiction over it. Moreover, the bureau will have a $500 million annual budget that will not require Congressional approval.

▶ **The "Volcker rule."** The rule largely prohibits any bank or other institution with FDIC-insured deposits from undertaking "proprietary trading"—i.e., trading for the banks' own behalf rather than for the benefit of a client—or from owning or sponsoring hedge funds or private equity funds. *The problem:* This rule will do nothing to reduce systemic risk, and will possibly increase it by decreasing the diversification of revenues that helps foster bank stability. The competitiveness of U.S. financial institutions will also be compromised. Clients will take their business to foreign banks offering the full range of financial services. Finally, the financial crisis wasn't caused by bank trading. As the subprime crisis proves, ill-advised lending carries greater systemic risk.

▶ **Debit card fees.** Fees paid by retailers to credit card companies will now be limited. *The problem:* Price controls never work as intended. The law will lead some issuers to drop their cards, cutting availability for consumers; or new bank fees to checking account customers will be levied. The net effect will be to force low-income people from the banking system and into the hands of pawnshops, payday lenders, and loan sharks whose interest rates make credit card fees look like giveaways.

▶ **Derivatives.** Greater transparency will be required when trading credit-default swaps and other derivatives. The bill calls for clearinghouses "to determine which contracts should be cleared." We agree with the need for clearinghouses. However, the objective should be to provide transparency, not to place undue restrictions on the functioning of the market. *The problem:* The new law goes beyond promoting transparency to aggressively regulating most derivatives, traders, and issuers—driving up the costs of these financial instruments, while curtailing their benefits.[11]

The bill has other downsides. Most notably, it was supposed to cure the so-called "too big to fail" doctrine that led to the bailouts of financial institutions. Americans hated the idea of big banks being saved by taxpayers instead of suffering for their allegedly egregious mistakes and speculations.

However, experts believe that Dodds-Frank codifies "too big to fail" by giving regulators enormous discretion over what institutions can and cannot do. In the Real World, this means that if a major firm gets into trouble, regulators—bureaucrats that they are—will be loathe to admit their errors. They'll be more likely to act to artificially preserve troubled institutions than to let market forces work.

Finally, there's the bill's destructive implications for community banks. Sarah Wallace, chair of the board of directors of First Federal Savings and Loan Association in Newark, Ohio, explained in the *Wall Street Journal* that the new regulations constitute a costly compliance and manpower burden that will devastate these small institutions, which provide a unique service to the small businesses and moderate and low-income customers.

> I have said to our employees many times, "We are in the business of helping people!" Sometimes, bad things happen to good people, people we see in the grocery store and at Little League baseball games. We used to believe that if someone hit a bump in the road of life and came to us for financing, we could often figure out a way to help them. I fear this kind of community-oriented banking will end. There will be credit-worthy borrowers who will no longer be able to get loans.

Congress intended financial reform to rein in Wall Street. But, as so often happens with government overregulation, big players end up doing just fine. It's the entrepreneurs and small businesses on Main Street that suffer.

The global panic and recession have been blamed on bank excesses. Excesses there were, but the issue was not free markets but the lack of them. Nicole Gelinas of the Manhattan Institute makes the point that the rise of the too-big-to-fail (or too-complex-to-fail) doctrine in fact helped to produce the crisis by encouraging increasingly dangerous levels of indebtedness.[12] After all, Washington and other central banks would be there to bail out big firms that got into trouble.

Friedrich Hayek, the great Austrian economist, wrote that economies need sensible rules of the road. The financial industry wouldn't have become so unhinged had regulators focused on the need to update rules in response to the creation of new instruments like mortgage-backed securities. Washington refused to recognize and respond to the enormous changes sweeping the financial world. When the crisis hit, politicos overreacted.

▲   REAL WORLD LESSON   ▲

Because government is ruled by politics and not the Real World needs of people, it usually overreacts in a crisis. Instead of fixing the real problem, it adds new layers of market distortion.

Q ► WASN'T THE SARBANES-OXLEY LEGISLATION NECESSARY TO CLARIFY "THE RULES OF THE ROAD" IN CORPORATE GOVERNANCE AND ACCOUNTING?

A ► NO. SARBANES-OXLEY SERVES AS A PRIME EXAMPLE OF HOW POORLY DESIGNED REGULATION PRODUCES DAMAGING, UNINTENDED CONSEQUENCES THAT HINDER ECONOMIC ACTIVITY.

Sarbanes-Oxley, or the Public Company Accounting Reform and Investor Protection Act of 2002, typifies the problems that can take place when politicians are pressed to "do something" in response to a crisis. Passed in 2002 in the wake of accounting and corporate-governance scandals that brought down Enron and other corporations, SOX was supposed to bring about better corporate accounting standards. But instead of improving corporate governance, the SOX legislation—as is typical of laws and regulations enacted in an emotional atmosphere—produced a host of economically destructive, unintended consequences.

Fraud, of course, is illegal. Executives from Enron and other corporations were indicted and convicted under existing statutes. Many experts thus believe SOX wasn't needed. "The SEC already had the authority to do everything the law demands about accounting or corporate boards," wrote Alan Reynolds of the Cato Institute in 2005.[13] SOX also has not prevented further scandalous corporate failures. One example: the sensational bankruptcy of the large commodities broker Refco, caused by the accounting criminality of its CEO. Banker and financial relations adviser Mallory Factor observed in the *Wall Street Journal* in 2006:

Over 700 prosecutions have been launched since 2002 to address corporate crimes. Nevertheless, not one conviction was a result of *Sarbox*. Sarbox clearly failed to prevent the massive accounting scandal at Fannie Mae.[14]

But haven't investors been helped by the elaborate, expensive bookkeeping tests and controls required by SOX? Reynolds of Cato says those rules weren't needed either:

> The market characteristically gets wind of what's going on inside companies and prices it into the stock: The bookkeeping obsession of Sarbanes-Oxley might nonetheless be defended as helpful to stockholders were it not for the fact that investors saw through Enron and WorldCom's exaggerated earnings and hidden debts long before accountants or federal regulators did.[15]

Another problem with the law was that it requires, in Reynolds's words, "that the audit committee of every corporate board be comprised entirely of independent directors with no company experience plus one financial expert who claims to grasp all 4,500 pages"[16] of GAAP. Yet as he points out, board independence was never an issue in the Enron scandal. The Enron board, he reminds us, "was 86 percent independent."[17]

T. J. Rodgers, founder, president, CEO, and a director of Cypress Semiconductor Corporation, complains that the FASB rules were created by a small group of ivory-tower experts with limited understanding of the Real World issues of corporate accounting:

> FASB is a group of seven theoretical accountants based in Norwalk, Connecticut. Its website shows that no FASB member ever started or ran a successful business and that only one member has even held a senior position in a prominent public company other than an accounting firm.[18]

According to Rodgers, GAAP's complicated accounting standards have only made it *more* difficult for even top executives to understand a company's financials.

> I first noticed the misleading nature of Generally Accepted Accounting Principles a few years ago when an investor called to complain about the small amount of cash on our balance sheet.

Since we had plenty of cash, I decided to quickly quote the correct figures from our latest financial report. But to my surprise, I could not tell how much cash we had either. With its usual—and almost always incorrect—claim of making financial reporting "more transparent," the Financial Accounting Standards Board had made it difficult for a CEO to read his own financial report.[19]

But the worst part of SOX has been its impact on the U.S. financial sector, driving up accounting and compliance costs—both in regulatory fees and man-hours. Audit costs for U.S. corporations have risen 30 percent or more as a result of more stringent accounting and audit standards. In the Board's first year of operation alone, the act's regulations resulted in more than $35 billion in compliance costs imposed on the nation's businesses.

The costs of being a U.S. public company are now more than triple what they were before the law passed, according to a study conducted by the Milwaukee-based law firm Foley & Lardner.

Fees required by the Public Company Accounting Oversight Board can run as high as $2 million annually for large firms. According to the accounting firm Deloitte, large companies have on average spent nearly seventy thousand additional man-hours complying with the new law.

But SOX has been hardest on smaller firms unable to shoulder the financial and manpower burden. According to one study, companies with annual sales below $250 million incurred a staggering $1.56 million, on average, in SOX compliance costs. Some smaller firms report that they are spending 300 percent more on SOX compliance than on health care for their employees. A survey by the American Electronics Association found that companies with sales of $100 million or less are spending 2.6 percent of their revenues on SOX compliance.

The gargantuan burden of SOX has driven public companies from U.S. stock exchanges and discouraged privately held companies, especially small ones, from going public. A 2006 study by the Committee on Capital Markets Regulation found that only 8 percent of new stock offerings are now executed on U.S. exchanges, compared with 48 percent in the 1990s. According to the report, SOX's compliance fees "are absolutely killing the U.S. in terms of maintaining listings dominance."[20]

A joint study by the Brookings Institution and the American Enterprise Institute found that the direct and indirect costs of SOX total a staggering $1 trillion.

Fears of criminal prosecution for governance and accounting transgressions have made corporations more risk averse. The result: fewer innovations and less growth. In 2006, a University of Rochester study concluded that the total effect of the law was to reduce the stock value of American companies by $1.4 trillion.

Rather than increasing transparency and creating a better environment for investors, SOX has done the opposite—it has added to the regulatory tangle, increasing balance-sheet confusion. SOX helped to create an environment that destroyed far more wealth than was ever destroyed through the prior corporate scandals put together.

▲   REAL WORLD LESSON   ▲

SOX illustrates the damage that can occur when regulators overreact and micromanage markets.

Q ► DOESN'T SOCIETY NEED LAWS TO PROTECT HEALTH, SAFETY, AND THE ENVIRONMENT?

A ► YES. BUT TOO LITTLE ATTENTION IS FOCUSED ON WHETHER THE BENEFITS OF THOSE LAWS ARE WORTH THE COST.

There's no question that many government regulations have worked to promote public health, safety, and a cleaner environment. But some haven't. Geology professor Seth Stein and engineer Joseph Tomasello write about the case of Memphis, Tennessee. The city is located in the New Madrid seismic zone, an area of the central United States prone to earthquakes. The region experiences really big quakes "only every 500 years or so, far less often than in California. As far as we know," they write, "no one has ever died in an earthquake in the New Madrid zone."[21] The last significant tremor to hit the area—a moderate 5.5— occurred a little more than forty years ago, in 1968.

Yet the Federal Emergency Management Agency wanted Memphis and the rest of the seismic zone to adopt anti-earthquake standards like California's. That meant using expensive antiquake construction methods on new buildings, and retrofitting existing ones.

According to Stein and Tomasello, meeting the new standards "could increase a building's cost 5 percent to 10 percent."[22] FEMA also wants to retrofit hospitals, highways, and bridges. Retrofitting just one of these projects, the Memphis Veterans' Hospital, they say, would cost about $100 million, "comparable to the cost of a new building."[23]

Stein and Tomasello raise the question, should hundreds of millions of dollars be spent on preparing Memphis for major earthquakes that occur only once every five hundred years? After all, so much spending on earthquake safety would divert funds from needs that are far more immediate:

> Money spent strengthening schools isn't available for teachers' salaries, upgrading hospitals may mean treating fewer uninsured patients, and stronger bridges may result in hiring fewer police officers. The proposed code may over time save a few lives per year, while the same money invested in health or safety measures (flu shots, defibrillators, highway upgrades) could save many more.[24]

FEMA's building codes are among countless regulations from numerous government agencies whose costs drastically outweigh their benefits. Among the latest measures, and one of the most draconian in some time, is the new Consumer Product Safety Improvement Act. Passed in 2008 after the panic over tainted Chinese toys and lead paint, it requires expensive third-party testing to verify the safety of all products primarily intended for children under twelve. As Manhattan Institute fellow Walter Olson explains,

> That includes clothing, fabric and textile goods of all kinds: hats, shoes, diapers, hair bands, sports pennants, Scouting patches, local school-logo gear and so on.
>
> And paper goods: books, flash cards, board games, baseball cards, kits for home schoolers, party supplies and the like. And sporting equipment, outdoor gear, bikes, backpacks and telescopes. And furnishings for kids' rooms.
>
> And videogame cartridges and audio books. And specialized assistive and therapeutic gear used by disabled and autistic kids.
>
> Again with relatively few exceptions, makers of these goods can't rely only on materials known to be unproblematic (natural

dyed yarn, local wood) or that come from reputable local suppliers, or even ones that are certified organic.[25]

In short, Olson says that the list includes almost everything—even older products sold at thrift shops and, possibly, books.

> Children's sections at libraries and bookstores will, at minimum, face price hikes on newly acquired titles and, at worse, may have to rethink older holdings.
>
> After all, no one has the slightest idea how many future violations lie hidden in the stacks and few want to play a guessing game about how seriously officialdom will view illegality. "Either they take all the children's books off the shelves," Associate Executive Director Emily Sheketoff of the American Library Association told the Boston *Phoenix*, "or they ban children from the library."[26]

Violators face criminal prosecution and fines of $100,000. Olson writes that the law promises "to wipe out tens of thousands of small makers of children's items from coast to coast, and taking a particular toll on the handcrafted and creative, the small-production-run and sideline at-home business, not to mention struggling retailers."[27]

How could such a heavy-handed, misguided piece of legislation have been passed by policy makers? Unfortunately, it is typical of the failure of bureaucrats to grasp how excessive, overbearing regulation can damage the economy and hurt people. Economist Robert W. Hahn estimates that more than 40 percent of American regulations impose costs on the economy that outweigh their benefits.

In a report for the American Enterprise Institute, Hahn asserts that insufficient analysis of the relative costs and benefits of health, safety, and environmental regulations has been a failure of both Republican and Democratic administrations.

He and others pose a sticky question: is it worth spending billions of dollars on rules that promise health, safety, or environmental benefits that, in some instances, may be realized by very few people?

Requiring third-party testing of library books and many other totally harmless items—as the new Consumer Product Safety Improvement Act does—is not only costly. It's just plain dumb. In 2008, the

Competitive Enterprise Institute published a list of "The Five Dumbest Product Bans." Among them: the lifesaving Cardio-Pump, whose use in the United States has been outlawed by the Food and Drug Administration. This lifesaving device is commonly used in Britain, France, Israel, Chile, and a dozen other countries. In fact, according to one study published in the prestigious *New England Journal of Medicine*, survival rates of heart attack patients resuscitated by the plungerlike heart pump were much higher than those treated with traditional techniques. Why did the FDA ban the device? Apparently, for bureaucratic reasons: the FDA was unable to carry out its own study of the device because patients in the throes of cardiac arrest are unable to give "informed consent" to participate.

In other words, the FDA decided that the mere possibility that the device might not work perfectly in a minority of cases outweighed its already demonstrated benefits—that it raised the likelihood of heart attack survival by most people.

We've already mentioned CAFE standards. Yes, today's cars burn less gas—they're 50 percent more efficient than they were in the 1970s. But CAFE standards have major downsides, too. They're a primary cause of the troubles that have hobbled the Detroit automakers. They've also resulted in lighter cars and more auto fatalities. A 2001 report from the National Academy of Sciences estimated that between 1,300 and 2,600 deaths a year may be attributed to the smaller passenger cars that were manufactured to improve fuel efficiency.

Increased fuel-efficiency standards actually encourage consumption. Believing their vehicles are energy efficient, people have fewer qualms about driving more and having bigger cars. The number of miles driven and the number of vehicles have virtually doubled since the mid-1970s. The same phenomenon has been observed with refrigerators. As they became more energy efficient, people bought bigger and bigger models. In other words, government regulations have improved fuel efficiency, but they haven't curtailed energy *usage*.

Robert Hahn says that regulation would be improved if lawmakers and others paid more attention to the Real World impact of proposed rules. Some laws are definitely more costly—or beneficial—than others. According to Hahn, laws mandating seat-belt use are a bargain, costing about $69 per "life-year" saved. Government-required airbag installation, meanwhile, costs about $120,000 per life-year saved. Requiring reductions in radiation exposure from X-ray equipment means $23,000 per life-year saved. All three regulations are more cost-effective than radiation controls at uranium fuel-cycle facilities—which require $34 billion per life-year saved. This doesn't mean expensive safeguards aren't needed, but the cost should be considered.

Cost-benefit analysis is receiving more attention in Europe, whose economy has stagnated under its regulatory burden. Hahn and his fellow economists have been criticized for placing a dollar value on human life. However, congressional economist Ike Brannon says that such analysis can be necessary in the Real World: "Because society has limited resources that it can spend on health and safety improvements, it should obtain the greatest benefit for each dollar spent, and ascertaining an appropriate value is necessary to that effort."[28]

Danish author Bjørn Lomborg maintains that a lack of cost-benefit awareness is the problem with many environmental regulations. Lomborg's controversial book *The Skeptical Environmentalist* gained notoriety for questioning the thinking of environmentalists. However, his critics miss the point. Lomborg acknowledges the possibility that man may have contributed to global warming. The problem, he says, is that the costs of the standard solutions far outweigh the benefits that may—or may not—be realized in the future:

> [W]e should first focus our resources on more immediate concerns, such as fighting malaria and HIV/AIDS and assuring and maintaining a safe, fresh water supply—which can be addressed at a fraction of the cost and save millions of lives within our lifetime.[29]

As congressional economist Ike Brannon points out, "society cannot spend an infinite amount of money to protect and extend each person's life." Hard as it may be for some to accept, "choices have to be made."[30]

▲   REAL WORLD LESSON   ▲

Cost-benefit analysis should be a greater part of the debate over proposed regulation, given the limitations on government and taxpayer resources.

Q ► Aren't cap-and-trade regulations a market-based way to
   control pollution?

A ► No. Cap-and-trade failed in Europe because it creates
   an artificial market that does not reflect Real World
   conditions or the needs of participants.

Cap-and-trade regulation is supposed to be a "market-based" way to control industrial emissions of carbon dioxide (CO_2), thought by many to
cause climate change. Here's how the system is supposed to work: Government sets a "cap" on how much carbon dioxide can be emitted each
year. Each company or institution is then granted a predetermined
number of permits. Companies that need to produce more emissions can
buy permits from others that don't need them. Another way to distribute
permits is for the government to simply auction them off. This avoids
the politically charged process of determining the number of permits
granted to each company or institution—and the auctions raise bundles
of money. Either way, say proponents, carbon emissions are controlled,
while a market is created that allocates the right to pollute according
to need.

Congress has so far failed to pass a national cap-and-trade program
despite intense pressure from President Obama. However, some believe
that the Environmental Protection Agency (EPA)—which in 2009 declared
carbon dioxide a "pollutant" and is dramatically increasing restrictions
on CO_2 emissions—will bypass Congress and institute a national program by regulatory diktat. Moreover, state cap-and-trade programs have
been proliferating. California has passed the first large-scale program. It
will cover all major industrial businesses, as well as distributors of transportation fuels, natural gas, and other fuels. Companies are required to
obtain allowances to cover their CO_2 emissions. The state is expected to
give away the allowances at first, auctioning more of them later.[31]

More limited cap-and-trade programs are in effect in the Northeast
through the multistate Regional Greenhouse Gas Initiative (RGGI). The
mandatory program covers power plants. Utilities must obtain an al-
lowance for each ton of CO_2 emissions. Other cap-and-trade networks
similar to RGGI are also due to launch within the next several years in
states in the Midwest and on the West Coast.

The real reason politicians love cap-and-trade is because it's "green"—as in lucrative. It's essentially a big tax increase that would rake in tens of billions of dollars each year. As of late 2010, RGGI raised some $729 million auctioning off its emissions permits. And that's only from selling permits to power plants. Imagine the potential of a national program.

The Real World problem with a cap-and-trade system is that it significantly boosts the cost of energy. Prices of CO_2-intensive products—including gasoline, electricity, and many industrial products—would soar. Dispassionate experts estimate that a national program could *double* electricity prices. Gas prices are expected to skyrocket almost 75 percent—or higher. Experts such as economist Martin Feldstein predict the cost of living for the average household will shoot up by $1,600 a year.

When all the *indirect* costs of a national program—such as higher taxes and slower economic growth—are added up, the Heritage Foundation estimates that the cost of living for a family of four, starting in 2012, will increase by some $4,300. And it will only go higher with subsequent CO_2 restrictions.

In Europe, the Emissions Trading Scheme (ETS) was put into effect in 2005 based on carbon emissions levels (caps) established by the Kyoto Protocol of the late 1990s. It is emerging as a major failure. European manufacturers have bitterly complained that the extra costs are making them uncompetitive, thus forcing them to consider moving facilities elsewhere.

Soundly based market initiatives can actually work. The problem with cap-and-trade is that it is a poorly conceived idea masquerading as a market solution.

The market for carbon emissions credits did not develop spontaneously, like the market for the pencil. It was dreamed up and imposed on people by bureaucrats. In other words, without government it would not exist.

In a sense, a marketplace is commerce's equivalent of an ecosystem. In economics, as in biological science, it is extremely difficult to successfully reproduce what spontaneously evolves in nature. In the early 1990s, oil billionaire Edward Bass poured $150 million into a miniature version of the world's ecosystem in the desert near Tucson, Arizona—Biosphere 2. It was essentially a giant, airtight terrarium that was supposed to contain the earth's ecosystem in miniature—an ocean stocked with fish and a dense forest in an oxygenated atmosphere that was supposed to be self-sustaining.

The idea was to create a self-sufficient environment where people, plants, and animals could survive without help from the outside world. The problem was that the scientists in charge of the project, some of whom had national reputations, couldn't possibly know all the conditions and components of a fully self-sufficient ecosystem. Starved for the right amount of oxygen, the fish in the ocean died. CO_2 levels in the air became too high. The big terrarium was overrun with an infestation of desert cockroaches. Several years after its much-publicized launch, Biosphere 2 was widely acknowledged to be a momentous failure.

Government attempts to create a cap-and-trade market for CO_2 permits are a little like the efforts of the scientists who tried to create Biosphere 2. There are inevitably distortions and unintended consequences because a handful of bureaucrats simply can't know all the workings of a marketplace "ecosystem."

Cap-and-trade failed in Europe because the market and its values were dreamed up by bureaucrats and were essentially arbitrary. Member states of the EU allocated permits free of charge to companies based on how many the government believed they needed. This arbitrary system resulted in an oversupply of permits. Politics polluted the allocation process. Large companies lobbied for more permits than they needed, only to sell them at a profit. Smaller organizations less effective at lobbying got too few permits and had to pay more than their fair share of fees. A December 2008 article in the *New York Times* reported:

> The European Union started with a high-minded ecological goal: encouraging companies to cut their greenhouse gases by making them pay for each ton of carbon dioxide they emitted into the atmosphere. But that plan unleashed a lobbying free-for-all that led politicians to dole out favors to various industries, undermining the environmental goals. Four years later, it is becoming clear that system has so far produced little noticeable benefit to the climate—but generated a multibillion-dollar windfall for some of the Continent's biggest polluters.[32]

Despite the immense expenditures, data are suggesting that the European program may even have had a negative effect on the environment. A 2007 report by the London-based think tank Open Europe found that across the EU, emissions from installations covered by the ETS actually rose by 0.8 percent.

Thus experts, such as highly regarded economist Martin Feldstein, believe that a U.S. cap-and-trade program is not likely to work any better:

> Since the U.S. share of global CO_2 production is now less than 25 percent (and is projected to decline as China and other developing nations grow), a 15 percent fall in U.S. CO_2 output would lower global CO_2 output by less than 4 percent. Its impact on global warming would be virtually unnoticeable.[33]

Even if a nominal benefit is achieved, Feldstein says that cap-and-trade will devastate the economic lives of Americans. The higher taxes, higher prices, and slower growth, he predicts, will kill the nation's chances of recovery from the 2009 recession. Everyone wants clean air. But cap-and-trade means diverting massive resources—billions of hard-earned taxpayer dollars and job-creating capital—into a government-created, politically driven artificial market that is, at best, an economic version of the Biosphere.

One final reason why cap-and-trade "greenhouse gas initiatives" are so much hot air is that because bureaucrats, being bureaucrats, inevitably divert the money for political purposes. This is currently happening with state programs. In 2010, the *New York Times* reported that New York, New Hampshire, and other states have used money generated by greenhouse gas initiatives to foot the bill for their bloated budgets. The *Times* reported that New York used some $90 million of its RGGI money "to deal with a projected state budget deficit of nearly $50 billion through March 2013."[34]

▲   REAL WORLD LESSON   ▲

Reflecting spontaneous decisions of thousands or even millions of people, markets are economic "ecosystems" whose behavior cannot be duplicated or controlled according to the preconceptions of a handful of bureaucrats.

Q ▶ Weren't the original antitrust laws needed to set the basic conditions of competition in free markets?

A ▶ No. Antitrust actions are most often examples of "rent seeking," attempts by large companies to strike back against their most successful competitors by using the legal system.

We've already discussed why, in a free-market economy, competition laws aren't needed. Sooner or later, natural forces of creative destruction undermine even the biggest players in a market. Unfortunately, free-market opponents have for generations failed to appreciate this basic Real World principle. This failed understanding has given us largely unnecessary and highly destructive antitrust laws.

Since the Sherman Antitrust Act of 1890 (see page 293), Congress has enacted laws ostensibly designed to ensure competition and protect consumers. They have resulted in antitrust actions or investigations—and often massive penalties—against companies ranging from the old Standard Oil and U.S. Steel to IBM, Microsoft, Staples, Toys "R" Us, and others.

Public antitrust debates generally center on whether the activities of a corporate giant—say, a Wal-Mart or a Google—are "anticompetitive" and deserve antitrust intervention. Take the widely debated Microsoft case, the most celebrated antitrust action in recent history. Some company supporters argued that government action wasn't needed, because high tech, with its ever-emerging new technologies, was a new competitive game. Microsoft was therefore different from early antitrust cases, such as Standard Oil, that involved low-tech marketplaces for more limited resources. Therefore, the argument went, Microsoft was not deserving of the antitrust prosecution inflicted upon those early industrial "monopolies."

But this skirts a far bigger question: were the Sherman Act and other early competition laws truly needed in the first place? Historians and economic and legal experts are now saying that the nation's earliest antitrust laws and court cases were then, as now, totally unnecessary—and economically destructive.

Ostensibly, antitrust laws are intended to preserve competition and to protect consumers from being harmed by overly powerful, monopolistic companies. But were the targets of those classic antitrust actions really hurting consumers? In other words, were they behaving as monopolies?

Antitrust historian Dominick Armentano examined fifty-five of the most famous antitrust cases in U.S. history. He found that the targets of classic antitrust actions rarely, if ever, could be considered monopolies. Armentano cites the classic case of Standard Oil of New Jersey, whose growth through mergers caused it to be broken up in 1911 by the government.

> Standard never even monopolized petroleum refining, let alone the entire oil industry (production, transportation, refining, distribution). Even in domestic refining, Standard's share of the market *declined* for decades prior to the antitrust case (64% in 1907) and there were at least 137 competitors (firms like Shell, Gulf, Texaco) in oil refining in 1911.[35]

Other supposed monopolies targeted in classic cases included IBM, which at the time had about 65 percent of the mainframe computer market. In the early 1960s, the government also ruled that Brown Shoe Company would become a monopoly if it acquired Kinney Shoes. But the two companies together would have had a 2 percent market share, a far cry from monopolistic dominance.

Were these goliaths hurting consumers? Far from it. Armentano says that in every single case, companies had been dropping prices, innovating, and expanding production. If they were any "harm" done, it was to less efficient competitors.

Standard Oil, for example, had been accused of controlling the market for kerosene. Yet kerosene prices during the period of supposed monopolization actually *fell*—from thirty cents a gallon in 1869 to about six cents a gallon at the time of the trial.

In the 1930s and 1940s, the Aluminum Company of America (ALCOA) was the subject of a thirteen-year-long antitrust case. What had the company done? Developed refining methods that had *lowered* aluminum ingot prices. Another target, the old American Can, was accused of "coercing" companies into signing long-term leases by offering attractive, generous price discounts for large orders of its cans.

Armentano and others say the classic antitrust cases weren't needed to protect consumers any more back then than they are now. The early cases, like most today, were brought about by a group of large competitors hoping to use the government to protect or enhance their interests. Economists have a term for this: rent seeking.

In the case of the Sherman Act, rural cattlemen and butchers hoped to use the law as a way to reduce the pricing power of the big meat packers in Chicago, whose size gave them immense power to negotiate lower shipping prices. Meanwhile, the Standard Oil antitrust case produced what Dominick Armentano has called a "government sanctioned cartel in oil"—a marketplace where players and pricing had to meet the approval of Uncle Sam.

In the case of American Can, the judge actually forced the company to raise its prices in order to help less productive, higher-priced competitors. None of these outcomes could be said to help consumers.

What antitrust true believers fail to appreciate is that, as we explained in chapter 2, even the biggest market players fall prey to new competition and marketplace creative destruction—often from unexpected quarters.

Government tried—and failed—to break up the mammoth U.S. Steel in another classic case in 1911. The free market did the job instead: the company's once-immense "market power" was gradually whittled away by competitors—not just by other steel makers but by alternatives like aluminum. U.S. Steel once made 67 percent of the steel produced in the United States. Today it produces only about 10 percent. Competition from foreign firms in countries like Japan and South Korea cut into the company's market share. New domestic competition came from so-called minimills, such as Nucor, which made steel from scrap.

The irony of antitrust is that the economy's only genuine monopolies are imposed or created by government. Think Fannie and Freddie, your local cable company, or, for those old enough to remember, "Ma Bell"—the old AT&T. Entities such as Medicare, the government's health insurer, have a far greater ability to set prices and eliminate competition than any antitrust target in the private sector. When a company does these things, it's accused of being "anticompetitive." But when government does them, it's ostensibly "a public good."

▲   REAL WORLD LESSON   ▲

Contrary to the view of antitrust believers, classic antitrust cases reflected market politics, not economics.

Q ► WHAT'S WRONG WITH MINIMUM-WAGE LAWS? DON'T THEY HELP
PEOPLE?

A ► NO. THE MINIMUM WAGE IS A PROVEN JOB KILLER FOR UNSKILLED
WORKERS.

What's wrong with a law requiring that unskilled workers get a decent wage? This question has long evoked intense and heated debate. The late senator Ted Kennedy, for one, went so far as to argue that a government-mandated minimum wage was no less than

> a defining issue about what our society is really about. Whether we reward work, whether we have respect for individuals that work hard and play by the rules, whether we are going to follow the great teachings of the Beatitudes, which inspire so many of us in terms of our responsibilities to our fellow human beings, and if we believe in those fundamental tenets of the Judeo-Christian ethic we cannot fail but to believe that the minimum wage must be a livable wage for all our fellow citizens.[36]

No doubt, emotional appeals like this can be persuasive. They're one reason that 90 percent of nations have instituted some kind of minimum wage. The problem is that studies have shown that a minimum wage does not help the poor in the Real World. Instead it increases joblessness among unskilled people.

Why? The answer comes down to basic Real World economics: if you make unskilled workers more expensive to employ, employers will simply hire fewer people.

Economist Thomas Sowell is one of many experts who warn that Americans need to pay close heed to the European experience with the minimum wage.

> Because minimum wage laws are more generous in Europe than in the United States, they lead to chronically higher rates of unemployment in general and longer periods of unemployment than in the United States—but especially among younger, less experienced and less skilled workers. Unemployment rates of 20 percent or more for young workers are common in a number of European countries. Among workers who are both younger and

minority workers, such as young Muslims in France, unemployment rates are estimated at about 40 percent.[37]

Sowell says that by reducing the number of jobs available to the lowest-skilled workers, minimum-wage laws have similarly hurt minorities in this country, making it harder for them to get a foothold in the economy: "Blacks in general, and younger blacks in particular, are the biggest losers from such laws, just as younger and minority workers are in Europe."[38] Few people today realize that the unemployment rate of black teenagers was at one time about the same as that of white teens. But after steady increases in the minimum wage it climbed to 40 percent by the late 1980s.

Sowell says that this was the intention of some of the supporters of the early minimum-wage laws, who had an openly racist agenda. "The last year in which the black unemployment rate was lower than the white unemployment rate in the United States was 1930. The next year, the first federal minimum wage law, the Davis-Bacon Act, was passed. One of its sponsors explicitly stated that the purpose was to keep blacks from taking jobs from whites."[39]

Concurring with Sowell, economist Walter Williams has called the minimum wage "one of the most effective tools in the arsenal of racists around the world."[40]

A Real World truth ignored by politicians is that minimum-wage jobs are basically starter jobs that allow workers to enter the workforce and learn skills. As Walter Williams points out, no one questions when "college students forego considerable amounts of money in the form of tuition and foregone income so that they may develop marketable skills. It is ironic, if not tragic, that low skilled youths from poor families are denied an opportunity to get a start in life."[41]

A Real World fact overlooked by well-intentioned advocates of minimum-wage laws: people do not make minimum wages for long. They quickly move up. According to the Heritage Foundation's James Sherk, an expert on the minimum wage,

> [B]etween 1998 and 2003—a time when the federal minimum wage did not rise—the median minimum wage worker earned a 10 percent raise within a year of starting work. During this period, over two-thirds of workers starting out at the minimum wage earned more than the minimum a year later. Once workers

have gained the skills and experience that make them more productive, they can command higher wages.[42]

Sherk and his colleague Rea S. Hederman Jr. also say that minimum-
wage workers rarely rely exclusively on their minimum-wage paychecks.
The majority of them are under twenty-five and "typically not their family's sole breadwinner. Rather, they live in middle-class households that
do not rely on their earnings."[43] As for older minimum-wage workers,
"the vast majority . . . live above the poverty line." Nor do they fit the
stereotype of a worker "living on the edge of destitution." They report,
"More than half—56 percent—work part-time jobs . . . while 45 percent
have incomes over twice the poverty line."[44]

In their study "Raising the Minimum Wage: Another Empty Promise
to the Working Poor," professors Richard V. Burkhauser of Cornell University and Joseph J. Sabia of the University of Georgia note that by 2003,
only 17 percent of low-wage employees were living in poor households
and only 9 percent of minimum-wage employees were actually the heads
of such households.[45]

Furthermore, studies also show that in addition to making it harder
to find jobs, minimum-wage increases have other unintended consequences. Michigan State University economics professor David Neumark
and Federal Reserve researcher William Wascher believe the minimum
wage encourages teenagers from lower-income families to drop out of
school. With fewer part-time minimum-wage jobs available, they're forced
to work full-time. The researchers found that a 10 percent increase in the
minimum wage caused teenage school enrollment in certain states to
drop by 2 percent.

Raising the minimum wage not only hurts the poorest of the poor, but
it burdens society with higher prices. Walter Williams believes it is at
least partly responsible for the decline in the services we associate with
a gentler era.

> When I was a kid growing up, neighborhood theatres had ushers
> to take you to your seats. . . . Now you don't see ushers in theatres,
> and that's not because Americans of today like to stumble down
> the aisles in the dark to find their seats. When you pulled into
> gasoline stations, there were young people out there to wash
> your windshield, fill your tank with gas, check the air in your

tires, and check the water in your radiator. Now we have self-service stations, not because Americans today like to smell gasoline fumes and get gasoline on their shoes while they fill up the car. The minimum wage destroyed those kinds of jobs.[46]

Minimum-wage supporters forget that in a free market, transactions take place based on mutual agreement and perceived benefit. If the wages for unskilled jobs were truly too low, there would be no takers. People who take minimum-wage positions clearly perceive that there is a benefit in taking these jobs, usually as a way to gain entry into the economy and as short-term employment. Remember, markets are spontaneous systems that behave in ways that bystanders may not always like. By imposing their ideas about what people should be making in low-skilled jobs, labor advocates have done their constituents a disservice by pricing out of the market the very neediest job seekers.

▲   REAL WORLD LESSON   ▲

Low-wage, unskilled jobs have more benefits than critics believe because markets do not always behave according to the preconceptions of bystanders.

Q ► Didn't deregulation wreck the airline industry?

A ► No, deregulation greatly benefited consumers. The problem is that government did not finish the job.

As we have seen in the case of the financial crisis, people often blame problems on a lack of regulation when the real culprit is bad regulation. This is true of the problems plaguing the airline industry.

Anyone who travels knows that airline travel can be a nightmare, with endless time spent on security lines, runways, and crowded planes and coping with lost luggage. No wonder everyone is angry, passengers and staff included. In 2008, the U.S. Department of Transportation received 40 percent more complaints about airline service than in December 2006.

These problems are usually blamed on airline deregulation. Writer Matthew Yglesias, a free-market critic, insists that airline quality has suffered because airlines are free to compete on price: "Previously, airlines barred from competing on the basis of price engaged in fairly vigorous competition on the basis of service quality. So while products generally get better over time, the quality of air travel has deteriorated rapidly as a low-cost, low-quality equilibrium has proven to be consistently more profitable."[47]

Is that really true? Airline delays and lost luggage are problems endured by passengers across the board, regardless of what they paid for their tickets. Is bad service really due to the fact that airlines make more money delivering poor quality? In most industries, the high-quality products usually offer the biggest profit margins, because they allow companies to charge more.

Washington's deregulation of airlines is not responsible for today's poor service. The problems stem from the fact that—contrary to what is believed—the entire airline industry was not deregulated. Airports and air-traffic-control systems that are critical to smooth and efficient flying were left under the control of government.

Writing in *Regulation* magazine, Robert Poole Jr. and Viggo Butler explain that government management of our airports and air-traffic-control systems has produced an antiquated, inefficient infrastructure unequipped to handle the explosion of air travel resulting from deregulation.

Government-run airports, for example, are unable to use market-based methods to reduce airport congestion—such as using peak pricing to direct some usage by carriers into off-hours. This would not only cut down on overcrowded terminals, it would generate much-needed fees to finance expansion and technological improvements both in air traffic control and in airport facilities.

Poole and Butler say that the misery of today's air travel is largely caused by an air-traffic-control system that relies on outdated 1950s technology. Only recently did the FAA announce that it would phase in more sophisticated NextGen air-traffic-control systems that use the kind of GPS satellite navigation technology consumers have had for years in passenger cars. The new systems would enable airports to handle at least twice as much traffic.

NextGen technology has existed for years. But the system has been bogged down in political debate. Not having to account to consumers, bureaucrats, as always, take their time at taxpayer expense. NextGen isn't expected to be fully in use until about 2025, at a total cost of some $35 billion.

Other countries already have more efficient, up-to-date air-traffic-control systems than the United States because they have given the management of airports and air-traffic-control systems to nonprofit corporations under industry control—and out of the hands of politically interested government bureaucrats.

The Rap on airline deregulation is anything but the truth. Airline deregulation actually has made service cheaper and more abundant. Adjusted for inflation, fares today are 25 percent to 44.9 percent lower than they were before deregulation three decades ago. Carriers offer far more service to more cities. And studies show travel is safer, too. The real problem in the United States isn't our airline traffic jam. It's the bureaucratic bottleneck in Washington.

▲   REAL WORLD LESSON   ▲

Government management, driven by politics and divorced from the realities of supply and demand, is not up to the task of managing the complex logistics of aviation infrastructure.

Q ► WHY IS NET NEUTRALITY A BAD IDEA?

A ► GOVERNMENT-MANDATED "NET NEUTRALITY" IS ESSENTIALLY RENT CONTROL FOR THE INTERNET. LIKE ALL PRICE CONTROLS, IT WOULD PRODUCE SHORTAGES AND LOWER THE QUALITY OF PRODUCTS AND SERVICES.

In December of 2010, the Federal Communications Commission voted to impose "net neutrality" regulations on the Internet. So what does this mean exactly?

Few economic policy discussions have been as muddied by technological jargon as the argument over net neutrality. We will spare you the mind-numbing lingo and technological details. The question, however, boils down to whether telecommunications companies should be able to set their own prices for the bandwidth they supply to Internet content providers. The dispute pits phone and cable companies like AT&T, Comcast, and Verizon—also known as Internet service providers or ISPs—against content providers such as Google, Yahoo!, and YouTube, among others.

Cable and telephone companies want to charge higher rates to those big customers because of the explosion of Web traffic clogging the information superhighway. Internet applications, such as video- and file-sharing networks, are rapidly taking up available space. A high-definition feature film, for example, requires as much data as 2,300 songs or 35,000 Web pages. According to the *Wall Street Journal*, bandwidth usage is growing at about 50 percent a year.

ISPs have traditionally relied on "all you can eat" pricing. Internet service companies assert that a tiered pricing system—where high-intensity users are charged more—will help to manage the congestion while encouraging companies to invest in more fiber-optic networks that expand their data pipelines.

But opponents of tiered pricing insist that it will force companies to "discriminate" against high-bandwidth users to control costs. For Web users, this means that some Web sites might suddenly operate more slowly or be less available. Some say this is already happening. The Internet service provider Comcast came under fire from net-neutrality advocates, who alleged the company blocked service to some of its customers.

Net-neutrality advocates have turned their campaign into a moral crusade to preserve the democratic heart and soul of the Internet. Yet no one argues when tiered pricing is used in other industries. The example most often given is FedEx. It seems reasonable that the parcel delivery giant charges more money to people who make use of its service by requesting quicker package delivery. Henry Blodget effectively draws this analogy in BusinessInsider.com:

> Imagine if the Post Office (or FedEx, or UPS, or DHL, or any trucking or transport company) were legally prohibited from charging more for delivering some stuff sooner than other stuff. Those shipping and transport companies spent billions of dollars building their transportation networks. They have every right to charge whatever the market will bear to deliver stuff via them. No one has any problem with the concept that the Post Office treats overnight packages differently than slow-boat ones. Importantly, they also charge *different rates depending on what is in the package*—see "book rate" and all pricing by weight. So why all this hullaballoo about "NET NEUTRALITY"?[48]

One can also argue that there has never been genuine net neutrality. For instance, individuals pay premiums to get high-speed DSL service.

Despite the vague, high-tech label, government-mandated "net neutrality" is essentially price control. And price controls, no matter what they're called, always end up harming the consumer. When companies are unable to generate sufficient profit, they have less money left over to invest in maintaining and improving operations. Enhancements are halted. Service eventually declines.

New York City's chronic housing shortage provides a powerful example of the perils of price controls. New York's rent-control laws were enacted in 1943, ostensibly to protect less affluent tenants against gouging by landlords. Other cities, including Boston, areas of Los Angeles, and San Francisco, followed New York's example. By the early 1980s, about 10 percent of the nation's renters were covered by rent-control regulations.

What happened? Less capital was available for real-estate development. The consequence: new housing in rent-controlled areas stopped being built or was sharply curtailed. By the 1990s, only about eight thousand new units were coming online each year in New York City, the lowest number since the Great Depression. Lower-income people had to make do with deteriorating rentals and more expensive nonrental housing.

Rent-control laws were loosened in the 1990s. But part of the market remains strictly controlled. To this day, New Yorkers are loath to move from rent-controlled apartments with cheap, below-market rents. The cost of housing in New York City today is about twice the national average.

Rent control did anything but bring more "neutrality" or fairness to the market. Affluent people were usually the ones who gained from hanging on to cheap, rent-controlled apartments. In one recent notorious case, an outcry ensued after it was disclosed that Charles Rangel, the one-time chairman of the House Ways and Means Committee, had at least four rent-controlled apartments. (These and other transgressions ultimately led to Rangel's being censured by the House of Representatives.)

Meanwhile, studies have shown that "free-market cities" with no rent regulations, such as Philadelphia, Chicago, San Diego, Phoenix, and Seattle, have almost perfectly competitive housing markets, with housing available at every price level.

Little wonder some have called net neutrality "rent control for the Internet." Net neutrality would turn the Internet broadband providers like Comcast and AT&T into the equivalent of New York City landlords.

According to the *Wall Street Journal*, the debate in Washington has already discouraged investment. It's one reason that the United States lags behind countries like South Korea and Japan in developing broadband capacity and is fifteenth in the world in bandwidth penetration.

Significantly, the new FCC rules do not overtly bar all tiered usage fees. Instead they require that FCC commissioners approve them. Internet service pricing will no longer be determined naturally based on supply and demand. It will be subject to the capricious forces of politics—i.e., the agendas of bureaucrats, FCC members, or others who may be influenced by rent-seeking corporations looking to squash competitors. In the words of Heritage Foundation analyst James Gattuso, "that will create an unpredictable atmosphere, with firms left unsure whether their activities will be deemed acceptable. At worst, it will lead to abuse and political gameplaying." He concludes:

> The overall result would be bad news not just for Web surfers but also for the economy as a whole. Investment in broadband today is one of the few bright spots of the economy, with providers expected to invest some $30 billion per year in private capital into their networks annually for the next five years, creating hundreds of thousands of jobs. Neutrality rules would threaten that investment and those jobs by hindering efficient network management and creating uncertainty.[49]

Net neutrality advocates should have learned from the regulatory failure of the 1996 Telecommunications Act. Under the guise of fostering competition, the legislation mandated that incumbent companies such as Verizon lease their wires to new phone companies at subsidized prices. No surprise, the incumbents then slashed capital spending. Why invest money in facilities that would benefit competitors? When these rules were lifted, the start-ups failed because they had been artificial creations of political legislation.

Unfortunately, "net neutrality" is the latest case of one industry group attempting to harness the powers of government to distort market behavior to suit its interests. Whether it's net neutrality or rent control, government-imposed price constraints only harm the economy and damage people and are anything but fair.

Promoting the interests of content companies over broadband providers, "net neutrality" is anything but neutral and is essentially price control.

Q ► Don't we need occupational licensing to protect consumers from bad or unethical practitioners?

A ► Most occupational licensing laws are not about preserving industry standards but about protecting incumbents from competition. They hurt both the economy and consumers.

In January 2005, a local news Web site in Miami featured the story of ten-year-old Carolyn Lipsick, who wanted to raise money for the victims of Asia's devastating tsunami—only to be shut down by city officials. Why? Because she lacked the appropriate license. The Web site recounts:

> Miami Beach city officials reportedly told [the] 10-year-old . . . , who wanted to sell cookies and drinks in her front yard to raise money for tsunami victims, that she could not hold the fundraiser because they could not grant her an occupational license.
>
> "I feel bad for them," said Carolyn. . . . "Some children have no clothes, no food, no water and no shoes and most important, that I want to help them, they can't find their parents. . . ."[50]

After the story got local news coverage, Florida's top officials were so embarrassed that they paid for Carolyn to set up her lemonade stand at the state capitol. She eventually succeeded in raising five hundred dollars—at the expense of taxpayers, who of course paid for her trip.

Carolyn's story illustrates what's wrong with most of the country's countless occupational licensing regulations—they're rigid, excessive, and often just plain dumb. And they end up costing the taxpayer and the economy.

According to a 2007 Reason Foundation report, more than one thousand occupations are currently regulated by the states (in addition to municipal and federal oversight). Certainly we want to license some of these professions—like doctors and maybe lawyers. Some may argue for licensing of real estate salespeople. But do we really need occupational licenses for interior designers, beekeepers, florists, and turtle farmers? The state of Maryland licenses fortune-tellers. Does that mean they're better equipped to predict the future?

Occupational licensing laws are billed as a means of protecting the public from negligent, unqualified, or otherwise substandard practitioners. But in many cases they were instituted to protect the interests of existing businesses. The Mackinac Center's Jack McHugh noted:

> The dirty little secret about state licensure is that the people who lobby for it are usually the stronger competitors of those who would be licensed. Their goal is not to protect the public, but instead to raise barriers to new competitors who might cut prices and lower profits.[51]

By limiting competition, licensing laws restrict job growth—by an average of 20 percent, according to the Reason Foundation report. The total cost of licensing regulations is estimated at between $34.8 billion and $41.7 billion per year.[52]

The laws also hurt consumers by reducing choice and enabling government-protected licensees to charge higher prices. Take the field of optometry. The Reason Foundation found that the average eye exam and eyeglass prescription is 35 percent more expensive in cities with more restrictive optometry regulations.[53]

Licensing regulations have also helped hike the price of funerals. Why are caskets so expensive? The industry's occupational licensing regulations have helped drive up prices by creating a "casket cartel."[54] In some states, it is illegal to sell caskets without a funeral director's license. This has led to enormous markups—as much as 600 percent above wholesale in states like Oklahoma and Tennessee.[55]

But don't we need occupational licensing laws to assure that practitioners of a profession deliver quality service? The answer is yes in the case of doctors and nurses. But as we've mentioned, the free market to a substantial degree is self-regulating. The average florist is not likely to keep your business or get recommendations if he or she constantly delivers wilted merchandise.

Most of us know from experience that occupational licensing is no protection against a bad plumber or even, in some cases, a bad physician.

That's why we still want to get referrals and recommendations before employing, say, a licensed electrician.

Licensing exams test knowledge that often has little or nothing to do with the real-world skills required by the profession. For example, it once took longer in Illinois to become a master plumber than for a newly graduated physician to become a Fellow of the American College of Surgeons—until the state court finally stepped in and changed the rules. And then there's the famous case of hair-braiding laws in Minnesota. We're not saying African hair braiding doesn't require specialized knowledge. Cosmetology in general requires training. But in parts of the state it takes more time to become a licensed hair braider than it does to become a certified emergency medical technician.

Getting a hair-braiding license can mean $15,000 in tuition and at least ten months of schooling.[56] Any braider who refuses to secure a government license can face up to one thousand dollars in fines and up to ninety days in jail. Defenders of these exams always say they're to ensure health and safety. But they're really intended to make it harder to enter a profession.

Little wonder that in some professions people, desperate for employment, ignore state licensing laws and operate illegally. In this way, overly burdensome licensing laws create black markets, turning law-abiding people into criminals in the eyes of our legal system. But even worse, some never enter a profession at all. They are denied their rightful opportunity to advance in a free-enterprise system that's not free enough.

▲   REAL WORLD LESSON   ▲

Occupational licensing, while necessary in some professions, raises prices and constricts employment.

CHAPTER SIX

"Aren't Free Trade and 'Globalization' Destroying American Jobs and the Economies of Other Nations?"

THE RAP ► American jobs have been destroyed and the economic welfare of people in poor countries has been harmed by the increasing globalization of business—through trade, industrialization, and the growth of multinational corporations. This global corporate juggernaut is bulldozing the cultures of other nations as well as the environment. The spread of the economic crisis from the United States to the rest of the world demonstrates the dangers of a global economy.

THE REALITY ► Since World War II, a historic era of free trade has brought unprecedented prosperity and opportunity to millions of people around the world, bringing greater freedom to many nations that were once dictatorships. The best way to expand the global middle class and increase prosperity is to continue reducing trade barriers—and establishing stable monetary policies. Bottom line: trade is a job creator, not destroyer.

What if the state of New York suddenly decided to boost employment during the recession by prohibiting residents from buying out-of-state products? You could buy only food, clothing, computers, furniture, and other products if they were made in New York. Most people would consider such a move unrealistic and unfeasible. For all its economic diversity, New York simply does not have the manpower and expertise to make everything residents need.

If New Yorkers could buy only state-produced products and services, their choices would be sharply reduced. Not many microchips are made in New York. There's no way the state could grow all the agricultural products that residents now take for granted. Sugar, for example, is a tropical crop. Tomatoes in the winter are imported from Florida and Mexico. And what about automobiles? Could a New York auto industry—if one managed to get started—possibly offer as many alternatives as three domestic and fifteen foreign carmakers? In this tightly confined market, many products would become expensive or unavailable. Companies would be unable to achieve economies of scale that make so many things affordable.

Facing higher costs, companies would generate less profit. Less wealth would be created for businesses and people. New York's standard of living would plummet. The Empire State would devolve into Honduras on the Hudson.

Let's hammer this point home: What if you *personally* had to produce at home everything you consumed? No longer could you pay outsiders to provide products and services. You'd have to make your own clothing, grow your own food, do your own home repairs, and everything else. This totally do-it-yourself lifestyle was how subsistence farmers lived at the time of our independence. Most people today would consider doing so grossly impractical and inefficient.

Think of all the people who never would have developed their skills had they been forced to devote their energies to meeting basic needs. What if Michael Jordan had had to spend time farming and sewing his own clothes? He never would have become the greatest basketball player in history.

Most of us can easily see the absurdity of prohibiting trade between states or individuals. Yet restricting trade between nations is equally foolhardy. Adam Smith realized this back in 1776 when he wrote *An Inquiry into the Nature and Causes of the Wealth of Nations:*

> It is the maxim of every prudent master of a family, never to attempt to make at home what it will cost him more to make than to buy. If a foreign country can supply us with a commodity cheaper than we ourselves can make it, better buy it of them with some part of the produce of our own industry, employed in a way in which we have some advantage.[1]

British economist David Ricardo described the benefits of international trade in his classic nineteenth-century work *On the Principles of Political Economy and Taxation.*[2] He explained that free trade enables countries with differing resources and capabilities to each produce more goods for lower cost than would be possible if each nation separately manufactured the same products. This is known as the theory of comparative advantage. It is the reason why trade between nations, when allowed to flourish, has been a powerful driver of economic growth throughout history.

Free-trade bashers forget that today's era of global trade was a response to the searing lessons taught by the Smoot-Hawley Tariff. Imposed in 1930, the levy raised import duties on a mind-numbing array of goods to record levels, igniting the worldwide trade war that plunged the world into the Great Depression.

Chastened by that experience, some 23 nations came together after World War II and signed the General Agreement on Tariffs and Trade (GATT) in 1947. In 1995, GATT was replaced by the World Trade Organization, which included 153 nations and nearly 98 percent of global trade.[3] Since the trend toward global trade began, most import quotas have been eliminated. According to Rod Hunter of the Hudson Institute, average tariffs fell from nearly 40 percent to 9.7 percent. America's import duties average a mere 3.5 percent. Europe's average is 5 percent.[4]

This loosening of trade barriers brought a thirtyfold increase in global trade that has been a boon to U.S. prosperity. In a widely cited 2006 study, economists Scott C. Bradford, Paul L. E. Grieco, and Gary Clyde Hufbauer estimated that overseas trade had added between $800 billion to $1.4 trillion in annual income to the U.S. economy since World War II.[5] That translates into a total gain in products, goods, and services of about seven thousand to thirteen thousand dollars per household. This enormous benefit far exceeds the cost of worker dislocations that trade produces—estimated at about $54 billion or less.

Much of this growth has occurred in the last thirty years. One of the reasons that the 1970s had a lower standard of living was that the United States did not trade with the world to the extent it does today. In 1970, imports and exports together made up only 12 percent of our gross domestic product. By the mid-2000s they made up 24 percent.[6]

The continuous move since World War II toward freer trade is a major reason that the United States has, over the past three decades, experienced a historic rise in its standard of living. Thanks to free trade, Americans of all income levels are now able to afford products from televisions to refrigerators to clothing that were once many times more expensive or considered luxuries.

But the benefits of trade with other nations go far beyond being able to afford "cheap" TVs, clothes, and toys. By making the iPod affordable, low-cost flash chips from South Korea, for example, have helped to make possible an entirely new mini-industry, along with tens of thousands of jobs. Economist Ana Isabel Eiras of the Heritage Foundation writes:

> Specialization and free trade allow the U.S. to become more competitive and innovative. Innovation constantly provides new technologies that allow Americans to produce more, cure more diseases, pollute less, improve education, and choose from a greater range of investment opportunities. The resulting economic growth generates better-paying jobs, higher standards of living, and a greater appreciation of the benefits of living in a peaceful society.[7]

Anyone who doubts the connection between free trade and innovation should look at the products of countries that don't allow competition from imported products. A well-known example is the Trabant, the auto produced in East Germany, where it faced no competition. Little wonder it became known for shoddy quality.

Anti–free traders, particularly organized labor, have bemoaned job loss resulting from corporations "outsourcing" or "offshoring"—using the lower-cost labor of other nations to manufacture goods once made in the United States. We've already noted that unemployment over the past three decades has been lower than when trade barriers were higher. And the trade bashers conveniently ignore the fact that foreign trade creates factory jobs in the United States. One out of every five American factory jobs is foreign trade related. Free trade also provides new markets for U.S. farmers, who export one-third of their crops.

Free trade has raised living standards around the globe. As Robyn Meredith and Suzanne Hoppough wrote in *Forbes* in 2007, "globalization"—international free trade—has done more to help the people in Asia and Africa than the $2 trillion of foreign aid that the United States and Europe have poured into those regions in the last half century.[8] According to the International Monetary Fund, some two hundred million people have been lifted out of poverty since globalization took off in the 1990s.

A study by the management consulting firm A. T. Kearney found that between 1980 and 1990 alone, global poverty rates fell by half—from 34 percent to 17 percent.[9] Within that decade, trade helped to lift 573 million people above the absolute poverty line. The middle class, meanwhile, saw its median income worldwide rise by roughly 15 percent.

Not only does free trade bring greater prosperity, but it also helps to usher in democracy—or the beginnings of it—to once-repressive dictatorships. No one would call China a democracy. But thanks to free trade and a more liberalized economy, that nation is nowhere near as oppressive as it was in the era of the Cultural Revolution under Mao Tse-tung. Daniel Griswold of the Cato Institute believes that the rise in global trade is related to the reduction of major armed conflicts. He cites a 2006 survey by the Stockholm International Peace Research Institute finding that since the early 1990s, "ongoing conflicts have dropped from 33 to 17, with all of them now civil conflicts within countries."[10] The reason?

> [D]emocracies tend not to pick fights with each other. Thanks in part to globalization, almost two thirds of the world's countries today are democracies—a record high. . . . War in a globalized world not only means human casualties and bigger government but also ruptured trade and investment ties that impose lasting damage on the economy. In short, globalization has dramatically raised the economic cost of war.[11]

Despite all the progress, free trade in the Real World is fragile. Protectionist pressures in all countries increase in hard times. During the 2004 presidential campaign, candidate John Kerry called companies that invested overseas "Benedict Arnolds."[12] Twenty years earlier, Walter Mondale raised the specter of America's becoming a "hollowed-out" nation of "hamburger flippers" because of the rise of Germany and Japan. Even in the last campaign, Hillary Clinton and Barack Obama competed with each other in denouncing the North American Free Trade Agreement.

Opponents of "globalization" fan the flames of fear by raising the specter of all sorts of doomsday scenarios. None have ever come to pass.

Former Michigan governor John Engler, president of the National Association of Manufacturers, points this out.

> The United States remains the world's largest manufacturing nation, accounting for more than 19.5% of global manufacturing output. In 2007, the U.S. produced more volume of products than ever before, and manufacturing represented $1.6 trillion of our economy, or about 11.6% of gross domestic product.
>
> Manufacturing in the United States accounts for more than 12 million jobs and supports millions more in other sectors. And manufacturing jobs are among the most highly compensated in the nation, paying on average about 20% more than those in other sectors.[13]

The real doomsday scenario would occur if trade were halted. The world economy would shut down.

Q ► But isn't it necessary to preserve American jobs in tough economic times?

A ► Protectionism destroys far more jobs than it saves.

The temptation for nations to turn inward inevitably grows in a down economy. Businesses and labor groups ramp up political pressure on legislators to eliminate foreign competition and—they think—save jobs. Hudson Institute trade policy analyst Rod Hunter reported that countries struggling with a worldwide recession in 2009 increasingly threw up trade barriers.

> World Bank staff report that G20 countries have implemented a raft of trade distorting measures since November [2008]—in many cases without violating their WTO commitments. Developing countries such as Ecuador and India have hiked up tariffs. Some have erected non-tariff barriers, sometimes camouflaged as consumer protection. China has banned Belgian chocolates, Irish pork, Italian brandy and Dutch eggs, and India has banned Chinese toys.[14]

The United States has shown similar protectionist impulses. Unfortunately, President Obama is the first president since Herbert Hoover who has not been a genuine free trader. Going into 2011, free-trade agreements with South Korea (which the president renegotiated), Colombia, and Panama still have not cleared Congress because the president has yet to push for passage. While the United States dithered, South Korea negotiated a very lucrative free-trade agreement with the European Union.

In 2009, one of the first acts of the new administration was halting a program that had allowed about one hundred Mexican trucks access to U.S. roads—a political payoff to the Teamsters union. (Two years later, after intense pressure from Mexico hinting the move had anti-Hispanic overtones, the administration backed down.) Meanwhile, stimulus legislation passed by the U.S. Congress featured a "Buy American" provision requiring that iron, steel, and manufactured goods acquired for infrastructure projects be produced in the United States.

Whether it is banning Belgian chocolates or foreign steel or Mexican trucks, protectionism is never a solution to hard times. The Real World fact of the matter is—and this is something that emotional free-trade bashers often don't get—even moderate sounding trade protections can be extremely damaging. And they really don't create many jobs; in fact, they destroy more than they save.

"Buy American" is a case in point. To some, the patriotically named measure may not sound particularly threatening. What's wrong with requiring that government projects use materials fabricated at home? Buy American, after all, is not an across-the-board tariff like the infamous Smoot-Hawley.

Economists Gary Clyde Hufbauer and Jeffrey J. Schott of the Peterson Institute for International Economics calculate that the number of jobs that would be created by both the House and Senate versions of Buy American would be minimal. The original Buy American provisions as passed by the House of Representatives would have resulted in the purchase of about 0.5 million metric tons of steel—creating about one thousand domestic jobs. In a labor force of 140 million people, this number is—as the authors put it—barely a "rounding error." They calculated that the total number of jobs created by the Senate version of the bill would be approximately nine thousand.[15]

Meanwhile, tens of thousands more jobs—directly and indirectly—would potentially be destroyed. Remember the classic case of Smoot-Hawley. That law was originally designed to help protect American farmers—and later, manufacturers and producers—from Canadian and other foreign competition. Yet within eighteen months of its enactment, unemployment had quadrupled.

Buy American provisions also promote unemployment by soaking up private-sector capital that would have created jobs elsewhere in the economy. Dartmouth economics professor Douglas Irwin describes the capital destruction that took place in the 1990s as a result of California regulations requiring the San Francisco–Oakland Bay Bridge to use more costly domestic steel.

> Because of the large amount of steel used in the project, California taxpayers had to pay a whopping $400 million more for the bridge. While this is a windfall for a lucky steel company, steel production is capital intensive, and the rule makes less money available for other construction projects that can employ many more workers.[16]

Then there's the job destruction that occurs when America's trading partners retaliate. According to Hufbauer and Schott of the Peterson Institute, Buy American as originally written could have provoked retaliation by any of twelve foreign nations that are U.S. trading partners—a group that includes Canada, the UK, Japan, and Germany, as well as China, South Korea, and Hong Kong. Based on our level of exports to those countries, the economists estimated that if "10 percent of those exports are lost, as many as 65,000 jobs could vanish."[17] They conclude:

> The negative job impact of foreign retaliation against Buy American provisions could easily outweigh the positive effect of the measures on jobs in the U.S. iron and steel sector and other industries. The difference is that jobs lost would be spread across the entire manufacturing sector, while jobs gained would be concentrated in iron and steel and a few other industries.[18]

Fortunately, Buy American was eventually watered down after free traders protested that the provision violated existing trade agreements.

Language was added that effectively neutralized the measure. However, the other protectionist move, the banning of one hundred Mexican trucks, resulted in Mexico slapping some $2.4 billion in tariffs on some ninety American products, from toilet paper and Christmas trees to fruit juices and deodorant. James Roberts of the Heritage Foundation writes that in Oregon alone, the tariffs will cost companies tens of millions of dollars, including $80 million in annual exports of french fries to Mexico. Canada, which doesn't have to pay the tax, would pick up the business.[19]

Bottom line: "protectionism" is really a euphemism for political favoritism that protects the jobs of a few at the expense of everyone else.

▲   REAL WORLD LESSON   ▲

Buy American and other protectionist provisions kill future job creation, raise costs, and hobble growth, hurting many more people than they help.

Q ► BUT DOESN'T OUTSOURCING OF JOBS OVERSEAS TAKE WORK FROM AMERICANS?

A ► ONLY A SMALL PERCENTAGE OF JOBS ARE DIRECTLY LOST DUE TO OUTSOURCING. AND, IN THE LARGER ECONOMY, MORE ARE ACTUALLY GAINED THAN LOST.

Everyone from Barack Obama to Pat Buchanan has assailed companies for "shipping jobs overseas." Such heated characterizations may win votes and viewing audiences. But they are misguided. As we note in the introduction to this chapter, America is still the world's largest manufacturer. In fact, relatively few jobs in the Real World U.S. economy are lost because of "outsourcing" or "offshoring."

According to a report by Forrester Research, not even 1 percent of jobs lost every quarter between 2000 and 2015 will likely be due to outsourcing. Contrary to popular perceptions, most American jobs can't be outsourced. A report by the McKinsey Global Institute pointed this out in 2003,

> [T]he evidence available . . . suggests that fears about job losses . . . tend to overplay the likely impact of offshoring. The vast majority—some 70 percent—of the economy is composed of services such as retail, restaurants and hotels, personal care

services, and the like spanning very broad wage and value added ranges. These services are necessarily produced and consumed locally—and therefore cannot be offshored.[20]

Much of the job loss blamed on "outsourcing" is actually part of the normal "churn," the ongoing process of job loss and new-job creation that takes place as the economy changes and grows. Even China, with its robust growth, has lost manufacturing jobs—including fifteen million between 1995 and 2002, according to the Conference Board.

What has really happened, as we explained earlier, is that jobs have shifted from one section of the economy to another, as America has increasingly become an economy specializing in services such as health care. This process is in fact helping our economy build wealth.

Outsourcing jobs overseas also helps create extremely lucrative markets for the products and expertise that drive our economy. Foreign companies buy our telecommunications equipment, computer hardware, and software. According to McKinsey, every dollar spent by American companies abroad generates additional revenue for the United States. They conclude that "far from being bad for the United States, offshoring creates net additional value for the U.S. economy that did not exist before."[21]

A Real World economic truth conveniently overlooked by outsourcing opponents: the United States is a major exporter of services. According to the American Enterprise Institute, American services provided to other nations represent about a fifth of the global trade in services and about 30 percent of U.S. exports. For those who care about trade deficits (and as we explain later, you shouldn't), our service economy is one place where we have had a trade surplus.

The most visible benefit of outsourcing is, of course, the production of cheaper goods for Americans and people around the world. Outsourcing in the tech sector, for example, helped reduce the cost of computer components by 10 percent to 30 percent between 1995 and 2002, according to Catherine Mann of the Peterson Institute for International Economics.[22] These declines help explain why laptops can now be bought for as little as five hundred dollars at the local Best Buy.

Outsourcing foes will dismiss this benefit—suggesting that we have sacrificed American livelihoods to feed a gluttonous national appetite for cheaper televisions and other consumer products. But lower prices have helped spark revolutions. Remember how Henry Ford transformed society. He made the Model T *affordable* to working Americans. People everywhere were able to travel longer distances faster than they could before. This meant not just greater personal convenience, but also the ability to travel to work and trade in places that were once out of reach.

If computers were as expensive now as they were in the 1960s and '70s, only a handful of researchers funded by corporations or government would be able to use them. We would never have experienced the technology revolution that has given us wireless computing, Bluetooth, Google, and countless other innovations that have made us more productive, informed, and connected than ever before.

▲   REAL WORLD LESSON   ▲

Outsourcing may destroy some jobs, but it ultimately results in more "creation" than "destruction" for the economy and Americans.

Q ► WHAT'S WRONG WITH "FAIR" TRADE?

A ► FAIR TRADE IS PROTECTIONISM LITE.

Fair trade means that the United States must go tit for tat regarding other countries' trade restrictions, even if those countries are in compliance with international bilateral trade agreements. "Fair trade" is supposed to be a middle-ground alternative to free trade. Its policies aim to achieve the benefits of trade—i.e., economic growth—while minimizing job loss and disruption.

Like all protectionists, advocates of so-called fair trade miss the Real World benefits of free trade to the broader economy. So if Thailand, with its lower-cost labor, can make a shoe at one-tenth of the cost that a U.S. shoemaker can, then that is not "fair." Fair traders believe we ought to impose a stiff tax on such nations, and in some cases even bar their products.

Tufts University professor Daniel Drezner has summed up the policy positions that fall under the heading of "fair trade." They include, in his words:

Slowing down the number of free trade agreements signed with developing countries; relying more on "managed trade" arrangements

and unilateral trade sanctions to promote U.S. exports; using escape
clauses and safeguard mechanisms to slow the flood of Chinese textile imports into the United States; implementing measures to
retard the pace of offshore outsourcing; and exploiting threats of
protectionist action against China to force a substantial revalua-
tion in the yuan.[23]

In the Real World, *fair trade* is a euphemism for protectionism. As
Drezner acknowledges, it is "impossible" to draw a clear line between
the two. In his book *U.S. Trade Strategy: Free Versus Fair*, he writes:

> The fair trade orientation assumes that policymakers will be able
> to discern when trade should be restricted because of concerns
> about social dislocation and when it should not be restricted. In
> point of fact, a fair trade orientation will encourage every special
> interest group to lobby harder for protecting its sector, using a
> fair trade argument to do so.[24]

In the Real World, Drezner writes, fair-trade policies end up having the
same effect as traditional protectionism—they save the jobs of a politically adroit few, while killing off many more jobs. And they raise prices
for consumers:

> Two recent examples illustrate the costs of the fair trade ap-
> proach. U.S. import quotas limit the amount of sugar the United
> States imports. As a result, U.S. sugar prices are 350 percent
> higher than world market prices. Although this policy has pre-
> served a few thousand sugar-producing jobs, it has also cost an
> estimated 7,500 to 10,000 jobs, as candy makers relocated pro-
> duction to countries with lower sugar prices. Similarly, when the
> United States raised the tariffs on steel in 2002–2003, it raised
> the costs of production for steel-using sectors. Because steel users
> employ roughly forty times the manpower employed by steel pro-
> ducers, an estimated 45,000 to 75,000 jobs were lost.[25]

Like other economic policies that tout "fairness," fair trade, in the Real
World, ends up delivering on that promise only to a politically favored
few. Opponents of free trade ignore fundamental principles not only of

economics but of Real World common sense. Less trade means a smaller economy—a net loss for workers and consumers. It means less prosperity for most people.

▲   REAL WORLD LESSON   ▲

Like all protectionism, "fair trade" results in favoritism, not fairness.

Q ► ISN'T CHINA MANIPULATING ITS CURRENCY TO GAIN AN UNFAIR
    TRADE ADVANTAGE?

A ► NO, CHINESE GOODS AREN'T CHEAPER BECAUSE OF "CURRENCY
    MANIPULATION" BUT BECAUSE THE CHINESE CAN MANUFACTURE
    MORE CHEAPLY WITH LOW-SKILLED LABOR.

Trade protectionists have lately targeted China for supposedly under-valuing its currency—making the value of the yuan too low against the dollar. Thus, they allege, imported Chinese products are made artifi-cially cheap, while American exports become more expensive. Before taking office as Treasury secretary, Timothy F. Geithner testified that President Obama "believes that China is manipulating its currency." The president, he promised, would do all he could to assure that "countries like China cannot continue to get a free pass for undermining fair-trade principles."[26] The Obama administration has since intensified the heat on China to radically revalue the yuan.

In fact, China has done anything but "manipulate" its currency. It has outsourced its monetary policy to the Federal Reserve: the value of the Chinese yuan has been pegged to the dollar since 1994. Both the yuan and the dollar fluctuate according to U.S. monetary policies. To appease U.S. protectionists, China has actually increased the value of the yuan some 20 percent against the dollar in recent years.

Currency protectionists have a hidden agenda: to do their own ma-nipulation by altering currency exchange rates to raise the prices of Chi-nese imports. Post–World War II trade agreements like GATT prohibit raising the cost of Chinese goods via protectionist tariffs. So fair traders want to pressure China to change the value of the yuan.

This would result in a de facto tax on Chinese products. Chinese exports to the United States would go up in price. The cost of those Chinese socks you bought would go, say, from $2.00 to $2.50. We'd buy fewer Chinese goods. Or the price of those computer motherboards imported from China would increase, driving up the price of American computers. People would be able to afford fewer PCs; the market for Chinese parts would shrink. Result: the U.S. trade deficit would be reduced.

Fair traders can't accept the fact that some countries have advantages over U.S. producers when producing certain types of goods. It's a fact of life in the Real World that Chinese goods are cheaper because China's low-cost labor enables Chinese companies to manufacture products less expensively. But this comparative advantage does not mean the United States is at a *disadvantage*. Remember, trade is about two parties making an exchange based on their respective strengths and capabilities—a trade that provides more benefit to both sides than what would have been possible if no transaction had occurred.

Importing less costly Chinese products may displace some American jobs in specific sectors of the economy. We've already noted that doing so creates jobs in other economic sectors, one of the reasons for low U.S. unemployment and increasing prosperity over the past several decades.

Saving on Chinese products enables American consumers and businesses to make their dollars go further. People—including many on lower incomes—are able to live better. Meanwhile, American companies buying cheaper Chinese-manufactured goods and equipment have more capital left over for investment in new operations and jobs.

Our trade with China also encourages the Chinese to invest here. Did you ever wonder what happens to those dollars Chinese companies get from trading with us? They exchange them for yuan from their own government, which ends up with vast pools of dollars. The Chinese government has to invest the greenbacks somewhere. Their best bet: bills and bonds from the U.S. Treasury, and also U.S. businesses.

Thus, U.S.-China trade not only expands the U.S. economy. It enables China to help underwrite U.S. government spending. Whether some of this spending should be taking place is another matter. But dollars from China ease the burden on the U.S. taxpayer.

Bloomberg News reported that when Hillary Clinton made her first visit to China as secretary of state in February of 2009, she urged China to keep buying U.S. Treasuries, "to help finance President Barack Obama's stimulus plan."[27] Mrs. Clinton explained that doing so was essential to both nations' economies. "It would not be in China's interest," she said, if the United States lost dollars vital to stimulating its economy. "We are truly going to rise or fall together."[28]

Ironically, the very same administration that sent Mrs. Clinton to urge China to continue investing in the United States raises the specter of currency protectionism. This is typical of free-trade bashers and other free-market opponents. They have a blinkered view of the workings of the economy. They focus on the destruction that occurs in one sector of the economy and don't recognize the greater creation also occurring.

Protectionists also fail to understand that currency values are not the fundamental determinant of global trade. Transactions that cross borders, like those between individuals, are about meeting one another's needs. That's why changing currency values over the long term have little impact on trade imbalances. Sooner or later, people go back to buying what they did before. Markets readjust the prices of products to reflect their intrinsic value.

Few people today recall that similar charges of currency manipulation were leveled against Japan during the Nixon administration in the late sixties. The yen-to-dollar ratio at that time was 360 to 1. Today it's about 100 to 1, a devaluation of almost 70 percent. But the trade deficit between the United States and Japan persists.

The only thing that currency protectionism accomplishes is wreaking havoc in an economy by increasing the supply of money. In the 1970s the Nixon administration thought that devaluing the dollar would improve our trade balance and lift the economy. Instead we got rip-roaring inflation and a chain of ever-more-serious recessions. Unemployment went higher and higher, peaking at almost 11 percent in 1982.

The administration of George W. Bush fell prey to the same misconception. It permitted the dollar to grow weak, thinking that would reduce our trade deficit. What happened? Most of that extra money printed by the Federal Reserve went into housing. The trade deficit was brought down, but at an enormous cost: a momentous housing bubble that produced stomach-churning volatility and the most severe recession in at least thirty years.

▲   REAL WORLD LESSON   ▲

Accusations of "currency manipulation" are a cover for anti–free trade policies, including U.S. currency protectionism.

Q ► Should we be afraid of China and India?

A ► Not in the near term. China and India have a long way to go before their economies pull ahead of the United States.

According to a 2008 Gallup poll, only 33 percent of Americans still see the United States as the world's foremost economic power. Four out of ten believe the most economically powerful nation in the world today is China. This is a big change from 2000, when 65 percent of Americans thought the United States led the global economy.

Increasingly, people see a growing threat to the United States, not only from China but also from India—or as some refer to them collectively, "Chindia." The rapid economic growth of these nations, their immense populations, and their industrious, well-educated citizens seem to point toward a future where Chindia will prevail and America will decline.

These fears are nothing new. Every ten or twenty years, new "threats" to U.S. economic power emerge. In the 1960s and '70s, it was the Germans. Fears of Japan were rampant in the 1980s. People were horrified when the Japanese bought New York's iconic Rockefeller Center. Worriers cried that we were losing our lead to Tokyo. Few people could have imagined back then that apprehensions about the Germans and the Japanese would seem almost quaint decades later.

However, to some, the 2009 economic crisis seems to offer compelling evidence that the United States really is growing weaker. But China and other nations have a long way to go before they become as economically powerful as the United States. With a gross domestic product of more than $14 trillion, the U.S. economy is in fact more than three times the size of Japan's. Despite our population being one-fourth the size of China's, our economy is about four times larger. In other words, China's per-capita income is barely one-sixteenth that of the United States.

Despite their considerable strides, China and India—and also Japan—still lack many of America's capabilities and advantages. India, for example, has had a protectionist bent. The country is still working to overcome its vast, stultifying regulatory regime, which severely hampered its economy for decades. Only in 1991 did India begin a sustained push for liberalization. Much of India is still connected by dirt roads. Its infrastructure is only now being developed. Paved highways, although expanding, are few and far between.

Japan hasn't really recovered from the recession of the nineties. Its conformist culture is not often conducive to entrepreneurship. Failure has a huge social stigma. China, too, has plenty of problems. It's made some progress. But the rule of law is far from established. It doesn't have an independent judiciary. It's hard to resolve disputes; decisions are often made for political reasons. China's capital markets are also in their infancy. Noted Columbia University economist Jagdish N. Bhagwati has written that China's problems include

> inefficient State Operating Enterprises, still much poverty, and a terribly weak financial sector. Its demographic structure, thanks to the draconian and effective one-child policy, also is lopsided, closer to that of Europe than of India. These problems cast a shadow over China's ability to sustain its high growth rate.
>
> But the prospects of China registering "miracle" growth rates for much longer are also cast in doubt by her communist politics. China lacks currently the four elements of a functioning democracy: NGOs, a free press, opposition parties and an independent judiciary. The result is growing social disruptions as commissars and their cronies grab land, for example.[29]

The Chicken Littles who predict our economic decline overlook a key American advantage: our unique entrepreneurial spirit and political traditions. They don't appreciate the role of America's system of democratic capitalism—i.e., a government with independent courts that enforce contracts and property rights and a political system that protects private ownership, as well as economic and political freedom.

These traditions set America apart from its competitors and are the foundation of our economic strength. Yet most of us take them for granted and underestimate their importance. Thus, journalist Robert Samuelson acknowledges, many wonder why the U.S. economy "doesn't do worse when there are so many reasons that it should."[30]

Those fearing America's decline might do well to recall history. Interviewed in *U.S. News & World Report*, Walter Russell Mead, senior fellow at the Council on Foreign Relations, notes that we've had many financial meltdowns. However, "those crises haven't sunk us in 300 years."[31]

▲   REAL WORLD LESSON   ▲

Experts have long underestimated the importance of America's entrepreneurial culture as a factor in its economic strength and world leadership position.

Q ► DID NAFTA HURT OR HELP THE UNITED STATES?

A ► NAFTA HAS CREATED A VIBRANT NORTH AMERICAN FREE-TRADE ZONE THAT HAS INCREASED JOBS AND OPPORTUNITIES NOT ONLY FOR THE UNITED STATES, BUT FOR CANADA AND MEXICO AS WELL.

Signed into law back in 1993, the North American Free Trade Agreement (NAFTA) continues to be controversial. Barack Obama and Hillary Clinton both criticized the agreement during the 2008 presidential campaign, going so far as to suggest it should be renegotiated. Critics allege that it has led to a loss of some one million American manufacturing jobs and has not achieved its goal of helping the U.S. economy.

In fact, NAFTA has supercharged trade among the United States, Canada, and Mexico, creating an immense, dynamic market. As historian John Steele Gordon has written on AmericanHeritage.com, NAFTA

> created a huge free trade area of more than eight million square miles, 430 million people, and almost uncountable economic resources. It is the largest free trade area in the world in terms of gross domestic product, $15.3 trillion in 2006.
>
> Since 1993, overall trade in goods between the three countries has almost tripled, from $297 billion in 1993 to $883 billion in 2006. American exports of goods to Canada and Mexico are up 157 percent, services up 125 percent.[32]

What about those one million jobs that were supposedly lost? In fact, since the agreement was signed and up until the recession, the nation's unemployment rate actually *fell*. Wages, on average, rose, too. According to a 2008 report from the National Center for Policy Analysis,

> U.S. employment rose from 110.8 million in 1993 to 137.6 million in 2007, an increase of 24 percent. The U.S. unemployment rate averaged 5.1 percent for the first 13 years after NAFTA, compared to 7.1 percent during the 13 years prior to the agreement.
>
> Moreover, increased openness to trade has been accompanied

by a more rapid rise in wages. For example, from 1979 to 1993 U.S. business-sector real hourly compensation rose at an annual rate of 0.7 percent each year, or 11 percent over the entire period. Between 1993 and 2007, however, real wages rose 1.5 percent annually, for a total of 23.6 percent.[33]

That massive exodus of American jobs and investment to Mexico that many feared simply did not happen. Between 1994 and 2001, American manufacturing companies invested more than $200 billion in new plants and equipment in the United States and invested just $2.2 billion in Mexico.

According to the Cato Institute's Daniel Griswold, "U.S. investment in Mexico did increase after NAFTA, along with trade, but those flows are a trickle compared to what we invest domestically."[34]

What NAFTA did do was help boost U.S. exports. According to Anil Kumar, a senior economist at the Federal Reserve Bank of Dallas, between 1993 and 2004, U.S. exports to Mexico more than doubled, rising from $42 billion in 1993 to $111 billion. American sales to Canada, meanwhile, nearly doubled—rising from $100 billion to $189 billion.[35] Exports from Mexico and Canada to the United States increased substantially. This has meant more economic activity. Remember, trade takes place between parties when both think it is beneficial.

Kumar says NAFTA has also helped encourage other overseas trade. He cites his own state of Texas, where "NAFTA also helped raise . . . exports to Asia, Europe and Latin America, making a strong case for net trade creation."[36]

By bringing down costs and pushing businesses to be more competitive, NAFTA has encouraged companies like J. H. Rose Logistics, a forty-six-million-dollar-a-year shipping logistics company in El Paso, to expand its trading horizons. President Amy Noyes initially feared that the free-trade agreement would make her company more vulnerable to lower-cost Mexican competitors. But instead of trying to beat them, she partnered with them to move freight in Mexico. Noyes told *BusinessWeek* magazine that becoming more competitive through these partnerships helped increase her business, as well as her U.S. workforce. In 2006 she opened a warehouse in New Mexico.

The benefits of NAFTA are clear. The real issue, as John Steele Gordon and others have written, is whether the United States can afford to turn inward in a world economy that technology has made increasingly global. It's impossible to withdraw from this world, Gordon believes, without "turning the United States into a modern version of pre-late-nineteenth-century Japan. So the real question is not whether we should continue with NAFTA and other free trade agreements. It is how we will manage the inevitable continuing creation of a single world economy."[37]

▲   REAL WORLD LESSON   ▲

The doomsday scenario predicted by NAFTA opponents never materialized and is based on political agendas and not economics.

Q ► IF FREE TRADE IS GOOD FOR POOR NATIONS, THEN WHY DO FARMERS AND OTHERS IN SOME COUNTRIES PROTEST "GLOBALIZATION"?

A ► THE REAL CULPRIT IS NOT "GLOBALIZATION" BUT U.S. GOVERNMENT FARM SUBSIDIES THAT CREATE ARTIFICIALLY CHEAP AMERICAN AGRICULTURAL EXPORTS THAT MAKE IT DIFFICULT FOR THE FARMERS TO COMPETE.

If free trade is making people around the world richer, then why do we see all those demonstrations against globalization in India, Mexico, Thailand, and other nations? In 2008, hundreds of farmers on tractors converged on Mexico City protesting the North American Free Trade Agreement. The reason? NAFTA's liberalized agricultural trade provisions resulted in cheap corn and grains flooding Mexico from the United States and Canada. Mexico's poor farmers were unable to compete.

The farmers had a legitimate beef. But unfortunately—as with so many other trade protests—this was another case of mistaken identity. The problem wasn't free trade or NAFTA but America's long-standing government farm subsidies.

Started in the 1930s as a way of helping family farmers during the Great Depression, Herbert Hoover's Farm Board fixed prices for wheat and cotton. If they dropped too low, the federal government would buy those crops and sell them later at a better price. Franklin Roosevelt later signed into law the Agricultural Adjustment Act, which paid farmers not to produce crops so that "oversupply" and overly low prices would be avoided.

Farm subsidies were supposed to be temporary. But they soon became permanent. Like other bad government policies, they have created a brutal imbalance in world agricultural markets: artificially cheap wheat and corn grown by government-subsidized U.S. producers are threatening the livelihoods of poor farmers who are priced out of the market. They're also hurting the U.S. economy—and American taxpayers.

The Heritage Foundation estimates that the U.S. government spends about $25 billion annually on farm subsidies.[38] Most of the money goes not to the small farmers championed by Depression-era policy makers but "to commercial farms with average incomes of $200,000 and net worths of nearly $2 million."[39]

Farm subsidies are helping today's politically powerful corporate farmers, while poor farmers abroad are suffering and U.S. citizens are paying higher taxes—and also higher food prices. Writing in *Reason* magazine in 2006, Daniel Griswold, Stephen Slivinski, and Christopher Preble calculated that the higher prices produced by agricultural subsidies resulted in a "food tax" of $146 per household.[40]

Particularly damaging are the subsidies going to U.S. corn farmers to encourage the production of corn for biofuel. According to journalist Robert Bryce, federal corn subsidies totaled $37.3 billion between 1995 and 2003, which he says is "more than twice the amount spent on wheat subsidies, three times the amount spent on soybeans, and 70 times the amount spent on tobacco."[41]

Even those who believe in the need for alternative fuel have doubts about whether ethanol-related farm subsidies are worth this enormous cost. For one thing, producing ethanol is a wasteful process that expends far more energy than it saves in our gas tanks. However, the greater cost is to people in underdeveloped countries, who have seen the price of corn, as well as soybeans and other vital food staples, skyrocket because of consumption by the biofuel industry.

The increasing use of corn for ethanol was a key reason that the price of tortilla flour in Mexico doubled in 2006, helping to stoke a massive public outcry. Writing in the journal *Foreign Affairs*, University of Minnesota economics professors C. Ford Runge and Benjamin Senauer called the government-subsidized biofuels industry "a grave threat to the food security of the world's poor."[42] Corn is now cheaper because of the recession. But its price remains inflated over what it would have been if not for corn-based ethanol. In addition, studies have raised environmental concerns about toxic runoff into the Mississippi River and the Gulf of Mexico resulting from the increased amounts of fertilizer used to grow ethanol corn.

Even Al Gore now admits that ethanol is a bad idea. In 2010 he confessed, "One of the reasons I made that mistake is that I paid particular attention to the farmers in my home state of Tennessee, and I had certain fondness of the farmers in the state of Iowa because I was about to run for president."[43]

Ethanol tax credits cost the government an estimated $7.7 billion annually. Even so, and in spite of bipartisan opposition, ending the program isn't easy. At the end of 2010, the U.S. Senate voted to extend ethanol tax credits to producers and a tariff on ethanol imports.

Unlike private-sector businesses, which rise and fall based on their ability to serve their market, farm subsidies are an example of how failed government programs don't go away. Even though they hurt millions more people than they help, farm subsidies continue—because the handful of people they help are the ones who most effectively wield political power.

▲   REAL WORLD LESSON   ▲

U.S. government farm subsidies are the "hidden" reason that some have been misled into believing free trade hurts the poor.

Q ► Aren't our national security and prosperity jeopardized by China, Japan, and other countries holding so much United States debt, not to mention growing stock in American companies?

A ► No, Americans benefit when foreign nations invest in the United States.

Why do countries like China buy U.S. Treasury bonds? As we explained earlier, it's largely because American companies buy Chinese goods with dollars. When their Chinese trading partners convert the dollars to yuan, their government ends up with pools of dollars. A natural place for them is in U.S. Treasury bonds.

Fifteen years ago, foreigners held only 14 percent of our publicly traded national debt. Today it is over 33 percent and rising. Free-trade critics commonly portray this in ominous terms. They worry that it represents a loss of U.S. economic virility and that this debt could be a weapon used against us.

However, in the Real World, foreign investments help us. How? By increasing the size of the potential market for U.S. Treasury bonds. The result is greater market liquidity and thus lower interest rates. If Americans were the only potential buyers, U.S. Treasury bonds would need higher yields to attract enough customers from this smaller market. Who pays for the higher interest the government would pay to bondholders? You, the taxpayer.

It's hard to see how a foreign nation could really use our debt as a weapon. If China dumped its $740 billion of Treasury securities, the price of Treasuries would plunge—which would mean China suffering a huge capital loss. But we would not lose our military strength. If anything, China's investment gives us the advantage. If we defaulted on our bond payments, China would experience a catastrophic setback, damaging its own economy.

Fears of foreign nations holding U.S. debt have traditionally proved groundless. Japan became a big buyer of U.S. Treasury bonds back in the eighties, and many people feared it would become stronger while America would decline. What happened? In the 1990s, Japan entered a decade-long recession because of its own domestic economic mistakes. By contrast, the United States enjoyed a long period of prosperity and an extraordinary wave of technological innovation. Companies such as Microsoft, Intel, Cisco, Apple, eBay, and Google emerged as vigorous examples of U.S. competitiveness.

What about other nations holding stakes in our companies? In recent years a number of countries in the Middle East and Asia set up so-called sovereign wealth funds (SWFs). They buy not only Treasury bonds, but also stocks and bonds of private-sector companies. The value of sovereign wealth fund holdings in the United States has been estimated at between $1.5 trillion and $2.5 trillion.

Many of these funds are investing on behalf of Middle Eastern governments—the largest sovereign wealth fund, for example, is in Abu Dhabi. Singapore and Norway also have major funds. Some feared SWFs would make investments or use their holdings for political purposes. So far these funds have been generally passive investors, and there has been little, if anything, to justify concerns. However, the key here is transparency—disclosing these funds' investment criteria and major holdings.

Congress sought to encourage this very transparency when it passed the Foreign Investment and National Security Act in 2007. The legislation provides a framework for greater scrutiny when a foreign government or entity attempts to take actual or de facto control of strategically sensitive corporations.

Such precautions are perfectly reasonable. However, SWFs mainly benefit investors. Their pools of money help lift stock prices. The banking crisis would have been infinitely worse if sovereign wealth funds hadn't poured tens of billions into beleaguered financial institutions such as Citigroup.

With the economic downturn, fears of foreign ownership have for the moment subsided; government has the opposite concern—foreigners cutting back on U.S. investment. The Bush administration's weak-dollar policy was intended to slow those cheap foreign exports. A disastrous, unintended consequence is that the cheap greenback has led investors and businesses to shift capital from the United States to Asia.

Unfortunately, the Obama administration has been no better than its predecessor at grasping the connection between foreign investment, free trade, and a strong, stable dollar. Why should investors and central banks around the world invest in U.S. assets when their value is steadily declining?

▲   REAL WORLD LESSON   ▲

Foreign investment in U.S. government bonds and corporate securities helps the economy and eases the burden on U.S. taxpayers.

Q ► WHY ARE FEARS OF TRADE DEFICITS SO MUCH BALONEY?

A ► BECAUSE TRADE DEFICITS ALONE SIGNIFY NOTHING ABOUT A COUNTRY'S ECONOMIC HEALTH AND WEALTH.

People care about America's trade deficit because they think it's a sign of weakness—like a company losing money. The financial press regularly runs stories like one from the Associated Press that announced in 2005, "Trade Deficit Hits $58.3 Billion in January." The story reported that this second-highest trade deficit in history was being caused by "Americans' appetite for foreign consumer products and automobiles."[44] The record deficit was cited as proof that trade policies of the Bush administration were not working. In the recession of 2009, the AP reported, "Trade Deficit Falls for 7th Straight Month in February," which was said to be "fresh evidence the economy's downward spiral may be easing."[45]

In fact, the story was the reverse. The smaller trade deficit was the result of anything but increased economic strength. Americans were buying fewer goods from overseas because they had less money in the recession. So what if the gap between imports and exports had narrowed? The United States was going through the worst recession in thirty years. How could that possibly be good news?

Trade deficits are meaningless. *Forbes* magazine has had a ninety-two-year trade deficit with its paper suppliers. We buy their paper so we can make money selling magazines. The company sells us paper because that's their business. They don't buy anything from us except, perhaps, a few subscriptions. What's wrong with that?

Nothing. The trade between *Forbes* and its paper vendor is only one aspect of our respective businesses. We're buying more from them than they buy from us. But the transaction is mutually beneficial: We're getting a product essential to the operation of our business. They're getting money. A "balance of trade" exists in this equal benefit.

Remember, for an exchange to take place in a free market, both partners have to benefit. Similarly, American companies buy from Chinese companies because it is mutually beneficial. Wal-Mart, for example, may import more goods than it sells in China. Nonetheless, it extracts a huge benefit. The retail giant has built a hugely profitable business based on being able to offer low-priced products to its price-conscious American customers. And the customers benefit, too, from getting more value for their money.

In other words, a trade balance may at first glance appear "lopsided" because one trading partner may realize the benefit elsewhere—in another area of a company's business, or in another sector of the economy.

Complaints about America's "trade deficit" ignore the benefit realized by the United States in the form of capital that returns to the economy—as foreign investment in either Treasury bonds or equities that help corporations expand their businesses. It also ignores American companies' exporting services and expertise overseas, such as Intel putting facilities in Malaysia that sell chips to Japan. People who decry trade deficits as an indicator that America is losing jobs often don't know that jobs are being created elsewhere.

Editor and author Sheldon Richman of the Foundation for Economic Education aptly sums up the absurdity of trade-deficit fears:

> If tomorrow Japan became the 51st state, we would no longer be aware of any trade deficit or surplus involving it and the United States. . . . Who knows what the trade picture is between Maine and New Jersey? Who cares? I don't either. If it makes sense to worry about the deficit between the United States and Japan, then maybe we should worry about the deficits among the states. But why stop there? Maybe Philadelphia has an intolerable deficit with Toledo that we're not being told about. Neighborhoods can have deficits too. Come to think of it, I have a huge deficit with the corporation that owns my favorite supermarket. I spend a couple hundred dollars a month there, but that corporation buys nothing from me. On the other hand, I rarely purchase things from the people who do buy from me. Are we wrong not to worry about these bilateral deficits? Would it make sense to strive to have all bilateral trade relations balance out? The fact is, if the balance of trade doesn't matter at the personal, neighborhood, or city level, it doesn't matter at the national level.

Free-trade bashers don't realize that America has had a trade deficit with the rest of the world for 350 of its 400 years. The only time America had a trade surplus was from World War I until the early seventies. If you looked only at trade flows, the U.S. economy could easily be mistaken for Zimbabwe writ large, and not the engine of the world's prosperity that it actually is.

When it comes to evaluating the health of an economy, you need to look at the whole picture. A focus on the trade deficit ignores an economy's ability to innovate. It overlooks flows of capital and the fact that foreign entrepreneurs and scientists and engineers still want to come to us by the hundreds of thousands each year.

▲   REAL WORLD LESSON   ▲

Because the nature of trade is to produce mutual benefit, there can be no such thing as a "trade deficit."

Q ► WHY WOULD A GOLD STANDARD BE BETTER FOR THE GLOBAL ECONOMY?

A ► BECAUSE IT WOULD PRODUCE MORE STABLE CURRENCIES AND LEAD TO MORE INVESTMENT.

Imagine how chaotic life would be if the government was always changing the number of minutes in an hour: Say you agree to work eight hours per day at twenty-five dollars an hour. Suddenly, the government decrees that an hour is seventy instead of sixty minutes. Instead of making two hundred dollars for working eight sixty-minute hours, you're working eight seventy-minute hours—eighty more minutes for the same money. Your work has been devalued by about 15 percent.

Think of the economic uncertainty this would cause. If you were a piano teacher, for example, how could you commit to giving lessons for one hundred dollars an hour each week when you could not be certain how long an hour would be—and how much you'd really be making?

Fluctuating currency produces the same kind of confusion. How do you know whether you should invest, say, in U.S. Treasury bonds, if the dollar value of your holding may soon decrease? Economist Judith Shelton has described the confusion of today's system:

> Price signals are distorted by gyrating currencies that create a "house of mirrors" atmosphere for asset valuation, leaving investors without an accurate reflection of global economic opportunity and risk. Misdirected capital flows and economic dislocations stem from distorted perceptions about the relative returns from seemingly productive investment projects.
>
> . . . You cannot build a new global financial architecture on a foundation of quicksand. Individuals who bring their goods and services to the marketplace need a meaningful unit of account and reliable store of value so they can make logical economic

decisions. Entrepreneurial endeavors should not be undercut by monetary manipulation. Government officials who insist on maintaining "flexibility" in the name of national autonomy are resorting to the last refuge of scoundrels. . . . Hardworking men and women simply want a form of money they can trust.[46]

We detailed earlier how the fluctuation of the dollar in today's system of "fiat currency" is a key cause of today's global recession. Alan Greenspan, who chaired the Fed for nearly twenty years, and his successor, Ben Bernanke, have allowed the dollar to be treated like a yo-yo. Compounding this destructive foolishness was the Bush administration's belief that a weak dollar would help improve our trade balance.

While our trade deficit shrank, George W. Bush's three Treasury chiefs all ignored the fact that volatile money damages business investment. Investing—in start-ups, existing businesses, securities, or anything else—is risky enough. Currency fluctuations are a deadly dampener on these necessary activities because they increase uncertainty, making investments even less attractive. Fear of the future decline of the dollar is one reason that China—despite the cajoling of Hillary Clinton and the Obama administration—has expressed fear of buying more Treasury bonds.

Today's global system of government-managed currency also permits political manipulation of exchange rates—the kind of "currency protectionism" we've described in this chapter.

We would not have these problems if the value of the dollar remained stable. That's why many free-market economists advocate constructing a new gold standard—setting the value of the dollar based on a fixed quantity of gold, or at least having it fall within a range of, say, $900 to $950 an ounce. Anchoring the dollar to gold would restore stability to global markets. It would sharply reduce the role of government and politics in determining currency values.

Today, for example, a country seeking to fund massive social spending will often do so by printing more money. What happens? The added money in circulation ends up lowering the value of its currency.

Gold is exceptionally well suited to anchoring currency values because its intrinsic value is constant. All the gold that has been mined is still in existence: gold cannot be destroyed. Even a major find wouldn't be large enough to dramatically alter prices. Thus, you don't get supply shocks and the kind of upheaval that, say, a drought might have on the price of wheat. In a report for the Cato Institute, University of Missouri economic historian Lawrence White writes that, while gold is not perfect, studies have shown it to be the best way to create an orderly global market.

> A gold standard does not guarantee perfect steadiness in the growth of the money supply, but historical comparison shows that it has provided more moderate and steadier money growth in practice than the present-day alternative, politically empowering a central banking committee to determine growth in the stock of fiat money.[47]

Fiat currency encourages inflation because governments can capriciously print more money. The opposite is true of gold: in the years that the United States maintained a classical gold standard—from 1880 to 1914—inflation was virtually zero.

In the old days, Washington was obligated to convert to gold the dollars that were presented to it. This became a problem in the mid-sixties and early seventies, when the Federal Reserve, attempting to lubricate economic growth, printed too many greenbacks. It became impossible to maintain the dollar's value at thirty-five dollars an ounce.

The United States abandoned the gold standard, as Lawrence White has observed, not because of any flaw in the system, but because of politics. Richard Nixon, like George W. Bush, was under pressure to do something about American's balance of payments and trade deficits.

For the gold standard to work today, Washington has to keep the value of the dollar pegged to gold at a value—as previously mentioned—of $900 to $950 per ounce. In today's modern markets, Washington doesn't need piles of gold to maintain a gold standard. Nor does the government need to promise to exchange gold at a fixed rate for dollars. All the Federal Reserve Bank has to do is look at the market price of gold: if it moves outside a certain narrow range, the monetary authorities should react by either tightening or loosening the money supply.

Today many economists ridicule the gold standard as "crazy." However, for centuries gold was the touchstone of money. From the days of Alexander Hamilton until the 1960s (except briefly in 1933–34), it was an article of faith that, barring a major war, the dollar should be fixed to gold in order to remain strong and stable.

The biggest objection to gold is that the fixed nature of the system restrains economic growth. But this thinking is based on the illusion that a central bank can create prosperity by running off more dollars. Another objection is that a major discovery could so increase the outstanding supply as to cause inflation. But experience demonstrates that even major finds such as the 1849 gold rush or the mammoth amounts of gold that Spain took out of Latin America led only to a mild increase in prices, and then not for very long. The disruptions of such discoveries are minimal compared to the damage politicians routinely wreak when a currency isn't anchored to gold.

An additional argument against gold is that it caused the Great Depression. This is also a myth. As we noted, the Great Depression was the product of bad policy—the Smoot-Hawley Tariff. Gold was a victim of the resulting global trade wars. Amidst an atmosphere of heightened economic and political uncertainty, people around the world exchanged their currencies for gold. With government supplies under pressure, nations led by Great Britain broke the link to gold. Its central role was restored at the end of World War II with the creation of the gold-based Bretton Woods international monetary system.

President Richard Nixon blew up the system in 1971 because of concern over the nation's increasing trade imbalance (remember, he and his advisers mistakenly thought an imbalance hurt the economy) and his declining poll numbers. So he succumbed to the temptation to try to "fix" the situation by devaluing the U.S. dollar. His unilateral abandonment of Bretton Woods and imposition of ninety-day wage and price controls were the "Nixon shocks." They left the United States and the world economy reeling and set the stage for the stagflation of the 1970s. Sadly, George W. Bush and his administration did not learn from this Real World lesson. And Americans in 2008 paid the price.

▲   REAL WORLD LESSON   ▲

Predictability and stability are necessary conditions for business investment in all markets. Stabilizing the dollar's value through a tie with gold is the best way to create a stable foundation in currency markets and the global economy.

Q ► Doesn't the economic crisis suggest the need for
international regulation of the global economy and
a single currency?

A ► No. Increasing "one-world" control of America's economy
makes the United States vulnerable to the political
interests of other nations.

As the 2008 financial crisis spread to nations around the globe, world
leaders like German chancellor Angela Merkel and then British
prime minister Gordon Brown called for more regulation of the global
economy. Writing in the *Washington Post*, Brown suggested expanding the
authority of the World Bank and the International Monetary Fund to
allow close scrutiny and greater control of financial institutions. At the
2009 World Economic Forum in Davos, Switzerland, Merkel called for
creation of a new international entity similar to the UN Security Council
and "a new charter for a global economic order" to make sure such a severe
worldwide financial crisis doesn't happen again.[48]

Weeks later, before the G-20 economic summit, both China and Russia
made another proposal—replacing the dollar as the world's international reserve currency with International Monetary Fund–issued Special
Drawing Rights (SDRs), a "globalized" currency under IMF control. It
would be based on the values of a group of national currencies. The selling
point was that it would not fluctuate as much as the dollar does today, providing a more stable global market for world business and investment.

Lofty-sounding proposals for world currencies and regulatory bodies
carry the weight of high authority, especially when made by heads of
state at global forums. But they're no more likely to work in the Real
World than any other bureaucratic solution that ignores markets.

If there is a Real World lesson to be learned from the present crisis,
it is that regulation, from any source, is no guarantee of protection. The
United States was once considered by the rest of the world to be a model
of regulatory best practices, particularly with the capital markets. The
Securities and Exchange Commission was a standard setter for securities
regulation. But none of these vaunted regulatory practices were able to
avert the financial crisis or Bernie Madoff's massive fraud.

There was also plenty of regulatory warning about the coming
mortgage-lending crisis in the United States. But as we've already noted,

policy makers chose not to listen. If the United States, the font of entrepreneurial capitalism, can make ghastly regulatory mistakes, why should
one assume that international bodies will do any better?

Merkel's proposal of a UN-based financial regulator—a possible UN
Economic Council—raises the question of what power such an institution would have and how it would actually function in the Real World.
Would an international body really have done a better job preventing
U.S. banks from making dodgy mortgages than American regulators,
who were on the scene and more familiar with local institutions? Are
banks now to have two sets of auditors, one from their home country and
another one from, say, Brussels?

Since 1988, the world banking system has had guidelines through
the Basel Accords. The chancellor's desire for an entity resembling the
UN Security Council was especially ironic, since the real-life UN body is
notorious for getting very little done, and then only after painful, time-
consuming, and generally useless compromises.

This is not to say global organizations and agreements can't be effective. Since World War II, the nations of the world have signed on to a
succession of major agreements that, by reducing tariffs and regulatory
barriers, facilitated an explosion in growth-producing world trade.

Two big successes have been the General Agreement on Tariffs and
Trade (GATT) and the subsequent World Trade Organization (WTO). Countries that have joined the WTO adhere to these trade agreements and
obey its rulings concerning trade disputes. The World Trade Organization
works because, beneath the political maneuvering, countries know that
reducing trade barriers and adhering to trade agreements and rulings
is good for them and for peaceful global commerce.

Putting aside the fact that the regulatory ideas bandied about by the
Merkels of the world are overwhelmingly vague, the truth is that existing
international organizations do not have an untarnished track record. The
World Bank, for example, has repeatedly been accused of corruption—
lending untold billions to governments whose politicians have looted
the treasuries of their own countries.

Do we really want to place our economic destiny in the hands of international bodies subject to the politics of other nations? Policy analyst
Brett Schaefer of the Heritage Foundation believes "any international
effort should be consultative and advisory, engaged in such matters as

the development of best practices standards, rather than bent on establishing new international regulatory authorities possessed of dictatorial or coercive powers over such matters."[49]

And what about the idea of a one-world currency? Ambassador Terry Miller, director of the Center for International Trade and Economics at the Heritage Foundation, rightly argues that it doesn't solve anything—and may even make matters worse.[50] For one thing, an IMF reserve currency has no intrinsic value. It has even less meaning to people in the world's marketplace than today's fiat dollar. World currency controlled by the International Monetary Fund would be vulnerable to even more political caprice than today's fluctuating greenback. The supply and value of money would be subject to the political desires of nations around the world whose interests might not always be in line with our own.

There would be new opportunities for corruption. IMF procedures for setting the value of money and interest rates would be less transparent than those of the U.S. Federal Reserve Bank. They would involve other countries whose representatives have different political agendas and are not as accountable to an open grilling by America's democratic government.

The best way to foster a healthy global economy is not through new global regulations or a single world currency, but through currencies that remain steady in value. Strong, stable currencies create a predictable environment that invites entrepreneurship and investment. Updating the gold-based Bretton Woods international monetary system, which served the world well from the end of World War II until the early 1970s, would go a long way toward ending economic volatility and restoring the stability sought by advocates of "one-world" economic solutions.

▲   REAL WORLD LESSON   ▲

A new Bretton Woods–style monetary system based on a gold standard and stable currency is a better way to reduce global economic volatility than politicized, "one-world" solutions.

CHAPTER SEVEN

"Is Affordable Health Care Possible in a Free Market?"

THE RAP ► Today's out-of-control health-care costs are the consequence of increasingly sophisticated medical technology and growing patient demand, compounded by greed throughout the system. Insurance and pharmaceutical companies, doctors, and hospitals all care more about profits than about patients. The only way to fix these complex problems is through a government-designed system with mandatory health insurance. Otherwise, health care will become totally unaffordable and beyond the reach of the poor and the middle class.

THE REALITY ► Today's health-care system is a case study of what happens when government dominance prevents the market from working. Federal policies have locked in a system of "third-party pay." The result is that you, the individual consumer, rarely directly pay for your medical care or insurance. Employers and insurers are the ones making the buying decisions. The market is therefore about meeting the needs of big companies and not those of the individual. Policy reforms allowing consumers to take charge of health-care buying decisions would correct this market distortion. Health-care and insurance providers seeking your business would lower prices, provide better service, and become more accountable.

American health care is the best in the world. Thanks to high-quality medicines and technologies, Americans have higher survival rates for illnesses ranging from cancer to heart disease. America leads the world in new drug development. We have greater access to care and advanced medical technology than patients in other advanced nations. The quality of U.S. health care draws people from countries with state-run health-care systems, who come seeking the best care medicine has to offer.

Some people who buy into the Rap on capitalism believe America's expensive advanced drugs and technology are a major reason that a "free market" simply can't work in health care. It's simply too expensive. They blame capitalism—namely, "greed" on the part of insurance and drug companies—for what they call "the health-care crisis" of upwardly spiraling medical and insurance costs. They're wrong. The problem in today's health-care market is not too much capitalism, but too little.

Our system has very real problems. Between 2004 and 2008, the cost of health-insurance premiums has skyrocketed by some 27 percent. Since 1999, it has increased a startling 119 percent. The average annual cost for an individual plan is rapidly approaching five thousand dollars, while the cost of a family policy is nearly thirteen thousand dollars. These staggering premiums are blamed for the existence of an estimated forty-six million uninsured Americans.

Not only the uninsured feel abused by the system. In 2008 the nation was riveted by the story of seventeen-year-old leukemia patient Nataline Sarkisyan, whose request for a liver transplant was denied by her insurer, CIGNA Health Care, on grounds that the procedure was too experimental. After headline-making demonstrations and calls from politicians, CIGNA eventually agreed to pay for the operation. Tragically, Sarkisyan died before it could take place.

More common is the story of fifty-four-year-old Tod Smith. The Connecticut children's book illustrator was denied coverage for forty thousand dollars in medical bills after his first heart attack. Smith was forced to sue his insurer, Assurant Health, after it claimed that his "angina episode" was a preexisting condition. Other people, meanwhile, are often stunned to discover their insurance doesn't fully cover expensive prescription drugs, which can reach six figures a year for the most costly medications.

Meanwhile, the quality of medical care seems to grow increasingly cold and impersonal. The house calls and personalized care of the 1950s and '60s are a distant memory. Patients endure hurried treatment by physicians and hospitals under cost pressure by insurers—or unnecessary testing by health-care professionals practicing "defensive medicine" out of fear of malpractice suits.

The combined pressures of low insurance reimbursement and increasing malpractice litigation are creating an unsustainable burden on physicians. Typical is Dr. Matthew Allaway, a urologist in rural Maryland who, according to the *Baltimore Sun*, starts at 7:00 a.m. and often sees as many as sixty patients a day in order to make ends meet. His office is often packed, with waits of up to ninety minutes. The reason: many colleagues have left the profession.

Little wonder so many people believe the system is a chaotic mess. Capitalism bashers are convinced that a Canadian- or European-style, government-run system is the only way to fix these problems.

They should think again. Many people blame today's health-care troubles on "greed" on the part of drug and insurance companies, and even some doctors. However, they miss a critical Real World truth: America's health-care system is anything but a "free market." It is the nation's most heavily regulated economic sector.

What people today call the "health-care crisis" is actually a massive economic imbalance created by bad government policy.

Today's health care can definitely be expensive and uncaring. That's because, as we pointed out, the patient really isn't the customer. The real customers are corporations: the *employers* that buy coverage from insurance companies—and the *insurers* that reimburse doctors and hospitals.

Remember, in a marketplace, people and companies seek to satisfy the needs and wants of their customers. Today's health-care system is about satisfying the needs of employers and insurers that are the primary customers—not your needs. In Milton Friedman's words, "The [physician] has become, in effect, an employee of the insurance company or, in the case of Medicare and Medicaid, of the government."[1]

Third-party payment has also driven up costs by artificially boosting the use of health-care services. The late Milton Friedman once put it very simply: "The patient—the recipient of the medical care—has little or no incentive to be concerned about the cost since it's somebody else's money."[2] Insurance may be expensive. But for people who have it, doctor's visits can seem "free." Patients end up making more visits to the doctor's office. Everyone knows what happens in the Real World when demand for anything goes up. Prices do, too. Health care is no different.

Third-party payment of health insurance was not the free market's response to patient need. Some may be surprised to learn that the system really owes its existence to an entirely unrelated government policy—the wage and price controls of World War II. They were enacted by FDR to control wartime inflation resulting from the government's printing so much money to pay for the war effort.

Companies needed to pay their employees more than government wage controls would allow. They couldn't do it with cash. So they did it through fringe benefits, principally health care.

The distorting effects of third-party pay were amplified many times over when government got into the health-insurance business in the 1960s, launching its two monster programs—Medicare insurance, its mandatory program for seniors, and Medicaid for low-income people. Medicaid has since been expanded with the State Children's Health Insurance Program (SCHIP), which began in 1997.

Both third-party payment systems, Medicare and Medicaid, increased the demand for health care even further. But unlike private insurers, government was less willing to pay for it.

Medicare and Medicaid only partially reimbursed doctors and hospitals. You couldn't really blame them. After all, they were paying with taxpayer money and had to control their own costs. Doctors and hospitals, squeezed by Medicaid and Medicare, started charging privately insured patients more. Private insurers today subsidize Medicare and Medicaid in excess of $90 billion a year.

Little wonder the cost of private insurance spiraled out of control after Medicare and Medicaid were established. Employers responded by offering plans that relied on cost-conscious health-maintenance organizations with networks of physicians who agreed to deliver care according to stringent guidelines set by insurers. The growth of Medicare and Medicaid since the 1960s thus led to the rise of bureaucratic managed care.

One more problem snarling this convoluted market that we explore later in this chapter is the tangle of state regulations that rigidly dictate what kind of health insurance you are allowed to buy in each state. What if government forced you to buy twice the number of groceries you needed when you went to the supermarket? Your bills would be enormous. That's essentially the effect that mandates have on the cost of insurance.

The bottom line in the Real World is that today's health-care economy is not only overregulated but essentially governed by price controls—those low reimbursement rates imposed not only by government but also private insurers. We've already talked about the consequences of price controls and command-and-control regulation in places like the old Soviet Union, and in Soviet-style countries like Cuba and Venezuela. You get declining quality, shortages, and rationing.

That's what's happened with health-care delivery in countries like Canada, Britain, and the nations of Europe—and it is happening today, in varying degrees, throughout our system. The worst example is Medicaid, where the quality of care is demonstrably lower. Many doctors won't treat Medicaid patients because of low reimbursement rates.

The answer to health care is to bring back the consumer and restore a normal market where individuals, and not corporations, make the buying decisions.

We see this starting to take place with the few consumer-driven solutions—like health savings accounts—that have managed to spring up despite the system and that are beginning to make health care more patient friendly and affordable.

The Real World bottom line: government-run economies result in monopoly and rigidities that work against innovation and productivity. Think post office, public education, Amtrak. Do you really want government bureaucrats in charge of your medical care?

Q ► What's so bad about a government health-care system?

A ► State-run health care is rationed. It's "free," but you often can't get it—or you have to wait too long.

In 2009, the actress Natasha Richardson, skiing in a resort in Quebec, Canada, hit her head and eventually died from massive brain injury. Days later, many speculated whether she might have been saved if a medical helicopter like those common in the United States had been able to transport her to a trauma center. There are no medical helicopters in the province of Quebec.

Fortunately, most of us won't ever need a medical helicopter. But we will need to see a doctor. And in countries with state-run health-care systems, needing to see a doctor, even for life-threatening conditions, can mean waiting months—or longer.

As one Canadian citizen, Esther Pacione of Ontario, told the *New York Times*, getting even basic care in Canada means being put on a waiting list. "If you are not bleeding all over the place, you are put on the back burner," Ms. Pacione said, "unless of course you have money or know somebody."[3]

That's because care in these systems is rationed. In Canada, rationing forced a Quebec man to wait a year for a hip replacement. He took his case to the Canadian Supreme Court, which ruled in 2005 that "access to a waiting list is not access to health care." The court struck down Quebec's law banning private health insurance.

It's not coincidental that two of the leading opponents of government-run care, Dr. David Gratzer and Sally Pipes of the Pacific Research Institute, are both Canadians. Gratzer decided to write a book, *The Cure: How Capitalism Can Save American Health Care*, after experiencing a harrowing epiphany as a med student walking into a Canadian emergency room.

> Swinging open the door, I stepped into a nightmare: the ER overflowed with elderly people on stretchers, waiting for admission. Some, it turned out, had waited *five days*. The air stank with sweat and urine. Right then, I began to reconsider everything that I thought I knew about Canadian health care. I soon discovered that the problems went well beyond overcrowded ERs. Patients had to wait for practically any diagnostic test or procedure, such as the man with persistent pain from a hernia operation whom we referred to a pain clinic—with a three-year wait list; or the woman needing a sleep study to diagnose what seemed like sleep apnea, who faced a two-year delay; or the woman with breast cancer who needed to wait four months for radiation therapy, when the standard of care was four weeks.[4]

And that's just in Canada. In a 2007 article for *City Journal*, Gratzer noted that more than one million Britons must wait for some type of care, with two hundred thousand in line for longer than six months. In Britain's state-run system, hospitals have been known to manage demand by imposing *minimum* waiting times of approximately six months.

The *London Daily Telegraph* reports that hospitals are penalized for "treating too many patients too quickly."[5] The paper reports: "One gynæcologist said that he spent more time doing sudoku puzzles than treating patients because of the measures."[6]

Things aren't any better in Sweden, where the wait for heart surgery can be as long as twenty-five weeks, and more than a year for hip replacements. According to Swedish policy analyst Johnny Munkhammar, some Swedes get so desperate they end up visiting veterinarians. Why? Because "veterinarians are private and there are many."[7]

Not only do patients in state-run systems have to wait for care, they have less access to advanced medical technology. CAT scans, for example, are three times more available in the United States than in Canada.

Yes, drugs may be cheaper in countries like Canada. But that's because their state systems keep the prices artificially low. (As we've noted, we pay for this in U.S. drug prices.) But people often don't get the drugs that can cure them—because they're banned by state health-care bureaucracies.

Sally Pipes has her own story about Canadian health care.

> [M]y uncle was diagnosed with non-Hodgkin's lymphoma. If he'd lived in America, the miracle drug Rituxan might have saved him. But Rituxan wasn't approved for use in Canada, and he lost his battle with cancer. A couple of years ago, I received an email from a woman in Ontario who had heard my uncle's story. Her reason for writing?
>
>   She wanted to let me know that Rituxan still wasn't available—so she was about to embark on a trip to Michigan for the drug. That's the grim reality of price controls—they lead to rationing. Similar tragedies have played out over and over again in Britain, France, Italy, and virtually every other country that imposes price controls on drugs.[8]

Labor shortages are a chronic feature of state-run health care in Canada, Britain, and France. A shortage of physicians and inadequate hospital capacity were said to be key factors behind the deaths of some fifteen thousand elderly citizens from a disastrous heat wave that struck France in August of 2003. Health-care policy analyst Linda Gorman wrote in 2008 that doctor shortages have been recently reported even in nations such as Germany and Switzerland, whose systems are considered successful by supporters of state-run medical care.

Why is rationing an inevitable consequence of state-run care? Because, as we've noted, state-run health care is a command-and-control system. In a market economy, consumer need drives what the market provides. But in a state system, politics determines what is produced—and who gets it. Practices and prices are rigidly imposed on the market—not developed spontaneously by people who are seeking to serve others' needs.

This is true whether the system is entirely state-run, like the British National Health Service, or state-financed, like Canada's single-payer system, where government pays for care provided by private entities.

The Golden Rule—"He who has the gold makes the rules"—applies to health care as it does to the rest of the Real World.

For health-care consumers, that means medical treatment is delivered based not on what you, the patient, need or want—but on what someone else thinks you should have. *Healthcare News* reported in 2007 that some British hospitals actually banned smokers and the obese from receiving treatments such as orthopedic surgery. Many people believe smokers and obese people have helped to put their own health at risk. That may be so. But should they actually be denied medical care?

We noted in the introduction to this chapter that the problem with American health care lies in the rigidities imposed on the marketplace by layers of government regulation and bureaucracy. Far from fixing the problems of American health care, a state-run system, with price controls, rules, and rationing, would multiply them many times over.

▲   REAL WORLD LESSON   ▲

By imposing price controls and bureaucratic constraints on the medical economy, state-run health care results in declining efficiency and quality throughout the system, as well as the rationing of medical care.

Q ► WHY IS A PRIVATE-SECTOR HEALTH-CARE SYSTEM CRITICAL TO QUALITY MEDICAL CARE?

A ► BECAUSE ONLY THE PRIVATE SECTOR CAN FULLY DEVELOP INNOVATIONS AND BRING THEM TO THE GREATEST NUMBER OF PEOPLE.

We noted before and need to emphasize again: U.S. health care is not a free market. It is government dominated and managed. But there is still a private sector. That is why U.S. health care, while expensive, is the most advanced in the world. Americans have higher rates of survival for a myriad of diseases. The highly respected British journal *The Lancet* found in 2008 that Americans have far higher survival rates for thirteen out of sixteen of the most common cancers—the reason that thousands of people come to the United States each year seeking medical treatment. But this lead in technology and quality will recede and ultimately vanish the more government control over health care expands.

This may sound like a political statement. But it is the Real World economics of command-and-control economies. As we have explained, the more government controls a market, the less innovative and quality-conscious people and companies become.

Why? Because state control means that government policies drive prices. Companies and people are prevented from generating the capital to invest in keeping up existing operations and also in developing new technologies. Government imposes rigid "protocols" that micromanage market activity. People are prevented from spontaneously developing new ways to respond to demand and meet patient needs.

This happens not only in health care, but in any market. Remember our example of the Trabant. A product of East German central planning, the smoke-belching sedan was considered advanced when it debuted in the late 1950s. Then it was manufactured unchanged for three decades. The Trabant was so shoddy that it was thought to be made of cardboard; attempts to sell it in Western markets failed miserably.

The Trabant may have started out as a decent car. But without any competition in East Germany's government-run market, there was no reason to keep improving it. The rest of the world pulled ahead in the auto technology race. In much the same way, the health-care systems of Canada and Europe stagnated after they fell under government control. Rigid government directives, minimal competition, tight funding constraints, and politically driven, punitive taxation kept doctors and hospitals from trying new ways to improve the delivery of health care.

David Asman, anchor of *Forbes on Fox*, experienced Trabant-style socialized medicine several years ago when his wife had a stroke in London. In the *Wall Street Journal*, Asman wrote that while he appreciated the caring staffers at the British Health Service, it quickly became apparent that their level of skill was far below U.S. standards. Even after administering an MRI, doctors at University College of London Hospital weren't certain of his wife's diagnosis. After much string pulling, he managed to get her admitted to Queen's Square Hospital for Neurology, considered the best neurological treatment center in England. Nonetheless, Asman reports,

> The conditions of the hospital were rather shockingly apparent. . . . [T]he smells wafting through the ward were often overwhelming.[9] . . . Compared with virtually any hospital ward in the U.S., Queen's Square would fall short by a mile. The equipment wasn't ancient, but it was often quite old. On occasion my wife and I would giggle at heart and blood-pressure monitors that were literally taped together and would come apart as they were being moved into place. The nurses and hospital technicians had become expert at jerry-rigging temporary fixes for a lot of the damaged equipment. I pitched in as best as I could with simple things, like fixing the wiring for the one TV in the ward. And I'd make frequent trips to the local pharmacies to buy extra tissues and cleaning wipes, which were always in short supply.
>
> In fact, cleaning was my main occupation for the month we were at Queen's Square. Infections in hospitals are, of course, a problem everywhere. But in Britain, hospital-borne infections are getting out of control. At least 100,000 British patients a year are hit by hospital-acquired infections, including the penicillin-resistant "superbug" MRSA. A new study carried out by the British Health Protection Agency says that MRSA plays a part in the deaths of up to 32,000 patients every year. But even at lower numbers, Britain has the worst MRSA infection rates in Europe. It's not hard to see why.[10]

After his wife got out of Queen's Square, she was briefly treated in one of the city's few remaining private hospitals. The contrast, Asman writes, was dramatic.

> Checking into the private hospital was like going from a rickety Third World hovel into a five-star hotel. There was clean carpeting, more than enough help, a private room (and a private bath!)

in which to recover from the procedure, even a choice of wines offered with a wide variety of entrees. As we were feasting on our fancy new digs, Dr. Cullen came by, took my wife's hand, and quietly told us in detail about the procedure. He actually paused to ask us whether we understood him completely and had any questions. Only one, we both thought to ask: Is this a dream?[11]

Upon returning to the United States, Asman writes that the contrast with even Britain's best hospitals was stark:

The cleanliness of U.S. hospitals is immediately apparent to all the senses. . . . Cornell and New York University hospitals (both of which my wife has been using since we returned) have ready access to technical equipment that is either hard to find or non-existent in Britain. This includes both diagnostic equipment and state-of-the-art equipment used for physical therapy.[12]

The innovation and quality gap between America's private-sector health care and European state-run systems is apparent in nearly every sector of health care. Europe once led the United States in drug development. But that is no longer the case, as Valentin Petkantchin, research director for the Brussels- and Paris-based Institut économique Molinari, writes.

During the last 20 years, the number of [drugs] launched by European drug firms has been reduced by half, going from an average of 97 [drugs] between 1988 and 1992 to 48 between 2003 and 2007.
     As a result, the center of drug innovation has shifted to the United States, where the drug market is generally less restricted than in Europe.[13]

Why did Europe lose its lead? Price controls and taxes intended to punish "greedy" drug companies choked off the profits that would have generated capital for new drug research. In biotech alone, U.S. private-sector investment between 1989 and 2002 was four times greater than that of Europe.

The fact that our health-care economy continues to permit some free enterprise is the reason that Americans benefit more from new technologies—even when they have been invented elsewhere. The CT scanner, which provides advanced, computer-enhanced X-ray imaging, was invented in the 1970s in Britain, the land of socialized medicine. But today Great Britain has half the number of CT scanners per patient than the United States has.

A study by the Organisation for Economic Co-operation and Development (OECD) in June 2007 found that the United States leads nearly every other nation except Japan in the availability not only of CT scanners but also of magnetic resonance imaging (MRI) machines.

According to the Cato Institute's Michael Tanner, far more Americans— 44 percent—have access to cholesterol-reducing statins, drugs that protect against heart disease, than patients in Germany, where only 26 percent can get these drugs, or Great Britain, where 23 percent can get them, or Italy, where just 17 percent can.

It is important to emphasize that America's health-care achievements come from the private-sector portion of its health-care economy. Creativity lags where there is more government involvement—for example, in Medicare and Medicaid. But where the market is least constrained, exciting innovations in health-care delivery are springing up.

According to John Goodman, founder of the National Center for Policy Analysis, these innovations include walk-in clinics in shopping malls that are providing fast, inexpensive service treating colds and providing immunizations and other routine care. No insurance is needed. Other entrepreneurial solutions include telephone consultation services, such as TeleDoc, which provide hard to get telephone consultations with a doctor, and mass marketing drugs through big chains like Wal-Mart, which has helped bring down the prices of many drugs.

Prices have come down, and service has improved in medical specialties not covered by insurance—such as cosmetic and LASIK eye surgery. That's because doctors work harder to please patients who are directly paying for their services. Not only that, Goodman says that prices in these specialties have fallen "despite a huge increase in volume and considerable technical innovation (which is blamed for increasing costs for every other type of surgery)."[14]

Innovation is flowering in less-regulated nations such as India, where an increasing number of Americans are seeking low-cost care. John Goodman says that these hospitals, which specialize in serving "medical tourists," provide "high-quality care in facilities (and by physicians) that meet American standards" at one-fifth to one-third the cost in the United States. In addition, they offer customer-friendly conveniences including "package prices that cover all treatment costs, including physician and hospital fees, and sometimes airfare and lodging as well; [and] electronic medical records."[15]

Why are such innovations produced mainly by free markets? Because government simply does not have the bandwidth of a marketplace where thousands of individuals and companies are testing myriad ideas until they come up with the best solution. Galen Institute president Grace-Marie Turner writes,

> No one in Washington, no matter how brilliant he or she may be, can possibly be smart enough to devise a centrally-controlled system that can meet the health care needs of 300 million Americans. Only the genius of a dynamic market can respond to the demands of consumers for better quality at more affordable prices.[16]

▲   REAL WORLD LESSON   ▲

In health care as in all markets, the free market is a better innovator than government because ideas are developed by many more people.

Q ► Don't we need government intervention because the health-care market is tipped against consumers, who aren't always in a position to choose when they need medical care?

A ► No. Health-care costs are high not because health care is "different," but because individual patients most often are not the ones making the buying decisions.

Illness isn't voluntary. For that reason, some argue that health care is not like other markets. You can't always choose when and how you will use medical care the way you can choose to take an airplane flight. You can't bargain for the best price, obviously, when you are being rushed to the hospital.

People who buy into the Rap on capitalism say the fact that health care is "different" is one reason why costs are so high and government involvement is needed. The balance is tipped unfairly against consumers. This is especially true, they say, when it comes to older and lower-income people, who need health care the most but who may be least able to make the right decisions about their care and coverage.

Yes, people may be incapacitated when they need care. There are unique conditions in every market. But the same Real World economic principles still apply: the best way to deliver the greatest level of benefit— i.e., quality services for the lowest cost to the most people—is through a market that allows people the broadest latitude to figure out ways to meet one another's needs, where both consumers and producers have the greatest number of options and free choice.

Such conditions do not exist for virtually anyone in today's state-dominated health-care system. The choices not only of consumers, but of doctors, hospitals, and insurers are dramatically restricted. Patients have to buy expensive insurance plans that limit how and where they see a doctor. Doctors and hospitals are locked in to making their money from third-party payments from both private and government insurers whose reimbursements function like de facto price controls and govern practice decisions.

This rigid system keeps them from coming up with better pricing solutions and new ways of delivering patient-friendly care. That's not just because hospitals and physicians have to answer to insurance companies—but because price controls prevent them from getting the information they need to respond efficiently to the market. Have you ever wondered why it can be so difficult to find out the cost of an individual hospital procedure? Or why, when you finally do get a price, it seems to be beyond all reason? It's not just because of Medicare-driven cost-shifting. It's because hospitals really don't know what it costs to serve an individual patient—because the individual patient is not their real customer. Thus, they don't keep track of the kind of information about consumer demand in the way that, say, Starbucks or Walgreens does.

But third-party pay and cost shifting are only part of the story. State governments have added yet another layer of distortion by locking in nonessential coverage with their own regulations. Known as "mandates," these regulations dictate the services your medical insurance must cover, whether you really want them or not.

Mandates vary from state to state. For example, about one-quarter of states today require that your health insurance cover acupuncture and marriage counseling. No matter if you're single—or if you view acupuncture as more mysticism than medicine. If you're in a state with this mandate, you still pay for this coverage. Insurance companies have to price their coverage on the assumption that you *might* avail yourself of these services—even if you never do.

Imagine if the government forced you to buy food you didn't want when you shopped for groceries. Your bills would be enormous. That's what's happening in health insurance. Because of mandates, the cost of insurance in heavily regulated New Jersey is seven times higher than the same coverage in innovation-friendly Tennessee. The Center for Freedom and Prosperity, a free-market think tank, calculates that mandates in heavily regulated states can boost premiums by more than 65 percent.

A last comparison: In 2007 the average annual family premium in Massachusetts—which has a heavily regulated state health-care system that served as a model for the plan proposed by the Obama administration—cost close to $17,000. In New York it cost more than $12,200. In lightly regulated Wisconsin, the average family premium is only about $3,000.

Heavy state regulation of insurance also means that coverage cannot be sold across state lines. The result: smaller insurance risk pools. The funds available to cover you are not based on your insurer's clients across the country. Risk pools are based on the size of your company's workforce or your insurer's clients within your state. The limited size of risk pools is one reason some patients with expensive conditions may get dropped by their insurers—their particular risk pool isn't large enough.

Keeping sales of insurance confined to individual state markets also means that there is less competition among insurance companies—and higher premium prices.

All of this would change if you, the patient, were directly buying your insurance and health care. We discuss on page 285 how consumer-driven reforms, such as making health savings accounts widely available and legalizing the selling of insurance across state lines, would restore sanity to the pricing of both medical care and insurance. Without the distortion of third-party payment, health care would not be so "different" and would begin to offer the variety and choice of other markets.

▲   REAL WORLD LESSON   ▲

Buying health care may not be the same as buying an automobile. But that's because government and private insurers—and not you, the consumer—buy most health care.

Q ► CONGRESS'S 2010 HEALTH-CARE LEGISLATION IS NEITHER A CANADIAN-STYLE SINGLE-PAYER SYSTEM NOR A BRITISH-STYLE NATIONAL HEALTH SERVICE. IT ALLOWS PRIVATE INSURANCE. SO WHY CAN'T IT WORK?

A ► BECAUSE IT ENORMOUSLY INCREASES GOVERNMENT BUREAUCRACY AND REGULATION, AND OBLITERATES THE VERY FORCES THAT COULD CREATE MORE AFFORDABLE AND HIGHER QUALITY HEALTH CARE— COMPETITION AND THE FREEDOM TO INNOVATE.

In the spring of 2010, after years of fierce political debate, Congress passed the Patient Protection and Affordable Care Act (PPACA). More than 2,500 pages and 500,000 words long, the new law is intended to make health care more abundant and affordable to millions of Americans. In fact it will do exactly the opposite, drastically changing almost every facet of American health care for the worse.

We've already started seeing these damaging consequences barely months after the law passed, in the form of higher insurance premiums.

But that's just the beginning. Physician Lloyd M. Krieger wrote in the *Wall Street Journal* in 2011 that the legislation, with its cutbacks in Medicare and Medicaid funding, has already resulted in "a wave of frantic consolidation" in the health-care industry. "Six years ago, doctors owned more than two-thirds of U.S. medical practices. . . . By next year, nearly two-thirds will be salaried employees of larger institutions." This consolidation, Krieger says, means "collectivization." He explains, "Government bureaucrats will be able to impose controls with much greater ease." The result: You, the patient, will get less care.

> Choices will be limited. Pathways to expensive specialist care such as advanced radiology and surgery will decline. Cutting-edge devices and medicines will come into the system much more slowly and be used much less frequently.[17]

Things only get worse from there. You're probably familiar with most of the bill's damaging features. For the record they include:

► **Individual and Employer Mandates.** The lynchpin of the bill is the requirement that every American obtain health-insurance coverage meeting government criteria. Starting in 2014, individuals must buy and companies must provide health insurance. If they don't, they pay a significant tax penalty to be collected with the help of some 16,500 new IRS agents.

The penalty is especially draconian for employers: Those with fifty or more employees will have to pay a $2,000 penalty per *each* full-time employee after the first thirty employees if at least one of those employees receives a tax credit. In a comprehensive report for the Cato Institute detailing the flaws of the new bill, noted health-care expert Michael Tanner estimates that as many as one third of employers will pay thousands of dollars in penalties under the law.[18] Certain employers, especially larger companies, will find it cheaper to pay the penalties and let workers fend for themselves on insurance exchanges. Aside from being an egregious violation of liberty—one that is currently under attack in the courts—this exceedingly harsh law, Tanner and others believe, will ultimately fail to produce the universal coverage its advocates want.

For one thing, the penalty is not enough to change the behavior of young, healthy people who tend to live in the here-and-now and often forgo insurance. That has been the experience in Massachusetts, which in 2006 adopted a mandatory coverage plan that's basically a smaller-scale version of the system just imposed by Congress. More than a third of those who remain uninsured in Massachusetts are younger people.[19]

Meanwhile, individuals and businesses, as well as the broader society, will pay a personal and financial price that will far outweigh the benefits of the bill.

Employers are already preparing to offset the law's enormous costs either by raising prices or by lowering wages, laying off workers or outsourcing. And each and every American will have to foot the bill for insuring 32 million more people. This burden, on government and the taxpayers, is simply horrific. Yet that has mattered little to the bill's zealous supporters, who have shamelessly used accounting methods to manipulate government budget projections. The *Wall Street Journal* pointed out in January 2011:

The accounting gimmicks are legion, but we'll pick out a few: It uses 10 years of taxes to fund six years of subsidies.

Social Security and Medicare revenues are double-counted to the tune of $398 billion. A new program funding long-term care frontloads taxes but backloads spending, gradually going broke by design. The law pretends that Congress will spend less on Medicare than it really will, in particular through an automatic 25% cut to physician payments that Democrats have already voted not to allow for this year.[20]

► **Insurance Regulations.** The new law dynamites the very concept of insurance, which is supposed to be bought ahead of time to cover big future expenses. It imposes on the market the idealistic but totally unworkable idea of *guaranteed issue*, whereby health insurers must, with minor limitations, accept all customers, regardless of their age or physical condition.

It also makes them charge people the same premium, regardless of age (again, with minor limitations) or health status. This is known as "community rating."

Under guaranteed issue and community rating, the young end up subsidizing the elderly. And people game the system. In Massachusetts, which has both guaranteed issue and community rating, increasing numbers of people are waiting until they become ill to buy insurance—dropping their plans when they no longer need or care to pay for them.

We discuss elsewhere in this chapter how states that have instituted guaranteed issue and community rating regulations have seen insurance companies leave the market and premiums skyrocket. A family policy in New Jersey, for example, costs about twice as much as a virtually identical one in neighboring Pennsylvania, and almost three times as much as one in Wisconsin. Before the passage of ObamaCare, Kentucky, New Hampshire, and Washington had partially or fully repealed these types of regulations because they more or less destroyed state insurance markets—making coverage dramatically more expensive and less available.

That's just the beginning. Michael Tanner points out that deductibles will be limited to no more than $2,000 for employer plans and $4,000 for family policies—unless you're under thirty.[21] But many people like high-deductible insurance, since it's a way of lowering premiums. Buyers should make their own decisions, not Washington bureaucrats.

The law also sets what is called the "medical loss ratio." This requires that insurance providers spend 80 to 85 percent of premium income on actual health-care benefits. The idea is to restrict insurance company spending on executive pay, advertising, and other administrative expenses—costs that are essential to running any business but that Congress, in its infinite bureaucratic wisdom, has deemed "wasteful."

But these rules make it harder for employers to offer lower-cost, limited-benefit plans with higher deductibles—the kind that allows them to insure large numbers of part-time transient workers. Many lower-wage earners will either be forced to buy more expensive insurance or else end up in Medicaid.

In 2010, McDonald's threatened it would have to drop the insurance it offers 30,000 of its restaurant workers because the plan violated the 80–85 rule. McDonald's eventually obtained a government waiver that allowed the company to keep providing its insurance.

Since then, the list of waiver recipients has been growing. As of January 2011, more than 222 organizations had gotten such exemptions. No surprise, many are labor unions. Congress's health-insurance regulations were supposed to bring "fairness." But, as inevitably happens in a centrally managed economy, favoritism and politics have ended up driving the system. Columnist Richard Epstein writes on Forbes.com:

> At least one million workers are now out from under Obama-Care, with more to come. The process vividly shows how unrealistic expectations can undermine the rule of law. Waivers are by definition an exercise of administrative discretion that benefits the party who receives its special dispensation. Yet nothing in ObamaCare explains who should receive these waivers or why.

▶ **Subsidies.** Along with forcing people to buy insurance through individual and employer mandates, the new law aims to achieve "universal coverage" by subsidizing the purchase of private health insurance and increasing eligibility for programs like Medicaid and the State Children's Health Insurance Program (SCHIP).

Michael Tanner writes that when Tennessee took a similar step, attempting to achieve universal coverage by expanding its Medicaid eligibility in the 1990s, the state's Medicaid costs increased by some 149 percent—twice as fast as in other states. "Despite this massive increase in spending, health outcomes did not improve. Even the state's Democratic governor Phil Bredesen called the program 'a disaster.'"[22]

Government subsidies and expanded Medicaid and SCHIP eligibility are also, in Tanner's words, "a 'poverty trap' for low-wage workers." Why bother to work harder to earn more if you're only going to lose your government benefits?

Tanner concludes, "All together, this law represents a massive increase in the welfare state, adding millions of Americans to the roll of those dependent, at least to some extent, on government largess."

▶ **Exchanges.** According to the law, one or more insurance exchanges would be set up by each state starting in 2014. The exchanges are supposed to function as a clearinghouse, matching customers with insurance providers and products that meet government standards.

The exchanges are supposed to lower insurance premiums, because people who buy from them become part of a single large risk pool. However Tanner reminds us this didn't happen in Massachusetts, which pioneered a similar "connector" program. Premiums only went up.[23]

If lawmakers had *really* been serious about the goal of providing more affordable health care and insurance, they would have taken steps to open up the market to competition by, for example, allowing people to buy insurance across state lines. This would create more lucrative national markets. Companies would rush in to serve customers, as they always do. Insurance prices would drop and service would improve.

It says something about this legislation that it penalizes people for having *too much* coverage: The law imposes a tax on so-called "Cadillac" insurance plans, the high-benefit plans offered by large employers. *Say that again:* Lawmakers want you to have insurance. Yet they're penalizing people who buy too much. Sounds an awful lot like rationing (more on that later).

The rules of ObamaCare also make it difficult for private insurers to keep offering Medicare Advantage, the alternative program now used by 22 percent of Medicare beneficiaries. Administration bureaucrats don't like that program because it's provided by private companies that receive government subsidies.

In addition to devastating the insurance market, the new legislation places a monstrous burden on the larger economy in the form of punishing taxes—more than $669 billion in new or increased taxes over the first ten years. These levies include: payroll tax hikes, high taxes on investment income, limits on itemized deductions, and taxes on medical devices and brand name prescription drugs. There's even a tax on tanning salons.

And, yes, there's more. As of 2012, the law required that all businesses, including the smallest coffee shop, file 1099 forms for any purchase over $600. Why? So that the newly expanded IRS will be able to recoup more tax dollars to pay for the government's enormous new health-care bureaucracy. This would lead to an avalanche of paperwork and accounting costs that would destroy many already-struggling small businesses. Little wonder that nearly everyone, including President Obama, agreed that this ridiculous rule should be repealed.

But the law doesn't just mean pricier health care. As we've said, it means less health care. Its cuts in already-paltry Medicare reimbursements to doctors will drive even more of them out of the profession. This will exacerbate the nation's growing physician shortage—expected to be more than 150,000 by 2025.

All of this will affect you even if you're not on Medicare. Remember, those stingy government reimbursement rates result in cost-shifting to the private market. And, since government is such a huge player in the health-insurance market, its policies heavily influence what private insurers decide to cover.

What this means for you, the health-care consumer, is that, increasingly, whether you are government- or privately insured, you will not get the medical care that you or your doctor believe you need. You'll get what the government thinks you should have.

Rationing has already begun. In 2010, the FDA rescinded its approval of Avastin, a widely used drug that has been found to prolong the life of breast cancer patients. The problem, the FDA alleged, wasn't that the drug didn't work, but that it didn't provide "sufficient" benefit. Yet

Avastin has been successfully used in the United States for years, and is approved even by normally stingy European government health-care systems. The real reason is that government insurers didn't want to be footing the bill for the drug, which costs $88,000 a year per patient.[24]

This is just for starters. The administration's first stimulus bill included funds to establish an Institute for Comparative Effectiveness. This new bureaucratic entity is charged with assessing the clinical and cost effectiveness of medical treatments, procedures, drugs, and medical devices. Its mission is to generate data that will be the foundation for government decisions on health-care rationing.

Those who may doubt the administration's intention to ration health care need only listen to Dr. Donald Berwick, head of the Centers for Medicaid and Medicare Services, the key entities that set government reimbursement policy. He has been famously quoted as saying, "The decision is not whether or not we will ration care—the decision is whether we will ration with our eyes open." Even worse, he implies that rationing may be based not only on cost considerations, but on more subjective (i.e., political) criteria: "We can make a sensible social decision and say, 'Well, at this point, to have access to a particular additional benefit [new drug or medical intervention] is so expensive that our taxpayers have better use for those funds.' "[25]

Writing in *Investors Business Daily*, Eric Singer describes what this Brave New World of government-dominated health care will mean when you go to the doctor:

> Having relentlessly thwarted a truly free market in health care, the government treats each patient as a liability to be managed. Once the government has a number in mind for the value of your life, your days will be numbered—and not by God, but by the government.
>
> What happens when you are worth more dead than alive? . . . You won't get meaningful treatment, but you will get some aspirin. That's the way it is in England and to an extent everywhere else medicine has been socialized.[26]

Congress's new legislation is worse than bad economics. Its soulless bureaucratization of health care has chilling implications for every American.

*Central planning, in health care as in any market, increases costs and creates
scarcity because it eliminates the forces of competition and innovation that
bring down costs and create abundance.*

Q ► But don't we need government to make sure health-
insurance companies cover the sickest patients?

A ► Regulations that force companies to insure everyone
actually hurt high-risk patients by making them more
expensive to cover.

Advocates of national, government-mandated universal coverage believe it should force companies to insure everyone. Otherwise, they
insist, insurers will "cherry pick" patients—they will keep healthier ones
and drop the sickest people, who need coverage the most. Some states already require insurers to accept everybody. Such regulations are known
as "guaranteed issue." Another kind of rule, known as "community rating," requires that insurance companies essentially charge everyone at
the same rate—regardless of their condition. Both guaranteed issue and
community rating rules are a key part of the massive health-care legislation passed by Congress in 2010. They're slated to become national law in
2014. The problem is that, in states where they have been in effect, such as
New York, New Jersey, Kentucky, Vermont, and Massachusetts, guaranteed issue and community rating requirements have been a disaster.

According to a 2005 report by the Heartland Institute, not only have
premiums soared, but the number of private insurance companies in
these states have dramatically declined: "Some 45 insurers, for example,
left Kentucky between 1994 and 1997."

> By contrast, states that did not adopt guaranteed issue and/or
> community rating have seen much smaller premium increases.
> For example, typical monthly insurance premiums for families
> in rural counties in Vermont are approximately five times as
> much as they are for families in rural counties in Illinois.[27]

Merrill Matthews, director of the Council for Affordable Health Insurance, describes what happened after New Jersey imposed guaranteed

issue laws requiring that insurers cover everyone, regardless of their condition. He notes that when the law was first enacted in 1994:

> A family policy could be purchased in the state for as little as $463 a month or as much as $1,076, depending on which of the 14 participating insurers a family chose. Now there are just 10 insurance companies offering plans in the state and the cost has soared to $1,726 per month on the low end and $14,062 on the high end.[28]

Well intentioned though they may be, Matthews says, guaranteed-issue regulations have so inflated the cost of coverage that "many states are 'protecting' their residents right into the uninsured camp." They are one of the reasons that there are forty-six million uninsured.

Unfortunately, politicians who drafted Congress's health-care legislation failed to consider free-market solutions to the problem of preexisting conditions. Matthews, for one, believes "the best solution is to let the health-insurance market work for the vast majority of Americans and create a safety net for those who can't get coverage."[29] For the small number of hard-to-insure individuals with preexisting conditions, he advocates high-risk pools that take all comers. The government, in partnership with the insurance industry, would fund these nonprofit insurance organizations.

Right now, some thirty-four states offer some kind of high-risk insurance to about two hundred thousand Americans. The problem has been high premium costs for those who enroll, which can make state funding difficult. High-risk pools are expensive for the same reason that ordinary health insurance is expensive—state mandates. Like private insurance, high-risk plans have to cover everything—not just catastrophic care but those nonessentials that people may not need. Merrill Matthews and others believe that high-risk pools would be less expensive and work better if the broader insurance market were deregulated and requirements like mandates were eliminated. One of the states where high-risk pools work, Matthews says, is Wisconsin, where there are fewer state regulations and consequently lower premium costs.

University of Chicago economist John Cochrane has proposed another way to pay for patients who suddenly develop "preexisting conditions" that prevent them from changing insurers or getting new insurance—supplemental health-status insurance. The coverage would be separate from the person's main policy. Cochrane explains: "Medical insurance covers your medical expenses in the current year, minus deductibles and co-payments. Health-status insurance covers the risk that your medical premiums will rise."[30] Health-status insurance would provide you with a large, lump-sum payment to cover future premium increases if you become sick. This supplemental plan would be portable and consumer driven. Cochrane estimates it could cost about seven hundred dollars per year at age twenty-five, rising to nine hundred dollars per year at age fifty-five. Not only would health-status insurance help to protect people from soaring premiums, but it would make insurers less likely to drop sick people.

Free-market economists say that a key solution to the problem of pre-existing conditions is a more competitive insurance market. As we have noted, permitting insurance to be sold across state lines would encourage this kind of cost-competition and also allow for larger risk pools. Both would help bring down premiums and make it easier to privately insure sick people. Fewer people would need to enter high-risk pools in the first place.

John Cochrane and others have also called for removing the tax deduction for employer-provided group insurance—the vestige of World War II–era tax policy that led to today's third-party pay system and all its distortions. Removing this artificial tax break would spur a new consumer-driven insurance market. More individuals would buy their own policies. Prices and services would be tailored to their needs. Insurers would do a better job of meeting the needs of sick people—if they were truly driving the market.

Cochrane summed up the situation: "Health care and insurance are service-oriented, retail businesses. There is only one way to reduce costs in such a business: intense competition for every customer. The idea that the federal government can reduce costs by negotiating harder or telling businesses what to do is a triumph of hope over centuries of experience."[31]

▲   REAL WORLD LESSON   ▲

The Real World consequence of forcing insurance companies to cover everyone is that it makes premiums less affordable—making it harder to insure the sickest patients.

Q ▶ DON'T DRUG MAKERS GOUGE CONSUMERS IN A FREE MARKET?

A ▶ NO. GENERIC AND OVER-THE-COUNTER DRUGS ARE USUALLY CHEAPER IN THE UNITED STATES. NEW DRUGS ARE EXPENSIVE BECAUSE OVER-REGULATION INFLATES THE COST OF DRUG DEVELOPMENT.

In 2008 the *New York Times* recounted the story of Robin Steinwand, a fifty-three-year-old Maryland woman who suddenly discovered that she would have to pay $325 a month for Copaxone, the drug she took to control her multiple sclerosis. The drug was so expensive that her insurance company could no longer afford to charge her the usual $20 copayment. Steinwand was devastated. She would have to pay $325 a month—or $3,900 a year—for the rest of her life.

Steinwand told the paper that upon receiving that first bill from her pharmacist, "I charged it, then got into my car and burst into tears."[32] Things would have been far worse, however, if she wasn't insured. She would have had to pay the entire $1,900-a-month cost of the prescription—or $22,800 a year.

Today's new drugs work medical miracles—that is, when people can afford them. In the words of the *New York Times*, even insured patients can end up "[having] to spend more for a drug than they pay for their mortgages, more, in some cases, than their monthly incomes."[33]

And prices keep going up. When Erbitux, a new, highly sophisticated therapy for colon cancer, reached the market, it was one of the most expensive cancer drugs ever—costing seventeen thousand dollars a month. Amazingly, medical journalist Robert Bazell reported in *Slate*, Erbitux isn't the most expensive medication. "That distinction is currently held by Zevalin, a $24,000-a-month treatment for a relatively rare type of lymphoma." Patients taking Zevalin have to somehow pay some $288,000 a year.[34]

What's going on? Many blame "rapacious" drug companies. Bazell, who has a degree in biochemistry, points out that, after all, drugs like Erbitux are not really that expensive to make: "True, these antibodies are more expensive to produce than most pills, but only slightly—the technology can be replicated in any college biology lab. Production costs amount to few dollars a dose at most."[35]

Even members of the medical establishment believe that drug companies are "gouging" consumers. Marcia Angell, former editor of the *New*

England Journal of Medicine, caused a public furor when she wrote a book charging that a common tactic companies use to boost prices is reinventing slightly altered versions of the same medication. This way, she asserts, they're able to extend a drug's period of patent protection, which permits a legal monopoly—avoiding competition from generics makers and keeping prices up. Angell insists that one of the biggest drugs of the decade, Nexium, was actually a slightly altered version of Prilosec, a cheaper, older drug.

Angell's claims were widely echoed by politicians. But her allegations, when you think about them, don't make sense in the Real World. Is it really in the interest of drug companies to gouge consumers? Companies in a normal market usually price their products so that they can get *more* customers, not fewer. In industries like electronics, for example, prices of new technologies come down fairly quickly. But like everything else in health care, the pharmaceutical industry is not a normal market.

One reason drugs are nearly unaffordable by individuals is that, as we've explained earlier, individuals are not usually the ones paying for them. Robert Bazell, for one, acknowledges this: "Few individuals purchase these drugs as they would a head of lettuce, say, or a refrigerator. In the case of cancer drugs, health-insurance companies are the consumers."[36]

But drugs are not exactly like those four-hundred-dollar hammers or seven-hundred-dollar toilet seats purchased by the Pentagon. They're genuinely costly to develop. Bazell, however, is right when he says that making the actual drug may not be all that expensive. It's not the manufacturing process itself but the rest of what's involved—developing and bringing a new medicine to market.

America's drug-approval process is the most stringent in the world. Only about one in a hundred potential new drugs end up in drugstores and doctors' offices. That tiny handful of successful drugs must throw off enough revenue to enable companies to recover the costs of the countless also-rans that never made it to market—as well as generate the capital to invest in developing the lifesaving drugs of the future.

As a result, experts estimate that the direct and indirect costs of bringing a single drug to market can be as high as $1.5 billion. Also driving up prices is the inability of drug companies to recover their costs from selling drugs in countries like Canada and Britain, where state-run health-care systems insist on artificially low prices. Drug makers are forced to shift costs to the only segment of the global market that will enable them to recoup expenses—the American market and you, the consumer. Americans end up subsidizing the state-run health care of other nations.

American patent laws add yet another layer of costs. A drug company has a patent for seventeen to twenty years on a new drug. After that, any company is free to jump in and produce a generic version. In other words, drug manufacturers have only a limited window to make the profits they need to cover their expenses.

What about Angell's claims that pharmaceutical makers seek to boost profits by subverting patent laws? *New Yorker* writer Malcolm Gladwell says the accusations by Angell and others are overblown. They ignore the Real World factors driving up the cost of drug production. New drugs in this country may be expensive. But the generic and over-the-counter drugs taken by millions of Americans are actually *cheaper* than in other countries:

> Because there are so many companies in the United States that step in to make drugs once their patents expire, and because the price competition among those firms is so fierce, generic drugs here are among the cheapest in the world. And . . . when prescription drugs are converted to over-the-counter status no other country even comes close to having prices as low as the United States.[37]

Detroit journalist Thomas Bray confirms this. Writing in the *Wall Street Journal*, he recounts visiting a Canadian pharmacy just over the U.S. border, only to discover that "aspirin and similar products like Tylenol and Advil were much more expensive than in the United States—up to 30% more expensive, in fact."[38] Why? Bray explains that Canadian price controls on prescription drugs force companies to recoup their costs from over-the-counter medications.

Those pushing Canadian- and British-style price controls forget a fundamental Real World economic principle: when you pay less for something, you end up with less of it. Price any product or service too cheaply, and you will end up with runaway demand and shortages. That's why in nations like Britain, where prices of medications are under strict control, drugs are often in short supply. British newspapers periodically carry headlines like "Cancer patients hit by shortage of drugs"—that we almost never see in the United States.

As in any market, overly low prices prevent producers—in this case, drug developers—from generating the capital for research and development. Pressure from state-controlled health-care systems is why European drug makers now lag behind American drug makers, which are still able to charge enough to make a profit. Günter Verheugen, vice president of the European Commission responsible for enterprise and industry, acknowledged this in a speech to the Pharmaceutical Forum in 2006.

> Over the last 15 years investment in pharmaceutical R&D has been growing in the US significantly and consistently faster than in Europe. . . . In the past, Europe was leading in developing the most successful breakthrough pharmaceuticals. This trend has reversed. In 2004, two thirds of the 30 top selling medicines in the world were developed in the USA.[39]

In state-controlled systems, drugs may be "cheap." But people who get fewer medications are paying a higher price—sometimes with their lives.

▲   REAL WORLD LESSON   ▲

Accusations of "price gouging" by the pharmaceutical industry ignore the importance of profit as a vital regulator of demand and a source of critical investment capital.

Q ► But can a free market work in all areas of health care? For example, isn't it wrong to buy and sell transplant organs?

A ► Not necessarily. Today's "altruistic" system, where people die waiting for donor organs, doesn't work.

In 2009, an uproar erupted when it was revealed that Apple founder and billionaire Steve Jobs obtained his life-saving liver transplant after temporarily relocating from his home state of California to Tennessee, where the wait for transplant organs is six weeks, far below the national average of ten months. Some observers suggested he might have registered on lists of potential transplant recipients in several states to reduce his waiting time. Was this fair?

The controversy over Jobs's liver transplant cast a spotlight on the nation's system of "altruistic" organ donation, which forbids the sale of organs on an open market. Even the most ardent supporters of free markets may feel squeamish about allowing people to buy and sell transplant organs. Won't this lead to unethical practices and exploitation?

Dr. Sally Satel says that we can't afford to be queasy. She believes that today's "altruistic" organ donation policy, which forbids the acquisition of organs in exchange for money, is killing people.

> There are about 78,000 people in queue for a kidney from a deceased donor. In places like California, the wait can be up to eight years. And unless a friend or relative gives a kidney to a loved one, he will weaken on dialysis. Four thousand people die each year because they cannot survive the wait.[40]

Satel speaks from experience as a physician, and a transplant recipient. She experienced the harsh reality of "altruism" firsthand in 2004 when she learned she had end-stage kidney disease.

> At the time, my prospects for a donation from family or friends looked bleak, and I would soon have to begin dialysis. I would be hooked up to a machine three days a week for four hours at a time. This would continue for at least five years—the time it would take for a kidney from a deceased donor to become available. Even with dialysis, the kidneys of many sick people deteriorate so quickly that time runs out. An average of 11 Americans die each day waiting for a renal transplant.
>
> Waiting for a kidney from a deceased donor is such a risky business that some people try publicly to convince strangers to give them live organs. Some put up billboards ("I NEED A KIDNEY, CAN YOU HELP? Call . . ."), start websites (GordyNeedsAKidney.org, whose opening page carries the plaintive headline, "Please Help Our Dad"), or go overseas to become "transplant tourists" on the Chinese black market with the frightful knowledge that the organ they get will almost surely come from an executed political prisoner.[41]

Satel writes that there was slim chance of getting a kidney from the United Network for Organ Sharing, which has a monopoly contract with the federal government. She found "60,000 other people ahead of me." After searching online, she finally found one prospective donor. But he soon changed his mind. Eventually she received a kidney from a friend. Had she not been so lucky, "I could have languished on dialysis for years."[42]

Satel is not alone in advocating a market for transplant organs. Other experts have proposed market-based approaches that incorporate financial incentives, while being designed to minimize potential abuses. Among the ideas: government paying potential donors to join a registry, with the promise of a larger payment to their estates if organs are used upon their death. Such a plan spares the family the discomfort of making a financial transaction when a loved one dies. Other proposals include having states waive driver's license fees if a person agrees to be an organ donor.

Allowing private contracts between individuals has also been proposed, though some fear this would end up creating a market where the poor sell organs to the sick people with the most money. Wouldn't this encourage abuse of poor people? Advocates answer that there would be rules and regulations in these market-based programs to protect donors, ensuring safety procedures, consent, and fair value. Organ donation could only take place in an accredited hospital, so that donors would be protected with top-notch care.

Satel and others believe that private, market-based exchanges would also help kill today's black-market demand for transplant organs from countries like India, where impoverished people sell their organs—or from China, which takes them from prisoners who have been executed.

As for Steve Jobs, Satel says that registering on several lists of potential liver recipients was totally legal. It was what anyone in his position would do.

One thing is certain, Satel says. Today's system doesn't work.

> Don't get me wrong. Altruism is a beautiful thing—it's the reason I have a new kidney—but altruism alone cannot resolve the organ shortage. . . . One doesn't need to be Milton Friedman to know that a price of zero for anything virtually guarantees its shortage.

▲   REAL WORLD LESSON   ▲

"Altruistic" organ donation may sound moral, but it ultimately takes lives by ignoring Real World economic principles.

Q ► WHAT'S WRONG WITH MEDICAID AND MEDICARE?

A ► WHILE WELL INTENTIONED, THESE MAMMOTH GOVERNMENT INSURANCE BUREAUCRACIES HAVE DRIVEN UP COSTS AND UNDERMINED INNOVATION AND THE QUALITY OF CARE—NOT ONLY FOR THEIR PARTICIPANTS, BUT INDIRECTLY FOR EVERYONE IN THE U.S. HEALTH-CARE ECONOMY.

Low-income and elderly people need health care. But the answer is not Medicare and Medicaid. Most of today's problems with health care are in fact market imbalances created by these two mammoth government insurers. As we've mentioned, they are the Fannie and Freddie of the health-care economy.

The problem was not the intent of these programs, but their fundamental structure. Take Medicare. Years ago, a person's so-called golden years could be a time of intense anxiety because of the difficulty of getting health insurance. Retirees didn't have employer-paid health care. Trying to get insurance in your sixties could be prohibitively expensive. In the 1950s and '60s, millions of Americans who were self-employed or worked for small and medium-sized companies did not have corporate pension plans. And Social Security payments were proportionately lower than they are today.

Medicare was supposed to do for health insurance what Social Security had done for retirement income—provide a backstop. The problem, however, is that this government system is also third-party pay. The patient does not directly control health-care dollars. You go to a doctor or hospital and the bill is sent to the federal government.

With government footing the bills, not only did usage soar but so did fraud. Doctors, clinics, home-health-care companies, and medical equipment makers have all been known to rip off the system—billing for services not performed, overcharging for treatment and medical equipment. One notable example: motorized wheelchairs. A recent study by the Department of Health and Human Services found that Medicare paid $5,297 for power wheelchairs that cost non-Medicare patients about $1,500 to $3,800.[43]

Instead, the government responded by imposing draconian Medicare reimbursement rates. One specialist with a New York City practice recently complained he gets only $18 from Medicare for a patient visit that costs $112. One would be hard put to find any place in America where a doctor can make ends meet with those kinds of fees.

A 2007 AMA survey of nearly nine thousand U.S. physicians found that 60 percent of doctors intended to limit the number of new Medicare patients and 40 percent of doctors said they'd cut down on treating even established Medicare patients if already-low reimbursement rates were reduced. An earlier study by the Association of American Physicians and Surgeons found that 66 percent of physicians said that they were considering retiring at an earlier age than expected because of increased bureaucratic hassle from government insurers.[44]

The problem is especially severe with Medicaid. Almost a third of U.S. doctors refuse to treat Medicaid patients because of inadequate reimbursements. With access to practitioners limited, studies have shown "health outcomes" for Medicaid patients to be far worse than for patients with private insurance and even Medicare.

Not only are many physicians refusing to see government-insured patients, but an increasing number are folding up shop because they can't make ends meet. A study in the *Journal of General Internal Medicine* concluded that the inadequacy of government reimbursements has helped produce a shortage of primary-care physicians and "unbalances the health care system and ultimately puts patients at risk."[45]

Doctors in the U.S. may not be government employees, as they are in Britain's government-administered National Health Service. But they have lost control of their self-determination. In the magazine *New American*, writer-physician Jane Orient describes the widespread demoralization within the profession:

> In the past decade, the number of U.S. medical graduates entering family medicine and internal medicine has fallen by half. And it's not just the money. Time pressures and increased demands for administrative work contribute to burnout.[46]

"I felt like I was becoming a guideline-following automaton and a documentation *drone*," said general internist Christine Sinsky, quoted in a November 27, 2008, article in the *New England Journal of Medicine*.[47] Medicare and Medicaid's paltry reimbursements are also a primary reason for the wild prices and shortfalls of today's health-care crisis. That's because, as we've mentioned, the privately insured end up footing the bill

when doctors and hospitals are underpaid by government insurance—
to the tune of $90 billion a year.

Like all underfunded government bureaucracies, Medicare and Medicaid have an institutional bias against innovation. Coverage decisions are
made based on budgets and political pressures—not the needs of patients. Both programs take decades to cover newer procedures and medicines. In an article for the National Center for Public Policy Research,
Edmund F. Haislmaier reports that Medicare did not cover sophisticated
pacemakers known as implantable cardioverter defibrillators (ICDs) until
nearly twenty years after they first became available. The reason, he says,
goes beyond the usual foot-dragging to something more ominous:

> The hard truth is that, like national health systems abroad,
> Medicare saves money by limiting the availability of life-saving
> care. This deadly delay is the program's default response to ad-
> vances in medical technology. . . . The inevitable political calculus
> of any government health program, even one for the elderly, is
> that at a relatively modest cost per person it can provide "free"
> care to the vast majority of its beneficiaries. The savings come
> from spending less on the few who need substantial or expensive
> treatment—and dead patients are a two-fer. Not treating them
> means the program not only saves money today, but also doesn't
> spend money on them in the future.[48]

In other words, without anyone's being explicit, the implied attitude is:
why bother treating the sickest people?

Medicare's paltry reimbursements have also encouraged inefficiency.
John Goodman of the National Center for Policy Analysis points out that
Medicare's refusal to reimburse doctors for e-mail and telephone consultations is one reason they're so seldom used. Medicare also refuses to reimburse doctors for educating patients on how to self-administer some
care at home—for example, the treatment of diabetes. Patients are forced
to go to the doctor's office or to the hospital, experiencing greater incon-
venience and adding unnecessary costs to the nation's health-care bills.

In the end, neither Medicare nor Medicaid fully delivers on the
promise of meeting the health-care needs of elderly and poor patients.
Medicare coverage is today so inadequate that participants have to purchase private "Medigap" insurance policies to pay for what's not covered.

Program participants today pay a greater percentage of their incomes for health-care expenses than they did in 1965, before Medicare began.

This already incomplete coverage is fated to get worse as the population ages and more people enter Medicare. Both free-market opponents and supporters agree the current system is heading for a Fannie- and Freddie-sized meltdown. The Cato Institute's Sue Blevins predicts that by 2030, just twenty years from now, only 2.3 workers will be available to support every Medicare patient—compared with today's 4 workers per beneficiary. Experts call the system "unsustainable."[49]

State-run Medicaid programs, meanwhile, are straining state budgets to the breaking point. In the state of Florida, with its high population of immigrants and elderly, Medicaid rolls ballooned 40 percent over five years, and the program in 2005 was 25 percent of the entire state budget.[50]

Many think that expanding government programs like Medicare and Medicaid will straighten out the health-care economy. But this would only exacerbate the mess these massive bureaucracies have caused. People will end up paying more for health care whose quality and innovation will continue to decline. The cost will be not only in dollars, but also, in policy lingo, in worsening "health outcomes," with greater risk to our health and our lives.

▲   REAL WORLD LESSON   ▲

By imposing a rigidly bureaucratic system of third-party payment with inadequate and capricious price controls, Medicare and Medicaid have massively distorted the entire health-care economy.

Q ► What is the Real World market solution to health care?

A ► Allowing consumers, not corporations or government, to control health-care dollars and make their own buying decisions.

The best way to fix health care is to allow the return of a healthier market, where consumers make the buying choices for health care and insurance. Doctors and hospitals will again become accountable to the individual patient. Do away with the regulations that are today currently driving up the cost of coverage. Make it easier for individuals to buy the plans and care that they want.

Enabling people to buy their own insurance and care would push insurers and caregivers to become more efficient and come up with new, less expensive ways of providing health care. We see this phenomenon in every other part of a free economy, including a market sector more basic than health—food. Food is more critical to life even than health care. Yet in real terms it is costing less and less.

With the patient in the driver's seat, you'd get better care and better service. Your insurer, doctors, and hospitals would treat you like a valued customer. New forms of health-care delivery would spring up as companies sought to serve individual buyers. More people would be able to afford medical insurance. Fewer would need a government alternative. But even if we still had Medicare and Medicaid, those programs would be easier to finance in a consumer-driven market because health-care costs would be lower.

The power of the individual consumer to bring down health-care prices is illustrated by the relatively low cost of medical services that people buy directly and are not covered by insurance. Two prime examples: plastic surgery and laser vision surgery. Neither is normally covered by traditional health insurance unless the surgery is needed because of accident or disease.

Plastic surgery has not experienced the kind of price inflation that has afflicted the rest of the health-care industry even though, in the last fifteen years, technological advances have proliferated and demand has rocketed sixfold. Conventional laser eye surgery that reshapes the cornea so a patient no longer needs to wear glasses costs a third less in real terms than it did a decade ago.

How do we get there from here? The following reforms would begin to untangle the system:

► **Allow people to buy health-insurance policies across state lines.** This would enable people to buy plans in states regulated by fewer costly mandates. You should be able to buy a policy offered anywhere, from Arizona to Vermont. Allowing sales of health insurance across state lines would enlarge risk pools, making sicker people easier to cover. And it would increase competition among insurers, bringing down costs. A couple of years ago, the Health Care Choice Act, introduced by then–Arizona congressman John Shadegg and South Carolina senator

Jim DeMint, would have allowed out-of-state insurance sales, while preserving the state's primary responsibility for regulating health insurance. The bill never made it out of committee. Had it passed, it would have enabled more people to have access to lower-priced insurance. Competition would have blossomed.

▶ **Remove restrictions on health savings accounts.** HSAs allow employers to offer health insurance with high deductibles. Companies—and workers, as well—put pretax money into health savings accounts. The account covers the lion's share of care—mainly routine expenses— that you would normally pay for before your insurance kicks in. That care is paid through the HSA. The money belongs to you. Like a savings or checking account, what you don't spend remains yours for future use. The HSA earns tax-free interest; funds can be invested, much like an IRA. This is the antithesis of flexible spending accounts, in which the worker loses whatever money in the account hasn't been spent by year's end.

HSAs allow people to use insurance for what it was supposed to be for—catastrophic expenses. Thus, they help lower the cost of premiums. Meanwhile, they let the patient directly buy routine medical care—creating a consumer-driven market.

For years, *Forbes* has provided employees what are, in effect, health savings accounts. The insurance itself is a bargain (relatively) because the policy deductible is high. What makes the plan so attractive, though, is that *Forbes* gives everyone who works at the company $2,500 each year, which covers most of the deductible. Money that isn't used is rolled over. If medical bills exceed both that $2,500 and the employee portion of the deductible, traditional health insurance kicks in. When companies initially put such a plan in place, they often see a decline in premiums. Over time, *Forbes*'s premiums have increased less than those of its peers.

Insurers are permitted to offer HSAs as a result of the Medicare Prescription Drug Improvement and Modernization Act, signed into law in 2003. So far, only about eight million people nationwide have signed up for them. One reason is because they're new. But also, people and insurers don't fully understand them. For people accustomed to prepaid coverage, shopping for health care can take getting used to.

Another problem is that the government restricts what deductibles are and how much money you can put in your account. If such restrictions were loosened, more people would sign up for HSAs. They would become a greater factor in the marketplace. The health-care system would have to respond to these new consumer-oriented pressures. A remarkable phenomenon would unfold: Growing amounts of money would accumulate in these accounts. The accounts would grow to become a significant asset for many people, thanks to the miracle of compounding interest.

If health savings accounts became a major factor in the marketplace for insurance, pricing of medical services would become saner and more affordable. We would finally see the return of genuine insurance—coverage for major risks, instead of the dollar-for-dollar kind of coverage we have now.

► **Institute Medicare and Medicaid health savings accounts.** Medicare and Medicaid participants would get their own HSAs, much like people covered by private insurance; government would provide a certain amount of money to cover basic expenses, along with a catastrophic policy. Medicaid participants would get food stamp–like vouchers or health debit cards. Medicaid and Medicare recipients would thus be encouraged to shop for health care like everyone else. To get people accustomed to the concept, the program could be phased in; it would be optional.

Health savings accounts would begin to bring the runaway costs of both Medicare and Medicaid under control. Participants would have a positive incentive to hold the line on spending—the prospect of building up their HSAs. HSAs would make government insurance consumer-centric instead of government-centric. It would create a consumer-driven market for health care; the need to please consumers would propel health-care providers to improve productivity and develop cheaper and better ways of providing health care.

► **Make it easier for small employers to pool together to buy health insurance for their employees.** This would enable them to spread the risk and pay lower premiums. Allowing small business pools would help to make health insurance affordable for the small employers that currently cannot afford to offer it to employees—and it would give formerly uninsured people access to coverage.

► **Allow individuals as well as employers to buy health insurance with pretax dollars.** Why shouldn't you be able to pay for health insurance in pretax dollars? Here's how it would work: Americans who wanted to buy their own insurance would be able to notify the government of their decision. They would then receive a refundable tax credit—which means either a tax credit or dollars—of, say, $2,500 for individuals, $5,000 or more for families. Equal tax treatment would encourage Americans who preferred to buy their own plans to do so without adverse tax repercussions. The market for individual plans would grow. Insurers would be under additional pressure to be accountable to individual patients. They would deliver more reliable coverage. You'd see a market developing for individual policies, instead of one-size-fits-all corporate policies. By encouraging free choice by individuals, equal tax treatment would allow individuals and insurers to free themselves from the burden of expensive mandates. There'd be more competition in the market for insurance. You'd see downward pressure on the price of coverage.

▲   REAL WORLD LESSON   ▲

In all markets, encouraging companies to compete for the business of individual consumers inevitably results in pricing and products designed to meet their needs.

Q ► Isn't malpractice litigation overblown as an issue?

A ► Absolutely not. Malpractice insurance is a huge cost for individual physicians and some hospitals. But many times greater is the cost of wasteful defensive medicine by lawsuit-fearing caregivers.

In the introduction to this book, we explained that two essential conditions to the successful operation of democratic capitalism are trust among individuals in the marketplace and a legal system that allows for fair and equitable resolution of disputes. Both trust and dispute resolution have broken down in the health-care economy. The reason: today's blizzard of malpractice litigation. It's not just a legal and medical problem, but a critical economic issue.

In New York City, for example, malpractice insurance premiums for obstetricians are an astounding $137,000 on average—and even more in some suburbs.[51] According to an article in the *New York Daily News*, the high cost of litigation and medical malpractice coverage is the reason why Long Island College Hospital in Brooklyn and other smaller hospitals in the area have closed their maternity wards and stopped delivering babies. It is why Thomas Middleton, a resident of rural Maryland, couldn't find a new doctor who would take him when his primary-care physician retired. He told the *Baltimore Sun*, "I had to go through three different doctor groups before someone would take me."[52]

A 2004 study by the *Journal of Medical Practice Management* estimated that runaway malpractice suits caused a 6 percent decline in physicians in the United States, many of whom work in critical specialty areas, depriving up to 14.4 million people access to critical medical services.[53] Malpractice suits increased the annual cost of employer-provided health insurance by as much as 12.7 percent. Researchers blame this malpractice-driven inflation for a decrease of 2.7 million in the number of workers and their families who were able to get coverage.

Philip Howard, chairman of Common Good, a nonprofit organization devoted to eliminating lawsuit abuse, explains that the direct costs of premiums and litigation are only a small part of the total toll malpractice exacts from the health-care economy. There's a much greater cost—the "defensive medicine" practiced by lawsuit-fearing doctors and hospitals. Howard says that all the wasteful and inefficient tests and examinations may cost as much as $100 billion. Howard testified before Congress about his personal experience having to go through such expensive, unnecessary tests:

> I was not allowed to have minor surgery recently until I'd gone through a complete pre-operative examination, complete with chest X-rays and other tests, at a cost to my insurer of $1500. This was basically the same exam I had undergone a few months before at my annual physical, but the hospital would not accept those results, or indeed, even allow me to waive any claim. This was $1500 not available for some person who needed care.[54]

Howard said that hospitals have become "a kind of slow motion zone." Every choice doctors make is "accompanied by forms in triplicate and precautionary procedures." He testified:

> A pediatrician in Charlotte recently told me that on a routine visit of a healthy child he used to write three lines on the patient chart. Now he writes twenty or thirty lines describing all the things which indicate that the child is not sick. Multiply these procedures by over 3 million doctors and nurses, and you have a system that is unaffordable.[55]

Defensive medicine is destroying the trust that is critical to the doctor-patient relationship and to the functioning of the market. Every patient is a potential plaintiff. As a result, Howard says, doctors and patients end up eyeing one another suspiciously: "Quality, cost, professionalism, patient empathy, accountability and effective compensation for injured patients are all adversely affected."

"The defensive culture," as Howard calls it, has other indirect costs: it discourages Good Samaritan physicians from donating their services to charitable organizations, such as the Medical Reserve Corps, for fear of being subject to a legal suit. Clinics, as a result, are having a harder time affording physician care for low-income patients. The proportion of physicians in the country providing any charity care fell from 76 percent to 72 percent between 1997 and 1999 alone.

No one denies that it can be necessary to sue a careless hospital or physician. According to the Institute of Medicine, avoidable medical errors take more than one hundred thousand lives each year. However, Philip Howard makes the point that the current system doesn't do a particularly good or consistent job of policing the profession or protecting patients.

> Accountability is inconsistent: inept doctors often keep their licenses while good doctors find themselves liable on baseless claims; [meanwhile,] one out of four baseless claims result in payment, according to a recent study by Professor Studdert and others in the New England Journal of Medicine.[56]

Emotion, not the facts of the case, is what drives lawsuits and settlement. According to the New England Journal of Medicine, amounts paid to malpractice plaintiffs were driven by the severity of the patient's disability, not by whether a provider was negligent, or even whether an injury had occurred.

Litigation also imposes an immense cost burden on pharmaceutical makers and is a key factor behind the high cost of drugs. According to the Manhattan Institute, the pharmaceutical manufacturer Wyeth (now part of Pfizer) maintains a $21 *billion* reserve for litigation related to its weight-loss drug fen-phen, which was taken off the market. Lawsuits over the anti-inflammatory drug Vioxx may end up costing Merck as much as $50 billion. The astronomical cost of these legal battles represents nine to twelve times more than each company's annual research and development budget.

The specter of a Vioxx- or fen-phen-sized legal nightmare is not only straining the financial resources of these medical care providers and drug makers. It is inhibiting them from taking risks on and investing in new drugs and technologies.

How do you reform this dysfunctional environment? One solution Philip Howard proposes is a specialized health court system that works the way bankruptcy court and tax courts currently do. Those courts would rely on judges with specialized expertise in medical issues to make decisions. They would eliminate juries, which are too often swayed by emotion and reach verdicts unsupported by medical evidence. Reforms that have been adopted by some states include subjecting lawsuits to expert review, instituting a statute of limitations on filing a claim, and limiting awards "for pain and suffering." Wider implementation of these changes would bring some sanity back to the system and restore some trust and common sense to the practice of medicine.

▲   REAL WORLD LESSON   ▲

Wasteful defensive medicine, which has distorted both the practice of medicine and the health-care economy, is the greatest cost of medical malpractice abuse.

CHAPTER EIGHT

"Isn't Government Needed to Direct the Economy?"

THE RAP ► Unfettered free markets are so brutal that millions would tumble into poverty without government intervention. We need government to shield people from the pain of boom-and-bust cycles through fiscal policies such as increased spending, changes in tax levies, and monetary policy that "fine-tune" the economy via the money supply and interest rates. Programs such as Social Security and Medicare are also necessary to provide a safety net.

THE REALITY ► The key to a healthy economy is creating a stable, predictable environment that encourages risk-taking innovations and new business formation in a free and open market. Government intervention too often distorts markets and inhibits economic activity. By draining individuals and businesses of the resources they need to build wealth and create jobs, government spending ends up slowing growth and keeping people from getting ahead.

I n May of 2009, the *New York Times Magazine* featured an interview with President Barack Obama. The magazine's cover line was "His Economy." The president discussed with reporter David Leonhardt how the United States would emerge "on the other side of the so-called Great Recession." He asserted that, in the reporter's words, "the country needed to break its bubble-and-bust cycle."[1]

Obama told Leonhardt, "Wall Street will remain a big, important part of our economy, just as it was in the '70s and the '80s. It just won't be half of our economy." He strongly implied that the government would be playing a greater role in its direction, with less influence from the private sector: "And that means that more talent, more resources will be going to other sectors of the economy."[2]

Condemning the "massive risk-taking that had become so common," the president said, "What I think will change, what I think was an aberration, was a situation where corporate profits in the financial sector were such a heavy part of our overall profitability over the last decade."[3]

Obama's words raised eyebrows among many, especially supporters of democratic capitalism. Not only was the president implying that the government would be stepping up its role in directing economic activity, but he did not seem to appreciate the processes—including normal business cycles and risk taking—that make possible economic progress.

What role should the government play in a democratic capitalist economy? The fight over this fundamental question helped give birth to this nation. Righteous anger over Britain's trampling of what North American colonists perceived as the traditional rights of Englishmen— especially "no taxation without representation"—sparked the American Revolution. In contrast to many of today's politicians, the Founding Fathers and framers of the Constitution saw the greatest threat to liberty as coming from an overly powerful government.

For the first hundred years of America's history, government for the most part had little role in the economic lives of Americans. The one exception during that time was the Civil War. This began to change in the late 1800s. Industrialization was transforming a previously agrarian society, bringing with it growing fear of big corporations, or "trusts." The Progressive movement sought to impose order on the threatening, seemingly chaotic forces of change. Progressives' efforts resulted in passage of the Sherman Antitrust Act and the creation of government agencies like the Interstate Commerce Commission and, later, the Food and Drug Administration and the Federal Trade Commission. In 1913, the Federal Reserve System was established. In the words of Florida State University economist and author Randall Holcombe,

the federal government had been transformed into an organization not to protect rights, but, ostensibly, to further the nation's economic well-being. . . . A government initially committed to protecting the liberty of its citizens now seemed to be just as firmly committed to looking out for their economic welfare.[4]

Until the 1930s, most economists believed that the economy would remain stable and self-correcting if the government largely stayed out of the way. But this view began to change amid the turmoil of the Great Depression. In 1936, economist John Maynard Keynes published *The General Theory of Employment, Interest and Money*. He advanced the idea, which must have been comforting to many at the time, that the nation's economic woes could be cured by an activist government. Keynes believed that the way to economic vitality was through heavy government spending during slumps. This spending, he asserted, had a "multiplier effect," creating more output than the dollars originally spent, increasing "aggregate demand" for products and services that would stimulate the economy and lead to "full employment."[5] No matter if the government had to pay for it by printing more money. Keynes famously called gold "a barbarous relic."[6]

Far from a believer in the efficacy of markets, Keynes believed that a group of wise economists could dispassionately direct the economy, independent of normal political pressures. Columbia University economist Edmund Phelps has written that Keynes, while not a socialist, was a "corporatist" and "an exponent of top-down growth."

Keynes rejected atomistic competition as an efficient market form. The policy he advocated called for the government to assist the ongoing movement toward cartels, holding companies, trade associations, pools and other forms of monopoly power; then the government was to regulate the affected industries.[7]

Keynesian beliefs became the economic mantra of FDR, and a major influence on the policies of presidents Kennedy, Johnson, Nixon, and Obama. The Keynesian mantle has long conveyed an air of seriousness and legitimacy in policy circles. President Nixon famously proclaimed, "We are all Keynesians now."[8] But when this mystique is put aside and Keynesian policies are viewed from the perspective of history, Keynes the high priest ends up looking more like the Wizard of Oz. Pull back the curtain and he's less than he's cracked up to be.

Over decades, Keynesian ideas have rarely worked and have done serious damage. A growing number of economists and historians—including Amity Shlaes, senior fellow at the Council on Foreign Relations and *Forbes* columnist, economic historian Burton Folsom, and University of Chicago professor John Cochrane—note that Franklin Roosevelt's Keynesian interventionism, along with his spending, did not end but rather prolonged the Great Depression of the 1930s.[9]

Decades later, Richard Nixon, the Keynesian convert who was ostensibly a conservative Republican, created an economic nightmare through Keynesian mismanagement. He severed the dollar's tie to gold so that he could print more money to boost the economy, along with the equally wrong-headed wage and price controls. All this did, however, was trigger a brief spike in demand, an artificial boom in 1972 that was instantly followed by more inflation and then a severe recession one year later. Price controls on energy suppressed oil and gas exploration and production, strangling supply. Everyday Americans suffered the consequences of these distorting policies. Drivers found themselves idling in gas lines that stretched for blocks. The economy stalled. We ended up with the "stagflation" of the 1970s—economic stagnation *and* rising prices.

Keynesianism's miserable record has continued under President Obama, which is why the recovery has been historically substandard. Amazingly, the administration's supporters refuse to learn from history. Many have insisted that the problem was that the government's spending wasn't big enough. In 2008, Paul Krugman declared that the economy needed $600 billion of stimulus. The president delivered far more—some $800 billion. Yet in 2010 Krugman nonetheless complained that the president did too little.

Keynes's most famous critic, Friedrich von Hayek, explained why Keynesian economic policies, with their emphasis on government solutions, were destined to fail. They were not that different from centralized planning. They distorted an economy and undermined growth because they subverted the natural processes of resource allocation and wealth creation that normally take place in a free market.

Hayek explained that prices in an open market function as "a mechanism for communicating information" or "a system of telecommunications" that tells both producers and consumers, buyers and sellers, how they should conduct their activities.

Without the mechanism of pricing, producers can't signal to the market how rare or available their product is, and consumers aren't given the knowledge they need to adjust their activities accordingly. With each side not knowing the needs of the other, the mutual benefit of a free-market transaction is not achieved, and you end up with distortions and imbalances—to cite some Real World examples, people waiting on those 1970s gas lines, or waiting even longer in a state-run health-care system for a doctor's visit.

Building on the work of his mentor, the eminent Austrian economist and philosopher Ludwig von Mises, Hayek argued that Keynes's analysis of boom-and-bust cycles neglected the degree to which government with its powerful central bank can adversely influence economic activity. Decades before Fannie and Freddie, he explained that a central bank, by lowering interest rates and printing money, produces economic bubbles. Overly abundant, loose money creates a heady, artificial environment where marginal business ventures that would not otherwise have existed spring up and even prosper. That is, until they inevitably collapse. Sound familiar?

In his book *The Road to Serfdom*, Hayek warned that government management of the economy is ultimately driven by the whims of politicians and not the needs of people.[10] He thought Keynes was fundamentally misguided in his belief that a knowledgeable few could successfully shepherd the economy; Hayek believed it opened up society to the political overreaching that threatens individual liberty.

Keynes himself acknowledged that his economic nostrums "can be much easier adapted to the conditions of a totalitarian state."[11] Hayek and Keynes debated each other in journals during the 1930s. Their famous exchange foreshadowed today's debate over the direction of the economy. Just as Keynes overlooked the role of government in producing the Great Depression of the 1930s, his current adherents, as we've previously noted, underemphasize the role of the Federal Reserve, Fannie Mae and Freddie Mac, and the SEC in producing the financial crisis and recession.

But what activist Keynesians miss altogether is that real growth comes not from theoretical assessments of a market that originate in an ivory tower, but from unmanaged activities where people are figuring out how to meet one another's needs and desires in the Real World. Government can command resources; it can redistribute them. But it cannot, long-term, *expand* an economy. That's because the kind of jobs and businesses that drive wealth creation and growth can emerge only from the trial-and-error process of innovation that takes place in the private sector.

How does capitalism's dynamism and innovation generate growth? By giving millions of people the latitude to come up with and try totally new ideas—from the iPod to selling groceries over the Internet. Government cannot do this, because it simply does not have the bandwidth—the expertise, imagination, and resources—of the millions of people who make up a free market. Its decisions are based on political influences. Government programs that don't perform can continue for decades—welfare, begun in the mid-1930s, wasn't reformed until 1996. But a company that fails promptly goes out of business.

As we explain later in this chapter, the core capability of government is mainly providing (1) services that maintain order through promoting the rule of law, (2) a sound defense, (3) protection of, as the Constitution puts it, "domestic tranquility," and (4) assuring basic education for its citizens. That is one reason why policy makers so often assail "unfettered" capitalism and attempt to score political points by promising to end routine business cycles. Capitalism, with its dynamic, ever-changing markets, can be chaotic. But it's this very disorder—the process of experimentations, success and failure, carried out among millions of people—that produces the new technologies and ways of doing business that lead to genuine growth in an economy.

Take the Home Depot. Founded about thirty years ago, the hardware chain pioneered a new approach to selling home-improvement products, offering a vast array of low-cost products out of enormous warehouses. The chain provided the convenience of one-stop shopping, allowing customers to save time and money. Its huge success created jobs for employees and business for its vendors. But that is not the only way it ends up creating wealth. The Home Depot's founders invested their personal wealth in unrelated sectors of the economy. Cofounder Bernard Marcus, moreover, donated a portion of his personal wealth to nanotechnology research at Georgia Tech that may eventually yield more growth-creating technologies.

Stanford Graduate School of Business economist Paul Romer has pointed out that wealth and growth are generated not only by the big breakthrough advances that everyone hears about, but also by minor improvements in the way people do things.

Take one small example. In most coffee shops, you can now use the same size lid for small, medium, and large cups of coffee. That was not true as recently as 1995. That small change in the geometry of the cups means that a coffee shop can serve customers at lower cost. Store owners need to manage the inventory for only one type of lid. Employees can replenish supplies more quickly throughout the day. Customers can get their coffee just a bit faster. Although big discoveries such as the transistor, antibiotics, and the electric motor attract most of the attention, it takes millions of little discoveries like the new design for the cup and lid to double a nation's average income.[12]

This free-market "dynamism" is why Hayek wrote that no government could contain the "know how" that existed throughout a free-market society. Government spending, with its increased taxation, drains businesses and people of the capital needed for this kind of innovation. Thus, it eventually ends up slowing an economy.

This is the very reason why massive federal government spending during the Great Depression failed to restore sustained growth. Yet when the federal government shrank its presence in the economy during the 1980s and '90s, the nation enjoyed its greatest expansion to date. The United States got closest to the Keynesian goal of "full employment" through cutting taxes and regulations.

The government does indeed have a critical role in democratic capitalism, not as a growth creator but as a facilitator—performing critical functions such as maintaining public order and enforcing commercial contracts. However, when it strays beyond this role, it usually destroys wealth.

The stock market, the foremost barometer of the future health of the nation's economy, seems to grasp this. (After all, what are markets but people?) A little-known but immensely revealing factoid is that the stock market tends to slump when Congress simply convenes. New York portfolio manager Eric Singer has tracked what he calls "the congressional effect." Between 1965 and 2008, he found that the S&P on average showed more than a 16 percent gain when Congress was out of session—in contrast to just 0.31 percent when it was at work. Singer founded the Congressional Effect Fund, a mutual fund that takes advantage of these gains for investors. Singer invests client money in stocks when Congress is on vacation, such as in the month of August or at the end of October. But he gets out of the market or reduces his positions when Congress is in session. Singer says that the congressional effect is remarkably consistent—but several years have been exceptions. One of them was 1997, when the market realized annualized average price gains of almost 60 percent when Congress was in session. What happened? Congress cut taxes, including on capital gains.

Q ► SHOULDN'T GOVERNMENT SPENDING BE SEEN AS AN INVESTMENT THAT AIDS THE ECONOMY?

A ► THE WORD *INVESTMENT* IS OFTEN USED BY POLITICIANS TO JUSTIFY GOVERNMENT SPENDING. HOWEVER, SUCH SPENDING, WHATEVER THE MERITS, RARELY PRODUCES THE RETURNS FOR THE ECONOMY THAT THE PRIVATE SECTOR WOULD.

When policy makers anticipate having to raise taxes, they often claim the increase is needed for government's "investment" in the economy. During his 2008 campaign, then-candidate Obama promised to "invest" in job and antipoverty programs. His administration has since lived up to that promise by raising government spending to a level unprecedented in the nation's peacetime history. Politicians know that the American public takes a dim view of spending, even if it likes particular programs. So they often substitute the word *investment* for *spending*—one has a good connotation, the other negative.

A case can be made that some government spending qualifies as an investment. In the early days of the republic—even with all the politics involved—government spending on the postal system was seen as a wise investment to speed communications and unite the country. The building of the Erie Canal was an investment that helped make New York City the commercial center of the nation by uniting it with the Great Lakes.

Infrastructure spending that spurs economic growth can also have the characteristics of a private-sector investment. Not only do such projects aid the economy, but people who buy transportation bonds to fund construction of highway projects get a real financial return.

However, government outlays for actual infrastructure projects make up a small portion of the federal budget. More to the point, a private-sector investment, when successful, produces a gain for investors. Investors in equities, for example, get dividends or make a profit on the sale of stock. Unfortunately, what is often billed as a government "investment" rarely produces a gain for the economy. Most often it's a no-growth proposition. It produces less economic activity—in other words, a loss. That's because to underwrite its investment, government has to tax the private sector. It absorbs—some would say "destroys"—capital that would have been used for genuine growth-producing investments. Jobs and businesses that would have been created never come into existence. And some—often many—existing jobs are also destroyed because of the slowing economy.

Even infrastructure projects funded by government borrowing end up destroying capital, because higher taxation can be needed to provide the funds to repay bondholders. True, bondholders get a return—at the expense of capital that is destroyed elsewhere. As we've seen from the ongoing scandal over congressional earmarks, most infrastructure projects are hardly as strategic as the Erie Canal. And many are anything but worthy "investments"—such as a $150 million airport that a powerful congressman recently built to help his commute (see page 313).

Few governments in the last twenty years have "invested" in their economies more than Japan. During the 1990s, the country implemented some ten infrastructure projects. Ronald Utt of the Heritage Foundation recalls,

> Japanese fiscal policy during the 1990s was flamboyantly unrestrained, and during that decade no other advanced industrialized country had expanded government spending by nearly as much. Starting in 1991, government spending (outlays) in Japan accounted for just 31.6 percent of the nation's GDP—one of the lowest among members of the Organisation for Economic Co-operation and Development (OECD). That year also marked the high watermark of Japanese prosperity.[13]

So what did the Japanese government—and taxpayers—get for their "investment"? According to Utt, after years of relative prosperity, they got a bum deal—a long, downward economic slide that was a net loss.

After peaking at 86 percent of U.S. income in 1991 and 1992, Japanese income continually fell behind the U.S., and by 2000, Japan's per capita gross national income had fallen to 73.7 percent of that of the U.S. despite the increased spending stimulus in Japan during the 1990s and into the 2000s. This decline in relative performance reflects the fact that the Japanese economy grew at an annual rate of only 0.6 percent between 1992 and 2007. In 1991, only the United States, Austria, and Switzerland had higher per capita incomes than Japan. By 2006 (the most recent OECD numbers), Japan's per capita income was surpassed by Austria, Australia, Belgium, Canada, Denmark, Finland, Ireland, Holland, Switzerland, Sweden, and the U.S.[14]

American fear of Japanese economic muscle has faded considerably since the 1980s. Japan's nonstop and wasteful government "investments," building unneeded projects and squandering vital taxpayer capital, produced few gains for the Japanese economy or its taxpayers.

▲   REAL WORLD LESSON   ▲

Most government "investments" produce few long-term economic gains because the taxes needed to fund them are wealth destroyers, not wealth builders.

Q ► IF GOVERNMENT SPENDING DESTROYS WEALTH, THEN WHAT DOES TODAY'S MASSIVE SPENDING MEAN FOR THE ECONOMY?

A ► IT MEANS THAT HIGHER TAXES AND GOVERNMENT BORROWING WILL DRAIN PEOPLE AND BUSINESSES OF CAPITAL, HOBBLING THE NATION'S ECONOMIC RECOVERY AND LEADING TO LONG-TERM ECONOMIC STAGNATION.

Even before the mind-boggling binge spending of the Obama administration, rising government outlays have been a concern. Experts have long warned of the unsustainable tax burden to be created when the Medicare and Social Security programs begin to buckle under the immense cost burden of caring for retiring baby boomers. Within the next decade, some seventy-seven million of them will be drawing on both of these entitlements. Social Security will soon be sending out more in benefits than it takes in from payroll taxes.

The national debt currently stands at more than $10 trillion. Yet the unfunded liabilities of Social Security, Medicare, and Medicaid are more than $70 trillion. And that's before the spending needed to fund the current administration's new and expanded programs.

The spending of the Obama administration is *in addition* to this entitlement time bomb. When the economic crisis is over, the Congressional Budget Office calculates that federal spending, as a proportion of the economy, will be about 25 percent higher than in 2007. America has never seen anything like it in peacetime before the economic crisis.

That's only federal spending. There's also state spending. State politicians were almost as profligate as those in Washington. Before the Obama administration, total government spending—states included—was equal to more than one-third of our gross domestic product. Now it approaches 40 percent.

Additional funding needed by those already-existing entitlements will ratchet our total government spending to breathtaking levels approaching those in economically laggard Western Europe—as high as 50 percent.

And then there's the huge tax burden coming as a consequence of the Obama administration's health-care plan, with its job-killing spending and regulations.

To place all of this in historical perspective, in 1929, when the United States was the largest and most complex economy in the world, the federal government spent only 3 percent of gross domestic product.

What this means for the economy, of course, is that individuals and businesses are likely to face a battery of new and higher taxes. Not only will the 2003 tax cuts be allowed to expire at the end of 2010, but FICA payroll taxes, which cover Medicare and Social Security, will substantially rise, making hiring people more expensive for employers.

Former Treasury Department economist Bruce Bartlett calculates that, based on current government budget projections, "federal income taxes for every taxpayer would have to rise by roughly 81 percent to pay all of the benefits promised by these programs under current law over and above the payroll tax."[15]

That's right. You read it correctly. He said "81 percent."

What does this mean? Higher income-tax rates will increase the cost of risk taking, productive work, and success. People talk about this spending having an impact "on future generations." However, experts like distinguished Harvard University economist Martin Feldstein believe that *the future is now.* Feldstein had been an economic adviser to President Reagan as well as to the Obama administration. He is the former head of the National Bureau of Economic Research—the nonprofit research organization that determines when recessions begin and end. He predicted that the expected rise in taxation under the current administration would "kill any chance of an early and sustained recovery."[16]

Because hiring people will become more expensive, fewer people will be hired. Higher taxes will soak up capital that would have been invested in new and existing businesses that create new jobs and innovate. The economy will slow. Feldstein writes that the very expectation of this happening will depress the economy:

> Households will recognize the permanent reduction in their future incomes and will reduce current spending accordingly. Higher future tax rates on capital gains and dividends will depress share prices immediately and the resulting fall in wealth will cut consumer spending further. Lower share prices will also raise the cost of equity capital, depressing business investment in plant and equipment.[17]

The seemingly dry numbers augur profound changes—not only in today's economy but also in America as a society—that would make the nation a radically different place than it has been in the previous 230 years. Imagine the future this holds for young people—instead of saving to buy a house, you have to pay off the pension and medical bills of Grandma and Grandpa because your payroll taxes are 30 percent instead of 15 percent.

What does it really mean when an economy stagnates? New jobs and opportunities aren't created. Businesses can't grow or come into existence.

We pointed out earlier in this book that the United States, from the early 1970s until the recession, has been a far better job creator than Western Europe and Japan. With high taxes draining capital away from job creation, we'll get what we already see in Western Europe—high unemployment among the young. Even before the current crisis, unemployment among young people in France and Germany was over 20 percent. With higher unemployment and more people needing government assistance, we will evolve into a European-style culture of dependence.

With less capital available for risk taking, entrepreneurship, and initiative, innovation will decline. Existing services—such as in health care—won't be able to be developed or even maintained and will start to deteriorate.

Another consequence: society will become even more politicized, as interest groups of various stripes fight over government benefits. We'll see the kind of generational conflict that is starting to occur in parts of Europe, where the elderly are increasingly looked upon as burdens. Several years ago, Holland was hit with scandals when it was discovered that hospitals short of beds were, not so coincidentally, euthanizing older, critically ill patients. Yes, this nightmare scenario actually occurred. Meanwhile, in Sweden, as we mentioned earlier, pressure has been exerted on the old to retire to "create jobs" for younger people.

Such episodes are extreme instances of what is essentially rationing. And rationing results when resources are limited and there isn't enough of something to go around—whether that may be health care, energy, or jobs.

Most of the time, of course, bureaucrats end up deciding who gets what and how much.

The Real World bottom line in a government-dominated economy is indeed the Golden Rule: he who has the gold makes the rules. In a state-run market or economy, that means the needs and wants of people—and often, their rights—take a backseat to the agendas of politicians. The government, for example, tells auto companies what kind of cars they're allowed to make, even if people don't want to buy them. We've seen with Fannie and Freddie and with TARPed banks and life-insurance companies that it can mean that lending will be directed to politically desirable projects and not to those that make economic sense.

Recall the cases of Chrysler and General Motors, where senior secured creditors were browbeaten into accepting a reorganization that harmed their interests in favor of the politically powerful United Auto Workers union. And we've experienced the economic disaster that can be caused when politics, and not the market, drives economic decisions—namely, the misdirection of hundreds of billions of dollars into subprime mortgages.

If government direction were the way to go economically, the Soviet Union, and not the United States, would have won the cold war.

▲   REAL-WORLD LESSON   ▲

Massive government spending and growing domination threaten not only the economic welfare of future generations, but also the recovery of the economy in the here and now.

Q ► ISN'T THE FEDERAL RESERVE BANK NEEDED TO LESSEN THE IMPACT OF BOOM-AND-BUST CYCLES AND KEEP THE ECONOMY FROM OVERHEATING?

A ► BY PRINTING MONEY, THE FED CAN DELIVER A SHORT-TERM BOOST TO THE ECONOMY. BUT IN TRYING TO PREVENT NATURAL BUSINESS CYCLES, IT CREATES DAMAGING—EVEN CALAMITOUS—MARKET BUBBLES.

In 2010, Federal Reserve Bank Chairman Ben Bernanke announced plans to buy $600 billion in Treasury bonds with newly created money. The move, known as Quantitative Easing, was intended to deliver one more charge to a sluggish economy—increasing the amount of money, thereby lowering interest rates and raising bond prices, making corporate financing easier. The result: more business activity. However, instead of being applauded, the Fed's latest move to manipulate the value of the greenback sent the dollar tumbling and commodities surging. Gold touched $1,400 an ounce. The move was widely condemned by world leaders. Not only did it raise the specter of inflation and boost prices of products sold to the U.S., it also increased the risk of new potentially dangerous asset bubbles.

A previous round of quantitative easing that began in 2008 had failed to deliver much of a charge to the economy. So why did Bernanke want "QE2"? Because Bernanke and others are enamored of a false axiom with weedlike durability: the Phillips curve. Back in the 1950s, a New Zealand economist posited the notion that there's a tradeoff between inflation and unemployment. If you want vigorous growth, you need to accept higher inflation—while lower inflation means accepting higher unemployment.

Underlying all of this is the even more insidious belief that the Fed is needed, especially during a downturn, to "fine tune" the economy by manipulating interest rates and the supply of money. It's simply not true.

The Federal Reserve, the nation's central bank, is charged with managing monetary policy and overseeing part of the banking system. It is not a wealth creator. However, throughout history, politicians and others have mistakenly believed that the Fed can soften the effects of business cycles. The notion has persisted that the Fed can cook up an economic expansion by simply printing more money, generating economic activity and more wealth for all.

Growth in a democratic capitalist economy is not produced by printing money. It comes from production and innovation. It comes from finding better ways of doing things—new technologies, new processes, and new ventures that increase productivity and allow jobs and capital to be created. A wealth-producing innovation can be a wireless device that helps diagnose disease, a retail store that sells merchandise in a new way, or, as we've noted before, a single-size lid for coffee cups.

Artificially changing the cost of money won't in the long term create more wealth. As we learned from Hayek, as well as from the events in the last few years, it will only distort economic activity and can potentially be dangerous.

Hayek could have written the lesson provided by recent events. By keeping the cost of money artificially low, the Fed stimulated a massive boom in housing. Millions of people who really couldn't afford a house ended up buying. Today we know that this proved to be disastrous for them, as well as for home builders, who became overextended, and a financial system that offered credit on the basis of inflated asset values. The boom in the housing and credit markets created by so much available money eventually collapsed, dragging the nation's and the world's economy down with it.

A similar scenario played out in the early 1970s. John Tamny, of Forbes.com and RealClearMarkets.com, writes that Richard Nixon sought to achieve the Keynesian goal of "full employment" by increasing the money supply by 8 percent. This worked for a time.

The money illusion gave the appearance of economic growth, and Nixon won re-election in a landslide in 1972. As late as January of 1973 unemployment was near [the] target at 4.6%, while GNP in the first quarter of '73 was rising at an annualized rate of 8.8%.[18]

But Tamny recounts that the balloon deflated.

Reality caught up with the illusion. GNP only rose at a 1.4% rate for the rest of the year, not to mention that all manner of commodities were rising in concert with the collapsing dollar.[19]

The following year both the economy and the stock market tanked. Remember our point in chapter 6 about attempting to manipulate the balance of trade with a weak dollar—the gains it produces are always temporary. Sooner or later, the market corrects. Same goes for the domestic economy. The market eventually seeks to correct artificially inflated prices of goods and services. And the results are traumatic.

The inflation that ensued in Nixon's second term inflamed nerves already frayed by the debate over the Vietnam War. In an angry atmosphere exacerbated by the Watergate scandal, Nixon was forced to resign. The economy suffered through a decade of "stagflation."

The Federal Reserve can't "manage" an economy for the same reason that the rest of government can't: there's no way that a handful of people—even smart people—in Washington can effectively guide the economic actions of three hundred million Americans or, for that matter, 6.5 billion people around the world.

The Fed suffers from the shortcomings of any government bureaucracy. While supposedly independent, it's vulnerable to political agendas. Nixon's Federal Reserve chairman, Arthur Burns, was accused of pumping up the money supply, not only to boost the economy but also to increase the president's chances of winning the 1972 presidential election. The Fed has made countless mistakes in regulating money. It was seen as undermining the value of the dollar in the fall of 1987, which helped precipitate the stock market crash that October. In the late 1990s, the Fed's tight money policy caused the collapse of agricultural commodities. This in turn created political pressure to substantially increase wasteful farm subsidies under President Bush in 2001.

The Fed's record regulating banks has been dreadful. Despite this, people have responded to the current financial crisis—a disaster that, as we've said, the Fed helped to cause—by wanting to endow the central bank with still more regulatory power. That would be a truly perverse mistake.

The Fed cannot prevent normal business cycles because they result from events that have nothing to do with the money supply—the economy's natural process of creation and destruction. Some people, like Representative Ron Paul, who made a credible run for president in 2008, question whether we need a central bank in the first place. The Fed was established in 1913 to prevent crises like the banking panic of 1907 from happening again. Ironically, that upheaval was solved by the private sector without the help of government. Financier J. P. Morgan brought together his fellow bankers to shore up beleaguered banks and shutter those beyond saving.

The Federal Reserve's prime function should be keeping the value of the dollar stable. A sound dollar would go a long way toward achieving the president's goal of minimizing the kind of violent economic gyrations that we recently experienced.

▲   REAL WORLD LESSON   ▲

The Federal Reserve cannot create prosperity or prevent normal cycles because wealth creation is about innovation, not the supply of money.

Q ► WOULDN'T IT BE TRAUMATIC TO RETURN TO A GOLD STANDARD AS IT WAS IN BRITAIN IN THE 1920S AND IN THE UNITED STATES AFTER THE CIVIL WAR?

A ► RETURNING TO A GOLD STANDARD WOULD BOOST THE ECONOMY BY REDUCING THE UNCERTAINTIES OF A FLUCTUATING CURRENCY. BUT IT MUST BE IMPLEMENTED CORRECTLY.

When governments allow the value of their currencies to fluctuate, it creates uncertainty and inhibits economic activity. Think about it: how easy would it be for a carpenter to build a two-thousand-square-foot house if the number of inches in a foot shifted frequently—from twelve inches one day to six the next, to eight the day after, et cetera.

It's as though an economist said: *If we change the size of a foot from twelve to fifteen inches, everyone will have a bigger house.* Really? In the Real World, you'll likely end up with a lot of confusion and fewer homes being built. Similarly, with a fluctuating dollar, you get less long-term investment, more speculation, and misdirected capital.

Prices are supposed to signal to producers and consumers what is plentiful (cheap) and what is rare (expensive). If prices are constantly changing because of government actions, then markets can't gauge—or respond to—the desires of consumers.

Economists and politicians complain that fixing the dollar to gold would mean that the Federal Reserve couldn't play a role in guiding the economy. We agree. However, that's a good thing. It should not be the Fed's role to guide the economy. Aside from the upheavals caused by natural disasters, pandemics, or major wars, the most severe economic disruptions—on the level we've experienced recently—are invariably the result of government errors. In a healthy democratic capitalist economy, the market is guided not by government fiat but by *people*—their wants, needs, and innovations.

Thanks to the misdiagnoses of economists like John Maynard Keynes, gold has gotten a bad rap, largely based on the mistaken notion that it helped trigger the Great Depression. And it was blamed for unemployment and price deflation after Britain reestablished a gold standard in 1925. The precious metal was also said to have caused a series of downturns in the United States after the Civil War.

We've discussed at length, however, that the trigger for the Depression was the calamitous outcome of global trade wars ignited by the Smoot-Hawley Tariff. With economic conditions deteriorating, people and financial institutions around the world became fearful. They began to turn in paper currencies for gold just as they do during wartime, putting pressure on government supplies. Some countries, attempting to maintain the link to gold, raised interest rates to induce people to keep their cash in the bank and not redeem their currency. But this only worsened the economic crisis. The British government, fearing it would run out of the precious metal, went off the gold standard in August 1931. Other countries followed. Gold was a victim of the Depression, not the cause. In the same way that a gold standard is suspended in a major war, it became impossible to maintain in the devastating global trade war that the United States unleashed in 1929–30.

What about the deflation that occurred after Britain returned to gold in the 1920s—and the misery that ensued after the United States went back to gold after the Civil War? Friedrich Hayek and his mentor, Ludwig von Mises, both pointed out that in each case, the mistake was incorrectly valuing currency in relation to gold.

In the case of the United States, we pegged the dollar to gold based on pre–Civil War price levels. But in the interim, the government had expanded the money supply to help pay for the war. When the value of the dollar was set according to preinflation prices, the result was a traumatic deflation.

Hayek wrote that Britain made a similar error in setting the pound-to-gold ratio after World War I. Prices by then had more than doubled. The British government should have reestablished the link at the new price level. Instead, the pound was relinked to gold at the pre–World War I level—the equivalent of $4.86 to the pound, instead of, say, $2.80. The drop in the money supply produced a severe recession, leading to a general nationwide strike. Millions of workers walked off their jobs. For over a week, economic activity came to a halt. The strikes were ultimately broken, but the anger and bitterness lingered.

Again, the wiser, less destructive course for the United States and Britain would have been to link the dollar and the pound to gold based on the existing postwar price levels. As the economist Ludwig von Mises pointed out, you don't undo the bad of an inflation by a subsequent deflation. Just accept that there is a new price level because of a crisis.

The United States could successfully return to a gold standard as long as we don't repeat those earlier mistakes. At this writing, the price of gold is around nine hundred dollars an ounce. The dollar-to-gold ratio when we last employed a gold standard in 1971 was thirty-five dollars an ounce. Pricing gold at that level today would produce a tsunami-sized depression and a massive deflation, with prices dive-bombing to 1971 levels. Even pricing gold at what it was in the early 1990s and in 2003—when it was around three hundred and fifty dollars an ounce—would produce a disruptive economic contraction.

However, if we went to a gold standard at a realistic dollar price—and not what it was years or decades ago—we could avoid such an economic upheaval. Bottom line: we should go to gold but do it wisely.

Even the best medicines won't work if used in the wrong doses. But if properly administered, a gold standard is the best cure for much of what ails the economy.

Q ► DOESN'T GOVERNMENT SPENDING BOOST THE ECONOMY? AFTER ALL, THE GOVERNMENT BUYS PRODUCTS AND SERVICES.

A ► GOVERNMENT SPENDING ONLY SHIFTS RESOURCES. THE TAXATION OR BORROWING REQUIRED TO SUPPORT THIS SPENDING DESTROYS FAR MORE ECONOMIC ACTIVITY THAN IT CREATES.

In the dark days of early 2009, the new Obama administration unveiled its solution to reviving the economy: the American Recovery and Reinvestment Act. It ushered in a breathtaking $862 billion government spending spree that was supposed to create jobs and return the country to prosperity.

One reason supporters gave to justify their out-of-this-world stimulus spending is that a dollar spent by government isn't just a dollar. Uncle Sam's money, they believe, has a "multiplier effect." The enormous flood of dollars into the economy not only helps recipients, it gets everyone moving.

In the Real World there's a word for this: hogwash.

In the case of the administration's multibillion-dollar stimulus spending, Obama's economic advisers asserted that the "multiplier" is 1.5; in other words, each dollar spent will generate a $1.50 increase in the gross domestic product.

Really? Economist Robert Barro is among those who believe spending has anything but a multiplier effect—just the opposite. His own research on the U.S. economy during World War II revealed that government spending resulted in less output and a lower gross domestic product. Every dollar spent by Uncle Sam resulted in only 80 cents being generated in GDP.

He concludes: "The other way to put this is that the war lowered components of GDP aside from military purchases. The main declines were in private investment, nonmilitary parts of government purchases and net exports—personal consumer expenditure changed little. Wartime production siphoned off resources from other economic uses—there was a dampener, rather than a multiplier."[20]

Barro takes on the whole idea that government spending is a net plus for the economy:

> The theory (a simply Keynesian macroeconomic model) implicitly assumes that the government is better than the private market at marshalling idle resources to produce useful stuff. Unemployed labor and capital can be utilized at essentially zero social cost, but the private market is somehow unable to figure any of this out.[21]

Some people may ask at this point: What about all the activity that's taking place as a result of all those government dollars flooding into the economy—going not only to the recipients of its largesse but to vendors, employees, and others who in turn spend and invest. Isn't that helping people and having a positive effect? It may be helping some people, yes. But it does not ultimately boost the economy.

In chapter 2, we discussed how the "broken-window effect" described by the nineteenth-century French economist Frédéric Bastiat shows that fixing a broken window doesn't create wealth. It may make jobs for the people who have to fix the tailor's window. But the tailor is out the money that he used to fix the window, as well as the business he would have had if his shop had not been damaged. In other words, fixing the window does generate some activity, but for the tailor and the community as a whole, there's a net loss.

Government spending fails to stimulate the economy because of the same broken-window effect. Spending may create jobs and economic activity. But at the same time, it drains capital from individuals and businesses, reducing the jobs and wealth that would have been created.

Dan Mitchell of the Cato Institute reminds us that "the federal government cannot spend money without first taking that money from someone."[22] That means siphoning off capital from the economy through either direct taxation or, perhaps later, the taxation needed to pay for government borrowing. There's less money in the economy for private-sector investment. There's less money available to put into new innovations, businesses, and jobs.

Every dollar that the government spends means one less dollar in the productive sector of the economy. This dampens growth since economic forces guide the allocation of resources in the private sector.[23]

Not only that, there are additional costs. That's because government spends money less efficiently than the private sector. The dollars are not allocated based on people's needs in the Real World.

Government all too often ends up spending the money for political and not economic objectives. Like a $150 million airport built in a remote city that has only three flights a day. That almost no one uses except the powerful congressman who flies back and forth on its tiny commuter airline to his job in Washington. This is not a hypothetical example. The late Pennsylvania congressman John Murtha (aka "the King of Pork") did this very thing. The John Murtha Johnstown–Cambria County airport may have generated construction jobs; it doesn't help create future wealth. It's a dead asset that sits virtually empty. Nonetheless, in 2009 it was slated to receive some $800,000 in "stimulus" funds.

Remember the 2010 report by Senators Tom Coburn and John McCain that documented the recipients of stimulus money? Other expenditures listed in their report included: $296,000 to fund a study of dog domestication at Cornell University; $141,000 to send students from Montana State University to China to study dinosaur eggs; and $762,000 to create interactive choreography programs at the University of North Carolina.[24] Not only are these temporary jobs, but they also benefit mainly young, educated individuals who, one might argue, generally need the least help finding employment.

John Cogan and John Taylor, both of the Hoover Institution, cite Commerce Department figures showing that only a tiny percentage of "stimulus" dollars spent under the 2009 American Recovery and Reinvestment Act went toward new purchases and infrastructure spending. Instead, much of the money went toward reducing existing government debt—what it owed for goods and services already purchased. They write:

> The bottom-line is the federal government borrowed funds from the public, transferred these funds to state and local governments, who then used the funds mainly to reduce borrowing

from the public. The net impact on aggregate economic activity is zero, regardless of the magnitude of the government purchases multiplier.[25]

Along with benefiting relatively few people, government spending on growing its own bureaucracy can drag down an economy by creating ever more costly market distortions. We've already seen the painful and costly consequences of domination of the health-care market by Medicaid and Medicare. Mitchell also gives the example of welfare programs that discourage work. He calls such outcomes a "behavioral penalty cost."[26] If there is a multiplier effect associated with government spending, he suggests, it's this long-term negative impact on the economy.

Keynesians always justify spending with the rationale that spending mobilizes idle resources. It's necessary during a downturn, they say, because consumers aren't buying; businesses aren't investing. However, government spending isn't going to cure this. The only way to do so is to address the reasons behind the decline in activity.

That's why stop-gap spending on initiatives like tax rebates always flops. Rebates typically produce a spike in consumer spending when the checks are issued—but little else. In 2008, as the economic crises deepened, the Bush administration sent out rebate checks—one-time payments of $600 for single filers, $300 per child, et cetera. The Obama administration sent out $250 checks to seniors, veterans, and supplemental security income recipients. In each case what resulted was very little.

According to Brian Riedl, "no new income is created because no one is required to work, save, or invest more to receive a rebate."[27] Riedl recalls that to boost the recessed economy in 2001, Washington borrowed billions of dollars from the capital markets. What happened? People bought more, but private domestic investment dropped more than 22 percent and the economy remained stagnant into the following year.

The economy's growth does take off, says Riedl, when the government spends less and not more.

In the 1980s and 1990s—when the federal government shrank by one-fifth as a percentage of gross domestic product (GDP)— the U.S. economy enjoyed its greatest expansion to date. Cross-national comparisons yield the same result. The U.S. government spends significantly less than the 15 pre-2004 European Union nations, and yet enjoys 40 percent larger per capita GDP, 50 percent faster economic growth rates, and a substantially lower unemployment rate.[28]

Keynesian notions about government spending gain credence during challenging economic times for the very human reason that people are comforted by the idea of government taking swift action and coming to the rescue. In fact, the money doesn't really get spent that quickly. By the time it leaks into the economy, a recovery is usually already occurring. By May 2009, for example, the Obama administration had spent only $31 billion of that "emergency" $787 billion stimulus package that was rushed through Congress soon after he took office.

▲   REAL WORLD LESSON   ▲

Government spending can't boost the economy because it drains businesses and people of capital for new business and job creation.

Q ▶ WILL ALL THIS SPENDING LEAD TO INFLATION—OR DEFLATION?

A ▶ DEPENDING ON HOW IT IS FINANCED, IT MAY LEAD TO BOTH.

Experts such as Martin Feldstein and *Forbes* columnists and economists Brian Wesbury and Robert Stein worry that the Obama administration's spending binge will lead to a severe inflation. They fear that with central banks around the world pumping the equivalent of hundreds of billions of dollars into their nations' economies, we may experience a hyperinflation similar to what unfolded in Argentina between 1975 and 1991. Overexpansion of the money supply to pay for spending by a succession of Argentine administrations caused prices eventually to soar at a rate of about 3,000 percent a year. Amid the chaos, Argentina's currency lost just about all its value. People shifted to barter, trading homemade wares, new and used clothes, and jewelry. Inflation was finally halted in 1992. Argentina pegged its currency to the U.S. dollar. But in 2001 the dollar-peso link was severed and another round of chaos followed.

Feldstein's concerns have particular resonance because he used to head the National Bureau of Economic Research, the nonprofit organization whose data marking the beginnings and ends of business cycles is considered definitive. The highly regarded economist believes that inflation is likely to hit "once we start to recover."[29] With credit tight, money sits in the banks. But Feldstein has voiced the fears of many that once lending resumes and money flows again, prices will skyrocket.

However, economist and *New York Times* columnist Paul Krugman fears the opposite scenario—deflation: "Falling wages are a symptom of a sick economy. And they're a symptom that can make the economy even sicker."[30] University of Munich economics professor Hans-Werner Sinn believes this deflationary death spiral could mean a future less like that of Argentina and more like that of Japan, whose economy has been crippled since the early 1990s. He explains,

> Japanese governments have tried to overcome the slump with . . .
> one Keynesian program of deficit spending after the other and
> pushing the debt-to-GDP ratio from 64% in 1991 to 171% in 2008.
> But all of that helped only a little. Japan is still stagnating. Not
> inflation, but a Japanese-type period of deflationary pressure
> with ever increasing public debt is the real risk that the world
> will be facing for years to come.[31]

So which is it—inflation or delation? That depends on how the government finances spending, as well as on what the Fed does. We won't get inflation if the government borrows the money on the open market; the money supply will remain constant. But if the Federal Reserve creates money out of thin air to cover the government's deficit, the money supply will expand. With more dollars in circulation, prices will eventually go up. Interest rates will go up immediately.

However, if the Fed doesn't create enough money for the economy—which is what happened between December of 2008 and the spring of 2009—deflation will result. The shortage of money will mean tighter lending; consumers and businesses will sell assets to generate cash. This wave of distress sales will put downward pressure on prices. The problem will be compounded by Uncle Sam's profligate spending, at levels never seen before in peacetime, and the time bomb of entitlements. These could suppress investors' appetite for U.S. government bonds. (After all, would you lend money to a guy who's not only broke but hopelessly overextended?)

What next? Real interest rates will soar. The higher cost of money will further cripple the private sector. The higher taxes needed to finance the interest payments and spending will only increase the pain—raising the cost of productive activity, draining people and companies of capital and savings. There will be less money in the economy to buy and invest. The result: falling asset values and prices.

It's very possible that we might actually experience both inflation and deflation—inflation in prices and deflation in wages. We've already seen a wage deflation during the 2008–2009 recession. Commodity prices went down. Credit was unavailable. People and businesses scrambled to get cash. Millions lost their jobs and millions of others had to take wage cuts. If, to finance spending, the administration lets the capital gains taxes go up by 33 percent and personal dividend taxes more than double, as they are scheduled to do at the end of next year, housing prices and stocks will be adversely affected. Moreover, the administration is toying with substantially increasing taxes on personal incomes by removing the cap on wages eligible for the 12.4 percent Social Security tax. Not only that, the health-care bill adds surcharges to high-income earners to help pay for "reform." When the Bush tax rates expire at the end of 2012, the highest effective federal tax rate could jump from the current 35 percent to well over 50 percent. The joblessness and hardship this would produce could be as disastrous as Argentina's currency chaos.

▲   REAL WORLD LESSON   ▲

Heavy government spending and the excessive printing of money produce inflation—but they can also produce equally disastrous deflation if the government taxes heavily to finance spending.

Q ► DOESN'T A DEMOCRATIC CAPITALIST SOCIETY NEED GOVERNMENT SAFETY NETS?

A ► SURE, BUT THERE ARE RIGHT WAYS AND DESTRUCTIVE WAYS TO PROVIDE THEM.

Yes, Virginia, even believers in free markets see the need for safety nets. The disagreement, however, centers on the size and scope of such government programs to help those who cannot help themselves.

Even the Founding Fathers, with their basic belief in limited government, felt government should assist the needy. But they thought the primary purpose of such aid should be to provide a lifeline at a time of crisis—to get people back on their feet.

Austrian school free-market economist Friedrich von Hayek considered meeting "the extreme needs of old age, unemployment, sickness" a "duty" in a democratic capitalist society.[32] Milton Friedman supported certain programs, such as the Earned Income Tax Credit (EITC), which basically transfers income to society's lowest earners. In his book *Against the Dead Hand: The Uncertain Struggle for Global Capitalism*, Brink Lindsey of the Cato Institute has written:

> There is no inherent conflict between the principles of economic liberalism [i.e., free-market economics] and a decent provision for the needy and unfortunate. . . . It is perfectly consistent with liberal precepts for government to supplement the charitable efforts of civil society with a more comprehensive and systematic safety net. Whether provided privately or by the government, social assistance lies outside the market, in the realm of public goods. That realm is not in conflict with the market; it is in addition to the market.[33]

However, helping the poor and sick at their time of need is different from what we have today; giant antipoverty bureaucracies that provide ongoing subsidies, and not just to the poor. In the case of Medicare, everyone has to accept assistance, needed or not. The program is mandatory.

Isn't it ridiculous that billionaires like Bill Gates or Ross Perot are forced to take Medicare or Medicare Part D, rather than government and taxpayer resources being focused on the 20 percent of the population that truly needs this insurance?

We have repeatedly noted that experts of all political stripes agree that Medicare and Social Security "entitlements" are not sustainable. Faced with unprecedented demands by the retiring baby boomer generation, today's government health-care system, even if it is not expanded, as well as Social Security, is in danger of collapse.

Social Security and Medicare were sold to the public not as welfare, but rather as government-run insurance programs. The idea was that you would put in money as you would into a 401(k) or annuity during your working lifetime. Then you'd draw the benefits when you retired.

The problem is that the cost of these programs continues to go up. Despite several extensions of Medicare coverage, millions of elderly Americans still need to buy more supplemental insurance.

Social Security and Medicare were supposed to be self-financing, just like your private health insurance and pension plan. But the government is not an insurance company. It didn't finance Social Security, for example, the way a private company would. There are no reserves. More and more taxes will be needed to finance these programs unless, as we have suggested, they are systemically reformed.

Medicare and Medicaid don't fully reimburse doctors and hospitals. So their costs are shifted to the private sector, which ends up subsidizing them in excess of $90 billion a year. And then there are those Fannie- and Freddie-sized distortions and the bureaucratic rigidities they create in the markets for health insurance and medical care. They also breed corruption, including fake claims and billing estimated to be in the billions of dollars.

These programs—and others—have become so big because government spending all too often lacks the market discipline, accountability, and transparency you'd normally have in the private sector. Funding is propelled by politics—i.e., who screams the loudest—and not by actual need.

This is true not only of the big entitlement programs. Writing in the magazine *City Journal*, Steve Malanga presented a compelling account of the little-scrutinized world of government-funded nonprofits. In New York City, they are a major part of the economy.

At one time, Malanga writes, such organizations were privately funded. They focused on serving the poor and did so without the help of government. All of this changed with the Johnson administration's War on Poverty:

> The feds allocated billions of dollars to nonprofits through direct grants or via money funneled through state and local government agencies. In the process, the federal government paid nonprofits to do everything from running homeless shelters and rehabilitation programs for drug addicts to opening job training centers and designing and operating preschool programs. In just a few years, the money turned many charities into government

contractors, reliant on public funding and serving an agenda set by Washington or local governments. The sudden availability of so much government money also prompted enterprising individuals to get into the public-contracting game and create new nonprofits of their own. . . .

Today, though the city's population has increased only slightly since the mid-1970s, social-services jobs number more than 160,000, making them one of the fastest-growing sectors. Indeed, private social services [even before the crash] now rival Wall Street as one of Gotham's biggest employers; three times as many people work in private social agencies as in publishing. But while these service jobs are counted as part of the private sector, they're financed almost entirely with government money. The industry continues to rely for its growth on expanding government budgets, fueled by tax collections.

Once narrowly focused on serving those in need, the social-services sector, Malanga writes, is today a government-supported industry. Inevitably politics enters the picture.

[M]any nonprofits have become political power bases, replacing the local political clubhouses of the 1960s. Executives and founders of nonprofits have used their agencies as launching pads for political careers, so that today a job in the nonprofit sector is as likely a route to the City Council or the state legislature as being a lawyer and member of a local political machine once was. And channeling money into nonprofit groups is a sure way for a legislator to win friends and influence people.[34]

Funded as they often are by pork-barrel spending, organizations have resisted reforms—like being made subject to competitive bidding to win government grants. Some have become enmeshed in scandal, Malanga says: "City Council staffers have created phony nonprofit groups and allocated money to them as a way of parking cash that could be dispensed later."[35]

The phenomenon Malanga describes is in no way limited to New York. The best known example of the politicized, post-'60s nonprofit was

ACORN, the Association of Community Organizations for Reform Now. The national network of activist nonprofits used community organizing to press for various goals, including "affordable housing." Their controversial voter registration tactics during the 2008 election got the group into hot water in several states. It was eventually defunded amidst scandal.

However, activist nonprofits continue to be politically powerful. For evidence, one need only look to the White House. Perhaps the best-known politician to rise out of the government-funded nonprofit circuit is none other than Barack Obama, who, Malanga writes, "launched a political career after heading up the Developing Communities Project, a social-service group that lived almost entirely off government grants."[36]

Indeed, one wonders whether political-activist groups like ACORN and others were really the kind of safety net the Founding Fathers or anyone else had in mind. Steve Malanga concludes: "While the taxpayer money has been great for the political careers of community activists, it's hard to see exactly what good these groups have done for the communities."[37]

Occasionally, it is possible to scale back and reform counterproductive government programs. President Bill Clinton realized the unsustainability of welfare in 1996 when he signed into law the Personal Responsibility and Work Opportunity Reconciliation Act. Welfare rolls dropped by nearly two-thirds. What happened? Sixty percent of the welfare mothers who left the program found employment.

What about Social Security and Medicare? Government can administer these programs. But they must be overhauled to make them sustainable. Younger people should directly own their Social Security and Medicare accounts. That way, the government won't be spending—and wasting—other people's money.

No one denies the need for safety nets for those who truly can't help themselves or for those who are victims of natural disasters. They're part of a humane democratic capitalist society. But they need to be economically sustainable in the Real World.

▲   REAL WORLD LESSON   ▲

A thriving market economy is the best answer to poverty. Social programs in a democratic capitalist society should not be so costly that they crush the private sector.

Q ► If innovation is critical to economic growth, then
    shouldn't government money be used to fund important
    yet unprofitable endeavors—such as basic medical
    and space research?

A ► There's nothing wrong with some government funding of
    certain kinds of basic research, as long as government
    doesn't control it completely.

Government funding of science constitutes a fraction of total spending
and is not a burden on the economy. Add up all government research
and development from defense to space to health to the sciences and it
all wouldn't come to 5 percent of the budget. What makes up the bulk—
40 percent—of domestic nondefense spending is actually entitlements—
Social Security, Medicare, and Medicaid.

It's all about proportion. Throughout our history, government has financed or engaged in many important endeavors. The Lewis and Clark
expedition was initiated by Thomas Jefferson to explore vast new territo-
ries the United States had acquired from France in the Louisiana Purchase. In the 1920s, the Department of Commerce helped set standard
measurements. Government engages in map making and has helped set
uniform time zones.

The United States has also encouraged ventures such as the building of
railroads with land grants. After World War II, Uncle Sam accorded
pipeline companies powers of eminent domain so that national gas networks could be built across state lines. Government has also supported
basic research in health and medicine that might not have been under-
taken by the private sector. Even Adam Smith believed that the government had a duty to maintain

> those public institutions and those public works, which, though
> they may be in the highest degree advantageous to a great society,
> are, however, of such a nature that the profit could never repay
> the expense to any individual or small number of individuals.[38]

The economy and society have benefited from many of these efforts.
Without government funding, we would probably never have had the
space program. No private company could have developed satellites.
The costs were prohibitive. Even today, what company could spend the

equivalent of tens of billions of dollars to send a man to the moon when there is no economic return?

However, this does not mean that the government should run technology or biotech companies or be in the business of dictating the direction of all science and health research via a cabinet-level "Department of Innovation," as some have recently suggested. Such a bureaucracy in the Real World would inhibit innovation.

Why? Because while government—most often, the military—can occasionally develop new technologies, innovation is not its core capability. At its heart, government is a bureaucracy. Its business is enforcing rules, managing and preserving what has been already been established. Risk taking, unless specifically sanctioned, is usually avoided. Why do anything that could get you criticized? Better to keep your head down.

In contrast, innovation is all about risk—experimentation, trial and error. Hayek recognized that open markets are more innovative by their very nature because they encompass a diversity of people and know-how. People in all kinds of unexpected places are developing and testing new ideas. Hayek wrote in *The Constitution of Liberty* that the disorder and freedom of capitalism are precisely what enables this. You never know where the next big thing will come from. In contrast, "the majority action" usually taken by government focuses on what has been tested and proven.

> We do not know how individuals will use their freedom. . . . If it were otherwise, the results of freedom could also be achieved by the majority's deciding what should be done by the individuals. But the majority action is, of necessity, confined to the already tried and ascertained, to issues on which agreement has already been reached in that process of discussion that must be preceded by different experiences and actions on the part of different individuals.[39]

Author Sheldon Richman also makes the point that the private sector's market discipline promotes better decisions about where to focus research efforts and resources. "Entrepreneurs . . . earn profits only by anticipating what people will find beneficial and be willing to pay for. They must take costs into account and have no taxpayers at their disposal."[40]

Thus, the National Institutes of Health has spent hundreds of billions of dollars on research over the last twenty years, yet it has developed only eighty-four new drugs. Most of the advances that have produced medicines for the broad population have come from pharmaceutical companies. And as we've already noted, the military created the mainframe computer and what became the Internet. But it was the private sector that developed these technologies into the revolutionary innovations they ultimately became.

NASA did indeed put a man on the moon in the 1960s and shuttles into space. But in recent years it has been criticized for bureaucratic afflictions, including poor cost control, inefficiency, and operational decline. The agency's research helped give birth to the computer-chip industry in the 1960s. But forty years later, by the early 2000s, the *New York Times* reported that the agency relied on "outdated computer chips, circuit boards and eight-inch floppy-disk drives" and had to search for replacement parts on eBay.[41]

One need look no further than the White House for examples of the backwardness of bureaucracy. The *Washington Post* reported that when the tech-savvy Obama administration took over its new digs at the White House in 2009, it "ran smack into the constraints of the federal bureaucracy . . . encountering a jumble of disconnected phone lines, old computer software, and security regulations forbidding outside e-mail accounts." The paper quoted an Obama spokesman who complained, "It is kind of like going from an Xbox to an Atari."[42]

▲   REAL WORLD LESSON   ▲

The fundamental disorder of free markets makes them more creative and innovative than a government bureaucracy.

Q ► Isn't the free-market prescription for the economy essentially to "do nothing"?

A ► Quite the contrary, it is to create the conditions that enable the dynamic market to work.

Shortly after taking office, President Obama responded rapidly to the financial crisis. He unveiled his massive stimulus package, calling on Congress to "act boldly and act now" to pass it immediately.[43] Even those who didn't agree with his breathtaking spending were impressed by his swift response. His decisive performance no doubt helped contribute to his initial high approval ratings.

When a crisis hits, most people are taught that the correct response is to "do something" to "fix" the problem. That impulse is ingrained in our collective psyche as a "can-do" nation. When something bad happens, we're supposed to come to the rescue with all the expertise at our disposal, doing what we know how to do best. For politicians, "doing what they do best" means making laws and spending lots of money. Not only politicians but also the public seem to want leaders who will act. So you can't entirely blame people when they assert that the response to a crisis in the economy is to intervene and "do something" to change the situation. To do otherwise is considered by many to be downright un-American.

In the 1930s, Friedrich von Hayek was asked what should be done about the Great Depression. Hayek famously said, "Do nothing. The economy will recover on its own."[44] Author and economist Mark Skousen writes that this was not what people wanted to hear. "When the economy didn't recover for years, Hayek and the Austrians lost the war of ideas to Keynes."[45]

What Hayek probably meant was that government should not impose artificial constraints on the market and instead allow it to work. That doesn't mean "doing nothing." Mark Skousen believes that Hayek might have won his debate with Keynes if instead of recommending that we "do nothing," he'd presented his ideas for what they most likely were: a plan to stimulate the economy by lowering taxes, eliminating draconian regulations, and creating an environment of sufficient certainty that businesses could invest, grow, and recover.

Hayek's words may not have been well chosen. But his ideas are constantly borne out in the Real World. Despite the chest beating of free-market critics over even normal business cycles, most recessions don't last very long and are self-limiting. Prior to the financial crisis, the average recession lasted an average of eleven months.

Again, remember the story of the pencil. The market's "invisible hand" responds spontaneously to meet the needs of people. When there is an imbalance in demand or supply, the market automatically works to restore equilibrium—without any bureaucratic diktat or government stimulus. That includes correcting the conditions that cause a recession. If too many people are out of work, for instance, prices drop. Lower prices and, eventually, pent-up demand spur people to start buying again. Entrepreneurs, including people who may have been laid off in the downturn, take advantage of cheaper prices and available manpower and start new businesses. The economy begins to recover.

Unfortunately, in the Real World, government efforts to "do something" and "fix" a down economy often end up creating additional imbalances and barriers that inhibit these forces. They make things immediately worse—or set the stage for a future market upheaval. People understood this in the early part of our history. As Robert Higgs, an economist at the Independent Institute, a respected market-based policy think tank, wrote recently,

> the United States managed to navigate the first century and a half of its past—a time of phenomenal growth—without any substantial federal intervention to moderate economic booms and busts. Indeed, when the government did intervene actively, under Herbert Hoover and Franklin D. Roosevelt, the result was the Great Depression.[46]

The Smoot-Hawley Tariff was far from the only government move responsible for the Depression. Economist and historian Amity Shlaes compellingly recounts in her landmark book *The Forgotten Man: A New History of the Great Depression* that a succession of interventions caused and prolonged the historic slump. She recently wrote in *Forbes*,

> [President Hoover's] tenure was marked not by laissez faire or respect for private property—indeed, Hoover had labeled property a "fetish" before he became president. The Great Engineer was in fact the Great Intervener, meddling in multiple areas, raising taxes and backing tariffs, to the economy's detriment. Mistrusting the stock market as unreal, Hoover berated short-sellers and exhorted businesses to keep wages high when they could ill afford it.
>
> International, monetary and banking factors all played a role in creating the Depression, but the counterproductive Hoover mattered as well. As economist George Selgin has noted, the most absurd of the Hoover increases was a 2% levy on checks, which

caused people to further drain money out of their bank accounts so they could pay their bills, untaxed.[47]

FDR took office in 1933 in the pit of the Depression. He immediately instituted a bevy of measures intended to boost the economy and create jobs—including public-works programs, wage and price controls, and enormous tax increases. Not only did they drain the economy of capital, they created an uncertain, hostile climate that crippled private-sector businesses and job creation.

> Roosevelt's National Recovery Administration, created in 1933, pulled wages up when perishing companies could not afford it; come 1935, the Wagner Act gave unions more bargaining power, forcing further wage increases on companies. Roosevelt's multiple tax increases caused businesses to postpone investment. Especially counterproductive was FDR's "undistributed profits tax," which punished firms for being cautious and forced them to disgorge cash at the worst possible moment.
>   . . . Other big players also saw what was going on. Week in, week out, the chief economist of Chase bank, Benjamin Anderson, penned a diary reporting the negative consequences of government regulation, taxation and prosecution. Lammot Dupont summed it up when he wrote, "Uncertainty rules the tax situation, the labor situation, the monetary situation and practically every legal condition under which business must operate."[48]

Shlaes writes that this uncertain climate caused the United States to rebound more slowly than France, Britain, and Canada. When it finally took place, our recovery was less than robust. American unemployment was higher than in those other countries. Before the Depression an American worker earned 30 percent more than his British counterpart. However, by the beginning of World War II, U.S. workers had lost their wage superiority.

Robert Higgs has noted that the "regime uncertainty" created by policy activism is "what Keynesians usually fail to grasp."[49] Whatever the intentions of such policies, in the Real World, "activism itself works against economic prosperity by creating . . . a pervasive uncertainty about the very nature of the impending economic order, especially about how the government will treat private property rights in the future."[50]

Higgs points out that similar economy-inhibiting regime uncertainty is being created today by "the government's frenetic series of bailouts, capital infusions, emergency loans, takeovers, stimulus packages, and other extraordinary measures crammed into a period of less than a year."[51]

▲   REAL WORLD LESSON   ▲

Attempts by well-meaning politicians to "do something" often exacerbate economic imbalances by creating uncertainty and imposing new, artificial constraints on a market.

Q ► What's the best way to fix the economy?

A ► Creating the optimum environment for the risk taking and entrepreneurship that produce job creation.

For starters, we should avoid repeating the mistakes that got us into this crisis. The Federal Reserve and the U.S. government must have a firm policy, codified into law, that assures a stable dollar. The way to do this is a link to gold. Gold's effectiveness in creating a healthy economy is borne out by history: George Washington and our first Treasury secretary, Alexander Hamilton, wisely recognized that a monetary policy based on a gold standard constituted the bedrock of a strong economy. Their prescience and insight helped give birth to America's economic miracle.

Along with going to a gold standard, we should fully privatize Fannie Mae and Freddie Mac. These monster government affiliates should be broken up into several parts and their ties to government severed. Breaking up Freddie and Fannie into smaller private mortgage entities would eliminate the market distortions created by these two giants; it would open the field to new companies that would not have to fear having to compete against the U.S. government. The smaller entities could perform Fannie and Freddie's role: raising private capital to buy mortgages from banks and mortgage bankers, then packaging and reselling them to pension funds and other investors. If one of these smaller companies got into trouble, the impact on the market wouldn't be as great.

Breaking up Fannie and Freddie and instituting monetary reforms would eliminate two key sources of today's problems—the excess money and the monopolistic, government-backed mortgage companies that artificially stimulated the housing markets. What about low-income people? Mortgages would be available for those who have the income to service them and who have saved up for a proper down payment. However, market sanity would be restored. Federal government agencies such as the Department of Housing and Urban Development and the Federal Housing Authority would no longer pressure banks to make dicey mortgages. There would be an end to politicians encouraging no-down-payment mortgages, as occurred in the administrations of Bill Clinton and George W. Bush. Subprime mortgages can work if proper lending standards are adhered to.

On the regulatory front, greater transparency in the derivatives market would have helped avoid the catastrophic growth of credit-default swaps (CDSs). In and of themselves, CDSs play a needed role in the market as a form of bond insurance. The idea of a bondholder purchasing insurance against a default is eminently sensible and desirable. However, inadequate transparency encouraged excessive risk taking among CDS providers. They were able to get away with having insufficient collateral or reserves to protect themselves from defaults.

Requiring an exchange or clearinghouses for these instruments would allow people to know how many are actually in existence. In spring 2009, the Obama administration announced support for such reforms. An exchange or clearinghouse would mean that trading in these instruments would be on public view, just as trading in stocks and bonds is now. We'd have a mechanism for warning of the level of risk that would help prevent the market from overheating.

Such reforms would also prevent fraud. During the credit crisis, there were strong suspicions that some hedge funds were engaging in what were, in essence, artificial trades of CDSs. The intent was to make it appear that the markets thought a particular company was in increased danger of defaulting on its bonds. Rating agencies would then give notice of a possible downgrade and regulators would then say the company had to come up with more capital. The whole process would undermine otherwise healthy corporations. This would be less likely to occur with an exchange or clearinghouses, where one could actually see the volume of particular CDS trades and thus better judge what the market was actually saying.

The uptick rule, prohibiting the short sale of a stock until it moves up in price, should also be reinstated. Mark-to-market accounting should be repealed. This would not eliminate transparency. Information about what bank and insurance assets might fetch in a distressed market would be relegated to the footnotes of a financial statement. Regulatory capital would again be treated as it was from 1938 until the fall of 2007, when mark-to-market accounting was reimposed. Otherwise healthy banks would therefore not be forced artificially and unnecessarily to write down the value of their regulatory capital.

Beyond these immediate measures, the goal of government should be to create a stable, hospitable environment for economic activity—allowing companies to do business and entrepreneurs to take risks and invest in job creation.

This is not to imply that such efforts will eliminate natural business cycles in the manner that President Obama has suggested. Nor should we attempt to. Experience has repeatedly demonstrated that the turbulence of creative destruction is critical to the process of growth and advancement in democratic capitalism. As new technologies and industries displace others, there will always be bubbles, shakeouts, and market fluctuations.

However, normal cycles generally are limited to particular sectors and rarely if ever the entire economy. Only government interventions are big and broad based enough to cause the nation to suffer the kind of systemic failure that we have just experienced. You might say it's the economy's version of the Newtonian principle of physics—that an action results in an equal and opposite reaction.

What government can—and must—do is avoid the kind of heavy-handed errors that can produce such cataclysmic consequences. What enables a troubled economy to rebound? Heeding the lesson of the pencil: allowing people to spontaneously rally, as they have always done, to meet one another's needs in a free and open market.

As we've noted, that does not mean "doing nothing." Quite the contrary, it entails policies devoted to ensuring that the following conditions are present in the economy:

The rule of law. A vibrant economy requires that terms of commercial contracts are respected and enforced, and that everyone, including politicians and government bureaucrats, abide by them. When rights are violated, people and businesses have recourse in a fair and judicious court of law. The rule of law should guarantee that officials cannot act arbitrarily, as Argentina's government did when it recently seized the private pensions of citizens in the country's national equivalent of a 401(k). Arbitrary, capricious government is a major reason that Argentina has a lagging, perennially troubled economy, and why it is no longer one of the richest nations in the world, as it was one hundred years ago.

The United States, in contrast, has long been a magnet for foreign investment because its legal system assured a relatively safe haven for investors. Government could not suddenly seize your property or nationalize your business.

Respect for property rights. Property rights are a critical part of the rule of law. If you own a business, an object, a piece of land, or a house or building, you should not have to fear that an envious or angry government might one day seize it arbitrarily. If a society does not have strong property rights, risk taking will decline. Entrepreneurs would be forced to protect their property by buying influence with the political powers that be, wasting time and resources that would otherwise be devoted to growth-producing enterprises.

Property rights help create prosperity because they allow people to use what they own as collateral. Land and buildings become not just utilitarian items but also sources of capital.

Early on, the United States developed a strong property-rights system, and we take its protections for granted. But property rights as we know them still do not exist in many countries, and not just communist countries like Cuba or North Korea. Until recently, for instance, Egypt had at least eight different property systems. No surprise that countries with Western-style property rights enjoy a far higher standard of living than those that don't. Studies by the World Bank and others have shown that weak property rights hamper economic development.

Several years ago, noted economist Hernando de Soto calculated that four billion people around the world owned real estate worth

$9 trillion. But because of weak property-rights systems, this real estate was, as de Soto put it, "dead capital."[52] Imagine how much of the world's poverty would be reduced if people were able to fully mobilize these trillions of dollars of assets.

China and other growth-oriented developing countries are starting to wake up to this.

Despite the widely acknowledged importance of property rights to a healthy economy, governments and politicians routinely find excuses for violating them—including in our own country. The U.S. Supreme Court in 2005 flouted the Constitution with its widely criticized decision in the case of *Kelo v. the City of New London, Connecticut*, which sanctioned the misuse of eminent domain law. Eminent domain has traditionally allowed government to forcibly buy property from owners for public purposes—such as a needed highway. But the court decision allowed the continuation of today's abuse of the law, whereby local politicians exercise eminent domain to condemn people's property to aid politically connected private developers.

Stable money. A strong and stable currency was why the United States did better after achieving independence than the nations of Latin America after they broke away from Spain and Portugal. For reasons we have explained earlier in this chapter, sound money is the bedrock of a prosperous economy.

A progrowth tax system. We have seen that taxes are a price and a burden. Low tax rates on income, profits, and capital gains foster more risk taking and higher growth, bringing about a richer economy with a higher standard of living—and with higher government revenues.

Ease of starting a business. We take this for granted in the United States. Starting a legal business here is fairly easy to do. That, of course, doesn't guarantee success, but there are virtually no obstacles to hanging out one's shingle. But in numerous countries, the process is time-consuming and expensive, involving multiple licenses, procedures, and government agencies.

Each year the World Bank puts out a survey called "Doing Business." It examines 181 economies around the world. One of the key factors it looks at is how difficult or easy it is to launch a legal commercial enterprise. It's no surprise that developed countries usually have the most streamlined procedures and underdeveloped ones the most onerous.

Several years ago, the new prime minister of Bulgaria was shocked to discover that an entrepreneur in his own country had to get seventeen legal permissions to start a business. One of his goals became making new-business formation easier through "one-stop shopping" for the necessary permits. Thanks to his reforms, Bulgaria simplified the process of starting a business, which helped to enlarge its formal economy.

Few barriers to doing business. Politicians may peddle protectionist tariffs, quotas, or "safety" regulations as "helping the economy." But as we've noted, they're more often acts of political favoritism, rewarding one or another special interest. They raise the cost of economic activity and allow less of it to take place. Japan was notorious for decades for barring imports of beef from the United States, ostensibly on the grounds of safety, when everyone knew it was for political purposes.

Barriers also exist within domestic economies. As we saw in chapter 5, the United States is hardly a paragon of virtue when it comes to states' abusing licensing procedures to protect politically connected incumbent businesses.

Bottom line: the best way for government to stimulate an economy is to make it easier for economic activity to take place. That means promoting a hospitable environment through protecting the rule of law and property rights, instituting low taxes, ensuring sound money, and removing obstacles to starting and building a business. These very simple steps would help to unleash the resources and brainpower of millions of people. Their energy and know-how would do more to galvanize our economy than any governmental stimulus.

▲   REAL WORLD LESSON   ▲

The best economic stimulus is creating an environment that allows companies and people to mobilize the vast resources and ingenuity of a free market.

EPILOGUE

What Now?

Q ► WITH THE GOVERNMENT VASTLY INCREASING ITS POWERS OVER
BANKS, INSURERS, AND AUTO COMPANIES, AND TAKING OVER
HEALTH CARE, ARE WE ON THE ROAD TO SOCIALISM?

A ► IT COULD HAPPEN—IF WE LET IT.

The introduction to this book quoted observers who declared American
capitalism, as we know it, a thing of the past. Others insist that the
prosperity and growth of the last three decades is over. Americans will
have to get used to a changed way of living—a "new normal." Economist
and *Forbes* columnist David Malpass has his own word for this economic
environment—"dismal." The new normal, he says, means,

> slower growth from a lower base, with higher unemployment
> and bigger government. Rather than a healthy frugality, the new
> norm implies an outright decline in median living standards, a
> disaster for both prosperity and fairness.

This dreary scenario seems well on its way to becoming reality. In 2009–
2010 joblessness already reached unexpected levels, and there are genuine
concerns as to how slowly it is coming down in the sub-par recovery. Still
more disturbing: the United States took an eye-opening drop in the 2010
Heritage Foundation–*Wall Street Journal* Index of Economic Freedom.

Is this government-dominated "new normal"—or what it truly is,
socialism—really our future? Given American history, this is an astonishing
question. Right up until 1929, the federal government was a small part of
the economy. Even though we had, by far, the largest, most developed economy in the world, the United States had the smallest government of any
developed country. Federal spending then was equal to 3 percent of GDP.

Uncle Sam's power over the economy expanded substantially during the Civil War and World War I. But in each case, the government's role receded once it was no longer needed, upon cessation of these conflicts.

For instance, the income tax enacted during the Civil War was eventually repealed. During World War I, the size and power of government again expanded—though to a far greater extent. The top income-tax rate grew from 7 percent to 77 percent. To mobilize for that war, Washington nationalized the railroads and the telephone companies and came to exercise enormous powers over whole swaths of the American economy. But again, the federal government's powers withered when the conflict ended. The top income tax rate was slashed to 25 percent. The national debt was reduced by one-third.

Everything changed with the Great Depression. We've discussed how this historic downturn was produced by catastrophic government errors. Then, as now, the impulse among policy makers was "never to let a good crisis go to waste." And so government's powers grew mightily. Through massive public-works spending, the launch of Social Security, and welfare programs, along with a blizzard of regulations, Uncle Sam extended an unprecedented reach into the workings of the economy.

We made the point earlier in this book that a growing number of experts, such as economist Amity Shlaes, have explained how most of these programs extended the Great Depression. Indeed, several years before that historic slump, America had experienced another depression, from 1920 to 1921. Government's response was minimal. What happened? The economy snapped back as major income-tax cuts were enacted. The great boom of the 1920s was under way.

So why was 1929 different? One major factor was the election of Herbert Hoover as president. Unlike his predecessor, Calvin Coolidge, and in opposition to America's long-standing political tradition, Hoover was an activist, in the mold of the Progressive school, whose standard-bearer was Teddy Roosevelt. A believer in interventionist government, Hoover didn't understand capital formation. As president, he pushed for high tariffs on agricultural products to help American farmers. The reaction of Congress was: Why stop at farmers? Why not help everyone else? Why not help industry? The resulting Smoot-Hawley Tariff devastated global trade and the flow of money around the world. When the market crashed, ushering in the Depression, Hoover's reaction was only to intervene further.

Like so much government intervention, this well-meaning activism produced Real World consequences that were the opposite of what was intended. Hoover made CEOs of the nation's largest companies pledge to avoid layoffs and wage cuts, a promise they kept for a year and a half. But with sales plummeting, companies somehow had to cut costs. So they ramped up pressure on their own vendors to slash their prices. The result: severe layoffs at those supplier companies. Unemployment still zoomed. Hoover's other mistakes, particularly his horrific tax increases, proceeded to shatter the economy.

Hoover's successor, Franklin Roosevelt, was also of the Progressive school. People he brought with him to his administration had been intoxicated by powers Washington exercised in World War I. They reasoned that if government could mobilize the nation to win the war, why couldn't it direct the economy to beat the Depression?

And so government involvement in the economy deepened. Roosevelt enacted extensive controls on how businesses could carry out their activities. They served to abort the recovery that was under way in mid-1933. By 1939, the New Deal was becoming a spent political force.

The American tradition of smaller government slowly began to reassert itself. Roosevelt Democrats were dealt a severe setback in the 1938 congressional elections. The rest of their party refused to go along with Roosevelt's tax increases and actually scaled them back a bit. This trend would have continued had it not been for World War II and the obvious need for unprecedented government powers.

But after the war, government began to contract. Spending was slashed. Labor laws were reformed to curb the power of unions. Taxes were cut, despite Truman's veto. No new social programs were established. Many feared that, without major government spending, the nation would slip back into a depression. Instead the economy blossomed.

Then came the Cold War. The game changed completely.

Events such as the Korean War and the Soviet blockade of Berlin fostered a growing conviction that America needed to take an active role in the world. We had to build our military to levels never before seen in peacetime. The federal government launched unprecedented social and economic initiatives. An interstate highway program that was the biggest public works project in history, federal aid to education (we needed more scientists and engineers), and the space program were all justified on the basis of "national security."

In 1960, John F. Kennedy spoke of the need to "get America moving again" to help combat the alleged slump in America's overseas prestige. One of the justifications for Kennedy's major progrowth tax cuts in the early 1960s was to show the world that America's economy was more dynamic than the Soviet Union's.

Both Democrats and Republicans supported a size and scope of government that were inconceivable before World War II. Not having learned the lessons of the thirties, policy makers had the hubris to believe that if we could put a man on the moon, we could solve all sorts of social and economic problems. Countless amounts of money were devoted to innumerable programs to fight a "war" on poverty. Instead they led to a proliferation of social ills, including welfare dependency, teenage pregnancies, and substance abuse.

But why didn't government recede after the fall of the Berlin Wall and the end of the Cold War? Actually, it did, but only to a degree. Military spending was scaled back. Even today, defense spending as a proportion of the economy still doesn't match the Reagan era of the mid-eighties. But the idea that government could guide the economy and provide an endless array of services for people became a given in American politics.

Today, two crises—the War on Terror and the "Great Recession"— are once again causing government to expand. Is socialism inevitable? No. You can have prosperity and entrepreneurship and sound safety nets without massive government domination. That doesn't mean eliminating government services that people have come to see as fixtures. It means structuring them based on free-enterprise principles so they are economically sustainable. The strength and prosperity of this nation were built on a free-market economy and a thriving private sector. Social Security, Medicare, and Medicaid, as we have discussed, can be reformed so that people have more control over their benefits and that funding these programs does not become an impossible tax burden.

Only by encouraging private enterprise will we be able to return to the growth we've seen in the past thirty years. But we can achieve this only if policy makers and the public have a greater appreciation of how the economy works in the Real World and the importance of economic freedom. We've summed up key principles below.

1 ▶ Free markets are best at serving the needs and wants of people. Adam Smith explained in his classic work *The Wealth of Nations* that transactions in a free market are about achieving the greatest possible mutual benefit. Because no one is forced to enter into a free-market transaction, it can take place only if both sides benefit. This is the opposite of "exploitation."

2 ▶ Self-interest—not "greed"—compels people in free markets to meet the needs and wants of others. There are greedy and unethical people in all societies. But greed, which means taking too much of something that you do not rightfully deserve, does not drive transactions in a free market. It undermines them. The bank robber's coercive demand, "your money or your life," is the exact opposite of a free-market transaction: there is no mutual benefit, and it deprives the other person of free choice.

3 ▶ Only a dynamic, entrepreneurial private sector is capable of producing the growth and prosperity that we take for granted in a free society. Government command-and-control economies simply can't do it. The deprivation of state-controlled economies—in nations from North Korea and Venezuela to the old Soviet Union—attests to the inability of state-run command-and-control economies to provide for the needs of their citizens. Bureaucrats and central planners cannot anticipate the vast and complex array of consumer desires we take for granted in a modern society—from cell phones to social-networking Web sites. With its focus on maintaining order and pleasing political interests, government bureaucracies are simply not capable of the risk taking and trial-and-error experimentation that produce growth-generating innovations. But in the open markets of democratic capitalism, if people have a need, entrepreneurs will fill it—if they're allowed to.

4 ▶ Entrepreneurial innovation is a free society's foremost "natural resource" and the true driver of a democratic capitalist economy. This is the Real World principle that even the "experts" can miss about democratic capitalism: the broadest prosperity is created in nations that give people the

greatest latitude to innovate. Entrepreneurial inventiveness and creativity turned Hong Kong, an area with few natural resources, into an
economic powerhouse. It is what transformed the mysterious black ooze
bubbling up from the earth into the fuel that powers our engines and
automobiles. And it is why the United States has consistently outper-
formed its competitors. Without the freedom to innovate in open markets,
society would never have advanced.

5 ►"The rich" make everyone richer. People become rich by meeting the
needs and wants of other people. They build or invest in the innovative,
job-creating businesses whose goods and services make life better. The
outsized wealth of many rich individuals reflects the risks they take as
entrepreneurs or investors. People who start businesses are the *last*
ones to benefit from the wealth they create. They reap their profits
after paying off their workers, suppliers, creditors, and investors—and
that's when things are going well. People who buy into capitalism's
bad Rap think rich and poor are fixed groups with opposing interests.
But in the Real World, rich people are not only necessary, they're vital
to a healthy economy. Their investment, entrepreneurship, and spending provide opportunities that enable other people to build their own
wealth. Throughout history, countries that have scapegoated and destroyed their merchant class—from Uganda to fifteenth-century Spain—
have seen their economies collapse or decline.

6 ►Profit is a vital barometer in a democratic capitalist economy and the key
source of investment capital. Profit does more than make some people
rich by generating dividends and capital gains. It is the way our economic system mobilizes people to provide for others. Profit is a critical
barometer of demand, telling producers where they should invest—or
where they should cut back. It keeps supply flowing smoothly. Profit is
also a key source of the investment capital that companies use to expand
operations, innovate, and create jobs. Contrary to what Marx believed,
profit is not just "surplus." It replaces what has been lost as a result of the
economy's creative destruction. Politicians like to think that punishing
profits serves the public interest. But the Real World economic truth is
that it does the opposite. Without the barometer profits provide, you end
up with shortages and other distortions. There would be no capital to

build the advances of the future. Nations that have banned profit have seen their economies—and societies—decline.

7 ▶ Government's role in the economy is not to "do nothing"; it's to help free markets work. Government does indeed have a critical role in democratic capitalism. Open markets cannot function successfully where there is no government to protect people's rights and assure the rule of law. Government's role in a democratic capitalist economy is to create hospitable conditions that give people the freedom to meet one another's needs. It should enable them to develop their talents and to innovate, with the least possible interference and protection from harassment. Government must create an environment of certainty and predictability, such as assuring stable money and instituting a pro-growth tax system. Government is also needed to respond to challenges created by change. One example: how should the law respond to the copyright issues raised by online distribution of music? Far from doing nothing, government should be essential to creating an environment that allows economic freedom, where people can advance and businesses can be established and thrive.

8 ▶ The most effective regulation in the Real World establishes the "rules of the road" and does not attempt to micromanage markets. People who buy into the bad rap on capitalism fail to recognize that, to a great extent, free markets are self regulating. Regulations may be designed with good intentions. But in the Real World too many rules are a drag on an economy. They stifle innovation, locking in the status quo and favoring established market players. They rarely if ever produce their desired results or deliver on the promise of fairness. Instead they impose artificial constraints on activities that produce marketplace imbalances—economic distortions that end up hurting the very people the rules were supposed to help. The most effective regulations in a free-market economy establish the "rules of the road." They establish basic guidelines for conduct and are not politically motivated or capricious.

9 ▶ Government tends to politicize and not solve economic problems. Innovations and solutions in a free market are developed by entrepreneurial people and businesses. They succeed or fail based on how well they provide what people want. In contrast, government policies directed at solving market problems, or achieving fairness, are developed by politicians seeking to please political constituencies and remain in power. Rather than fostering open markets with the greatest degree of competition, government, in the name of protecting favored groups, more often imposes rigidities—restricting activity or imposing costs that limit the number of market players. The result is less innovation and growth—and often, market imbalances that hurt people. With government's political solutions, you often get rationing, shortages, and higher prices for most consumers. Think rent control—where a few people get cheap apartments, with costs shooting through the roof for everyone else—and the wild prices of today's heavily regulated health-care market.

10 ► The best economic stimulus results when government unleashes the private sector by lowering tax rates and opening up markets. Government efforts to "stimulate" or "fine-tune" the economy—through spending or monetary policy—have never produced sustained long-term growth. Big government spending failed to lift the United States out of the Great Depression, which lasted more than a decade. And it failed to revive the economy of Japan in the 1990s, despite ten stimulus spending programs. That's because the taxes and borrowing needed to fund government's "investment" suck job-creating capital from the economy. Similarly, government attempts to artificially "fine-tune" the economy through increasing the money supply may deliver a short-term boost. But as the financial crisis has demonstrated, it also creates disastrous economic distortions like the housing bubble. The way to lasting economic growth in the Real World is for government to reduce impediments to productive economic activity—cutting taxes and regulations and unleashing the energies of entrepreneurs. When the federal government shrank as a portion of the U.S. economy during the 1980s and '90s, the economy enjoyed its greatest expansion to date.

11 ► The best way to boost tax collections is to enlarge the tax base through progrowth tax policies—namely, meaningful cuts in tax rates. Economic growth means that people and businesses earn more. That, in turn, means a larger tax base and higher tax collections. Tax collections rose, not fell, after the tax cuts of the 1980s. Tax increases may produce

an initial spike in revenues, but they ultimately slow growth and shrink an economy. Remember, taxes raise the cost of constructive economic activity. Therefore less of it takes place. The best way to bolster an economy and increase tax collections is through reasonable tax rates that allow for optimum business investment and job creation.

12 ► **Protectionism kills more jobs than it saves.** People who buy into capitalism's bad rap miss the bigger picture of the benefits of global trade. They focus myopically on certain "jobs being shipped overseas." Meanwhile, in the past three decades up until the recession, the opportunities created by global trade helped reduce America's overall unemployment levels to record lows. Remember the lesson of the Smoot-Hawley Tariff. It didn't save jobs in the 1930s. Instead we got a terrible global trade war and a long Depression. After World War II, many nations of the world came together to liberalize global trade and put such destructive policies in history's rearview mirror. The lesson? Protectionism kills an economy. Free trade means not less but more job creation, competition, innovation. Relatively few jobs in the Real World are lost because of outsourcing or offshoring.

13 ► **It's easier to see the destruction that occurs in free markets than the creation and growth that are simultaneously taking place.** People who decry the destruction of jobs and industries that occur in capitalism's open markets are missing the bigger picture of the creation that also takes place—often because it happens elsewhere in the economy. For example, automotive manufacturing jobs "shipped overseas" are denounced as "irreplaceable" losses, while thousands of well-paying manufacturing jobs are simultaneously being created by foreign automakers building facilities in the United States. The development of the iPod and iTunes undoubtedly destroyed some jobs—but it created thousands of others, not only in the Internet industry, but also in retailing and manufacturing. Even in good economic times, there is "churn," the destruction and creation of jobs, as new technologies and industries displace others in open markets. If this process of "creative destruction" could not take place, the economy and society would not advance. We'd still be using typewriters instead of computers and making operator-assisted calls instead of using cell phones and cheaper fiber-optic landlines.

14 ►Only government, with its immense power, is capable of causing systemic economic upheaval on the scale of history's greatest economic failures. Through its ability to tax, regulate, and control the supply of money, as well as its political influence, government has more power than many Wal-Marts and Googles put together. The creative destruction of free-market capitalism can create job losses and disruption within specific economic sectors. But only the actions of government have the kind of impact on the national—indeed, global—economy capable of producing a system-wide meltdown on the scale of the Great Depression of the 1930s, the Great Inflation of the 1970s, and the economic crisis and recession of 2008–2009. Yet politicians and others who buy into the Rap on capitalism almost always blame these traumas on "unfettered markets"—responding with still more government "solutions" that only make matters worse.

Bottom line: Trust we the people. We *are* the economy!

ACKNOWLEDGMENTS

We are deeply grateful to the following individuals for helping to make this book a reality. The encouragement and enthusiasm of our agent, the spirited Larry Kirshbaum, were critical in pushing this project forward. At Crown, John Mahaney's superb editorial instincts and deft judgment were indispensable. His colleague Jo Rodgers also earns our gratitude. All three represent the publishing industry's gold standard.

This project required extensive research. Juliette Fairley spent countless hours fact-checking the manuscript. Deroy Murdock provided invaluable recommendations for a first-rate editorial research and checking team that included the tireless Jacob Laksin, as well as Ilya Laksin, RiShawn Biddle, and David Feith. Scott Bistayi, Elizabeth Gravitt, and Susan Radlauer cheerfully handled numerous requests for information. Audrey Wecera painstakingly helped prepare this manuscript.

Rich Karlgaard's insights on entrepreneurial innovation were inspiring and invaluable. Over the years, George Gilder has provided profound insights into the moral basis of entrepreneurial capitalism. Without the ever-patient assistance of Jackie DeMaria and Maureen Murray, Steve would never have been able to find the time for this project. Steve is also grateful for the moral support of Merrill Vaughn and the always wise counsel of Bill Dal Col.

On a personal note, we would like to express our profound appreciation to our families, without whose encouragement and patience this project would have been well-nigh impossible.

NOTES

Preface to the Updated and Revised Edition

1. Interview with Ben Bernanke, *60 Minutes*, December 5, 2010. http://www.cbsnews .com/stories/2010/12/03/60minutes/main7114229.shtml.
2. Charles Gasparino, "Obamanomics: Only Fat Cats Prosper," *New York Post*, December 7, 2010. http://www.nypost.com/p/news/opinion/opedcolumnists/obamanomics_only_ fat_cats_prosper_H7iJkddKctP5hA9rG7sNhK.
3. Court Huber, conversation with Elizabeth Ames, December 12, 2010.

Introduction: Why Capitalism Is the Answer

1. Committee on Oversight and Government Reform, "The Financial Crisis and the Role of Federal Regulators," hearing, 10:00 a.m., Thursday, October 23, 2008. http:// oversight.house.gov/story.asp?id=2256.
2. Joseph Alois Schumpeter, *Capitalism, Socialism and Democracy*, 5th ed. (New York: Routledge), originally published in 1976, p. 143.
3. Business and Media Institute, "Bad Company: For the American Businessman, Primetime Is Crimetime," special report, June 21, 2006. http://www.businessandmedia.org/ specialreports/2006/badcompany/badcompany_execsum.asp
4. Stephen Moore and Julian L. Simon, "The Greatest Century That Ever Was: 25 Miraculous Trends of the Past 100 Years," Cato Institute Policy Analysis No. 364, December 15, 1999. http://www.cato.org/pubs/pas/pa=364es.html.
5. Schumpeter, *Capitalism, Socialism and Democracy*, p. 143.
6. Ibid.
7. Thomas Sowell, "Is Anti-Semitism Generic?" *Hoover Digest*, no. 3, 2005. http:// www.hoover.org/publications/digest/2931421.html.
8. Ibid.
9. George Roche, "Education and the Free Society," *The Freeman*, vol. 46, May 5, 1996. http://www.thefreemanonline.org/featured/education-and-the-free-society-2/.
10. Bryan Caplan, *The Myth of the Rational Voter: Why Democracies Choose Bad Policies* (Princeton University Press, 2007), ch. 3, pp. 30, 36, 40, 44. See also Wikipedia summary, http:// en.wikipedia.org/wiki/index.html?curid=13081323.
11. *The Fortune Encyclopedia of Economics* (Time Warner, 1993), David Henderson, ed., pp. 636–39. http://www.lewrockwell.com/rothbard/rothbard106.html.
12. Leonard E. Read, "I, Pencil: My Family Tree as told to Leonard E. Read," *The Freeman*, December 1958. http://www.econlib.org/library/Essays/rdPncl1.html. First published in the December 1958 issue of *The Freeman*, it was reprinted in *The Freeman* in May 1996 and as a pamphlet entitled "I, Pencil" in May 1998.
13. Read's influential story, "I, Pencil," has over the years inspired others to imagine in a similar vein what would happen if government—or a single individual—attempted to make a pencil.

14. Rob Walker, "The Guts of a New Machine," *New York Times Magazine*, November 30, 2003. http://www.nytimes.com/2003/11/30/magazine/the-guts-of-a-new-machine.html.

15. Fredrik Reinfeldt, Prime Minister of Sweden, "The New Swedish Model: A Reform Agenda for Growth and the Environment," address delivered at the London School of Economics and Political Science, February 26, 2008. http://www.sweden.gov.se/sb/d/10296/a/99193.

16. John Mackey, "Winning the Battle for Freedom and Prosperity," *Liberty*, June 2006, Vol. 20, No. 6. http://libertyunbound.com/archive/2006_06/mackey-winning.html.

17. David Mamet, "Why I Am No Longer a 'Brain-Dead Liberal,' " *Village Voice*, March 11, 2008. http://www.villagevoice.com/2008-03-11/news/why-i-am-no-longer-a-brain-dead-liberal/2.

18. Milton Friedman, "The Hong Kong Experiment," *Hoover Digest*, no. 3, 1998 (reprinted from *National Review*, December 31, 1997, from an article entitled "The Real Lesson of Hong Kong.") http://web.archive.org/web/20060220030940/www.hooverdigest.org/983/friedman.html.

19. Andrew P. Morriss, "Freedom Works: The Case of Hong Kong," *The Freeman*, November 2008, vol. 58, no. 9. http://www.thefreemanonline.org/featured/freedom-works-the-case-of-hong-kong/.

Chapter One: "Is Capitalism Moral?"

1. Michael Novak, "Wealth and Virtue: The Moral Case for Capitalism," *National Review Online*. Text of a speech delivered before the Mont Pelerin Society in Sri Lanka, January 11, 2004. http://www.nationalreview.com/novak/novak200402180913.asp.

2. Milton Friedman and Rose Friedman, *Free to Choose: A Personal Statement* (New York: Harcourt, 1980). *Free to Choose* was also a PBS television series. See http://www.ideachannel.tv/; and http://en.wikipedia.org/wiki/Free_to_Choose.

3. Novak, "Wealth and Virtue."

4. Walter E. Williams, "The Argument for Free Markets: Morality vs. Efficiency," *Cato Journal*, vol. 15, nos. 2–3, fall/winter 1996. http://www.cato.org/pubs/journal/cj15n2-3-3.html.

5. Charles H. Green, "Charles H. Green's Trust Matters" blog, October 31, 2007. http://trustedadvisor.com/trustmatters/255/Weve-Got-the-Hamburgers-a-Customer-Service-Classic.

6. Ayaan Hirsi Ali, "Does the Free Market Corrode Moral Character? Not at All." Essay written for the John Templeton Foundation, October 1, 2008. http://www.aei.org/article/28734 or http://www.templeton.org/market/.

7. Ibid.

8. EBay's seller ratings are critical to maintaining trust in this system. When problems surfaced with the reliability of a small percentage of sellers, eBay responded immediately with a more detailed seller-rating system in order to protect its brand. Its efforts have helped to maintain users' faith in eBay and keep the company in business.

9. Sen. Bernie Sanders (Ind-VT), "No on Nussle," *Huffington Post*, September 3, 2007. http://www.huffingtonpost.com/rep-bernie-sanders/no-on-nussle_b_62902.html.

10. Doug Bandow, "Demonizing Drugmakers: The Political Assault on the Pharmaceutical Industry," Cato Policy Analysis No. 475, May 8, 2003.

11. Kerry Capell, "Europe Pays a High Price for Cheap Drugs," *BusinessWeek*, February 17, 2003. http://www.businessweek.com/magazine/content/03_07/b3820139_mz034.htm.

12. Gerald P. O'Driscoll Jr., "Subprime Monetary Policy." Originally appeared in *The Freeman: Ideas on Liberty*, November 2007. http://www.cato.org/pub_display.php?pub_id=8849.

13. Stephen Koepp, "Having It All, Then Throwing It All Away," *Time*, June 24, 2001. http://www.time.com/time/magazine/article/0,9171,146704,00.html.

14. Ibid.

15. David Adams, "Cuba's Economy Rife with Corruption," *St. Petersburg Times*, January 15, 2007. http://www.sptimes.com/2007/01/15/Worldandnation/Cuba_s_economy_rife_ w.shtml.

16. Ibid.

17. Paul Rosenzweig, "The Over-Criminalization of Social and Economic Conduct," Heritage Foundation Legal Memorandum and Executive Summary, April 17, 2003.

18. 2009 Index of Economic Freedom from the Heritage Foundation and the *Wall Street Journal*. http://www.heritage.org/Index/Country/Russia. Russia's economic freedom score is 50.8, making its economy the 146th freest in the 2009 Index. Its score is one point higher than last year, reflecting improved scores in four of the ten economic freedoms, especially trade freedom. Russia is ranked forty-first out of forty-three countries in the Europe region, and its overall score is below the world average. Russia scored lowest on Property Rights (25 compared with a global average of 44.0) and Freedom from Corruption (23 compared with a 40.3 global average).

19. "Interview with Grigory Yavlinsky," *Moskovsky Komsomolets*, September 2, 2003. Yavlinsky was chairman of the YABLOKO party from 1993 to 2008. http://eng.yabloko.ru/ Publ/2003/PAPERS/9/030902_mosk_koms.html

20. Heritage Foundation and *Wall Street Journal*, 2009 Index of Economic Freedom. http:// www.heritage.org/Index/Country/Russia.

21. Arch Puddington, "Freedom in the World 2009: Setbacks and Resilience," Freedom House. http://www.freedomhouse.org/template.cfm?page=130&year=2009.

22. Daniel Griswold, "Trade, Democracy, and Peace: The Virtuous Cycle," speech to the Peace Through Trade Conference, World Trade Centers Association, Oslo, Norway, April 20, 2007. http://www.freetrade.org/node/681.

23. Ibid.

24. Ibid.

25. Howard W. French, "In Chinese Boomtown, Middle Class Pushes Back," *New York Times*, December 18, 2006. http://query.nytimes.com/gst/fullpage.html?res=9401E3DA1331 F33DA9grgr(r0g6ngC8R6g

26. Andrew Jacobs, "In China, Child's Day Without the Children," *New York Times*, Sunday, June 1, 2008. http://www.nytimes.com/2008/06/01/world/asia/01iht-quake.4.13375989 .html.

27. According to the Bureau of Labor Statistics.

28. Jerry Kirkpatrick, *In Defense of Advertising: Arguments from Reason, Ethical Egoism, and Laissez-Faire Capitalism* (Westport, Conn.: Quorum Books, 1994), p. 21. PDF ebook available at http://www.tljbooks.com/ebook.html.

29. John Kenneth Galbraith, *The Affluent Society* (New York: Mariner Books, 1998; 40th-anniversary edition), p. 223.

30. Radley Balko, "Don't Blame SpongeBob for Child Obesity," FOXNews.com, February 21, 2005. Radley Balko was a policy analyst for the Cato Institute specializing in vice and civil liberties issues. He is a columnist for FOXNews.com. http://www.cato.org/pub_ display.php?pub_id=3696.

31. Kirkpatrick, *In Defense of Advertising*, p. 17.

32. Ibid, p. 31.

33. Jane Gross, "Millionaire's Mega-Mansion Shocks Even the Hamptons," *New York Times*, Sunday, August 23, 1998. http://www.nytimes.com/1998/08/23/nyregion/millionaire-s -mega-mansion-shocks-even-the-hamptons.html.

34. Ibid.

35. Rita Healy and P. G. Sittenfeld, "Making McMansion Owners Pay," *Time*, July 12, 2007. http://www.time.com/time/nation/article/0,8599,1643151,00.html.

36. Dinesh D'Souza, *The Virtue of Prosperity: Finding Values in an Age of Technoaffluence* (New York: Free Press, 2001), p. 73.

37. Ibid, p. 74.

38. "And Luxury for All," *Wired*, January 2005.

39. Randy Cohen, "When Layoffs Are Immoral," *New York Times Magazine*, May 26, 2009. http://ethicist.blogs.nytimes.com/2009/05/26/when-layoffs-are-immoral/.

40. Ibid.

41. "Layoffs and CEO Compensation," University of Arkansas press release, October 3, 2006. http://dailyheadlines.uark.edu/9365.htm.

42. Pietro Garibaldi and Paolo Mauro, "Job Creation: Why Some Countries Do Better," working paper, International Monetary Fund (2000). http://www.imf.org/external/pubs/ft/issues/issues20/index.htm

43. Cohen, "When Layoffs Are Immoral."

44. Bob Sutton, "When Layoffs Are Immoral: Randy Cohen in the *New York Times*," posted on his blog, "Work Matters." http://bobsutton.typepad.com/my_weblog/2009/05/when-layoffs-are-immoral-randy-cohen-in-the-new-york-times.html.

45. Ibid.

46. Mark Thornton, "Alcohol Prohibition Was a Failure," Cato Institute Policy Analysis, no. 157, July 17, 1991. http://www.cato.org/pub_display.php?pub_id=1017.

Chapter Two: "Isn't Capitalism Brutal?"

1. W. Michael Cox and Richard Alm, "The Great Job Machine," *New York Times*, November 7, 2003. http://www.nytimes.com/2003/11/07/opinion/the-great-job-machine.html.

2. Daniel Gross, "What Makes a Nation More Productive? It's Not Just Technology," *New York Times*, December 25, 2005. http://www.nytimes.com/2005/12/25/business/yourmoney/25view.html?pagewanted=print.

3. Jeff Jacoby, "Frank's Fingerprints Are All Over the Financial Fiasco," *Boston Globe*, September 28, 2008. http://www.boston.com/bostonglobe/editorial_opinion/oped/articles/2008/09/28/franks_fingerprints_are_all_over_the_financial_fiasco/.

4. Barney Frank, Committee on Financial Services Letter Addressing Predatory Lending, March 29, 2007. http://www.americansecuritization.com/story.aspx?id=1589.

5. Rick Klein, "McCain Blames Greed for Wall St. Mess; Obama Blames GOP," ABC News, September 16, 2008. http://abcnews.go.com/Politics/5050/story?id=5812268&page=1.

6. Bureau of Labor Statistics, "Employment Situation," July 2, 2009. http://www.bls.gov/news.release/empsit.htm

7. Bureau of Labor Statistics, "Business Employment Dynamics Summary," May 19, 2009. http://www.bls.gov/news.release/cewbd.nr0.htm.

8. Clair Brown, John C. Haltiwanger, and Julia I. Lane, *Economic Turbulence: Is a Volatile Economy Good for America?* (University of Chicago Press, 2006).

9. Cox and Alm, "The Great Job Machine."

10. Ibid.

11. Clayton M. Christensen, *The Innovator's Dilemma: When New Technologies Cause Great Firms to Fail* (Cambridge, Mass.: Harvard Business Press, 1997). Introduction, pp. x–xvii.

12. Ibid.

13. Ibid.

14. Ibid.

15. Clayton Christensen, Thomas Craig, and Stuart Hart, "The Great Disruption," *Foreign Affairs*, p. 84. http://www.self.org/news/Great_Disruption.pdf.

16. Holman W. Jenkins, Jr., "Yes, Detroit Can Be Fixed: A CAFE Tweak Can Bust the UAW Labor Monopoly," *Wall Street Journal*, November 5, 2008, p. A2. http://online.wsj.com/article/SB122584326266699163.html.

17. Jerry Flint, "They Can Build Them; Why Can't We?" *Forbes.com*, May 28, 2009. http://www.forbes.com/2009/05/27/auto-manufacturing-detroit-business-unions.html.

18. Ibid.

19. Mark Modica and Hal John, "Model Corruption: The Truth About the GM 'Rescue,'" *New York Post*, August 13, 2010.

20. Joann Muller, "Poof! $20B Likely Lost on GM, Says Former Auto Czar," Forbes.com, September 20, 2010, http://blogs.forbes.com/joannmuller/2010/09/20/poof-20b-likely-lost-on-gm-says-former-auto-czar/.

21. Barack Obama, "Remarks in Detroit, Michigan," September 28, 2008. http://www.barackobama.com/2008/09/28/remarks_of_senator_barack_obam_123.php.

22. Henry Hazlitt, "Economics in One Lesson." http://jim.com/econ/chap02p1.html.

23. Ibid.

24. Ibid.

25. John Stossel, "Real Jobs Create Wealth," RealClearpolitics.com, February 19, 2009. http://www.realclearpolitics.com/articles/2009/02/real_jobs_create_wealth.html.

26. Ibid.

27. Amity Shlaes, "The New Deal Jobs Myth," *American Enterprise Institute*, January 2008. http://www.aei.org/docLib/20080116_0722579OTIShlaes_g.pdf.

28. Ibid.

29. Ibid.

30. Brian S. Wesbury and Robert Stein, "Government, the Anti-Stimulus," *Monday Morning Outlook*, published by First Trust, January 10, 2011.

31. Stossel, "Real Jobs Create Wealth."

32. Greg Mankiw, "Create or Save," Greg Mankiw's Blog, February 19, 2009, http://gregmankiw.blogspot.com/2009/02/create-or-save.html.

33. Jim Angle, "House GOP Wants Stimulus Input Following Critical Report," FOXNews.com, January 9, 2009. http://www.foxnews.com/politics/first-100-days/2009/01/09/house-gop-wants-stimulus-input-following-critical-report/.

34. Robert Reich, "Don't Blame Wal-Mart," *New York Times*, Febuary 28, 2005. http://query.nytimes.com/gst/fullpage.html?res=9C07E2DA153DF93BA15751C0A9639C8B63.

35. "Overall, Has Wal-Mart Been Good or Bad for the American Economy?" *Wall Street Journal*, October 2, 2007. http://forums.wsj.com/viewtopic.php?t=858.

36. Al Norman, "Wal-Mart Cancels 45 Superstore Projects," *Huffington Post*, March 30, 2008. http://www.huffingtonpost.com/al-norman/wal-mart-cancels-45-super_b_94112.html.

37. Andrea M. Dean and Russell Sobel, "Has Wal-Mart Buried Mom and Pop?" Spring 2008, Cato Institute. http://www.cato.org/pubs/regulation/regv31n1/v31n1-1.pdf.

38. Ibid.

39. Robert McNatt, "Who Says Wal-Mart Is Bad for Cities?," *BusinessWeek.com*, May 10, 2004. http://www.businessweek.com/magazine/content/04_19/b3882083_mz017.htm.

40. Gwendolyn Bounds, "The Long Road to Wal-Mart Shelves," *The Wall Street Journal Online*, September 20, 2005.

41. Byron York, "The Wal-Mart Movie: Buyer Beware," *Huffington Post*, November 21, 2005. http://www.huffingtonpost.com/byron-york/the-walmart-movie-viewer-_b_11025.html.

42. John C. Bogle, "Strengthening Worker Retirement Security," Statement before the Committee on Education and Labor, U.S. House of Representatives, Washington, D.C.,

February 24, 2009. http://www.nextstepdc.com/assets/pdf/20090224JohnBogle
Testimony.pdf.

43. David John and Robert Moffit, "Medicare and Social Security: The Challenge of Giant
Entitlement Costs," Heritage Foundation, March 25, 2008. http://www.heritage.org/
Research/Budget/upload/wm_1867.pdf.

44. Michael Tanner, "A Real Lockbox for Social Security," *Cato.org*, July 1, 2005. http://
www.cato.org/pub_display.php?pub_id=3970.

45. David C. John, "2009 Social Security Trustees Report Continues to Show the Urgency of
Reform," Heritage Foundation, May 13, 2009. http://www.heritage.org/Research/
SocialSecurity/upload/wm_2439.pdf.

46. Jeremy Siegel, "Stock Market," *The Concise Encyclopedia of Economics*. http://www.econlib
.org/library/Enc/StockMarket.html.

47. Ray Holbrook and Alcestis Oberg, "A Model for Social Security Reform," *USA Today*,
March 15, 2005. http://www.usatoday.com/news/opinion/2005-03-15-benefits-reform
-galveston_x.htm.

48. Jeffrey Sachs, "The Social Welfare State, Beyond Ideology," *Scientific American*, November, 2006. http://www.scientificamerican.com/article.cfm?id=the-social-welfare-state.

49. Ibid.

50. Daniel Mitchell, "What Can the United States Learn from the Nordic Model?"
Cato Institute Policy Analysis, November 5, 2007. http://www.cato.org/pubs/pas/
pa-603.pdf.

51. Bruce Bawer, "We're Rich, You're Not. End of Story," *New York Times*, April 17, 2005.
http://www.brucebawer.com/rich.htm.

52. Ibid.

53. Daniel Mitchell, "Hoping to Restore Growth, Voters Rebel Against Sweden's High-Tax
Welfare State," Heritage Foundation, September 24, 2006. http://www.heritage.org/
research/taxes/wm1219.cfm.

54. Martin De Vlieghere, "The Myth of the Scandinavian Model," *Brussels Journal*, November 25, 2005. http://www.brusselsjournal.com/node/510/print.

55. Mitchell, "What Can the United States Learn from the Nordic Model?"

56. Per Bylund, "How the Welfare State Corrupted Sweden," *Mises Daily*, May 31, 2006.
http://mises.org/story/2190.

57. Mitchell, "Hoping to Restore Growth."

58. Mitchell, "What Can the United States Learn from the Nordic Model?"

59. Daniel Mitchell, "Sweden Repeals Wealth Tax," *Cato@Liberty.org*, March 31, 2007.
http://www.cato-at-liberty.org/2007/03/31/sweden-repeals-wealth-tax/.

Chapter Three: "Aren't the Rich Getting Richer at Other People's Expense?"

1. Barbara Ehrenreich, "The Trouble with the Super-Rich," *The Nation*, June 12, 2007.
http://www.thenation.com/doc/20070625/ehrenreich2.

2. Daniel Gross, "Don't Hate Them Because They're Rich," *New York Magazine*, April 11,
2005. http://nymag.com/nymetro/news/culture/features/11721/.

3. Ibid.

4. Daniel Henninger, "The Obama Rosetta Stone" (Wonder Land column), *Wall Street
Journal*, Opinion, March 12, 2009, p. A13. http://online.wsj.com/article/
SB123681860305802821.html.

5. Nancy Pelosi, House Floor Speech in support of Emergency Economic Stabilization Act
of 2008, House of Representatives, September 30, 2008. http://speaker.house.gov/
newsroom/speeches?id=0149.

6. Alan Reynolds, "Fannie Mae and Freddie Mac Should Be Cut Down and Cut Loose," *U.S. News and World Report*, July 21, 2008. http://www.usnews.com/articles/opinion/2008/07/21/fannie-mae-and-freddie-mac-should-be-cut-down-and-cut-loose.html.

7. Ibid.

8. Terry Jones, "How a Clinton-Era Rule Rewrite Made Subprime Crisis Inevitable," *Investor's Business Daily*, September 24, 2008. http://www.ibdeditorials.com/IBDArticles.aspx?id=307149667289804.

9. Ronald Utt, "Time to Reform Fannie Mae and Freddie Mac," Heritage Foundation, June 20, 2005. http://www.heritage.org/research/governmentreform/upload/79741_1.pdf.

10. Brink Lindsey, "How Real Is Real Income?" "Age of Abundance" blog, May 30, 2007. http://www.brinklindsey.com/?p=77.

11. Diana Furchgott-Roth, "Richer Than You Think," Hudson Institute, December 11, 2006. http://www.hudson.org/index.cfm?fuseaction=publication_details&id=4355.

12. Robert Frank, "The Mobile Rich," The Wealth Report, Wall Street Journal.com (blog), November 14, 2007. http://blogs.wsj.com/wealth/2007/11/14/the-mobile-rich/.

13. Michael Barone, "Personal Well-Being Overshadows Income Inequality," *Washington Examiner*, January 1, 2011, http://washingtonexaminer.com/politics/2011/01/personal-well-being-overshadows-income-inequality.

14. Hedrick Smith, "The Russians: Intro," *HedrickSmith.com*. http://www.hedricksmith.com/books/bookTheRussianIntro.shtml.

15. Douglas J. Besharov, "Measuring Poverty in America." Testimony Before the Committee on Ways and Means in the U.S. House of Representatives, August 1, 2007. http://www.welfareacademy.org/pubs/poverty/Pov_Meas_House_testimony_07_0801.pdf.

16. Ibid.

17. Nicholas Eberstadt, "The Poverty Rate," *AEI Online*, March 1, 2002. http://www.aei.org/issue/13711.

18. Robert Rector, "The Myth of Widespread American Poverty," Heritage Foundation, September 18, 1998. http://www.heritage.org/research/welfare/bg1221es.cfm.

19. Robert Rector, "Understanding Poverty and Economic Inequality in the United States," Heritage Foundation, September 15, 2004, http://www.papillonsartpalace.com/poverty.htm

20. Eberstadt, "The Poverty Rate."

21. Brian Wesbury, "Rising Wage Gap, But No Squeeze," *RealClearPolitics.com*, February 5, 2007. http://www.realclearpolitics.com/articles/2007/02/rising_wage_gap_but_no_squeeze.html.

22. Marc Hodak, "CEOs Aren't Overpaid," Forbes.com, May 8, 2008. http://www.forbes.com/2008/05/08/ceos-not-overpaid-ent-competition08-cx-mh_0508hodak.html.

23. Gary Weiss, "The Man Who Made Too Much," *Portfolio*, February 2009. http://www.portfolio.com/executives/features/2009/01/07/John-Paulson-Profits-in-Downturn.

24. Ibid.

25. Ibid.

26. Ibid.

27. Hunter Lewis, *Are the Rich Necessary?* (Mount Jackson, Va.: Axios Press, 2007), pp. 19–20.

28. Hunter Lewis, "Are the Rich Necessary? Great Economic Arguments and How They Reflect Our Personal Values," *The Mises Review*, fall 2007. http://mises.org/misesreview_detail.aspx?control=316.

29. Barbara Ehrenreich, "The Rich Are Making the Poor Poorer," *The Nation*, June 13, 2007. http://www.alternet.org/workplace/53962/.

30. Ibid.

31. Ibid.

32. Una Galani, "Uganda: Return of the Exiles," *The Independent*, August 26, 2005. http://www.independent.co.uk/news/world/africa/uganda-return-of-the-exiles-504325.html.

33. Thomas Sowell, "Is Anti-Semitism Generic?" *Hoover Digest*, 2005. http://www.hoover.org/publications/digest/2931421.html.

34. David Fintz Altabe, "The Significance of 1492 to the Jews and Muslims of Spain," *Hispania*, September 1992. http://www.millersville.edu/~columbus/data/his/ALTABE01.HIS.

35. "Spain Honoring Jews 500 Years After Expulsion," *New York Times*, June 3, 1990. http://www.nytimes.com/1990/06/03/world/spain-honoring-jews-500-years-after-expulsion.html.

36. D. V. Ranarajan, *Sura's Quotable Quotes, Adages and Sayings* (India: Sura Books, 2004), p. 62.

37. Ben Stein, "Democrats Fan Dangerous Envy," *USA Today*, Editorial/Opinion, March 7, 2001.

38. Lynn Stout, "Why Carl Icahn Is Bad for Investors," *Wall Street Journal*, August 1, 2008. http://online.wsj.com/article/SB121754688222002635.html.

39. Bruce Bartlett, "New York Times Twists Good News into Bad," *Human Events*, August 31, 2004. http://www.papillonsartpalace.com/newnyork.htm.

40. Department of the Treasury, "Income Mobility in the U.S. from 1996 to 2005," November 13, 2007. http://ustreas.gov/offices/tax-policy/library/incomemobilitystudy03-08revise.pdf.

41. Todd Zywicki, "It's Not the Mortgages, It's the Taxes," *Washington Post*, April 29, 2008. http://www.washingtonpost.com/wp-dyn/content/article/2008/04/28/AR2008042802486.html.

42. Todd J. Zywicki, "The Two-Income Tax Trap," *Wall Street Journal*, August 14, 2007, http://www.law.gmu.edu/news/2007/803.

43. Ibid.

44. Laura Rowley, "Can You Live on One Income? It's Worth a Try," *Yahoo Finance*, May 7, 2008. http://finance.yahoo.com/expert/article/moneyhappy/81176.

45. *WiseBread.com*, August 9, 2008. http://www.wisebread.com/is-living-on-one-income-a-status-symbol#comment-132008.

46. Curt, "Dual-Income Families Have Less Money," *WiseBread.com*, August 7, 2008. http://www.wisebread.com/is-living-on-one-income-a-status-symbol#comment-131660.

47. *WiseBread.com*, August 19, 2008. http://www.wisebread.com/is-living-on-one-income-a-status-symbol#comment-133916.

Chapter Four: "Aren't Higher Taxes the Price We Pay for a Humane Society?"

1. Steve Forbes, *Flat Tax Revolution: Using a Postcard to Abolish the IRS* (Washington, D.C.: Regnery Publishing, 2005), p. 13.

2. Andrew Chamberlain, Gerald Prante, and Patrick Fleenor, "Death and Taxes: The Economics of the Federal Estate Tax," special report, Tax Foundation, May 2006, No. 142. www.taxfoundation.org/files/sr142.pdf.

3. David R. Henderson, "Will the Real Christina Romer Please Stand Up?" *Forbes.com*. January 7, 2009. http://www.forbes.com/2009/01/07/romer-obama-stimulus-oped-cx_dh_0107henderson.html.

4. Tax Foundation, 2009 Survey of U.S. Attitudes on Taxes, Government Spending, and Wealth Distribution, Special Report no. 166. http://www.taxfoundation.org/files/sr166.pdf.

5. Yaron Brook, "Life and Taxes," *Forbes.com*, April 17, 2008. http://www.forbes.com/2008/04/16/yaron-taxes-campaign-oped-cx_ybr_0417yaron.html.

6. Tom Bawden, "Buffett Blasts System That Lets Him Pay Less Tax than Secretary," *The Times* (London), June 28, 2007. http://www.timesonline.co.uk/tol/money/tax/article1996735.ece.

7. Mark Robyn and Gerald Prante, "Summary of Latest Federal Individual Income Tax Data," Tax Foundation Fiscal Fact No. 249, October 6, 2010. http://www.taxfoundation.org/news/show/250.html.

8. Stephen Moore, "How to Soak the Rich (the George Bush Way)," *Wall Street Journal*, p. A14. http://online.wsj.com/article/SB114670305012743294.html.

9. "Excerpts from the Debate," *New York Times*, October 16, 2008. http://query.nytimes.com/gst/fullpage.html?res=9D03E0D81631F935A25753C1A96E9C8B63.

10. Scott A. Hodge, "U.S. States Lead the World in High Corporate Taxes," March 18, 2008, Fiscal Fact No. 119. http://www.taxfoundation.org/publications/show/22917.html.

11. David Cay Johnston, "Enron's Collapse: The Havens; Enron Avoided Income Taxes in 4 of 5 Years," *New York Times*, Thursday, January 17, 2002. http://www.nytimes.com/2002/01/17/business/enron-s-collapse-the-havens-enron-avoided-income-taxes-in-4-of-5-years.html.

12. Alan Reynolds, "Obama's '$4 Billion for Exxon' Myth: Why Haven't the 'Fact-checkers' Done a Better Job?" *Wall Street Journal*, November 1, 2008, p. A11. http://online.wsj.com/article/SB122549399683189495.html.

13. Tax Foundation, "American Families Bear Large Burden from Corporate Income Tax: Growing Consensus Says Corporate Taxes Are Most in Need of Reform," August 26, 2008. http://www.taxfoundation.org/news/show/23547.html.

14. Scott A. Hodge and Gerald Prante, "Personalizing the Corporate Income Tax," Tax Foundation, Fiscal Fact No. 106, October 25, 2007. http://taxfoundation.org/research/show/22694.html.

15. N. Gregory Mankiw, "The Problem with the Corporate Tax," *New York Times* (Business), June 1, 2008. http://www.nytimes.com/2008/06/01/business/01view.html.

16. Steve Forbes, *Flat Tax Revolution* (Washington, D.C.: Regnery Publishing, 2005), p. 7.

17. Ibid, p 7.

18. Brook, "Life and Taxes."

19. Chamberlain, Prante, and Fleenor, "Death and Taxes."

20. Ibid, p.3.

21. Victor Mavar (former vice president of Mavar Shrimp & Oyster Co.), Statement for the Record, U.S. Senate Finance Committee, "Federal Estate Tax: Uncertainty in Planning Under the Current Law," November 14, 2007. http://www.nodeathtax.org/resources/testimonies/mavar.

22. Henry J. Aaron and Alicia H. Munnell, "Reassessing the Role for Wealth Transfer Taxes," *National Tax Journal* 45, no. 2 (June 1992), p. 139. Study cited in "The Economics of the Estate Tax," a Joint Economic Committee Study, December 1998. http://www.house.gov/jec/fiscal/tx-grwth/estattax/estattax.htm#endnot132.

23. Herman Cain, written testimony for U.S. Senate Finance Committee hearing, "Federal Estate Tax: Uncertainty in Planning Under the Current Law," November 14, 2007. http://www.nodeathtax.org/resources/testimonies/cain.

24. David Cay Johnston, "A Texas Bid to Shift School Finances to 'Sin Taxes'" *New York Times*, April 21, 2004. http://www.nytimes.com/2004/04/21/national/21TEXA.html.

25. Elizabeth Karasmeighan, "State Tax Trends over Twenty-Five Years: Tax Increases Down, Revenue Sources Shifting," Americans for Tax Reform, August 14, 2006. www.atr.org/pdf/2006/august/081406ot-statetrendspaper.pdf.

26. Rev. Robert A. Sirico, "The Sin Tax Craze: Who's Next?" *Acton Commentary*, April 28, 2004. http://www.acton.org/commentary/commentary_196.php.

27. Ibid.

28. "Cigarette Tax Burnout," *Wall Street Journal*, Review & Outlook, August 11, 2008. http://online.wsj.com/public/article_print/SB121841215866128319.html.

29. National Center for Policy Analysis Task Force on Taxing the Poor, "Taxing The Poor," no. 300, June 22, 2007. http://www.ncpa.org/pub/st300?pg=2.

30. Sirico, "The Sin Tax Craze."

31. Stephen Moore, "Capital Gains Taxes," *The Concise Encyclopedia of Economics*, Library of Economics and Liberty. http://www.econlib.org/library/Enc/CapitalGainsTaxes.html.

32. Ibid. Alan Blinder, a former member of the Federal Reserve Board, noted in 1980 that, up until that time, "most capital gains were not gains of real purchasing power at all, but simply represented the maintenance of principal in an inflationary world." Alan S. Blinder, "The Level and Distribution of Economic Well-Being," in Martin Feldstein, ed., *The American Economy in Transition* (Chicago: University of Chicago Press, 1980), p. 48.

33. Donald Luskin, "The 2003 Tax Cut on Capital Gains Entirely Paid for Itself (I'm Not Just Saying It—CBO Is.)" *National Review Online*, January 27, 2006. http://www.nationalreview.com/nrof_luskin/luskin200601270946.asp.

34. Stephen Moore, "The Bush Capital Gains Tax Cut after Four Years: More Growth, More Investment, More Revenues," National Center for Policy Analysis, http://www.ncpa.org/pub/st307.

35. Brian M. Riedl, "The Myth of Spending Cuts for the Poor, Tax Cuts for the Rich," Heritage Foundation, February 14, 2006. http://www.heritage.org/research/budget/bg1912.cfm.

36. John Tamny, "A Dearth of Taxes?" RealClearPolitics.com, October 27, 2007. http://www.realclearpolitics.com/articles/2007/10/a_dearth_of_taxes.html.

37. Brian M. Riedl, "CBO Budget Baseline Shows Historic Surge in Spending and Debt," Heritage Foundation, WebMemo no. 2193, January 7, 2009. http://www.heritage.org/research/budget/wm2193.cfm.

38. Ibid.

39. Daniel J. Mitchell, Ph.D. "Ten Deceptive Myths About Social Security, the Budget, and the Economy," Heritage Foundation, Backgrounder no. 1467, August 23, 2001. http://www.heritage.org/research/socialsecurity/bg1467.cfm.

40. Brian M. Riedl, "Top 10 Examples of Government Waste," Heritage Foundation, Backgrounder no. 1840, April 4, 2005. http://www.heritage.org/research/budget/bg1840.cfm.

41. Riedl, "CBO Budget Baseline Shows Historic Surge in Spending and Debt."

Chapter Five: "Don't Regulations Safeguard the Public Good?"

1. Friedrich Hayek, *The Road to Serfdom* (New York: Routledge, 2001).

2. Milton Friedman, *Free to Choose* (New York: Houghton Mifflin Harcourt, 1990), p. 29.

3. William Anderson, "A Primer on Regulation," Mises Institute, 2004.

4. Friedman, *Free to Choose*, p. 188. Regulation ended up crippling the railroad industry, preventing needed mergers and other productivity-enhancing measures. By the 1970s, the industry was in as bad a shape as the Detroit automakers are today. The industry faced bankruptcy. The government had taken over the bankrupt Penn Central. But instead of more bailouts and takeovers, Washington did something right. At the behest of President Jimmy Carter, Congress passed a sweeping deregulation bill that ended up abolishing the Interstate Commerce Commission and gave railroads the freedom to set

prices and do mergers. Almost overnight the industry rebounded and became profitable and vibrant.

5. Indonesia, "2009 Index of Economic Freedom," Heritage Foundation. http://www.heritage.org/index/country/Indonesia.

6. James S. Henry and Laurence J. Kotlikoff, "Financial Reform, R.I.P." *Forbes.com*, July 15, 2010. http://www.forbes.com/2010/07/15/dodd-frank-failure-regulation-opinions-contributors-james-henry-laurence-kotlikoff-wall-street.html.

7. Ibid.

8. Ibid.

9. "Brief Summary of the Dodd-Frank Wall Street Reform and Consumer Protection Act." http://www.banking.senate.gov/.../070110_Dodd_Frank_Wall_Street_Reform_comprehensive_summary_Final.pdf.

10. Douglas J. Elliott, "Financial Reform: Now It's Up to the Regulators," paper written for the Brookings Institution, July 12, 2010. http://www.brookings.edu/papers/2010/0712_regulators_elliott.aspx.

11. David C. John and James Gattuso, "Financial Reform in Congress: A Disorderly Failure," Heritage Foundation Web Memo #2942, published on June 28, 2010. http://www.heritage.org/research/reports/2010/06/financial-reform-in-congress-a-disorderly-failure.

12. Nicole Gelinas, *After the Fall: Saving Capitalism from Wall Street and Washington* (New York: Encounter Books, 2009).

13. Alan Reynolds, "The Sarbanes-Oxley Tax," *Investor's Business Daily*, March 14, 2005. http://www.cato.org/pub_display.php?pub_id=4240.

14. Mallory Factor, "Two Cheers for Nancy Pelosi," *Wall Street Journal*, March 19, 2006. http://www.opinionjournal.com/extra/?id=110008110.

15. Reynolds, "The Sarbanes-Oxley Tax."

16. Ibid.

17. Ibid.

18. T. J. Rogers, "FASB: Making Financial Statements Mysterious," Cato Institute Briefing Papers, August 19, 2008. http://www.cato.org/pubs/bp/bp105.pdf.

19. Ibid.

20. John Fund, "Escape from Wall Street," *Wall Street Journal*, December 4, 2006. http://www.opinionjournal.com/diary/?id=110009339.

21. Seth Stein and Joseph Tomasello, "Safety Costs Too Much," *New York Times*, January 10, 2004. http://www.aei-brookings.org/policy/page.php?id=171&printversion=1.

22. Ibid.

23. Ibid.

24. Ibid.

25. Walter Olson, "Scrap the Consumer Product Safety Improvement Act," *Forbes.com*, January 16, 2009. http://www.manhattan-institute.org/html/miarticle.htm?id=4303.

26. Ibid.

27. Ibid.

28. Ike Brannon, "What Is a Life Worth?" Cato.org, winter 2004–2005. http://www.heartland.org/custom/semod_policybot/pdf/16936.pdf.

29. Bjørn Lomborg, *Cool It: The Skeptical Environmentalist's Guide to Global Warming* (New York: Alfred A. Knopf, 2007).

30. Brannon, "What Is a Life Worth?"

31. Debra Kahn, "State Regulators Approve the Nation's Biggest Cap-and-Trade Plan," ClimateWire, *NewYorkTimes.com*, December 17, 2010. http://www.nytimes.com/

cwire/2010/12/17/17climatewire-state-regulators-approve-the-nations-biggest-84198
.html.

32. James Kanter and Jad Mouawad, "Money and Lobbyists Hurt European Efforts to Curb
Gases," *New York Times*, December 11, 2008. http://www.e3network.org/resources/
Money%20and%20Lobbyists%20Hurt%20EU%20ETS%20(NYT).pdf.

33. Martin Feldstein, "Cap-and-Trade: All Cost, No Benefit," *Washington Post*, June 1, 2009.
http://www.washingtonpost.com/wp-dyn/content/article/2009/05/31/
AR2009053102077.html.

34. Mireya Navarro, "States Diverting Money from Climate Initiative," *New York Times*,
November 28, 2010. http://www.nytimes.com/2010/11/29/nyregion/29greenhouse
.html.

35. D. T. Armentano, "A Politically Incorrect Guide to Antitrust Policy," *Mises Daily*, September 15, 2007. http://mises.org/story/2694.

36. Quoted in Amanda Carpenter, "God Says Raise the Minimum Wage, According to Ted
Kennedy," *Human Events*, November 8, 2005. http://www.humanevents.com/article
.php?id=10140.

37. Thomas Sowell, "The Imitators: Part I," *Capitalism Magazine*, June 23, 2008. http://
www.capmag.com/article.asp?ID=5214.

38. Ibid.

39. Ibid.

40. Ali Abdiweli, "Unvarnished Views of a 'Radical' Economist: Walter E. Williams on More
Innovation, Less Regulation, and the Entrepreneur as an American Hero," *Journal of
Applied Management and Entrepreneurship*, July 2005. http://findarticles.com/p/articles/
mi_qa5383/is_200507/ai_n21364336/pg_6/.

41. Quoted in Roger Koopman, "The Minimum Wage: Good Intentions, Bad Results," *The
Freeman*, March 1988. http://www.thefreemanonline.org/columns/the-minimum-wage
-good-intentions-bad-results/.

42. James Sherk, "Minimum Wage Workers' Incomes Rise When the Minimum Wage Does
Not," Heritage Foundation, July 28, 2006. http://www.heritage.org/research/economy/
wm1181.cfm.

43. James Sherk and Rea Hederman, "Who Earns the Minimum Wage? Suburban Teenagers,
Not Single Parents," Heritage Foundation, January 23, 2007. http://www.heritage.org/
research/economy/wm1320.cfm.

44. Rea Hederman and James Sherk, "Who Earns the Minimum Wage—Single Parents or
Suburban Teenagers?" Heritage Foundation, August 3, 2006. http://www.heritage
.org/research/economy/wm1186.cfm.

45. Richard V. Burkhauser and Joseph J. Sabia, "Raising the Minimum Wage: Another
Empty Promise to the Working Poor," Employment Policies Institute, August 2005.
http://www.heartland.org/custom/semod_policybot/pdf/19638.pdf.

46. Ali Abdiweli, "Unvarnished Views of a 'Radical' Economist: Walter E. Williams on More
Innovation, Less Regulation, and the Entrepreneur as an American Hero," *Journal of
Applied Management and Entrepreneurship*, July 2005. http://findarticles.com/p/articles/
mi_qa5383/is_200507/ai_n21364336/pg_6/.

47. Matthew Yglesias, "Airline Deregulation," *Think Progress*, September 14, 2008. http://
yglesias.thinkprogress.org/archives/2008/09/airline_deregulation.php.

48. Henry Blodget, "Oh, Please, 'NET NEUTRALITY' Zealots Are Just Looking Out for
Their Own Self-Interest," Business Insider.com, December 21, 2010, http://www
.businessinsider.com/all-bits-are-not-created-equal-and-you-net.

49. James L. Gattuso, "Red Tape Under the Tree: FCC Plans Internet Regulation for Christmas," Heritage Foundation Web Memo No. 3086, December 17, 2010. http://www

.heritage.org/research/reports/2010/12/red-tape-under-the-tree-fcc-plans-internet
-regulation-for-christmas.

50. "Problem Solvers Get Involved When City Refuses Lemonade Stand," Local10.com,
January 10, 2005. http://www.justnews.com/news/4053892/detail.html.

51. Jack McHugh, "Proposed Legislation a License to Kill Competitors for Big Auto Dealers,"
Mackinac Center for Public Policy, January 2002. https://www.mackinac.org/article
.aspx?ID=3925.

52. Adam Summers, "Occupational Licensing Laws Protect Special Interests, Not the Public," Reason Foundation, April 1, 2008. http://reason.org/news/printer/occupational
-licensing-laws-pr.

53. Cited in Morris M. Kleiner, "Occupational Licensing and the Internet: Issues for Policy
Makers," University of Minnesota and the National Bureau of Economic Research,
October 1, 2002. http://www.ftc.gov/opp/ecommerce/anticompetitive/panel/
kleiner.pdf.

54. Jacob Sullum, "Coffin Break," *Reason*, December 31, 2004. http://www.reason.com/
news/show/35973.html.

55. Clark Neily, "IJ Takes on Oklahoma Casket Cartel," Institute for Justice, May 2001.
http://www.ij.org/index.php?option=com_content&task=view&id=1707&Itemid=245.

56. Valerie Bayham, "A Dream Deferred," Institute for Justice, September 2006. http://
www.ij.org/index.php?option=com_content&task=view&id=1631&Itemid=246.

Chapter Six: "Aren't Free Trade and 'Globalization' Destroying American Jobs and the Economies of Other Nations?"

1. Adam Smith, *An Inquiry into the Nature and Causes of the Wealth of Nations* (T. Nelson, 1852),
p. 185.

2. David Ricardo, *On the Principles of Political Economy, and Taxation* (New York: Penguin, 1971).

3. Rod Hunter, "An Unwinnable War," *Weekly Standard*, March 31, 2009. http://www
.weeklystandard.com/Content/Public/Articles/000%5C000%5C016%5C347aehbf
.asp?pg=1.

4. Ibid.

5. Scott C. Bradford, Paul L. E. Grieco, and Gary Clyde Hufbauer, "The Payoff to America
from Global Integration," Peterson Institute for International Economics, 2006.
http://www.iie.com/publications/papers/2iie3802.pdf.

6. Daniel Drezner, "U.S. Trade Dilemma: Free or Fair?" *Washington Post*, September 15,
2006. http://www.washingtonpost.com/wp-dyn/content/article/2006/09/14/
AR2006091401140.html.

7. Ana Isabel Eiras, "Why America Needs to Support Free Trade," *Heritage Foundation*,
May 14, 2004. http://www.heritage.org/research/tradeandeconomicfreedom/
bg1761.cfm.

8. Robyn Meredith and Suzanne Hoppough, "Why Globalization Is Good," *Forbes.com*,
April 16, 2007. http://www.forbes.com/free_forbes/2007/0416/064.html.

9. Cited in Nathan Gardels, "Globalization Bites Back," *National Perspectives Quarterly*,
April 5, 2004. http://www.digitalnpq.org/global_services/global_ec_viewpoint/
04-05-04.html.

10. Daniel Griswold, "Trade, Democracy, and Peace: The Virtuous Cycle," Presentation
at World Trade Centers Association, April 20, 2007. http://www.freetrade.org/node
/681.

11. Ibid.

12. *Washington Times*, editorial, May 16, 2004. http://www.washingtontimes.com/news/
2004/may/16/20040516-102448-2933r/.

13. John Engler, "Forging A Second American Century," *Forbes.com*, May 28, 2009. http://www.forbes.com/2009/05/27/john-engler-manufacturing-business-america.html.

14. Rod Hunter, "An Unwinnable War," *Weekly Standard*, March 31, 2009. http://www.weeklystandard.com/Content/Public/Articles/000%5C000%5C016%5C347aehbf.asp?pg=1.

15. Gary Hufbauer and Jeffrey Schott, "Buy American: Bad for Jobs, Worse for Reputation," Peterson Institute for International Economics, February 2009. http://www.iie.com/publications/pb/pb09-2.pdf.

16. Douglas Irwin, "If We Buy American, No One Else Will," *New York Times*, January 31, 2009. http://www.nytimes.com/2009/02/01/opinion/01irwin.html.

17. Hufbauer and Schott, "Buy American."

18. Ibid.

19. James Roberts, "Elimination of U.S. Pilot Truck Program Triggers Mexican Tariffs," Heritage Foundation, March 24, 2009. http://www.heritage.org/research/latinamerica/upload/wm_2357.pdf.

20. McKinsey Global Institute, "Offshoring: Is It a Win-Win Game?" McKinsey and Company Inc., August 2003. http://hei.unige.ch/~baldwin/ComparativeAdvantageMyths/IsOffshoringWinWin_McKinsey.pdf.

21. Ibid.

22. Catherine L. Mann, "Globalization of IT Services and White Collar Jobs: The Next Wave of Productivity Growth," Peterson Institute for International Economics, Policy Brief 03-11, December 2003. www.iie.com/publications/pb/pb03-11.pdf.

23. Daniel Drezner, "U.S. Trade Strategy: Free Versus Fair," Council on Foreign Relations, 2006. http://www.cfr.org/content/publications/attachments/CPCTrade.pdf.

24. Ibid.

25. Ibid.

26. "Hearing on Confirmation of Mr. Timothy F. Geithner to be Secretary of the U.S. Department of Treasury," Finance Committee Questions for the Record, United States Senate Committee on Finance, p. 81, January 21, 2009. finance.senate.gov/.../LEG%202009/012209%20TFG%20Questions.pdf.

27. Indira Lakshmanan, "Clinton Urges China to Keep Buying Treasuries," *Bloomberg.com*, February 22, 2009. http://www.bloomberg.com/apps/news?pid=20601087&sid=ahowJ.dThUNs&refer=home.

28. Ibid.

29. Jagdish Bhagwati, "U.S. Trade Policy: The China Question," Testimony before the Senate Finance Committee, March 27, 2007. http://74.125.95.132/search?q=cache:l_3DWelupFIJ:www.columbia.edu/~jb38/Testimony%2520March%252027%252007.doc+longer+are+also+cast+in+doubt+by+her+communist+politics.+China+lacks+currently+the+four+elements+of+a+functioning+democracy:+NGOs,+a+free+press,+opposition+parties+and+an+independent+judiciary.+The+result+is+growing+social+disruptions+as+commissars+and+their+cronies+grab+land,+for+example.&cd=1&hl=en&ct=clnk&gl=us.

30. Robert Samuelson, "U.S. Shouldn't Fear Rise of China, India," *Business Times*, May 26, 2005. http://yaleglobal.yale.edu/article.print?id=5762.

31. Thomas Omestad, "Does Financial Crisis Threaten America's Central Role in Global Economy?" *US News & World Report*, October 10, 2008. http://www.usnews.com/articles/news/2008/10/10/does-financial-crisis-threaten-americas-central-role-in-global-economy.html.

32. John Steele Gordon, "Why NAFTA Was a Very Good Thing," *AmericanHeritage.com*,

December 17, 2007. http://www.americanheritage.com/articles/web/20071217-north-american-free-trade-agreement-canada-mexico-george-h-w-bush-globalization.shtml.

33. Heidi Sommer, "The Economic Benefits of NAFTA to the United States and Mexico," National Center for Policy Analysis, June 16, 2008. http://www.ncpa.org/pub/ba619.

34. Daniel Griswold, "NAFTA at 10: An Economic and Foreign Policy Success," Center for Trade Policy Studies, Cato Institute, December 17, 2002. http://www.freetrade.org/node/87.

35. Anil Kumar, "Did NAFTA Spur Texas Exports?" Federal Reserve Bank of Dallas, March/April 2006. http://www.dallasfed.org/research/swe/2006/swe0602b.html.

36. Ibid.

37. John Steele Gordon, "Why NAFTA Was a Very Good Thing," *AmericanHeritage.com*, December 17, 2007. http://www.americanheritage.com/articles/web/20071217-north-american-free-trade-agreement-canada-mexico-george-h-w-bush-globalization.shtml.

38. Daniella Markheim and Brian Riedl, "Farm Subsidies, Free Trade, and the Doha Round," Heritage Foundation, February 5, 2007. http://www.heritage.org/RESEARCH/BUDGET/wm1337.cfm.

39. Brian Riedl, "How Farm Subsidies Harm Taxpayers, Consumers, and Farmers, Too," Heritage Foundation, June 20, 2007. http://www.heritage.org/research/agriculture/upload/bg_2043.pdf.

40. Daniel Griswold, Stephen Slivinski, and Christopher Preble, "Six Reasons to Kill Farm Subsidies and Trade Barriers," *Reason*, February 2006. http://www.reason.com/news/show/36207.html.

41. Robert Bryce, "Corn Dog," *Slate.com*, July 19, 2005. http://slate.msn.com/id/2122961/.

42. C. Ford Runge and Benjamin Senauer, "How Biofuels Could Starve the Poor," *Foreign Affairs*, May/June 2007. http://www.foreignaffairs.com/articles/62609/c-ford-runge-and-benjamin-senauer/how-biofuels-could-starve-the-poor.

43. Gerard Wynn, "U.S. Corn Ethanol 'Was Not a Good Policy'—Gore," *Reuters.com*, November 22, 2010. http://af.reuters.com/article/energyOilNews/idAFLDE6AL0YT20101122?sp=true.

44. Martin Crutsinger, "Trade Deficit Is 2nd Highest Ever," Associated Press, March 11, 2005. http://www.usatoday.com/money/economy/trade/2005-03-11-trade-deficit_x.htm.

45. "Trade Deficit Falls for 7th Straight Month in February," Associated Press, April 9, 2009. http://blog.cleveland.com/business/2009/04/trade_deficit_falls_for_7th_st.html.

46. Judith Shelton, "Time for a New Bretton Woods," *Wall Street Journal*, October 15, 1998. http://www.imfsite.org/operations/shelton.html.

47. Lawrence White, "Is the Gold Standard Still the Gold Standard Among Monetary Systems?" Cato Institute briefing paper, February 8, 2008. http://www.cato.org/pub_display.php?pub_id=9181.

48. Carter Dougherty, "Merkel, at Davos, Calls for a 'Global Economic Charter,'" *New York Times*, January 30, 2009. http://www.nytimes.com/2009/01/30/business/worldbusiness/30iht-davos.4.19817885.html.

49. Brett Schaefer, "Gordon Brown's Financial Folly: The Global Economy Does Not Need More Regulation," Heritage Foundation, October 17, 2008. http://www.heritage.org/Research/internationalorganizations/wm2107.cfm.

50. Ambassador Terry Miller, "New Global Currency Proposal: Good Diplomatic Theater but Bad Policy," Heritage Foundation, http://www.heritage.org/Research/tradeandeconomicfreedom/wm2364.cfm. March 26, 2009.

Chapter Seven: "Is Affordable Health Care Possible in a Free Market?"

1. Milton Friedman, "How to Cure Health Care," *Hoover Digest*, 2001. http://www.hoover.org/publications/digest/3459466.html.

2. Ibid.

3. Clifford Krauss, "Canada Looks for Ways to Fix Its Health Care System," *New York Times*, September 12, 2004. http://www.nytimes.com/2004/09/12/international/americas/12canada.html?position=&pagewanted=print&position=.

4. David Gratzer, "A Canadian Doctor Describes How Socialized Medicine Doesn't Work," *Investor's Business Daily*, July 26, 2007. http://www.ibdeditorials.com/IBDArticles.aspx?id=270338135202343.

5. "Hospitals Punished for Their Success," *The Telegraph*, August 2, 2006. http://www.telegraph.co.uk/comment/personal-view/3626813/Hospitals-punished-for-their-success.html.

6. Karyn Miller, Adam Lusher, and Tom Harper, "Too Successful: The Hospitals Forced to Introduce Minimum Waiting Times," *The Telegraph*, August 7, 2006. http://www.telegraph.co.uk/health/healthnews/3342361/Too-successful-the-hospitals-forced-to-introduce-minimum-waiting-times.html.

7. Johnny Munkhammar, "Markets Are the Answer to Health Care Problems," Heartland Institute, August 2007. http://www.heartland.org/policybot/results/21701/Markets_Are_the_Answer_to_Health_Care_Problems.html.

8. Sally Pipes, "Drug Importation Is a 'Reform' We Can Do Without," *Washington Examiner*, October 19, 2008. http://m.washingtonexaminer.com/dcexam/db_8610/contentdetail.htm;jsessionid=B3851A2BA7300FAE0C29D2EBCAFD62BC?full=true&contentguid=wT4PUmMI&pn=8&ps=5.

9. David Asman, "There's No Place Like Home," *Wall Street Journal*, June 8, 2005. http://www.opinionjournal.com/extra/?id=110006785.

10. Ibid.

11. Ibid.

12. Ibid.

13. Valentin Petkantchin, "How Europe Stifled Medical Innovation," Institut économique Molinari, March 27, 2009. http://www.institutmolinari.org/editos/20090327.htm.

14. John Goodman, "Health Alert," *John Goodman's Health Policy Blog*, January 23, 2009. http://www.john-goodman-blog.com/where-the-medical-markets-actually-work/.

15. Ibid.

16. Grace-Marie Turner, "The Value of Innovation in Health Care," Galen Institute, January 13, 2009. http://www.galen.org/component,8/action,show_content/id,13/category_id,2/blog_id,1145/type,33/.

17. Lloyd M. Krieger, "ObamaCare Is Already Damaging Health Care," *Wall Street Journal*, February 23, 2011.

18. Michael Tanner, "Bad Medicine: A Guide to the Real Costs and Consequences of the New Health Care Law," The Cato Institute, 2010. http://www.cato.org/bad-medicine/.

19. Ibid.

20. "ObamaCare's Reality Deficit," editorial, *Wall Street Journal*, January 8, 2011. http://online.wsj.com/article/SB10001424052748704415104576065723458609678.html.

21. Tanner, "Bad Medicine."

22. Ibid.

23. Ibid.

24. "ObamaCare Rationing Begins," *Investors Business Daily*, December 22, 2010. http://www

.investors.com/NewsAndAnalysis/Article/557595/201012221907/ObamaCare-Rationing
-Begins.aspx.

25. Interview with Donald Berwick, "Rethinking Comparative Effectiveness Research."
    Biotechnology Healthcare, June 2009; 6(2): 35–36, 38. http://www.ncbi.nlm.nih.gov/
    pmc/articles/PMC2799075/?log%24=activity.

26. Eric Singer, "When You're Worth More Dead Than Alive," Investors.com, August 14,
    2009, http://www.investors.com/NewsAndAnalysis/ArticlePrint.aspx?id=503472.

27. Conrad F. Meier, "Destroying Insurance Markets: How Guaranteed Issue and Commu-
    nity Rating Destroyed the Individual Health Insurance Market in Eight States," pub-
    lished by the Council for Affordable Health Insurance and The Heartland Institute,
    2005. http://www.heartland.org/books/Destroying.html.

28. Merrill Matthews, "A Health-Insurance Solution," *Wall Street Journal*, December 12, 2007.
    http://www.drugwonks.com/blog_post/show/4445?eid=774065bc8b95932f826a65ccab63
    aaac.

29. Merrill Matthews, "The 'Uninsurable,'" *Washington Times*, June 16, 2008. http://www
    .washingtontimes.com/news/2008/jun/16/the-uninsurable/.

30. John Cochrane, "Health-Status Insurance: How Markets Can Provide Health Security,"
    Cato Institute Policy Analysis, February 18, 2009. http://www.cato.org/pubs/pas/
    pa-633.pdf.

31. John H. Cochrane, "What to Do About Pre-Existing Conditions," *Wall Street Journal*,
    August 14, 2009. http://online.wsj.com/article/SB10001424052970203609204574316172 5
    12242220.html.

32. Gina Kolata, "Co-Payments Soar for Drugs with High Prices," *New York Times*, April 14,
    2008. http://www.nytimes.com/2008/04/14/us/14drug.html?pagewanted=print.

33. Ibid.

34. Robert Bazell, "Strange Medicine," *Slate.com*, June 23 2004. http://www.slate.com/id/
    2102844/.

35. Ibid.

36. Ibid.

37. Malcolm Gladwell, "Need, Not Greed, Is What's Causing High Prices for Prescription
    Drugs," *The New Yorker*, October 25, 2004. http://www.heartland.org/publications/
    health%20care/article/15909/Need_Not_Greed_Is_Whats_Causing_High_Prices_for_
    Prescription_Drugs.html.

38. Thomas Bray, "Premium Pain Relief," *Wall Street Journal*, July 23, 2002. http://www
    .opinionjournal.com/columnists/tbray/?id=110002025.

39. Günter Verheugen, "Delivering Better Information, Better Access and Better Prices,"
    Speech at the European Pharmaceutical Forum, September 29, 2006. http://www
    .montesquieu-instituut.nl/9353000/1/j9vvh6nfo8temvo/vhefjfs6y9q2?ctx=vgg6ig6
    cels8&start_tabo=20.

40. Sally Satel, "Organs for Sale," *The American*, October 14, 2006. http://www.american
    .com/archive/2006/november/organs-for-sale/article_print.

41. Ibid.

42. Ibid.

43. Office of Inspector General, "A Comparison of Prices for Power Wheelchairs in the
    Medicare Program," Department of Health and Human Services, April 2004. http://
    oig.hhs.gov/oei/reports/oei-03-03-00460.pdf.

44. "A Testimony on Kyle Medicare Contracting Bill," Association of American Physicians
    and Surgeons. http://www.aapsonline.org/medicare/kyltest.htm.

45. Karen Lasser, Steffie Woolhandler, and David Himmelstein, "Sources of U.S. Physician

Income: The Contribution of Government Payments to the Specialist-Generalist Income Gap," *Journal of General Internal Medicine*, September 2008. http://www.springerlink .com/content/ql727j6357270761/?p=61e20debe5e2441db52ae70e5347682a&pi=3.

46. Kurt Williamsen, "SCHIP of State: President Obama and Most of the Press Cheered the Passage of the State Children's Health Insurance Program, but Can SCHIP Stay Afloat Long-Term?" *The New American*, March 2, 2009. http://findarticles.com/p/articles/mi_ m0JZS/is_5_25/ai_n31438421/.

47. Susan Okie, "Innovation in Primary Care—Staying One Step Ahead of Burnout," *New England Journal of Medicine*, November 27, 2008. http://content.nejm.org/cgi/content/ full/359/22/2305.

48. Edmund F. Haislmaier, "Medicare's Fatal Weakness: Expensive New Technologies are Rationed," *National Policy Analysis*, March 2005. http://www.nationalcenter.org/ NPA525MedicareRationing.html.

49. Sue Blevins, "Let Seniors Get Off the Sinking Medicare Ship," Cato Institute, April 7, 2004. http://www.cato.org/pub_display.php?pub_id=2600.

50. Steven Malanga, "How to Stop Medicaid Fraud," *City Journal*, spring 2006. http://www .city-journal.org/html/16_2_medicaid_fraud.html.

51. "Legislative Malpractice," *New York Post*, August 25, 2008. http://www.nypost.com/ seven/08252008/postopinion/editorials/legislative_malpractice_126025.htm.

52. Stephanie Desmon, "Doctors in Short Supply in Rural Maryland," *Baltimore Sun*, February 17, 2009. http://www.baltimoresun.com/services/newspaper/printedition/sunday/ ideas/bal-id.rural01mar01,0,6046663.story.

53. "Medical Malpractice Litigation Raises Health-Care Cost, Reduces Access, and Lowers Quality of Care," *Journal of Medical Practice Management*, 2004. https://www.researchgate .net/publication/8217146_Medical_malpractice_litigation_raises_health-care_cost_ reduces_access_and_lowers_quality_of_care.

54. Philip K. Howard, "Hearing on Medical Liability: New Ideas for Making the System Work Better for Patients," Testimony before the Senate Committee on Health, Education, Labor, and Pensions, June 22, 2006. http://help.senate.gov/Hearings/2006_06_ 22/howard.pdf.

55. Ibid.

56. Ibid.

Chapter Eight: "Isn't Government Needed to Direct the Economy?"

1. David Leonhardt, "After the Great Recession," *New York Times Magazine*, April 28, 2009. http://www.nytimes.com/2009/05/03/magazine/03Obama-t.html.

2. Ibid.

3. Ibid.

4. Randall Holcombe, "Federal Government Growth Before the New Deal," *The Freeman*, September 1, 1997. http://www.independent.org/publications/article.asp?id=360.

5. John Maynard Keynes, *The General Theory of Employment, Interest, and Money* (New York: Harcourt, Brace & World, 1964).

6. Quoted in Robert A. Mundell and Paul J. Zak, *Monetary Stability and Economic Growth: A Dialog Between Leading Economists* (Cheltenham, UK: Edward Elgar Publishing, 2002), p. 3.

7. Edmund S. Phelps, "Corporatism and Keynes: His Views on Growth," May 16, 2007. http://www.columbia.edu/~esp2/CorporatismAndKeynes2007May16rev2.pdf.

8. Ike Brannon, "We Were All Keynesians Then," Cato.org, January 9, 2006. http://www .cato.org/pub_display.php?pub_id=5362.

9. Amity Shlaes, *The Forgotten Man: A New History of the Great Depression* (New York: HarperCollins, 2007).

10. Friedrich August Hayek, *The Road to Serfdom* (New York: Routledge, 2001).

11. Ronald Hamowy, *The Encyclopedia of Libertarianism* (Thousand Oaks, Calif.: Sage Publications, 2008), p. 138.

12. Paul Romer, "Economic Growth," *The Concise Encyclopedia of Economics* (Indianapolis: Liberty Fund, 2007). http://www.stanford.edu/~promer/EconomicGrowth.pdf.

13. Ronald Utt, "Learning from Japan: Infrastructure Spending Won't Boost the Economy," Heritage Foundation, December 16, 2008. http://www.heritage.org/research/economy/bg2222.cfm.

14. Ibid.

15. Bruce Bartlett, "The 81% Tax Increase," *Forbes.com*, May 15, 2009. http://www.forbes.com/2009/05/14/taxes-social-security-opinions-columnists-medicare.html.

16. Martin Feldstein, "Tax Increases Could Kill the Recovery," *Wall Street Journal*, May 14, 2009. http://online.wsj.com/article/SB124217336075913063.html.

17. Ibid.

18. John Tamny, "The Fed Cannot Create Economic Growth," *Forbes.com*, December 29, 2008. http://www.forbes.com/2008/12/28/fed-gold-growth-oped-cx_jt_1229tamny.html.

19. Ibid.

20. Robert J. Barro, "Government Spending Is No Free Lunch," *Wall Street Journal*, January 22, 2009. http://online.wsj.com/article/SB123258618204604599.html.

21. Ibid.

22. Daniel Mitchell, "The Impact of Government Spending on Economic Growth," Heritage Foundation, March 15, 2005. http://www.heritage.org/research/budget/bg1831es.cfm.

23. Ibid.

24. U.S. Senators Tom Coburn, M.D. (R–OK), and John McCain (R–AZ), "Summertime Blues: 100 Stimulus Projects that Give Taxpayers the Blues," August 2010. http://coburn.senate.gov/public/index.cfm?a=Files.Serve&File_id=a7e82141-1a9e-4eec-b160-6a8e62427efb.

25. John F. Cogan and John B. Taylor, "The Obama Stimulus Impact? Zero," *Wall Street Journal*, December 9, 2010. http://online.wsj.com/article/SB10001424052748704679204575646603792267296.html.

26. Mitchell, "Impact of Government Spending."

27. Brian Riedl, "Why Government Spending Does Not Stimulate Economic Growth," Heritage Foundation, November 12, 2008. http://www.heritage.org/research/budget/bg2208.cfm.

28. Ibid.

29. Julia A. Seymour, "Obama Economic Adviser Warns Spending Could Create Double Digit Inflation," Business & Media Institute, April 22, 2009. http://www.businessandmedia.org/printer/2009/20090422154308.aspx.

30. Paul Krugman, "Falling Wage Syndrome," *New York Times*, May 3, 2009. http://www.nytimes.com/2009/05/04/opinion/04krugman.html.

31. Hans-Werner Sinn, "Forget Inflation, Deflation Is the Real Worrier," *Financial Week*, March 2, 2009. http://www.financialweek.com/apps/pbcs.dll/article?AID=/20090302/REG/902279982/1028&template=printart.

32. Quoted in Brink Lindsey, *Against the Dead Hand: The Uncertain Struggle for Global Capitalism* (Hoboken, NJ: John Wiley & Sons, 2002), pp. 217–218.

33. Ibid.

34. Steven Malanga, "Doing Well Off Do-Gooders," *City Journal*, April 22, 2008. http://www.city-journal.org/2008/eon0422sm.html.

35. Ibid.

36. Steven Malanga, "ACORN's fruits: Billions to Help Pols, Not the Poor," *New York Post*,

February 24, 2010. http://www.nypost.com/p/news/opinion/opedcolumnists/acorn _fruits_n7hQfh2ljHxFernyowvQil.

37. Ibid.

38. Adam Smith, *The Wealth of Nations* (New York: Penguin Classics, 1999), p. 310.

39. Friedrich Hayek, *The Constitution of Liberty* (Chicago: University of Chicago Press, 1960).

40. Sheldon Richman, "Government Should Find Science? It Just Ain't So!" *The Freeman*, March 2005. http://www.fee.org/pdf/the-freeman/richman0305.pdf.

41. William Broad, "For Parts, NASA Boldly Goes . . . on eBay," *New York Times*, May 12, 2002. http://www.nytimes.com/2002/05/12/us/for-parts-nasa-boldly-goes-on-ebay.html.

42. Anne Kornblut, "Staff Finds White House in the Technological Dark Ages," *Washington Post*, January 22, 2009. http://www.washingtonpost.com/wp-dyn/content/article/2009/01/21/AR2009012104249.html.

43. David Espo and Jennifer Loven, "Obama: Congress Must Act Boldly and Now on Economy," Associated Press, January 8, 2009. http://abcnews.go.com/Business/wireStory?id=6601988.

44. Mark Skousen, "Is 'Do Nothing' the Right Response?" *Human Events*, Febuary 11, 2009. http://www.humanevents.com/article.php?id=30641.

45. Ibid.

46. Robert Higgs, "Instead of Stimulus, Do Nothing—Seriously," *Christian Science Monitor*, February 9, 2009. http://www.csmonitor.com/2009/0209/p09s01-coop.html.

47. Amity Shlaes, "Fifteen Minutes of Pain," *Forbes.com*, April 30, 2009. http://www.forbes.com/2009/04/30/1930s-great-depression-business-shlaes.html.

48. Ibid.

49. Robert Higgs, "Why the Great Depression Lasted So Long and Why Prosperity Resumed After the War," *Independent Review*, spring 1997. http://www.independent.org/pdf/tir/tir_01_4_higgs.pdf.

50. Robert Higgs, "Recession and Recovery: Six Fundamental Errors of the Current Orthodoxy," Independent Institute, March 5, 2009. http://www.independent.org/newsroom/article.asp?id=2448.

51. Ibid.

52. Hernando de Soto, "Citadels of Dead Capital," *Reason*, May 2001, http://www.reason.com/news/show/28018.html.

INDEX

ABOUT THE AUTHORS

STEVE FORBES is chairman, CEO, and editor in chief at Forbes Media and an internationally respected authority in the worlds of economics, finance, and corporate leadership. He campaigned twice for the Republican nomination for the presidency. His previous books include *Flat Tax Revolution*, *A New Birth of Freedom*, and the *New York Times* bestselling *Power Ambition Glory*.

ELIZABETH AMES is founder of BOLDE Communications, which advises corporate and individual clients on communications strategies. Her work as a journalist has appeared in *BusinessWeek*, *New York*, *Vogue*, and other publications.

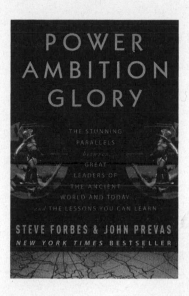